VARIORUM COLLECTED STUDIES SERIES

The Sources of Beneventan Chant

Thomas Forrest Kelly

Thomas Forrest Kelly

The Sources of Beneventan Chant

ASHGATE
VARIORUM

ML
93
.K33
2011

Published in the Variorum Collected Studies Series by

Ashgate Publishing Limited
Wey Court East
Union Road
Farnham, Surrey
GU9 7PT
England

Ashgate Publishing Company
Suite 420
101 Cherry Street
Burlington, VT 05401–4405
USA

www.ashgate.com

ISBN 978–1–4094–0530–6

British Library Cataloguing in Publication Data
Kelly, Thomas Forrest.
    The sources of Beneventan chant.
    – (Variorum collected studies series)
    1. Beneventan chants – Italy, Southern – History – Sources.
    2. Beneventan chants – Italy, Southern – History and criticism.
    I. Title II. Series
    782.3'222'009457–dc22

    ISBN 978–1–4094–0530–6

Library of Congress Control Number: 2011924378

VARIORUM COLLECTED STUDIES SERIES CS980

The paper used in this publication meets the minimum requirements of the American National Standard for Information Sciences – Permanence of Paper for Printed Library Materials, ANSI Z39.48–1984. ∞ ™

Printed and bound in Great Britain by
TJ International Ltd, Padstow, Cornwall

CONTENTS

This volume contains xii + 390 pages

PUBLISHER'S NOTE

The articles in this volume, as in all others in the Variorum Collected Studies Series, have not been given a new, continuous pagination. In order to avoid confusion, and to facilitate their use where these same studies have been referred to elsewhere, the original pagination has been maintained wherever possible.

Each article has been given a Roman number in order of appearance, as listed in the Contents. This number is repeated on each page and is quoted in the index entries.

INTRODUCTION

The studies gathered here, published over a span of twenty-five years, share an interest in the musical world of southern Italy in the early Middle Ages.

This area of the world is noted for its cultural independence, its political identity as the domain of the southern Lombards, and for the characteristic writing, called the Beneventan script, which was used in Latin southern Italy from the eighth century well into the sixteenth.

The Beneventan script is named for the city of Benevento, the political and cultural capital of Lombard southern Italy in the eighth century. During this time the Lombard dukes (later princes) of Benevento ruled an extensive area coterminous with the Beneventan cultural zone. Originally linked with the Lombard kingdom of Pavia, the area ruled from Benevento cultivated its independence, and later independent after the fall of Pavia to Charlemagne in 774.

This Beneventan script is in fact the continuation of a local style of writing; many other regional scripts were abandoned in favor of the newer ordinary, or Caroline, minuscule. The Beneventan script was brought to its perfection in the eleventh and twelfth centuries at the nearby abbey of Montecassino, the mother house of Benedictine monasticism and a cultural and religious center of the first importance in the eleventh and twelfth centuries; the monastery was powerful and influential, the source of bishops, abbots, and popes for the Roman Church.

This cultural zone has a particular musical profile: southern Italy developed and cultivated a liturgy and music of its own. The musical repertory, developed in the seventh and eighth centuries, was allied with the Lombards in that it shares some characteristics of the northern Lombard music known as Ambrosian chant, from the region around Pavia and centered on Milan. The southern Lombard chant, however, is so distinct that it is clearly recognizable as having its own remarkable style. We now call it Beneventan chant.

The Beneventan chant coexisted for a time with the Franco-Roman chant; known also as Gregorian chant, this imported and imposed repertory was part of an attempt, on the part of emperors and popes, to secure uniformity and universality for the Roman Church. The Beneventan chant was suppressed in the course of the eleventh century, and as a result it survives mostly in fragments, in palimpsests, and in books of Gregorian chant where its origin is disguised or no longer remembered.

* * *

A first group of studies (Chapters I–III) introduces this Beneventan chant and the challenges presented by efforts to recover it. The musical style of the chant, and of the other music of the area, is presented, and a survey of the musical manuscripts surviving from early-medieval southern Italy provides some physical context.

A second group of studies (Chapters IV–X) presents a series of cases: individual sources, mostly fragmentary, that reveal aspects of the Beneventan chant's extent and demonstrate that the sources were once very extensive indeed. It becomes clear, also, especially in Chapter V, that the famous abbey of Montecassino in earlier times had practiced the Beneventan chant; by the late eleventh century, however, the abbey had become a powerful center of influence for the Roman Church, and actively suppressed the local music; a few palimpsests and fragments are our only witnesses to a rich earlier practice.

A third section (Chapters XI–XVII) presents some studies that provide a broader context for the Beneventan chant, the Roman chant in southern Italy, and the context in which for a time they coexisted. The earliest datable musical notation in the area comes from about 930 (Chapter XI), which gives us a date before which this music was probably not transmitted in written form.

The coexistence of the Beneventan and Gregorian repertories is noted in several studies of sources which preserve both repertories; these are usually books of Gregorian chant which include smaller or larger portions of the local repertory. The only complete surviving antiphoner in Beneventan script includes, here and there among its mostly-Gregorian contents, elements of Beneventan, and indeed of Ambrosian, chant (Chapter XII). The same is true of other sources mentioned in this section (Chapter XIII).

The extent of the Beneventan chant can be observed from its presence in Lucca, Venice, and elsewhere, as Chapters XIV and XV demonstrate. Its local persistence, in an antiphoner of the fourteenth century, witnesses something of Lombard pride in local culture (Chapter XVI).

A final study (Chapter XVII) provides some context for this musical repertory. The Lombard invaders, who made of southern Italy a cultural zone of character and permanence, left their mark in a number of aspects of their liturgy and music as it survives to us. The conflict of traditional, local, and Lombard with the imperial, the papal, and the universal, was felt nowhere more strongly that at Montecassino; its greatest abbot, Desiderius (later Pope Victor III), was himself a native of Benevento, and knew and practiced the Beneventan chant. During his abbacy the close relations he maintained with the Roman Church led to the reform of the liturgy of the abbey, and by the end of his time the Beneventan chant had virtually been eradicated at one of its most important centers.

Most of these studies are detailed views of a larger picture. That picture is delineated in four larger monographs of mine, which are not part of this volume, but which are the result of the sort of individual study represented here. *The Beneventan Chant* (Cambridge, 1989) is a comprehensive study of the repertory, it sources, its history, and its style; it draws on many of these studies, but cannot provide the detail that is given in this volume.

Le chant bénéventain: le répertoire subsistant de l'ancienne liturgie de l'Italie du sud reproduit d'après tous les témoins manuscrits connus: Paléographie musicale, Volume XXI (Solesmes, 1992), provides facsimiles of virtually every piece of Beneventan chant from each of its sources, with brief introduction and commentary on the plates.

The Exultet in Southern Italy (Oxford, 1996) is a comprehensive treatment of the very interesting case of the Beneventan version of the blessing of the paschal candle; this is one of the most characteristic and widespread survivals from the Beneventan liturgy, having the unusual feature of singing this chant from highly decorated scrolls.

The Ordinal of Montecassino and Benevento: Breviarium sive ordo officiorum, 11th century, Spicilegium Friburgense 45 (Freiburg, 2008) is an edition with substantial commentary of the liturgy of the divine office as practiced at Montecassino at the time of Desiderius, in its several Cassinese versions and in the versions transmitted to and used at Benevento. They represent the (almost) absolute triumph of the Roman chant and its liturgy in an area that once proudly sang in its own voice.

The studies presented here, I hope, will permit interested readers to delve deeply into details of a fascinating and important area of the early-medieval musical landscape. The picture we now have of medieval music is more varied and richer than we once thought, since we have now begun to pay close attention to these regional varieties of music.

THOMAS FORREST KELLY

Cambridge, Massachusetts
January 2011

ACKNOWLEDGEMENTS

Grateful acknowledgement is made to the following persons, institutions, journals and publishers for their kind permission to reproduce the papers included in this volume: the Hungarian Academy for Sciences, Budapest (for Chapters I and XVII); Harrassowitz Verlag, Wiesbaden (II); Ludion, Ghent (III); *Kirchenmusikalisches Jarbuch* (IV); Cambridge University Press (V, X); the Pontifical Institute of Mediaeval Studies, Toronto, Ontario (VI, VII, IX); LIM Editrice, Lucca (XI); L'Archivio do Montecassino (XII); Carocci Editore, Rome (XIII); University of California Press, Berkeley (XIV); Brepols, Turnhout (XV); and Fondazione Levi (*Rivista Musica e Storia*), Venice (XVI). Thanks also go to Herman F. Holbrook, co-author of Chapter VI, and to John Z. McKay for the preparation of the three indexes for the volume.

For the illustrations in this volume, thanks go to: L'Archivio do Montecassino (figs 4 and 5 in V; part of fig. 4 in XVII; and figs 1 and 2 in XI); Archivio Diocesano di Bisceglie (figs 1–4 in VII); Biblioteca Apostolica Vaticana (fig. 2 in V); Biblioteca Vallicelliana, Rome (figs 1–4 in IV; fig. 1 in V); Archivio Capitolare della Cattedrale di Altamura (figs 7–10 in VI); Archivio di Stato di Lanciano (fig. 1 in IX); Biblioteco comunale "Ruggero Bonghi" di Lucera (fig. 2 in IX); Archivio Storico dell'Archidiocesi di Pescara-Penne (figs 3 and 4 in IX); Archivio di Stato Venezia (fig. 1 in XVI); Biblioteca Capitolare, Benevento (figs 1–3, part of fig. 4, and figs 5, 6 in XVII); and Stiftsbibliothek Melk (part of fig. 4 in XVII).

Every effort has been made to trace all the copyright holders, but if any have been inadvertently overlooked the publishers will be pleased to make the necessary arrangement at the first opportunity.

I

The Beneventan Chant*

On the twenty-third of December, 1908, the diocesan newspaper *La Settimana* of Benevento carried the first report by Dom Raphaël Andoyer of his visit to the liturgical manuscripts of the chapter library. Andoyer was the first modern scholar to appreciate the importance of the archaic regional music he discovered there. Fifty years ago, Dom Hesbert and his colleagues made a thorough study of the Beneventan rites for Holy Week, and published a series of facsimiles in *Paléographie musicale*. More recently, studies by Bonifacio Baroffio, Michel Huglo, John Boe, Terence Bailey, and others including myself, have expanded our knowledge of this repertory. But there is still no comprehensive study, and no complete list of sources.

The Beneventan chant is the liturgical music of Latin south Italy before the spread of Gregorian chant; it is preserved in manuscripts from the medieval Lombard duchy of Benevento. My own census shows some eighty manuscripts which preserve at last some musical remnant of the Beneventan chant.

The manuscripts preserving Beneventan chant are like pearls: they are precious, of course, but also their composition is a series of superimposed layers of musical style and liturgical and historical influence. To peel back these layers is no easy matter, but they are important in understanding the context of the Beneventan chant as it survives.

Chief among the sources are the five graduals in the Biblioteca capitolare of Benevento. Of these, two (Benevento 38 and 40) are the principal sources of Beneventan chant. But they, like their shelfmates, reveal many more layers of musical development; we can very roughly identify five.

1) At the center — the seed of the pearl, to continue the analogy — is the common foundation of Western liturgy, elements shared alike by all the many musical and liturgical areas of the West; this is a substratum difficult to detect and almost impossible to define, but the common language of litur-

* Study Session VII: Tradizioni periferiche della monodia liturgica medievale in Italia.

I

gical shape, of musical form, of widely used texts, as well as the early history of Christianity in the West, make it clear that such a foundation is the basis of the other layers.

2) Next comes the music of the Beneventan chant, originating in the seventh and eighth centuries; this is the principal subject of this report. But overlaid on this is a third early layer — 3) the so-called Gregorian chant; this repertory arrived in south Italy, in a fully developed form, in the course of the eighth century. To this the local liturgists and musicians added 4) a substantial body of music in Gregorian style, composed for local needs and used only in the area. This 'Romano-Beneventan' chant fills gaps in the received Gregorian tradition, and provides music for feasts of purely local importance; it is a repertory worthy of a study of its own. The creative spirit of the tenth, eleventh, and twelfth centuries, however, turned from liturgical chant, by now essentially fixed, to the creation of 5) a rich body of tropes and sequences. Some of these are borrowed, but many are local products, witnesses to a thriving musical culture. (The tropes are the subject of an edition by John Boe and Alejandro Planchart, and the south Italian sequences have been studied by Lance Brunner). It is worth noticing that there is relatively little effort to preserve the Beneventan chant itself by disguising Beneventan pieces as tropes; and Beneventan pieces themselves do not bear tropes.

All of these layers, then, are present in the graduals of Benevento and in many other regional manuscripts; they are presented together, so that, for example, the mass of the Holy Twelve Brothers of Benevento in manuscript Benevento 40 includes standard Gregorian elements, local Romano-Beneventan pieces, a rich selection of tropes, and an entire alternative mass in Beneventan chant. The material is rich, and the Beneventan chant is only one of many elements preserved together.

The Beneventan chant itself is linked closely with the fortunes of the Lombards, who made in south Italy a political and cultural sphere of influence that lasted until the eleventh century. The history of the Lombards is reflected in music, for there is another ancient chant connected with the Lombards, equally distinct from the Gregorian: the Ambrosian chant of Milan — from the region, that is, of the Lombard kingdom of Pavia, whose kings in principle also ruled Benevento until the late eighth century. Despite their many differences, the Beneventan and Ambrosian chants have so many characteristics in common as to suggest that the Lombard areas, north and south, once shared a similar liturgy and music, whose separate development produced the related repertories of Milan and Benevento. The Beneventan scribes were in a way aware of this link, for when they labeled their local music they inevitably called it 'Ambrosian'.

It is in this 'Lombard' aspect of the Beneventan liturgy that we can see its connections with politics; its preservation, over several centuries, as an artistic patrimony, and its ultimate suppression, in a much weakened Benevento peopled still with proud Lombard nobles, under the joint forces of Norman invasion and Papal reform.

What is the Beneventan chant like ? How do we recognize it as a separate repertory ? For us, familiar with the Gregorian repertory, a Beneventan chant is most readily recognized by liturgical or musical anomalies. The Beneventan chant almost never uses the same text in the same function as the Gregorian. Thus an unusual liturgical text (particularly a non-Biblical one) in a south Italian manuscript, or a familiar text in the wrong place, immediately arouses interest in the hunter of Beneventana.

And there are other instant clues: any music in Beneventan writing which is labeled 'Ambrosian' is Beneventan: this is its only local name, used to distinguish it from Gregorian chant. The Beneventan begins with an *ingressa*, not an introit; almost all Alleluia verses have the same melody.

Musically, the Beneventan chant jumps to the eye. This is not to say that it is paleographically different; it survives in the hands of the same scribes who wrote Gregorian chant. But the music itself has its own style, its own methods of procedure, its own turns of phrase, that set it apart from other chant dialects. It has a very standardized group of cadences; a limited stock of frequently-used melodic turns of phrase; and a tendency in many cases to form longer pieces from several repetitions of a single phrase. And, unlike the Gregorian repertory, these cadences, formulas, and repeated elements are not separated by liturgical category or by mode (a fact that would not be evident, of course, from looking at a single piece), so that their number is smaller, and their occurrences proportionately more frequent. The Beneventan chant, regardless of liturgical category, proceeds at a uniform, rather ornate pace, with much stepwise motion and relatively few dramatic melodic contours. Every piece ends either on G or on A, but there are no other differences to be seen between the two groups.

It is in this simplicity and regularity that the repertory has much of its value for us. An undifferentiated modality; a very limited number of melodic formulas; an archaic liturgical usage; and a small number of surviving pieces: these make of the Beneventan chant an important specimen to compare with the 'modern' features of more developed chant repertories. But there is much charm in its simplicity, much to observe about its arrangement of very limited materials, and much to learn from its position as a cultural artifact.

There remains much to be done. The Beneventan liturgy as it survives is incomplete: as to its chant it is entirely different from the Roman liturgy;

I

but we have no lectionaries, sacramentaries, or missals of the old Beneventan rite; we are not now sure how the mass was said, nor how the calendar was arranged. Hints of Beneventan practice can be gained from the chant, from a few surviving rubrics (notably a long *ordo* for Holy Week in Vatican lat. 10673), and perhaps also from some of the unusual liturgical practices surviving in Gregorian books from south Italy: the use of three readings at mass, a prayer after the Gospel, a large number of proper prefaces, and so on: but these features, preserved not with Beneventan masses but with Gregorian, may in fact be early or regional varieties of the Roman liturgy.

Geography remains a problem. Though we have many manuscripts, there are significant lacunae. We have almost nothing from the great abbey of San Vincenzo al Volturno, whose Beneventan Lombard foundation and subsequent Frankish leanings should make it an ideal place to study the conflict of the two liturgies; we know little of other important centers: Salerno, the second capital of the great Beneventan prince Arichis II; Capua, the first metropolitan archbishopric of southern Italy.

The details of transmission need much careful study. A curious example is the survival of the Beneventan vespers of Good Friday, a rare specimen of Beneventan music for the office; this office is found in the principal central sources: Benevento 38, 39, and 40; but it is found also, with much other Beneventan material, in an addendum to the eleventh-century missal Lucca 606; and it survives complete also in the thirteenth-century missal Subiaco XVIII. A monastic conduit leading north from Montecassino through Subiaco and Lucca is to be imagined here, for the northern sources have Beneventan notation; Subiaco, with its close connections with St. Benedict, has further materials in Beneventan script and notation; and Montecassino 175 includes a precious tenth-century ordo for Good Friday whose rubrics match almost exactly those in the Lucca manuscript. Montecassino itself is a vexing problem; for although we have much evidence that the Beneventan chant was used there, the growing power of the monastery, and increased contact with Rome, led to a liturgical purification, and a renewal of liturgical books under abbot Desiderius, that substantially obscures the earlier liturgical history of this important monastic center.

And perhaps the most vexing question of all is among the most difficult: how was this music used by those who wrote it in the eleventh century, so long after its creation? Was it merely a memory of a glorious past, preserved by proud Lombard scribes who had no other real use for it? Or were there separate churches which practiced the Beneventan chant as an alternative or an adjunct to the now universal Roman liturgy? Was the Beneventan chant a real alternative for the high feast days for which masses are preserved?

Lacking further information we cannot be sure. But there is at least some evidence that the Beneventan chant was a real alternative, at least at certain places and occasions. An example is the rubric first published by John Boe from Vat. Ottob. 145, a manuscript connecting Montecassino with the important church of Santa Sofia of Benevento, describing antiphons used for a monastic *mandatum* ceremony: 'when we do not sing these antiphons according to the Roman (rite, liturgy) as they are written above, we sing them according to the Ambrosian (we would say, "Beneventan"), as follow' *(Quando non canimus ipse an. secundum romano. quo modo supra scripte sunt canimus secundum Ambro[sianum] hoc modo)*. And then follow six antiphons, all of them used elsewhere in the Beneventan rite as communions.

The scribes of the eleventh century made the effort to preserve at least a portion of the older local liturgy. For us it remains to unravel its history, and to uncover, as far as we can, the full breadth of this important repertory.

II

Notes on a Census
of Beneventan Manuscripts

The term 'Beneventan' refers to the area of the old Lombard duchy of Benevento, a very particular part of the European landscape in the earlier Middle Ages. Despite contacts, not always friendly, with Rome and Byzantium, and despite the hostile visits of a series of German emperors beginning with Charlemagne, the region once ruled from Benevento retained a measure of independence throughout the Middle Ages; it produced the characteristic Beneventan script that was brought to perfection at the abbey of Montecassino in the eleventh century, and it developed a cultural and musical tradition largely independent of the rest of Europe.

Professor Roger Reynolds has estimated that some 60 percent of the surviving materials in the Beneventan book-hand is liturgical in nature. That is, of some 1300-1400 documents surviving, around 800 are liturgical. I have lately been engaged in making a census of musical notations in Beneventan documents, and I have a list of some 600 separate items. This is a rather large number, being more than half the total number of liturgical items, but it is a number that needs to be explained and qualified.

But even before that, it might be well to suggest ways in which the study of musical documents like these is of interest at all. First of all, of course, as a musicologist I am interested in the music itself: how does it sound? what is it for? and how does the repertory change over time? And then there are questions about the writing of music: the beginnings of music writing in Italy; what music was written down; how it was recorded – what performance details the scribes try to preserve, and what was so well-known, or so difficult to write down, that it is lost to us.

But there are many other uses to which information about musical manuscripts can be put. For one thing, manuscripts are mirrors of history: we can sometimes isolate details that reflect changing political and cultural values. Let me give two examples from southern Italy.

Sometimes musical notation can give us historical hints that might not otherwise be noticed: the Lamentations of Jeremiah in the lectionary Naples VI AA 3 were notated by the same late-eleventh-century Beneventan scribe who wrote the text; but a portion of the notation was somehow omitted, and a scribe using Aquitanian notation has filled in the gap using a melody not otherwise known in southern Italy.[1] Likewise, a twelfth-century

---

1   A facsimile of the manuscript showing both notations is in *Paléographie musicale* 2 (Solesmes 1891, repr. Basel 1974), pl. 24.

breviary fragment at Altamura has Beneventan writing of the Bari-type; but the notation is surely French – the work of a foreigner transported, perhaps through Norman influence, far from home.[2]

Musical manuscripts seem to be the only sources of information about the old Beneventan liturgy. Most of the sources of this older liturgy have been destroyed – many of them deliberately. It survives almost entirely in fragments, palimpsests, and in an occasional musical piece or group disguised by a nostalgic Lombard scribe in a manuscript of the now-official Gregorian chant. Without these musical survivals we would not even know of the existence of this earlier liturgy – a liturgy which dates back at least to the eighth century, which reflects the political and cultural independence of the Lombards, and which is in itself an important cultural artifact.[3]

My census attempts to assemble all surviving witnesses of Beneventan musical notation. In its current form the list includes the evidence of surviving fragments, and presents a picture very different from what we see when we consider only entire manuscripts. The numbers must be approximate, of course. New fragments are discovered frequently;[4] it is difficult to be sure that a fragment really represents a whole lost document; there is the question of *membra disiecta* – one doesn't want count five scattered fragments from the same manuscript as five manuscripts. Conversely, many books that today bear a single shelf-number are in fact assemblages of elements from different times and places; where possible I have separated these and given them separate entries in the census. What I have tried to do is to record the evidence of how often someone sat down with the intention of making a document (rather than altering, correcting, or adding to one).

From this larger census I should like to consider here the musical books, saving the many other cases of musical notation for another occasion. For the moment we will concentrate on the central music-books of the mass and the office.

Some preliminary observations can be made on the basis of the Table opposite, which counts the surviving books and fragments in each of these categories.

2 See Thomas Forrest Kelly, 'Beneventan Fragments at Altamura', *Mediaeval Studies* 49 (1987), 465-479.

3 On the Beneventan chant in general see Thomas Forrest Kelly, *The Beneventan Chant* (Cambridge 1989); facsimiles of the sources of Beneventan chant are found in *Paléographie musicale* 21 (Solesmes 1992).

4 The collecting of information about manuscripts is Beneventan script is facilitated by the indispensable work of Virginia Brown, who revised the list of manuscripts in Elias Avery Loew, *The Beneventan Script; A History of the South Italian Minuscule* (Oxford 1914; Second Edition prepared and enlarged by Virginia Brown, 2 vols (*Sussidi eruditi*, 33-34, Rome 1980); Professor Brown has regularly reported new Beneventan discoveries: Virginia Brown, 'A Second New List of Beneventan Manuscripts (I)', *Mediaeval Studies* 40 (1978), 239-280; 'A Second New List of Beneventan Manuscripts (II)', *Mediaeval Studies* 50 (1988), 584-625; 'A Second New List of Beneventan Manuscripts (III)', *Mediaeval Studies* 56 (1994), 299-350; 'A Second New List of Beneventan Manuscripts (IV)', *Mediaeval Studies* 61 (1999), 325-392.

Summary of Surviving
Beneventan Musical Manuscripts by Type

	Complete	Fragments	Total
Office			
Antiphoner	3	80	83
Breviary			
notated	2	34	36
no notation	5	10	15
Total office	10	124	134
Mass			
Gradual	7	54	61
Missal			
notated	11	37	48
no notation	6	54	60
Total mass	24	145	169
Total	34	269	303

First, we can note that a very small percentage of books survives complete. Of the 303 manuscripts known to have existed, most survive only as fragments; only about 12 percent are in anything like their original form. A great many surviving fragments are from liturgical books; this may be partly because liturgical books go out of date, but also because they are heavily used, and really do wear out. The tattered state of many fragments, and of many surviving books, gives clear evidence of repeated use.

As to the relative frequency of copying the various types, the census changes our picture. Judging only from complete books, we would never know that antiphoners once existed in such great numbers, or indeed that graduals, of which only a few survive, were once far more plentiful.

This raises the question of why books are discarded, and why certain volumes survive. It looks as though purely musical books are discarded more readily than others. Advances in notation may account for this in part, for the earliest books are not so accurate in some details as later ones: succeeding generations might wish to discard older volumes in favor of newer ones meeting newer notational requirements.

It is possible that musical books wear out faster than missals and breviaries; but more likely, I think, is that many breviaries and missals are preserved mainly for their texts, not their music. It is certainly true that most examples of the oldest Beneventan musical notations come from books where musical notation is not essential to the purpose of the manuscript: homiliaries and gospel-books with a few neumes added; Exultet rolls preserved for their beauty; missals whose texts and prayers retain their usefulness even when the notation is hopelessly old-fashioned.

Let us now look briefly at each of these four main types of music book. We have evidence of 83 antiphoners in Beneventan script, but only three survive more or less complete. Of these, the oldest are both from the later 12th century: Benevento 21[5] and Montecassino 542, the latter having less than half the original manuscript. The only other substantial survival is in Capua, and dates from the 14th century.[6] But there are fragments of 80 further antiphoners, twenty of them dating from before the twelfth century. It is surprising that so few antiphoners survive, since they seem indispensable for the full performance of the choral office. Although reponsories are sometimes sung by soloists, and the antiphons could conceivably be memorized by the choir, it would seem that at least one antiphoner would be needed in *any* monastic or collegiate church; and yet they have almost all disappeared, leaving only fragments behind. Such books would wear out with constant use, and perhaps the last Beneventan antiphoners were replaced with books in a more up-to-date script, and, ultimately, with printed antiphoners.

A notated breviary can, of course, substitute for an antiphoner. The history of the breviary, generally viewed as the amalgamation of separate books - antiphoner, lectionary, homiliary, collectar - is a complicated one, and it appears that the breviary is a relatively late phenomenon in southern Italy. The oldest surviving Beneventan noted breviary is Benevento 22, from the 12th century, but it includes only the first half of the year. A very incomplete manuscript in the Vatican is our only other notated breviary:[7] we have only fragments to tell of the existence of 35 more such manuscripts.

But is a breviary really designed to replace an antiphoner? Breviaries without musical notation raise this question even more strongly. A breviary might serve as a traveling book, for clerics unable to be present at the office of their communities. This seems particularly possible in the case of breviaries without musical notation, for an itinerant monk might not be expected to sing the music allotted to the choir and its soloists.

Beneventan breviaries without notation are fewer in number than notated breviaries, and they are not a perceptibly later phenomenon. Five such breviaries survive, two of them in the Biblioteca Capitolare at Benevento.[8] Fragments of only nine other such manuscripts also remain: the oldest, now in Giessen, is a single leaf containing portions of the office of the dead: we cannot even be sure that it was part of a whole breviary.[9] On

---

5 Manuscripts of Benevento referred to here are kept in the Biblioteca capitolare. This manuscript is edited as MS L in René-Jean Hesbert, *Corpus antiphonalium officii*, 6 vols. Rerum ecclesiasticarum documenta, series maior, fontes 7-12 (Rome 1963-79); a facsimile edition is *Paléographie musicale* 22 (solesmes 2001).

6 Capua, Biblioteca Arcivescovile MS VI F 34; see Brown, 'A Second New List (II)', 594.

7 Vatican City, Biblioteca Apostolica Vaticana MS Vat. lat. 14446, 13th century. The incomplete secular breviary consists of 65 folios (numbered 1-63 plus 23A and 23B). It includes the end of the *psalmista*, parts of Lent, and part of the proper of the saints (Purification to St. Benedict).

8 Manuscripts 23 and 25, of the 13th and 12th centuries. The other notated breviaries are Rome, Biblioteca Vallicelliana MS C 51 (11th/12th c.); Vatican City, BAV MS Chigi C VI 176 (early 12th c.); Montevergine, Biblioteca dell'Abbazia MS 6 (late 13th c.).

9 Universitätsbibliothek MS NF 444; see Brown, 'A Second New List (II)', 598.

the whole, the surviving breviaries without notation seem sometimes to be books of reference (like those at Benevento), and only occasionally to be personal books.

For the mass, there are seven surviving manuscript graduals; five are at Benevento and were written in that city.[10] The oldest gradual, now in the Vatican, dates from the late tenth or early eleventh century, and is unfortunately incomplete and of unknown provenance.[11] Fragments of some fifty-one other graduals survive, but only one of them – actually only a few binding scraps at Montecassino – may be older than the Vatican gradual.[12]

Apparently as old as graduals, and more numerous, are missals – at least in southern Italy. Like breviaries, missals are compendia: they group all the texts needed for the celebration of the mass: lectionary, sacramentary, and gradual are combined in a single codex. The reasons for this amalgamation of separate books are complex and not well understood. Contributing factors include the need for portable books for itinerant priests; the growing proportion of monastic priests and the increasing practice of private daily mass; and the celebrant's obligation, from the late 11th century onward, to recite all the texts of the mass, including the musical pieces even when they are also sung.

But what is the use of musical notation in a missal to be used in traveling, or in saying a private mass at a side altar, or indeed celebrating at the main altar when the notation is not available to the choir? As important as its function as an altar-book, it seems to me, is the missal's function as a synoptic book of reference.

If missals result from the combination of sacramentaries with other books, why do we not have a great many sacramentaries in Beneventan script? I know of only four – the beautiful Desiderian sacramentary Montecassino 339, and three small later fragments.[13] All three fragments are later than the earliest missals. But Montecassino 339 is not a sacramentary in an older tradition that later flowed into the missal, but just the reverse: note this remark in the Chronicle of Montecassino about books made by the great abbot Desiderius (1058-87):

---

10 Manuscripts 34 (first half of 12th century; facsimile in *Paléographie musicale* 15, Tournai 1937), 35 (11th century); 38 (first half of 11th century); 39 (late 11th century); 40 (11th century; facsimile in *Benevento Biblioteca Capitolare 40 Graduale*, ed. Nino Albarosa and Alberto Turco [Padova 1991]).
11 Vatican City, BAV MS Vat. lat. 10673; facsimile in *Paléographie musicale* 14 (Tournai 1931, repr. Bern 1971).
12 Three fragmentary remains probably from the same gradual of the late tenth or early eleventh century: (1) an orange envelope in Montecassino Compactiones XXII contains a fragment (about 95 x 70 mm.) with Gregorian Alleluias and their verses; (2) a leaf (marked "3" in pencil) also in Compactiones XXII shows in its margin the reversed offset impression (about 64 x 32 mm) of texts and neumes probably from the same manuscript; (3) in Compactiones VII, which contains some 217 folios of a twelfth-century missal (studied in Alban Dold, 'Umfangreiche Reste zweier Plenarmissalien des 11. und 12. Jhs. aus Monte Cassino', *Ephemerides liturgicae* 53 (1939), 114-144), one of two leaves marked '7' is repaired with a fragment (58 x 40 mm) from the same gradual.
13 Rimini, Giovanni Luisè collection S. N. 11th/12th c. (Brown, 'A Second New List (II)', 612); Milan, Biblioteca Ambrosiana, MS Q 43 sup. and Q 57 sup., whose back flyleaves seem to be from a sacramentary of the first half of the twelfth century; Geneva, Bibliothèque Publique et Universitaire, MS Comites Latentes 271, four small scraps from a sacramentary of the second half of the 12th century (see Brown, 'A Second New List (III)', 312.

'Likewise he made one and the other sacramentary of the altar; and no less than two gospel-books, and one epistle-book. For up to that time both the gospel and the epistle had been read from a plenary missal; and what had been unsuitable was now put right'.[14]

Apparently missals in Beneventan script continued to be used at the altars of Montecassino well into the fifteenth century, when a detailed inventory was made of the books which are used in the church; it lists:

Libri qui tenentur in ecclesia:

[1] In primis missale pro maiori altari cum sequentiis in littera long[obarda – that is, in Beneventan script]

[2] Item aliud simile sine sequentiis in dicta littera pro s. Gregorio

[3] Item aliud simile pro altari s. Marie

[4] Item aliud simile pro s. Iohanne

[5] Item aliud simile pro s. Nicolao

[6] Item aliud simile

[7] Item aliud simile

[8] Item aliud grossius pro s. Bartolomeo

[9] Item aliud in littera latina cum sequentiis

[10] Item aliud parvum sine sequentiis ... [15]

The list goes on to enumerate several more small missals: these may be modern, personal books; one of them is listed as a *missale notatum*, suggesting that the other minuscule or Gothic missals were without musical notation.

This list apparently names eight missals in Beneventan script, of which one, with sequences (does that mean, with musical notation?) was used at the main altar of Montecassino; four others (without sequences, nos. 2-5) were used at the other main altars of the basilica, where masses would be said, not sung. We cannot say whether these books had always been used at the altars where they were inventoried in the 15th century, but there was clearly a large number of missals kept in the church and evidently used there, even though their musical notation would not usually be sung.

The oldest surviving missal in Beneventan script is Benevento 33, probably from the early 11th century;[16] it shows signs of heavy use. The manuscript did not originate at Be-

---

14 'Similiter fecit et sacramentoriis altaris uno et altero et duobus nichilominus evangeliis et epistolarium uno. Nam usque ad illud tempus in plenario missali tam evangelia quam epistole legebantur, quod, quam esset tunc inhonestum, modo satis advertitur.' *Chronica monasterii Casinensis* [*Die Chronik von Montecassino*], ed. Hartmut Hoffmann, Monumenta Germaniae Historica Scriptores 14 (Hannover 1980), p. 384.

15 From the 15th-century inventory of the books of the abbey of Montecassino, Vatican City, BAV Vat. lat. 3961, f. 21r, reprinted in Maurus Inguanez, *Catalogi codicum casinensium antiqui (saec. VIII-XV)* (Montecassino 1941), p. 43.

16 Facsimile with introduction and tables in *Paléographie musicale* 20 (Bern 1983); the musical portions reproduced in *Die Handschrift Benevento: Biblioteca capitolare 33*, Monumenta palaeographica gregoriana 1 (Munsterschwarzach [1984?]). A summary edition is Sieghild Rehle, 'Missale Beneventanum (Codex VI 33 des Erzbischöflichen Archiv von Benevent)', *Sacris erudiri* 28 (1985), 469-510.

Benevento, however; we know that it has some connection with Salerno.[17] Both this and the next oldest missal - the Canosa missal now in Baltimore[18] - have musical notation. The only other surviving missal of the 11th century is Montecassino 127, which is without notation.[19] We do have evidence of four missals, all with musical notation, that are as old as, or older than, Benevento 33;[20] unfortunately they are mostly palimpsests or small fragments: if they had survived we might know a great deal more than we now do about the arrival and the transmission of the Franco-Roman liturgy in southern Italy.

We have talked here only about the most central types of musical book, and only in general terms. Let me just mention two other musical types.

There is only one manuscript devoted to tropes in Beneventan script, and it comes from Montecassino. There is in fact no real evidence that any other manuscript of tropes was ever made. Four surviving fragments might be from tropers, but we cannot tell.[21] Tropes were generally transmitted in graduals, along with the musical pieces they embellish. The five graduals of Benevento are the richest, and almost the only, sources of tropes from southern Italy.

One last type of musical book should not go unmentioned. This is the combined missal-breviary: a book containing texts and music for both mass and office, arranged in a single series. This sort of multi-volume compendium is rare in liturgical manuscripts: but it is typical of the liturgical books of the Ambrosian rite of Milan (which, as it happens, is closely allied with the old Beneventan liturgy),[22] and it is to be found also sometimes in

17 On the presence of the manuscript in the region of Salerno in the thirteenth century see Jean Mallet and André Thibaut, *Les manuscrits en écriture bénéventaine de la Bibliothèque capitulaire de Bénévent*, vol. 1 (Paris 1984), p. 90, and vols. 2-3 (Paris and Turnhaut 1997); 2: 168-173; 3: *passim*.

18 Baltimore, Walters Art Gallery MS W 6; see Sieghild Rehle, *Missale beneventanum von Canosa (Baltimore, Walters Art Gallery MS W 6)*, Textus patristici et liturgici 9 (Regensburg 1972).

19 The missal Montecassino 426 of the second half of the eleventh century consists only of ferial and votive masses without musical notation).

20 Montecassino, Compactiones XXII: on a leaf marked '3' in pencil is the offset of 13 lines of a missal of the 10th/11th century; Montecassino Compactiones VI contains a fragment of a notated missal of similar date; two fragments used to repair manuscripts at Benevento, one extracted from MS 22 folio 99r/103v, the other still attached in MS 23 folio 63v/70r, are from a late tenth-century missal, and have been given the provisional number of Fragment F (they are described in 2: 316-317 Jean Mallet and André Thibaut, *Les manuscrits en écriture bénéventaine de la Bibliothèque capitulaire de Bénévent*; one palimpsest bifolium in a manuscript in St. Petersburg is from a missal perhaps of the early eleventh century: Sobranie inostrannykh Rukopisei Otdela Rukopisnoi i Redkoi Knigi Biblioteki Akademii Nauk SSSR MS F. No. 200, folios 78 and 83; see Kelly, *The Beneventan Chant*, pp. 304-305.

21 Vatican City, BAV MS Barb. lat. 681 contains in the binding after folio B a vertical strip (11th c.) including a portion of a sequence; the miscellany BAV Vat. lat. 14733 includes an 11th-century page of Gloria-tropes as folio 31; pages 377-78 of Montecassino MS 194 contains a single sequence of the second half of the eleventh century; Montecassino Compactiones V contains a single leaf with sequences of the twelfth century; these fragments might have been individual leaves, or survivors from sequentiaries, graduals with tropes, or tropers.

22 On the relationship of the Milanese rite to the Beneventan, see Terence Bailey, 'Ambrosian chant in southern Italy', *Journal of the Plainsong & Mediaeval Music Society* 6 (1983), 1-7; Kelly, *The Beneventan Chant*, 181-203; Thomas Forrest Kelly, *The Exultet in Southern Italy* (New York 1996), 208-11. For a list of Milanese chant books see Michel Huglo, Luigi Agustoni, Eugène Cardine, and Ernesto Moneta Caglio, *Fonti e paleografia del canto ambrosiano*, Archivio ambrosiano 7 (Milan 1956).

Spain. Only one example of this type survives: the remarkable pair of volumes Benevento 19 and 20, from the 12th century.[23] But there is a fragment at the Vatican from another such book;[24] and based on certain patterns of copying, there is reason to believe that still other such volumes once existed, particularly for the old Beneventan liturgy.[25]

From this brief tour of an ongoing census, what can we conclude? For one thing, we should not disregard the evidence of fragments, no matter how small, in helping to establish patterns of distribution and chronology. For another, I might just underscore a point that is already well known but that is brought home very forcefully by this census: the enormous importance of the manuscripts in the Biblioteca capitolare at Benevento.

Benevento does not have a large library, but just let me recall the manuscripts we have mentioned here:

- the oldest notated missal in Beneventan script is Benevento 33;
- one of the few surviving missals without notation was in the library of Benevento as manuscript 29 until it mysteriously disappeared during the Second World War; it is now in the British Library as MS Egerton 3511;
- five of the seven surviving graduals are in the same library - and two of them, manuscripts 38 and 40, are the only substantial sources for the old Beneventan liturgy;
- the oldest complete antiphoner is Benevento 21;
- the only surviving witness of what may once have been a Beneventan phenomenon - the multi-volume combination of mass and office - is Benevento manuscripts 19 and 20;
- the richest surviving repertory of tropes from southern Italy is contained in the graduals of Benevento.

Montecassino may have one of the greatest libraries surviving from the Middle Ages; but the liturgical renewal in the late eleventh and early twelfth centuries under abbot Desiderius swept away much documentation of earlier times. The chapter library of Benevento provides us the best, the earliest, and often the only examples, of complete musical books. If a dozen of its manuscripts had not survived, our picture of music in southern Italy would be vastly different: we might not even know of the existence of the old regional liturgy; the poetry and music of the tropes of southern Italy would be reduced to less than half of the surviving repertory; and our picture of manuscript types and history would be falsified beyond hope of rectification.

---

23 See Kelly, *The Beneventan Chant*, 299, and the bibliography cited there; a complete description is in Mallet and Thibaut, vol. 2 (above, note 19), 2: 61-70.

24 The miscellany Vatican City, BAV Vat. lat. 10645 contains as folio 63 a twelfth-century page containing texts and music for the mass of the Sunday after Pentecost followed by vespers antiphons.

25 See Kelly, *The Beneventan Chant*, 50-52.

III

Music of Benevento Cathedral

Introduction: local and universal repertories and styles

The music of Benevento Cathedral is as varied as the history of the building and the city itself. The sucessive and overlapping musical styles and practices provides a picture, or a confirmation, of the long and varied history of the city.

The chief interest in the music of medieval Benevento is usually in the so-called Beneventan chant, the music of the liturgy practiced in southern Italy before the adoption there of the standardized "Gregorian" chant of the Roman church. But this is just one of several layers of music that survive to us from medieval Beneventan manuscripts, and each of them has a historical and artistic importance of its own. Let us summarize briefly the nature of these layers.

1. The music of Benevento shares basic elements with the many musical and liturgical areas of the West; this is a substratum difficult to detect and almost impossible to define, but the common language of liturgical shape, of musical form, of widely used texts, as well as the early history of Christianity in the West, make it clear that such a foundation is the basis of the other layers. The poetical text of the entrance chant of the Beneventan Easter mass, "Maria uidit angelum," is found (without music) in the ninth-century antiphoner of Compiègne; this may be one of several elements of a pan-Italian, or a pre-Gregorian, layer.

2. The invasions of the Lombards from the north in the sixth century brought a wave of destruction and paganism, but resulted in planting on southern soil the seeds of a culture that was to endure for centuries, and which developed its characteristic writing, its own liturgy and music. The political capital of this area was the city of Benevento, and the liturgy and music developed there was in many respects independent of parallel developments in the Roman church. This liturgy and its music spread throughout the south from Benevento, and was practiced from the seventh century until its suppression in the course of the eleventh.

3. The Gregorian chant which was ultimately adopted throughout the Latin west arrived at Benevento as early as the eighth century, although the Beneventan chant continued to be practiced for a time as well. The Gregorian chant transmitted to Benevento is essentially that used elsewhere also: but its early arrival at Benevento is attested by characteristics that are musically and historically very interesting; the Beneventan version of the Franco-Roman chant preserves archaic melodic elements, and the version transmitted to Benevento does not include certain formularies of later adoption, with the result that the Gregorian liturgy as received at Benevento contains certain lacunae which needed to be filled on the spot.

4. Romano-Beneventan chant is music composed at Benevento or in the region to provide for occasions of local importance or for feasts where the received Gregorian chant was aliturgical. Composers produced, in the Beneventan zone but in what they understood to be Gregorian style, masses, antiphons, responsories, entire formularies for local feasts. In this music we can get a view of how the Gregorian chant was appreciated and understood.

5. The creative spirit of the tenth, eleventh, and twelfth centuries, however, turned from liturgical chant, by now essentially fixed, to the creation of a rich body of tropes and sequences. Some of these are borrowed, but many are local products, witnesses to a thriving musical culture.

The manuscripts that preserve the music of Benevento cathedral are not divided into specific repertories. Generally the most valuable and oldest manuscripts, those of the tenth through the twelfth centuries, include a series of superimposed layers of musical style and historical influence. To peel back these layers is no easy matter, but they are important in understanding the context of the music of Benevento as it survives. The Feast of the Holy Twelve Brothers in the eleventh-century gradual Benevento 40, for example, contains a mass in Beneventan chant, a local mass in Gregorian style, and a rich selection of tropes and sequences. Such a variety of music did not arise all at once, and perhaps was never meant to be used on a single occasion; but it provides a view of the variety and the history of the music of Benevento.

Liturgical music in southern Italy before the Lombards

There was certainly a Latin liturgy practiced in southern Italy before the Lombard invasion, and it surely involved chant. However, we know very little about its shape, and almost nothing about its music. Among the liturgical anomalies of such "Roman" books as the tenth-century missal Benevento 33 there are non-standard characteristics which may survive from an earlier time; these may well be remnants of what some have called a "Campanian" liturgy, versions of a Latin liturgy practiced in southern Italy before the Lombard invasion. Such characteristics include a unique system of lections at mass; the occasional use of hagiographical lections at mass; an unusually large number of proper prefaces; the use of three lections at mass; a prayer *post euangelium*; and a prayer *super populum*. (On these, Thomas Forrest Kelly, *The Beneventan Chant*, Cambridge 1989 [hereafter TBC], 63–5).

That there was a Latin liturgy in southern Italy before the Lombards is without doubt; we know almost nothing of its music, however. The poetic text of the entrance chant of the Beneventan Easter mass, "Maria uidit angelum," is found (without music) in the ninth-century antiphoner of Compiègne, suggesting that this may be one of several elements of a pan-Italian, or a pre-Gregorian, layer.

Beneventan chant

Lombard aspects of the Beneventan chant

The chant of the Beneventan rite and its chant are to a large extent aspects of the Lombard culture of southern Italy. We can determine this from a variety of indirect evidence. First, the chant seems to have developed, as we shall suggest, in the course of the seventh and eighth centuries, at a time when Lombard power was at its height. Second, the Beneventan chant seems centered on the city of Benevento. It includes music for Saint Barbatus, bishop of Benevento; for the apparition of St Michael on Monte Gargano, a saint and a shrine particularly dear to the Lombards and the Beneventans; and for the Holy Twelve Brothers of Benevento, whose remains were interred by Duke Arichis II in his palace church of Santa Sofia: it was surely from Benevento that the cult of the Twelve Brothers spread to Montecassino and elsewhere.

The surviving sources of Beneventan chant, numbering almost a hundred manuscripts and fragments, describes a geographical area which matches very closely the range of Lombard domination in the south at the height of Lombard political influence. No other center could serve so well as a model for imitation than the capital city of the southern Lombards.

III

The influence of secular authority on the church in the seventh and eighth century is well known, and it seems certain that the rulers of Benevento gave considerable impetus to the local variety of chant. Under the early Beneventan princes the church was closely subjected to the ruler; bishops from early Lombard times were accustomed to providing political services for the dukes and princes of Benevento; and the foundation of churches and monasteries by many Lombard princes and nobles enriched the city and extended far beyond it. Arichis II (or his predecessor Gisulf) founded Santa Sofia in Benevento; Theoderada (pious consort of Romuald) founded the monastery of St Peter's *extra muros*. Three nobles of Benevento founded San Vincenzo on the Volturno. Many other examples could be cited of Lombard princes and nobles establishing churches and monasteries. Lombard political presence was strongly felt also at Montecassino. The rebuilding of Montecassino begun under Petronax of Brescia (ca. 718) owes much to the support of the Beneventan dukes Romuald II (706–730) and Gisulf II (742–751). Abbot Gisulf (796–817), who was responsible for a significant building campaign at Montecassino, was of "the noble family of the dukes of Benevento" and had presumably therefore been close to the court of Arichis II and his successors.

There is a curious further Lombard aspect to the Beneventan chant: whenever it is given a name by scribes, that name is "Ambrosian": *Cantus ambrosianus, responsorium ambrosianum, antiphona ambrosiana*, and so on. Indeed, the rite itself is called Ambrosian: "sicut in ambrosiano scripte sunt"; "canimus secundum ambro.," etc. And yet this is not the Ambrosian chant of the church of Milan. There is indeed much evidence of a relationship between the Beneventan and the Ambrosian chants, but they are not the same; Beneventan chant and Ambrosian are related, but not identical. The use of the term "Ambrosian" in the south has the effect of invoking the authority of Saint Ambrose, who perhaps alone can stand against the oncoming influence of the chant associated with Saint Gregory the Great. The southern scribes acknowledge a Lombard link, for the Ambrosian chant of Milan is the chant of the Lombards of the North, and Ambrose is thus claimed as the ancestor of both rites. There is indeed a link, and it seems likely that the Lombards, north and south, once shared a similar liturgy and music, which gradually grew apart as a result of geographical and political separation, particularly after the fall of the Lombard kingdom of Pavia to Charlemagne in 774.

Chronology

The Beneventan rite and its music grew in southern soil from imported Lombard seed. It was developed in the course of the seventh and eighth centuries, and was still being written, and sung, in the eleventh, though not without considerable resistance.

The pagan, and then Arian, Lombard invaders of sixth-century southern Italy destroyed much of the ecclesiastical life of the region, and it was only after their conversion to Catholicism that a regular religious life derived from Lombard culture developed in the south. The final conversion to Catholicism after one of many relapses into paganism is recounted in the ninth-century life of St Barbatus, bishop of Benevento in the 670s, which describes the pagan practices of the Lombards; it was Barbatus who reclaimed the backsliding duke Romuald (661–71?) for the Catholic fold, but not without the help of Romuald's pious consort Theoderada.

The development in the eighth century of an independent principality under Arichis II and of an elaborate court ceremonial must have marked a high point in the development of Beneventan liturgy: the chant was already securely in place in Arichis' Lombard capital but not so fixed that new music could not be composed. The Beneventan mass of the Holy Twelve Brothers points clearly to the Benevento of the second half of the eighth century. The relics of these saints were gathered by Arichis himself and interred by him in the ducal church of Santa Sofia in 760. Such a mass would not have originated elsewhere and been adopted later at Santa Sofia, and since the cult of these saints did not exist at all until their remains were collected by Arichis we can be certain that the mass was not composed before 760, nor probably much later. At that time what we call the Beneventan chant was already in use at Benevento, since the ingressa of the Holy Twelve Brothers is an adaptation of the ingressa of the Beneventan Easter mass. The cult of these martyrs, intended by Arichis as "patroni patriae," spread throughout the region, and indeed entered the Roman calendar. This diffusion witnesses not only the spread of the Beneventan chant, but more directly, the importance of Benevento as the political and cultural focus of its region, at least in the eighth century.

The Holy Twelve Brothers were an aspect of the princely aspirations of Arichis II, who sought in them and in other relics which he acquired to focus on Benevento and Santa Sofia the religious nationalism of the southern Lombards. The center of the ecclesiastical life of Benevento under Arichis was the court church built by him – that is, Santa Sofia. Like many other monasteries and churches founded by Lombard nobles, it was effectively a private church, exempt from episcopal authority; Santa Sofia was intended by Arichis as a national Lombard shrine – "ecclesia sancte Sophie, quam a fundamentis edificavi pro redemptione anime mee seu pro salvatione gentis nostre et patrie" – and it certainly served that purpose, at least for a time.

Arichis enriched it with gifts and relics; he attached to it a convent of nuns; he established a special group of clergy to assure the regular performance of the liturgy; and he himself is reported to have prayed there regularly.

Santa Sofia, the palace church, was probably the source for the creation and dissemination of the Beneventan liturgy, at least in its earlier stages. But whereas Santa Sofia continued to be an important cultural asset in Benevento for many centuries, the growing importance of the bishop and the cathedral soon caused the Beneventan liturgy to be supplanted. It may be the cathedral which first received the "Gregorian" chant, and which worked to achieve its adoption. Of this we cannot be sure, however, owing to the small number of surviving musical and liturgical sources.

Sources

No Beneventan chant survives in sources of the seventh, eighth, and ninth centuries; there is no music written down at the time of Arichis and his successors. We must develop our understanding of the early musical history of Beneventan chant from musical sources that begin in the late tenth century, which persist for only about a century, and which are often suppressed, erased, or destroyed by later generations.

The chief sources of the Beneventan chant are manuscripts whose main purpose is to record the Gregorian chant; these manuscripts sometimes include some additional, non-Gregorian music, whose liturgical anomalies and consistent musical style point them out as pieces of Beneventan chant. The Beneventan chant survives, then, as doublets, appendices, and supernumerary additions in manuscripts dedicated to the chant which ultimately replaced it.

Three manuscripts of the Biblioteca capitolare of the cathedral of Benevento contain almost all the surviving Beneventan chants for the Mass. Two of these are eleventh-century graduals (manuscripts 38 and 40), including an annual series of masses in Gregorian chant, together with a supply of tropes and sequences. But a number of the principal feasts in these manuscripts have not just the Gregorian chants, but also a second mass, beginning with an *ingressa* (not an introit), whose unusual texts and musical style indicate that these are part of the music we now call Beneventan. A particularly important document is the final flyleaf of the twelfth-century gradual Benevento 35; this final leaf is a single unerased page from what must have been a whole Beneventan mass-book: it contains the end of the Christmas mass and the beginning of the mass for the next feast in the calendar (St Stephen); although there is plenty of evidence of the existence of other complete Beneventan music-books, the books themselves do not survive; we have only a few literary references and a small number of palimpsest fragments.

There are other sources of the Beneventan chant: two fragments have portions of Beneventan offices for St John the Baptist and for the Epiphany; music in Beneventan style survives in some later office books, though the music is not identified by the scribe as being Beneventan (what the scribe would call "Ambrosian"). And there is a large number of manuscripts which retain one or more elements of the special rites of Holy Week as practiced in the Beneventan liturgy. These manuscripts give us a good sense of the spread of the Beneventan rite, or of parts of it, and of its chronological persistence, but they do not add significantly to the repertory known from the three manuscripts just above.

Among the sources ought to be mentioned also the magnificent illustrated Exultet rolls of southern Italy, which were used in major monasteries and cathedrals for the blessing of the paschal candle on the vigil of Easter. Such rolls, when they contain the special Beneventan text of the Exultet, or the Beneventan melody which persisited long after most churches had converted to the imported Franco-Roman text, give further evidence of the extent and influence of the Beneventan ritual.

Liturgical characteristics

The shape and function of the Beneventan liturgy must remain to some extent uncertain. The musical sources are incomplete, and there is no surviving sacramentary, missal, lectionary, or antiphoner.

Calendar

To judge from the surviving materials, the shape of the Beneventan year was much like that of the Roman Church. Centered on Christmas and Easter, the principal feasts of Our Lord (Nativity, Epiphany, Holy Week, Easter, Ascension, Pentecost) provide a framework for feasts of saints of universal significance (Stephen, John the Baptist, Peter and Paul, Lawrence, All Saints, Martin, Andrew) and those of local importance (Michael, the Holy Twelve Brothers), as well as the Assumption, and feasts of the Holy Cross. Most major feasts are present, but there is little evidence that the Beneventan rite included a specific set of chants (with readings and prayers) for every Sunday in the year, as in the fully-developed Roman calendar. There are no surviving masses for the Sundays and weekdays of Lent, even though the two main sources do contain the Gregorian propers to which the Beneventan might well

III

have been appended had they existed. We know less still about the Sundays of Advent, or those of the ordinary time following Epiphany and Pentecost. Most likely is that a fully-specific and independent mass for each Sunday was never part of the Beneventan system.

Mass: shape and texts
The surviving mass-music for the Beneventan rite indicates that the Beneventan mass had a shape analogous to that of Rome. An entrance chant, chants to follow lections, offertory and communion chants, provided a shape familiar from the other Latin liturgies.

Chants of the ordinary are relatively rare in the surviving sources, but they indicate that the creed was frequently present in the Beneventan mass (a Lombard symptom, perhaps, in that the fact or the memory of Lombard arianism meant that orthodoxy could not be taken for granted), and the a single threefold *Kyrieleyson* was sung after the *Gloria in excelsis* (as in the Milanese rite).

Beneventan chants have a high frequency of non-biblical texts, and of texts which rearrange biblical phrases and ideas; this is a sharp contrast to the Roman rite, which in its mass texts is almost exclusively biblical and predominantly psalmic. Such a variety of texts at Benevento recalls the Milanese rite, which likewise allows a greater range of textual sources, and it suggests parallels with the poetry of the Byzantine church. Although some Beneventan texts have parallels at Milan or in the Greek rite, most do not.

Mass: chant functions
The chants of the Beneventan mass consist of at least four elements: ingressa, Alleluia, offertory, communion; sometimes a gradual is present. In this arrangement the mass is similar to the chants of other Latin rites. But the Beneventan chant is unusual in its flexibility of liturgical assignment, and in the presence of additional pieces duplicating the communion or the offertory.

The *ingressa* is the opening chant of the Beneventan mass. Like the ingressa used for the same function at Milan, the Beneventan ingressa is sung without the accompanying psalmody characteristic of the Roman introit. The Beneventan ingressae are among the most elaborate chants of the repertory; each serves for one feast only, although melodies and formulae can be adapted from one ingressa to another: the ingressa for the Holy Twelve Brothers is based on the melody for Easter; and there is a group of three ingressae, for Sts Peter and Paul, the Assumption, and All Saints, which share the same group of melodic formulae.

The *gradual* is present in only six Beneventan masses; they are not replaced with another chant in the remaining masses. The gradual may often have been omitted; however, there is evidence of four graduals in fragmentary sources, and perhaps the gradual was once a more regular feature of the Beneventan mass than appears from later manuscripts. There are three *responsoria* (*Ante sex dies, Amicus meus, Tenebrae*) used in Holy Week rites in the manner of a gradual following a lection, and perhaps they ought to be part of this group of pieces. All these chants have a single verse, and sometimes indicate a partial repetition of the opening portion.

The *Alleluia* is present in all the surviving masses except for those of Holy Week (we can presume that the Alleluia was omitted in Lent). There is a single melody which is adapted for most of the masses of the year. A second melody is used for St Stephen, and was perhaps used for other saints as well. A third melody is used for Holy Saturday and is adapted, perhaps in a later stage, to other texts for Christmas, St Peter, the Transfiguration, and the Epiphany (the last surviving only in a manuscript of Old Roman chant).

The *offertory* is present in each mass, though the offertory is often a piece used elsewhere, either in another mass or in another function (as communion or antiphon). In two masses there are two offertories. The Beneventan offertory is brief and relatively simple, unlike the elaborate compositions with long verses found in the Gregorian repertory.

The *communion* of the Beneventan mass has a wide range of musical styles, from the extremely elaborate communion of the Easter mass to the very simple antiphon-like communions found elsewhere. Many masses have two communions, either because a manuscript gives both, or because two sources give different pieces for the same function. (Perhaps there was once a tradition of two chants for the communion rite like the Milanese *confractorium* and *transitorium*). Some pieces used as communions are found in other sources as offertories, or as antiphons.

Flexibility of liturgical assignment

A number of Beneventan chants serve multiple funcions: these pieces may appear as antiphons, offertories, or communions. In addition, there are many places where sources do not agree about the chant to be assigned to a certain function in the mass, particularly in the case of offertories and communions. These phenomena may be a sign that some of these pieces may not be in their original place; it may indicate that when Beneventan chant is recorded in a Gregorian format requiring a fixed chant for every liturgical function, it becomes necessary to misrepresent the less-fixed and more flexible nature of the Beneventan repertory.

It is possible that the Beneventan mass never had, and never was intended to have, the fixity which we associate with the Roman mass. The Beneventan mass begins with fixed elements and moves to areas of more flexibility. Each mass begins with a unique ingressa, which is in some sense the signature, the marker, of this mass. To make a mass as complete as most of those that survive, it is sufficient to add an Alleluia, whose verse is easily adapted to a standard melody, and then to choose from a general pool of pieces we might call antiphons to provide music for the offertory and the communion rites. This general pool is suggested also by the fact that there are pieces used as offertories and communions which are found also as antiphons of the office, or as individual antiphons without psalmody.

Thus the ingressa, the elaborate chant, is the only fixed element in such a system, and the masses that survive in the Gregorian graduals of Benevento misrepresent the situation when they need to choose specific pieces for the offertory and the communion; in such a situation it would not be a surprise if one scribe assembled a mass differently from another. A palimpsest Beneventan book now in the Biblioteca Vallicelliana (MS C 9) has a series of ingressae, one following the other, without their accompanying masses. What could be the function of such a series? Perhaps this was one way of presenting Beneventan music: a cantor provided with the ingressa could adapt an Alleluia verse and choose a couple of antiphons (perhaps from memory), and the mass would be as complete as most of those that survive. It stands to reason that when Abbot Theobald of Montecassino presented a book of Beneventan chant to the dependent house of San Liberatore, he called his book an *ingressarium*.

Holy week

The rites of Holy Week are especially well documented in the Beneventan rite. Some are given with full rubrics beginning with manuscripts of the late tenth century, and elements of Beneventan Holy Week practices survive in many sources which retain nothing else of Beneventan music; these persist far longer than anything else in the Beneventan rite.

Surviving masses for *Palm Sunday* and for *Maundy Thursday* are relatively straightforward; they are similar to other Beneventan masses, but different from their Roman counterparts. For Palm Sunday there is additional music for the ceremony of the palms, and for Maundy Thurday there is a series of pieces for the washing of feet at the *mandatum*.

Good Friday has three functions. (1) The adoration of the cross which is performed at the third hour and repeated at the ninth hour, each time followed by a fore-mass including elaborate canticles and the reading of the passion. The adoration includes a series of antiphons performed in Greek and in Latin. There is also a bilingual antiphon (*Panta ta etni / Omnes gentes*) for processional use at the second (public?) adoration. (2) The afternoon liturgy consists of the solemn prayers and the communion of the presanctified; no music survives. (3) Vespers of Good Friday follows the afternoon liturgy.

Holy Saturday is difficult to reconstruct in its entirety, but there are clear Beneventan characteristics that distinguish this rite. In the western liturgies the vigil consists of a series of lections and prayers, recounting the history of God's relation to humankind. As a moment of renewal, Holy Saturday has traditionally been a time for the admission of new members by baptism, and this rite, with the accompanying blessing of baptismal water, is a feature of the vigil in most churches, though often not in monasteries. The vigil concludes with the first mass of Easter.

The Beneventan vigil of Easter begins, in the earliest sources, with a litany; it continues with lections, followed by the blessing of the candle; this in turn is followed by a final lection from Isaiah, "Hec est hereditas"; then follow the procession to the font, the baptisms, and the mass. Beneventan music consists of an opening antiphon, a series of four tracts, the Exultet, further antiphons (including one in Greek), the deacon's dismissal of those who are not to participate in the mass ("Si quis catechumenus est, procedat!, etc."), and the music for the vigil mass.

The Exultet

Beneventan characteristics

In most Western liturgies the blessing of the paschal candle is the first public event of the many actions of the vigil. New fire is blessed and used to light the great candle which in turn is consecrated with a prayer of particular solemnity (in the Franco-Roman, Milanese, and Beneventan rites, with versions of a prayer beginning "Exultet iam angelica turba celorum"). Often there is a procession with the announcement *Lumen christi*. These actions are found in many but not all rites; the ceremony is not used in the papal liturgy at all, for example, until relatively late. The blessing of a candle, but with other texts, is found in the Old Spanish rite and the Gelasian sacramentary; and the *Exultet* itself has a variety of texts: Franco-Roman, Beneventan, Milanese.

Only in the old Beneventan liturgy is the Exultet placed elsewhere, and this sets the Beneventan practice apart from all other Western liturgies. The Exultet comes after the lections, not before; or more precisely it is placed before the last lection, which in turn serves as a transition to the baptisms.

The Beneventan liturgy has a particular version of the prayer of blessing, the *Exultet*, which shares its opening portion with the blessings used at Milan and in the Franco-Roman liturgy, but which continues with a specifically Beneventan second portion.

This Beneventan Exultet is sung to a melody closely allied to the Beneventan liturgy, a very simple recitation used also for other rites of Holy Week. This is a special tone used within a normal lection when the text quotes a prayer (or, as the manuscripts call it, a Canticle): the prayer of Jonah, the prayer of Jeremiah, the prayer of the three children in the fiery furnace. The Exultet is not in itself a lection, and it is not a quotation of a biblical prayer, like those of Jonah, Jeremiah, or the three children; but it is, of course, itself a prayer, at least in its second part. This Beneventan melody of the Exultet persists long after the Franco-Roman text was adopted in the course of the twelfth century. Thus when we find Exultets that preserve the Beneventan melody, even when their text is the imported Franco-Roman version, we can be certain that the Beneventan liturgy has had its influence in that place.

Exultet rolls

The importance of the Exultet in the ceremonies of the Easter vigil can be judged from the value of the manuscripts prepared especially for this one moment in the year, much as the luxury of many gospel-books is a measure, at least in part, of the importance of the Gospel reading in the ceremonies of the mass. These southern Italian Exultets are documents of almost unparalleled luxury, and they take the rare form of the roll. Rolls are uncommon in the tenth and eleventh centuries; parchment membranes, attached end to end, and written in a single long column, were unusual in the manufacture of written documents. The Exultet was written on a scroll in order to lend importance, solemnity, and magnificence to the occasion. The fact that something is in scroll form gives it a special significance, and the use of a scroll in the liturgy of the Easter vigil is particularly suitable. The illuminated Exultet rolls of southern Italy were extraordinary objects when they were made, and even now they fascinate us on account of their beautiful miniatures, sometimes painted upside down with respect to the liturgical text with its musical notation.

The earliest and arguably the most important surviving Exultet roll (now Vatican City, Vat, lat. 9820) is from Benevento, made in the late tenth century for the use of the convent of San Pietro extra muros, Benevento. An illustration with a legend shows Iohannes presenting the roll to St Peter; and in the text of the original roll the concluding invocations include prayers for the abbess and her congregation ("necnon et famulam tuam abbatissam nostram cum universa congregacione beatissimi petri sibi commissa"). The roll is generally understood to be a copy, executed for St Peter's, of a roll originally made for Archbishop Landolf of Benevento (969–982); the existence of other liturgical rolls evidently made for Landolf (those at the Biblioteca Casanatense), and the extraordinary attention given to the archibishop in the illustrations, make a strong case for the present roll being a copy of an archiepiscopal original. The part of the text which differs from the original is written after the presentation scene, suggesting that a final presentation scene, but different from this one, may have been present in the archiepiscopal original, on the model of the "LANDOLFI EPISCOPI SUM" found at the end of the Casanatense benedictional Biblioteca Casanatense 724 (B I 13) 1.

The practice of using a roll for the Exultet was not unique to Benevento; but it is only in southern Italy, in the area which practiced the Beneventan liturgy, that elaborately-illustrated Exultet rolls were used. Thus the area has unique practices which connect the Exultet rolls with the particular characteristics of the Beneventan liturgy. The practice of using a roll for the Exultet survived the change from the Beneventan text to the Franco-Roman; indeed some old rolls were re-manufactured to meet new needs. Thus the Vatican roll from Benevento was reversed and a substitute Franco-Roman text was written upside down to provide inverted pictures. An Exultet roll now in the Biblioteca Casantense, and which was once attached to two tenth-century liturgical rolls of Landolf mentioned above, is also of Beneventan manufacture; it bears the Franco-Roman text, and its pictures are based on those of the Landolf scroll as preserved in Vat. lat. 9820. This series of pictures influences Exultet rolls through the thirteenth century manufactured for Montecassino, Salerno, Mirabella Eclano, and elsewhere. Altogether there are some twenty-five Exultet rolls from southern Italy, most of them with the newer Franco-Roman text.

Office music and other survivals

There are three substantial survivals of Beneventan music for the divine office: the Vespers of Good Friday preserved in several manuscripts as part of the special Beneventan rites of Holy Week; the Vespers of St John the Baptist preserved in the so-called "Solesmes flyleaves," and what appears to be a Vespers of the Ephiphany in a fragment from Bisceglie. The Beneventan office, so far as we can determine from these fragments, was similar to that of other Latin liturgies. Antiphons with psalms sung to regular psalm-tones, a responsory, and a canticle (Magnificat), are preserved from all three of these Vespers offices. In addition, office books from southern Italy sometimes preserve groups of antiphons which are in Beneventan style even though they are transmitted in Gregorian books as though they were part of the received Roman liturgy. Important series of antiphons for Saint Barbatus, bishop of Benevento, and for the Holy Twelve Brothers of Benevento (including the mass-communion as one of the antiphons), suggest that these are survivals of a local liturgy of the office, used in later books for local saints. Other "Gregorian" offices have one or two antiphons whose style seems Beneventan, and in these cases we can do no more than wonder whether such pieces might not be the remnants of a larger repertory of old Beneventan antiphons. Likewise there are occasional antiphons among the pieces for rogations, and a pair of pieces for the Purification, whose style seems decidedly Beneventan even though there is nothing in their transmission to suggest that the scribe knows their Beneventan origin.

Musical characteristics

General aspects of Beneventan musical style

The old Beneventan chant has a uniform style. Although there are a few simple pieces, and a few melismas, the music generally proceeds at a regular, rather ornate pace, using mostly stepwise intervals. Scattered throughout the chant are repetitions of melodic formulas, small invariable turns of phrase that are repeated vastly more often than are their counterparts in other chant dialects. Unlike the situation in Gregorian chant, there are few stylistic distinctions to be made in the repertory on the bases of liturgical function or modal category. There are no clear distinctions between music for the choir and music for the cantor. Even though the surviving repertory is small, we have several pieces preserved in multiple sources, and in such cases the sources agree with only the smallest discrepancies. On a superficial level the pieces are all alike.

There are archaic features in the Beneventan chant. The tonal range is considerably restricted. There is no evidence that the Beneventan chant was ever subject to the systematizing effects of the eight-mode system imposed on much other music. There is a remarkable economy of means in this music; the same few cadences and melodic formulae, the use of a very limited range; a tendency to immediate repetition, both at short range and for long musical periods. These may be characteristics of music carried for a long time in oral transmission. The Beneventan chant was written down substantially later than the Gregorian repertory among the Franks, and it is certainly true that the other repertories written rather late – the Old-Roman and the Ambrosian – share the surface prolixity, and some of the musical characteristics which are often called archaic, but which are perhaps typical of oral tradition.

Musical examples

We may take as examples of Beneventan chant the music for the mass of Easter. Example 1 shows the Easter offertory, the simplest chant of this mass. Divided into three phrases, the melody is full of Beneventan musical formulae which appear throughout the repertory; though they are not repeated within this offertory, many of these formulae can be detected by comparison with other chants.

Example 1: Angelus Domini

The Easter Alleluia is only slightly more elaborate. The same melody is used for at least fourteen Beneventan Alleluias, of which two examples are presented in Example 2. Note that the two verses, which otherwise share the same melody, end on different pitches; of the fourteen Alleluias sharing this melody, five end, like the Easter *Pascha nostrum*, on A, while nine end, like

Territus Andreas, on G. If we assume that the Alleluia is repeated after the verse, then the final note will always be that of the Alleluia, but it still seems unusual – and in Gregorian chant it certainly is unusual – for a verse to end on a different pitch from that of the Alleluia. The final note seems not to be significant to the melodic structure of the Alleluia.

Example 2: Two Alleluias

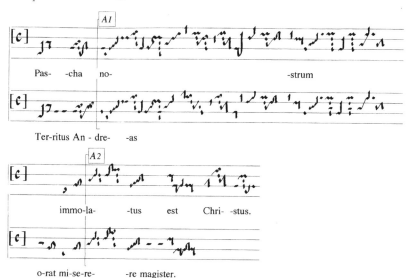

The Alleluia melody is not made in reprises (like the Communion and Ingressa below), but is a standard melody used for many verses; the two parallel versions presented here give a good idea of the fixity of its notes. We can recognize some short formulae that by now may be familiar, and begin to see how the text is adapted to the melody.

The melody of the Alleluia is adjusted to the text on the basis of two accents (marked A1 and A2). The first brief portion of text that can stand alone ("Pascha nostrum") accommodates recitation at the beginning, and closes the first half with two melismas beginning on the accent at A1. The first melisma is essentially invariable; the second ("-strum") is sometimes omitted. The remainder of the text is set to the second portion; an opening recitation leads to a shorter melisma on accent A2; two possible endings are shown here; a third, used for longer texts, includes an extension of the longer melody.

Example 3 is a transcription of the Beneventan communion for Easter.

Example 3: Easter Communion

This communion is unique in the repertory in that it has two long verses of a doxology; these are the only Beneventan communion-verses. The transcription is arranged to show the regular repetition which is characteristic of this piece, and of many others in the repertory. A large-scale repetition shapes the whole communion. Lines 6 through 8 (the first of the two verses) are paralleled by lines 9 through 11 of the second verse. But this repetition is not a recitation-formula like that of a Gregorian responsory-verse: the same pattern is used in the communion itself, as can be seen in lines 2 through 5, where the central section is repeated as lines 3 and 4. And also unlike a responsory-formula, this repeating melody is unique to this piece, although similar repetition-plans are found in other pieces. Thus the communion as a whole is made of three long reprises, preceded by the introductory phrase *Qui manducauerit*. In addition to the larger pattern which tailors this piece, a mosaic of smaller melodic formulae links this communion with the whole repertory. The lettered columns in the transcription indicate short melodic units that recur not only here but throughout the Beneventan chant.

This formulaic construction on two levels – on the one hand, the structuring of individual pieces in multiple reprises of a long melody, and on the other hand, the presence throughout the repertory of short melodic fragments – is characteristic in the Beneventan chant. There is very little chance of mistaking a Beneventan melody of this kind for an unknown piece from the Gregorian repertory.

The Beneventan ingressa for Easter (Example 4), like the communion, is made by reprises. There are six repetitions of a central melody, to which different beginnings and endings are attached. These can be further grouped into two larger cycles of three phrases each. Lines 1 and 4, which open the cycles, share an initial melody not found in the other phrases of each group; and lines 3 and 6, which close the two cycles, share a cadence unique to these phrases. To these two groups are added two Alleluias, standing outside the repetition structure, and which close the piece.

The musical style of the Beneventan chant is relatively uniform; unlike the Gregorian chant, it does not vary much from one liturgical category to another; it is a sort of pre-modal music, almost every piece ending on one of two notes (A or G); the regular repetition of single phrases throughout a piece recalls the structure of the Gregorian tracts (which are also made in reprises, and have only two modes). These unified stylistic attributes give us a view on a specific and localized musical practice of the eighth century, a

Example 4: Easter ingressa

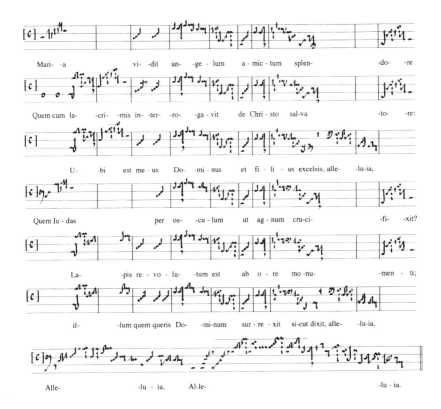

Mari- -a   vi- -dit an- -ge - lum   a - mic - tum   splen-   -do- -re

Quem cum la-   -cri- -mis in- -ter- -ro- -ga - vit   de Chri - sto   sal-va   -to- -re:

U- -bi   est me - us   Do- -mi- -nus   et   fi - li - us excelsis, alle-   -lu-ia,

Quem Iu - das   per os- -cu - lum   ut   ag - num   cru-ci-   -fi- -xit?

La-   -pis re - vo - lu- -tum est   ab   o - re   mo -nu-   -men - ti;

il-   -lum quem queris Do-   -mi-num   sur - re - xit   si-cut dixit, alle-   -lu-ia,

Alle-   -lu - ia,   Al-le-   -lu - ia.

valuable repertory in itself and a possible paradigm for the early stages of
chants which are found in more evolved forms in other repertories.

Roman chant at Benevento

Early arrival

When did Gregorian chant arrive in South Italy? Judging only from the age of
the southern Italian manuscripts it might have arrived with the millennium; the
oldest sources are essentially those that preserve the vestiges of Beneventan
chant. Much internal evidence, however, suggests that the Gregorian chant
had actually been in use for a long time before the surviving sources were

written. The Franco-Roman, or "Gregorian" chant was in use in South Italy by the end of the eighth century.

This is a very important piece in the puzzle of the early history of western chant, but the matter can only be summarized here. Essentially, the eighth-century date arises from the presence in the Gregorian chant of the Beneventan region of elements which had disappeared from the Gregorian liturgy elsewhere by the end of the eighth century. There is much to be taken into consideration: the retention of the older Roman psalter in chant texts which elsewhere use texts from the later "Gallican" psalter adopted in the ninth and tenth centuries; the melodic archaisms of the Gregorian chant of Benevento, which match in many ways the oldest Carolingian sources; details of the lectionary, which preserve features which had disappeared elsewhere by the middle of the eighth century.

Particularly interesting is the Beneventan treatment of feast days which were without a proper liturgy in early Carolingian stages of the Gregorian rite, for they show that the received version of Gregorian chant was an early one. Here one example must serve for many. The mass for the seventh Sunday after Pentecost (Introit *Omnes gentes*) is omitted in some Beneventan manuscripts. Some early witnesses of the Roman tradition also lack this mass. It is omitted in the 8th-century Cantatorium of Monza; the 8th–9th century Mont-Blandin antiphoner includes it, but with the rubric *ISTE EBDOMATA NON EST IN ANTEFONARIOS ROMANOS*; and the manuscripts of the Old-Roman tradition also omit this mass. But the mass is otherwise uniformly present in the Gregorian tradition, with the sole exception of a group of manuscripts with ties to southern Italy. The absence of this mass, evidently added to the Gregorian repertory in the eighth century, testifies to a particularly archaic aspect of the received tradition at Benevento.

Evidently, then, the Gregorian chant did not arrive at Benevento at the end of the tenth century; for then it would not have preserved these archaic elements; the early liturgical lacunae would already have been filled, and the Beneventan manuscripts for these feasts would match versions found elsewhere in Europe. But there are so many liturgical features that had disappeared elsewhere by the end of the eighth and the early years of the ninth century that a Gregorian liturgy including these features must already have been present at Benevento before changes took place elsewhere. The Gregorian chant must have been in place in South Italy in the eighth century.

The arrival of musical notation

Did this music arrive in a form with musical notation? Musical notation is particularly interesting in the South, because it appears that it was not invented in Italy, but was imported. There are several reasons for thinking so. First, it is highly unlikely that what is essentially the same system of neumes should be invented independently in more than one place. And the oldest musical documents we have are not Beneventan but Frankish. It may be that musical notation came to southern Italy as a part of the influence that also brought the Frankish version of the Roman liturgy which ultimately became the standard for all of Italy.

The earliest Beneventan musical notation known to me is in the colophon written before 949 by the monk Iaquintus at the end of Montecassino manuscript 269. Iaquintus' musical writing is fluent, and very similar to the other examples of early Beneventan music-writing from the late tenth and the very early eleventh century.

The thin, spidery early Beneventan notation gave way in the early eleventh century to a style which is more vertically oriented, and which matches the Beneventan script in many particulars: it includes many more strictly vertical strokes; it uses the contrasting thin and thick lines typical of the script; and it is written with a pen of generally the same breadth as that used for the text.

The very rapid development of musical notation in the Beneventan zone suggests its importation and assimilation to the Beneventan script. By the eleventh century the music looks like the script; and from then onward, music and text go hand-in-hand, reaching a height of elegance and refinement in the twelfth century. The Beneventan notation *looks* foreign at its beginnings, and only at a second stage becomes assimilated to the style of the local script.

Kenneth Levy has argued, on the basis of graphic similarities, that Gregorian chant, *with neumes* (and the neumes are Levy's chief point) arrived in South Italy in the late eighth century (See Kenneth Levy, "Charlemagne's Archetype of Gregorian Chant," *Journal of the American Musicological Society*, 40, 1987, 1–30). We have suggested reasons for agreement with Professor Levy about the date of the arrival of the liturgy itself, but the question of musical notation is problematical. While the musical aspect of the liturgy might have been transmitted orally using books containing texts only, it seems unlikely that a notational system imported in the eighth century would by the beginning of the eleventh have changed so little in its paleographical aspect. Already in the first half of the eleventh century the notation has adapted itself to the norms of Beneventan writing, and makes further changes rapidly thereafter; that the notational style should have been static, the notation looking different from the script, from the late eighth century until the eleventh seems incompatible both with the later continuous changes and with the substantial developments in the Beneventan script itself during the same period. More consistent with the available evidence, it seems to me, is that musical notation was received only shortly before the time of Iaquintus; that it rapidly gained a foothold on account of its great utility; and that it changed, almost as rapidly, into the clearly Beneventan notation of the eleventh century that so well matches the idiosyncrasies of the local script. We cannot say that there was no musical notation in the eighth century: only that there is no evidence of its use in southern Italy until the middle of the tenth. Indeed, it may be the arrival of a useful system of notation that prompted the writing of the local chant in the same style of writing used to record the Gregorian melodies.

Paul the Deacon

Exactly how this Gregorian influence came to South Italy, how it was received, and how it gradually overshadowed the Beneventan chant, will probably never be fully explained. But, as a paradigm of Frankish influence on the southern Italian church – perhaps, indeed, as a direct cause – we can consider the career of the eminent Paul the Deacon, whose connections with Carolingian cultural circles and with the southern centers of Benevento and Montecassino puts him squarely in the center of the period in which the northern chant arrived in the south.

Paul, the famous historian of the Lombards, an important poet and teacher, is also a significant figure in eighth-century liturgical matters. He is credited with assembling a liturgical homiliary, and was connected with the mass-book which Charlemagne requested from Pope Hadrian I. After his years at the Lombard royal court of Pavia, Paul was present at the court of Benevento from 763 to 774; his *Historia romana* is dedicated to Arichis' consort Adelperga with an elaborate acrostic, and his own epitaph for Arichis transcends funerary rhetoric to describe the loss of a friend. When Pavia fell in 774 Paul became a monk of Montecassino, where he remained until his death in 799 except for three years at the court of Charlemagne (782–785/6). He was thus closely associated both with the Carolingian world and with the centers of primary importance to South Italy in this period.

We cannot be certain that Paul himself was the intermediary of the Roman rite in the South; but his career exemplifies the cultural currents which brought the Gregorian liturgy from the Carolingian North to the Lombard South.

When we consider the saints of Benevento below we cannot fail to notice the coincidence: The Twelve Brothers in 760 have a Beneventan mass; St Mercurius, whose relics were brought to Benevento in 768, has none; and the arrival of Paul the Deacon falls betwen between the two, in 763.

And it is after Paul moves to Montecassino that that great abbey begins its active role as the recognized fountainhead of western monasticism; its practices are studied as models; and perhaps under his influence it begins a rapprochement with the liturgy of Rome. That the Gregorian chant was used at Montecassino seems certain; but what is equally clear – but not mentioned – is that the Beneventan chant was used there also.

Archaic qualities of the "Gregorian" chant at Benevento

The Franco-Roman chant was received at Benevento in the eighth century, and survives in manuscripts from no earlier than the end of the tenth century, and mostly from the eleventh and later. Nevertheless, the versions of the Gregorian chant preserved in the later manuscripts – later, but the earliest we have from the region – retains many qualities which indicate both its early arrival in the South, and the faithful transmission of the received version for two centuries and more. Indeed, this quality of fidelity to early versions of the chant strengthens the supposition that the Roman chant arrived in the South at an early date.

Particular characteristics of the Beneventan version of Gregorian chant have been studied in considerable detail in Volume 14 of the *Paléographie musicale*, but it is worth reviewing some of the principal characteristics that give a particular value to the Roman chant as written at Benevento.

We have already mentioned the evidence of liturgical archaisms in the received versions of the Roman liturgy. In the matter of chant, Beneventan manuscripts continue to transmit the Roman psalter, whereas most of the rest of Europe altered received Roman-psalter texts to the Gallican psalter widely adopted in the ninth century. A word of explanation may help here.

The Gregorian chant is closely bound up with its texts; these texts are largely psalmic, and the Roman chant was evidently formulated using text from the Roman psalter (that is, from St Jerome's first translation of the book of psalms). In the course of the ninth century much of Europe adopted the use of the Gallican psalter (Jerome's second translation, usually named for the wide use it received in the north). Where chants were inextricably linked to their texts – as with the music of the mass, the antiphons and responsories,and so on – there was no question of altering the traditional Roman psalter to the

Gallican version. But where a psalm was sung to a formula, as with the psalms of the office, or the individual psalm-verses sung with introits (and sometimes communions) at mass, it was frequently decided to use the Gallican version: this is the case in many northern chant manuscripts, where the same text may appear in Gallican form as the introit-verse, and its original Roman form as the text of another piece in the same mass. (This is the case, for example, with the introit-verse for the first Sunday of Advent, which in St Gall manuscripts is "Vias tuas Domine **demonstra** mihi et semitas tuas **doce** me" (Gallican version), while the gradual of the same mass includes "Vias tuas domine **notas fac** mihi et semitas tuas **edoce** me" (Roman psalter). Clearly the Roman chant was conceived using a single version of the psalter, and the substitution of the Gallican psalter – only where the formulaic quality of the music makes it possible – is a later alteration. The Beneventan manuscripts, however, retain the Roman psalter everywhere. They remain faithful to their received tradition, and are not tempted to substitute the newer version of the psalter. The Gallican psalter never had much currency in southern Italy, but it is at least clear that the Roman chant, when it arrived in its Frankish redaction, did not yet have the Gallican psalm-verses; and that Benevento was never tempted to insert them.

There are distinct qualities in the melodic versions of the Roman chant transmitted in the Beneventan manuscripts which suggests that the melodies remain faithful to received tradition, and pass along a musical version closer to their Frankish original than many manuscripts of earlier date and arguably more central tradition. This cannot be fully demonstrated here, but the reader can refer to the extensive study of melodic variants in the Beneventan tradition carried out in Volume 14 of the *Paléographie musicale*, pages 153–196. That study, comparing Beneventan manuscripts with versions of chants in the St Gall tradition (notably the manuscript Einsiedeln 121 of the late tenth or early eleventh century, taking this to be close to the tradition received from Rome). At a striking number of places the Beneventan manuscripts agree with Einsiedeln 121 where many others do not. Dom Hesbert, writing at the conclusion of that study, writes:

> . . . we noted the very special, one might even say strange, character of the Beneventan tradition. We have shown that in analyzing this first impression, we were led to observe that in all these domains: paleographical and liturgical, semiographic and melodic, this characteristic note was to be explained in the same way, by the archaism of this particular tradition and its truly unique fidelity, on certain points, to the purest Roman and Gregorian tradition; with the result that, if *originality* at first appears to be the characteristic of the

Beneventan tradition, there is nothing to retract from this judgement, provided that the term be understood in its most strictly etymological sense.

Saints at Benevento: court and cathedral, Beneventan and Roman chant

How did Beneventan chant give way to Gregorian chant at Benevento? Was Beneventan chant specifically suppressed at a given moment? Did they coexist for a time? Was there a portion of the city and of the region that maintained Beneventan chant, while others adopted the imported liturgy and music more readily?

These questions will probably never be fully answered. In general terms, however, it appears that the growing importance of the cathedral of Benevento in the ninth century reflects the growing significance of the idea of a universal church, of adherence to the authority of Rome and to the liturgy and music which represent that general authority. It may be that the Beneventan chant persisted among those who felt a loyalty to Lombard tradition, and was retained in places, perhaps like Santa Sofia in Benevento, which had a long and proud Lombard heritage.

We can trace some elements of the changing influence of Lombard and Frankish, Beneventan and Roman, court and cathedral, by examining the cult of saints in the city of Benevento.

An important patron of the Lombards was St Michael the archangel, the warrior prince of angels who protected the Lombards of the South. St Michael's apparition at Monte Gargano was celebrated on May 8th, and his shrine on Monte Gargano was an important place of pilgrimage for the Lombards from at least the seventh century; but the shrine was not near Benevento, and it was not always easy for the dukes of Benevento to retain control of it. Nevertheless it was always arranged that the diocese of Siponto, in which the Gargano shrine was located, remain under the jurisdiction of the bishops of Benevento. A Beneventan mass for the feast of May 8th survives.

Arichis II, as he assumed independent power as Prince of Benevento, assembled relics to glorify and embellish his court church of Santa Sofia, and to exemplify in ecclesiastical terms the importance of an independent Benevento. He gathered from throughout the region the remains of twelve martyrs – whom tradition quickly made into brothers – and interred them in Santa Sofia in 760. The cult of the Holy Twelve Brothers, intended as "patroni patriae," spread throughout the region; and the only datable music in Beneventan style is the Beneventan mass for these newly-"invented" saints.

Eight years after the translation of the Holy Twelve Brothers, in 768, Arichis II acquired another apt patron for the warrior Lombards. The relics of Saint Mercurius, one of the great military saints of Byzantium, were enshrined with great pomp in a special altar in Santa Sofia. Mercurius, like the Twelve Brothers, was intended by Arichis to be a patron of the court, of the church of Santa Sofia, of the city, and of the Lombard people. His cult was strong in the Middle Ages, well beyond the time of the suppression of the Beneventan chant; the relief over the doorway of Santa Sofia, probably of the twelfth century, includes Christ with the Virgin and Saint Mercurius with a kneeling figure who may be Arichis II. Curiously, there is no surviving Beneventan mass for Mercurius, though one was created only eight years earlier for the Holy Twelve Brothers. Nor is there a newly-adapted Gregorian mass, as there was to be in 838 for St Bartholomew.

In ninth-century Benevento itself, as the political power of the capital waned the relative importance of the church increased. We can trace this in the relics of the local saints.

The body of St Januarius, who was wrongly identified with a historical bishop of Benevento, was robbed from Naples about 831 and brought to Benevento by duke Sico. The relics were interred first in the church of St Festus and later transferred to the church of "Hierusalem," said to have been the seat of the early bishops of Benevento before the cathedral of St Mary. Though he was a patron of the ducal family, Januarius was a bishop, and connected more with the cathedral than with the court church of Santa Sofia. Liturgical material for St Januarius is not abundant, and none of the chant is in Beneventan style.

A few years later (838) the relics of the apostle St Bartholomew were brought to Benevento, and the feast of his translation entered the calendar the following year. His relics, which were to remain at Benevento for 160 years, were interred in a church adjoining the Cathedral, and Bartholomew became the chief saint of the city and a second patron of the cathedral. A mass for St Bartholomew, in Gregorian style, is unique to Beneventan manuscripts.

The cult of St Barbatus, though he was a seventh-century bishop of Benevento, seems to have gathered strength only in the early ninth century. He was not "invented," like the Twelve Brothers and Mercurius, nor stolen, like Saints Januarius and Bartholomew; he was a local saint who had long been venerated; but the resurgence of his cult in the ninth century was doubtless related in part to his being a bishop; and the ninth-century *vita* takes pains to justify an anomalous situation in the organization of the church – namely that the diocese of Siponto, which included the sanctuary of St Michael the

Archangel at Monte Gargano, had long been subordinated to the diocese of Benevento without any Papal ratification. The *vita*, by asserting that St Barbatus originated this arrangement, may have sought to explain a state of affairs that became increasingly awkward as the church of Benevento sought closer connections to Rome.

The Holy Twelve Brothers are martyrs found and translated by Arichis to the court church; St Mercurius is a Byzantine military saint likewise interred in Santa Sofia – these are the eighth-century patrons of the new Lombard principality. But the saints of the ninth century are different; they are connected with the cathedral and with the bishop. This shift of emphasis, over less than a hundred years, from court-centered to church-centered cults is paralleled by the shift from composition in Beneventan style to Gregorian.

Co-existence of Beneventan and Roman chant

How was the Beneventan chant used by those who wrote it in the eleventh century, so long after its creation? Was it merely a memory of a glorious past, preserved by proud Lombard scribes who had no other real use for it? Or were there separate churches which practiced the Beneventan chant as an alternative or an adjunct to the now universal Roman liturgy? Was the Beneventan chant a real alternative for the high feast days for which masses are preserved? Lacking further information we cannot be sure, but there is some evidence that the Beneventan chant was a real alternative, at least at certain places and occasions. An example is in the monastic book Vat. Ottob. 145, a manuscript based on Montecassino practice but connected with the important church of Santa Sofia of Benevento; its litany includes the Holy Twelve Brothers named individually, and Saints Graficus and Quineclus, "martyres in Sancta Sophia" according to other books from the Beneventan church. A rubric describing a monastic *mandatum* ceremony states "when we do not sing these antiphons according to the Roman (rite, liturgy) as they are written above, we sing them according to the Ambrosian (we would say, 'Beneventan'), as follows" (*Quando non canimus ipse ant. secundum romano. quo modo supra scripte sunt canimus secundum Ambro[sianum] hoc modo*). And then follow six antiphons, all of them used elsewhere in the Beneventan rite as Communions.

There are several churches which as late as the eleventh century posessed books of Gregorian chant as well as Beneventan. The monk Theobald, who was provost of San Liberatore alla Maiella and later became abbot of its mother house, Montecassino, in 1022, provided many books for the church.

In his *Commemoratorium*, partly written in his own hand, which was begun in 1019 and continued in subsequent years, Theobald lists the objects provided at his behest for San Liberatore; he names many types of book: ymnuarium, antiphonarium, and so on. The last item, added to the document after Theobald had been elected abbot, reads "et unum ingressarium," doubtless a book of Beneventan masses, whose opening chant is always called "ingressa." Evidently both kinds of chant were useful at San Liberatore.

In tenth-century Salerno, the princely church of Santa Maria listed the following among its possession: "codices: duobus liber comites unum indifanario [=antifonario] de die et unum de nocte et alium ambrosianum"; and a list from Bari in 1067 lists "omelia et feriale cum gestis de sanctis; antifomarium de dia et alium de nocte (unum ambrosianum)."

And there are eleventh-century fragmentary remains of books of Beneventan chant: not a few masses tucked into a Gregorian book, but whole "ingressaria ambrosiana." The flyleaf from Benevento 35 (f. 202) is one example, but there are others. Codex C 9 in the Biblioteca Vallicelliana contains several palimpsest folios from an "Ambrosian" mass-book; Vat. lat. 10657, the cartulary of Santa Maria di Mare in the Tremiti Islands, and Montecassino 361, written in the twelfth century, likewise contain leaves from formerly complete Beneventan books.

How does it happen that the Gregorian chant arrives as early as the eighth century, but the local variety of liturgical music, the Beneventan chant, continues to be written, and presumably sung, well into the eleventh? It is possible, indeed likely, that some places were more attached to the old Lombard music than others. One imagines that at Benevento the church of Santa Sofia, long a princely chapel palatine, and the repository of so many "patroni patriae," would continue the use of the local chant. However, we have no books of Beneventan chant which we know to have originated at Santa Sofia. We do know, however, that Santa Sofia was viewed as having its own performing tradition, to judge from the marginal addition to the Gregorian-Beneventan communion *Lutum fecit* in the gradual Benevento 34, f. 94. A melodic version different from that shown in the manuscript is marked "in Sancta Sophia." By the twelfth century, when two copies of a Santa Sofia *ordo officii* were made (Naples VI E 43, Vat. lat. 4928) there is no remaining trace of the Beneventan liturgy, except for the placement of the Holy Saturday Exultet in the old Beneventan position after the lections. At some point before these documents were made (or indeed perhaps at just this point), any remaining traces of Beneventan chant were banished from Santa Sofia.

The ordinals of Santa Sofia just mentioned are closely modeled on ordinals of Montecassino; and it was shortly before the twelfth century "reform" of Santa Sofia (if that is what happened) that a similar process happened at Montecassino. We know from the Chronicle of Montecassino that in 1058 Pope Stephen IX visited the monastery, of which he had been made abbot shortly before his recent elevation to the papacy, and strictly forbade the singing of "Ambrosian" chant: "Tunc etiam et Ambrosianum cantum in ecclesia ista penitus interdixit." This pronouncement confirmed what had already been taking place at Montecassino and elsewhere. Desiderius, Pope Stephen's designated successor as abbot, carried out a renewal of the abbey's liturgical books. Desiderius was born of a noble family in Benevento, and he had been a monk of Santa Sofia; he surely knew the Beneventan chant, and perhaps had sung it many times. Desiderius' reform at Montecassino had the effect of eradicating the Beneventan chant, whether his purpose was liturgical renewal or embellishment; we have no musical books from Montecassino from before the time of abbot Desiderius, and those made in his time reflect a complete adherence to the Roman rite. Only a few fragments give evidence that Beneventan chant was once regularly used at Montecassino.

It is at Benevento that some effort was made to preserve the older repertory alongside the new, and two manuscripts (Benevento 38 and Benevento 40) now in the Biblioteca capitolare preserve the great majority of the surviving repertory.

On occasion an effort was made to create a sort of hybrid rite, combining elements of the Gregorian and the Beneventan rites in a single liturgical function. The scribe of Vat. lat. 10673, writing a manuscript whose provenance is unfortunately unknown, tried to produce an amalgamated Gregorian-Beneventan order for Good Friday. But unsatisfied with his hybrid results, he began again, and wrote a long rubric detailing the pure Beneventan rite for the day; he begins "Likewise the manner in which the function of Good Friday is carried out according to the Ambrosian rite," and gives us our clearest view of a whole Beneventan ceremony. For Holy Saturday a number of scribes (including those of Benevento 38 and Benevento 40) have attempted to insert Beneventan elements – particularly the Beneventan tracts – into the Gregorian rite for the Easter vigil; the solutions are never satisfactory, and the scribe of Vat. lat. 10673 acknowledges the difficulty when he writes "The lection *Hec est hereditas*, which is placed fifth according to the Roman rite should be read here; according to the Ambrosian it should be read after the blessing of the candle." Occasionally Beneventan chants survive in series of optional pieces, for the *mandatum* of Maundy Thurdsay, in series of Rogation and Purification antiphons. But the attempt to combine the two rites seems to have had little success, and the deliberate suppression of the Beneventan rite can be seen in the physical mutilation of most of the surviving sources.

A "sententia" attached to a poem about Gregorian and Ambrosian chant in an eleventh-century miscellany at Montecassino perhaps describes the mixed feelings, and perhaps the wistful longing for simpler times, that must have accompanied the demise of the Beneventan chant in at least some worshippers: "It is not to be understood in such a way that the Ambrosian chant is to be despised; but by God's favor, the Roman chant is to be preferred, for brevity and the disdain of the people."

Romano-Beneventan chant

The received Gregorian chant was faithfully sung and transmitted in southern Italy, but in cases where the received repertory was lacking music for a feast instituted later it was necessary to provide suitable music. These lacunae are of two sorts: feasts which were originally without proper liturgies in the Roman order, and those feasts which were celebrated only locally, and for which the Roman repertory therefore contained no music.

In the first case, we have already mentioned the fact that Benevento does not have music for certain feasts generally provided elsewhere in manuscripts of the ninth century and later: this is, we have said, a sign of the early arrival of the Gregorian chant in the south. But these feasts needed to be kept, and in order to do so it was necessary to provide music on the spot. This is what gives rise to a group of chants composed at Benevento (or in the region) in Gregorian style, but of purely local circulation. Music of this kind is found, for example, for days that were aliturgical in the Roman rite (usually because they were the day after another important celebration). Thus the second Sunday in Lent (DOMINICA VACAT) was originally without a liturgy of its own, since it followed the ordination mass of the previous day, whose extent was such that it pre-empted the rites of the following Sunday. Similar situations are to be observed with the Saturday after Ash Wednesday and the Saturday before Palm Sunday. Many other traditions fill the gap in various ways, often by adopting music already used for other days.

At Benevento the same processes were followed. Sometimes pieces were repeated from elsewhere; but often new music was composed for these lacunae, and their composition gives us a look at how musicians of the Beneventan zone understood and appreciated the style of Gregorian chant.

There is a substantial body of this Romano-Beneventan chant, and much of it has been considered in Volume 14 of the *Paléographie musicale*. Here we can take only a sampling of Beneventan composition in Gregorian style.

Chants for vacant feasts

Example 5 shows two Beneventan compositions, along with material from standard Gregorian pieces to which they are related.

Example 5: Romano-Beneventan introits

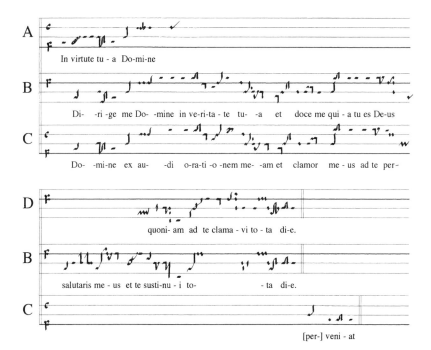

The introit *Dirige me domine* (Ps. 24:5) is the introit for the Romano-Beneventan mass for the second Sunday of Lent, whose other pieces are also adaptations of Gregorian melodies or new compositions. This introit seems to be a new composition, inspired at its beginning by a number of Gregorian pieces which open with similar melodies (two of these openings are transcribed here). The composer may have been reminded by the word *domine* in his text of the introit *In uirtute tua domine*, whose opening melody he borrows. This beginning is generally used for pieces in the seventh or eighth mode, which will end on G; but the Beneventan composer soon goes his own way, and makes a handsome melody. Coming to the end, he notes the similarity of his text (*tota die*) to the close of the introit *Inclina*, and borrows its ending; this latter introit is in the first mode; and yet the Beneventan composer has produced an original melody whose mode is that of neither of his models, but the second mode, as is confirmed not only by its melody but by the psalmody which accompanies the introit. (There are some Beneventan manuscripts which transmit a slightly different ending on G).

At a second stage in Romano-Beneventan composition it was necessary for someone to produce an introit for the Saturday before Palm Sunday, also originally without a liturgy of its own. The Beneventan composer of this introit *Domine exaudi* modeled his piece on the already-existing Romano-Beneventan introit *Dirige* we have just seen. But this new piece is surely not the work of the same composer as that of *Dirige*; he is an unworthy successor. Here the composer takes his text *Domine exaudi orationem meam* (Ps. 101:2) and follows along with *Dirige*; he may have been reminded of *Dirige* by the common word *domine*, or he may have chosen to adapt a local piece rather than a hallowed member of the canon. However, he errs considerably in his work. The beginning matches fairly well; and he then aligns the beginning of his second phrase (*et clamor meus ad te ueniat*) with the *et* found also in his model. But in the model, which is also divided into two phrases (though longer ones), the *et* of *et doce me* is not a beginning, but the end of the first half. The result is that the second adapter, following along mindlessly, arrives at *clamor* and gives it the music of *edoce me*. But *edoce me* is a moment of repose, the close of a very important subsection, after which a pause and a breath should occur. Our adapter, however, continues right through this, as he must do to connect the adjective *meus* with its noun. The result is that the music for *meus*, which in the original is a vigorous new beginning, is tacked on to the previous musical phrase at the expense of the harmony of music and text. By the time our hapless adapter arrives at *ad te*, he realizes that he has only four syllables left, and he abandons his model and adds music to bring the piece to a close on G. What started well ends awkwardly. Not every adapter at Benevento was equally adept.

Chants for local feasts

Of particular significance for Benevento is the music in Gregorian style composed for saints of the city: Bartholomew, Mercurius, and others. This too is part of the repertory of Romano-Beneventan chant.

Saint Bartholomew
A mass for Saint Bartholomew survives in manuscripts of Benevento, and it is in Romano-Beneventan style. The pieces, with the exception of the Alleluia, are adapted from the repertory of Gregorian chant by the process we have seen in the better example of composition above. The introit, *Geadeamus omnes in domino*, adapts the text used for St Agatha and for All Saints, but instead of adopting their melody it is based on the introit *In uoluntate*. The Alleluia has a melody found with this text (*O quam beatus est dei apostolus*) only in Beneventan manuscripts, though with another text (*O quam beata es uirgo*) it is found for the Assumption in the northern Italian manuscript Rome, Angelica 123 in addition to Beneventan sources. The melody is probably of Beneventan origin, and in its form for Saint Bartholomew it is certainly a local product. The relics of the saint were translated to Benevento in 838, and remained there only until the end of the tenth century, when they were transferred to Rome. This Romano-Beneventan mass, then, is surely not composed after the tenth century, and seems most likely a creation for the institution of the feast at Benevento in the early ninth. The sequence – whose borrowed melody is widely known in Europe, has a local text which includes *Iamque tripudiant ciues samnie quam leti pangentes nectarea carmina deuote regi regum debitas grates ferentes inmensas*. The absence of an old Beneventan mass for St Bartholomew suggests that the Beneventan chant was no longer being composed at Benevento – at least not for use in the Cathedral – when Bartholomew's relics were placed in an adjoining church.

Saint Mercurius
Translated to Benevento in 768 and buried in Santa Sofia, the Byzantine military saint Mercurius became another patron of the Lombards. It is perhaps surprising that no Beneventan mass survives for this feast, instituted just eight years after the arrival of the relics of the Holy Twelve Brothers in the same church. There is no Romano-Beneventan mass surviving for his feast, though there is special office music composed at Benevento. Not until the renewal of Santa Sofia in the twelfth century would elaborated special music be composed in his honor.

Saint Januarius
Venerated as an early bishop of Benevento after the theft of his relics from Naples, about 830, there is no local mass, Beneventan or Gregorian; there is however a collection office music in Gregorian style which is unique to Benevento.

III

Saint Barbatus

Revered as an early bishop of Benevento, the cult of St Barbatus seems to have gathered strength in the ninth century, when the saint's *uita* was composed. Surviving music for Barbatus is limited to music for the office, and curiously for a ninth-century creation, it is in Beneventan style. Perhaps the Beneventan antiphons date from an earlier time, when the saintly bishop was celebrated not so much as bishop but as converter of the pagan Lombards.

New music in the twelfth century

A group of new liturgical compositions in the twelfth century suggests the presence at the monastery of Santa Sofia of a school of educated writers and composers. We have already suggested the probability of a liturgical renewal at Santa Sofia in the twelfth century, to go along with the renewal of the fabric taking place at the same time. It is in the twelfth century that the two surviving ordinals, based on Montecassino models, are drawn up, leaving no place for the older Beneventan chant.

A group of liturgical materials included in Naples XVI A 19 (ff. 39–48) is a twelfth-century collection of materials for saint Mercurius and for the Holy Twelve Brothers. Although there is music for Saint Mercurius and for the Holy Twelve Brothers in other earlier manuscripts, this music is new, found nowhere else. There is a first group of Vespers music for the Translation (26 August) and the Passion (presumably the feast – *natiuitas* – of 25 November, and not the feast of the dedication of the altar in Santa Sofia, of 18 August) of Saint Mercurius (ff. 39–41v). A second fascicle (f. 42–45) includes music for the translation of the Holy Twelve Brothers (a Vespers hymn and a mass assembled from existing Gregorian pieces), a mass for the two feasts of Saint Mercurius just named, and a mass for the Passion of the Holy Twelve Brothers. These last two masses include much music set to (newly-composed) rhyming texts, many of which are specific to Benevento. An example is the offertory for Saint Mercurius *Letare felix Samnium*, Example 6.

A final bifolium (f. 47–48) adds a hymn and a sequence for the Holy Twelve Brothers. Such a rich collection of liturgical materials for these saints could only derive from Santa Sofia itself, the church where their relics repose.

The composition of new chants in Gregorian style at Benevento seems not to have been a regular or a systematic occurrence. Such music was made when and where it was needed, and sometimes the job was done by persons without exemplary skill in music. But the collection from Santa Sofia suggests that new artistic creation for the liturgy was still possible in the twelfth century.

Example 6: Offertory Letare felix Samnium

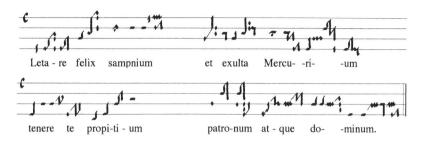

Leta - re felix sampnium   et exulta Mercu- -ri- -um

tenere te propi-ti - um   patro-num at - que do- -minum.

Indeed it had been going on for a long time, but not so much in new pieces of official chant as in the rich repertory of tropes and sequences.

Tropes and sequences

A trope, particularly as used at Benevento, is a musical and textual addition to a liturgical chant. Generally tropes are used for important feasts; at Benevento they are often attached to the introit of the mass, where they serve as introductions and sometimes as further interpolations in the course of the chant, so that sections of liturgical chant alternate with sections of trope. Many other tropes are provided for chants of the ordinary of the mass, especially for the *Kyrie* and the *Gloria in excelsis*.

In cases like the introit, where in a single performance the chant itself is sung more than once, several trope elements, or sets of trope elements, may be provided, all of which might be used in a single highly extended performance. Most elaborate at Benevento is the set of tropes provided in Benevento 40 for the introit of Easter. A normal performance of the introit involves alternating the introit antiphon itself, *Resurrexi*, with a psalm-verse, a doxology, and a further verse called *uersus ad repetendum*, the resulting performance being antiphon/verse/antiphon/doxology/antiphon/versus ad repetendum/antiphon. There are thus four performances of the antiphon, and four occasions when tropes or sets of tropes may be used to decorate it. And in Benevento 40 there are four sets of tropes, corresponding perhaps to the four times the introit antiphon is sung. Such a collection, however, may equally plausibly be a set of alternatives used for varying arrangements of the introit.

An example

The complete set of tropes as presented in Benevento 40 is as follows (texts of the introit and its verses are in italics)

DOM S PASCHA
Quem queritis in sepulcro christicole.
Iesum nazarenum o celicole.
Non est hic surrexit sicut predixerat; ite nuntiate quia surrexit.
Alleluia resurrexit dominus.

TRO
Hodie exultent iusti resurrexit leo fortis Deo gratias dicite omnes
Resurrexi et adhuc tecum sum, alleluia.
Lux mundi Dominus resurrexit hodie.
Posuisti super me manum tuam, alleluia.
Manus tua Domine saluauit mundum hodie et ideo
Mirabilis facta est scientia tua.
Scientia Domini mirabilis facta est hodie.
Alleluia alleluia.
V. *Domine probasti me et cognouisti me; tu cognouisti sessionem meam et resurrectionem meam.*

ALI TRO
Mulieres que ad sepulcrum uenerant angelus dixit iam surrexit dominus.
Resurrexi et adhuc tecum sum, alleluia.
Cito euntes dicite discipuli quia surrexit sicut dixit Dominus
Posuisti super me manum tuam, alleluia.
Ve tibi Iuda qui tradidisti Dominum et a iudeis accepisti pretium
Mirabilis facta est scientia tua, alleluia alleluia.
V. *Cum resurrexisset filius Dei tertia die a mortuis, glorianter dixit ad patrem*

ALI
Hodie resurrexit leo fortis Christus filius Dei Deo gratias dicite illi eia
Resurrexi et adhuc tecum sum, alleluia.
Victor resurgens manet in secula deus
Posuisti super me manum tuam, alleluia.
Omnes confringens Tartara uictor exiit ad supera
Mirabilis facta est scientia tua, alleluia alleluia.
Gloria omnes in excelsis domino dicite fratres

V. *Gloria patri et filio et spiritui sancto, sicut erat in principio et nunc et semper, et in secula seculorum. Amen.*

ALI
Eia karissimi uerba canite Christi eia.
Resurrexi et adhuc tecum sum, alleluia.
Qui dicit patri prophetica uoce
Posuisti super me manum tuam, alleluia.
Mirabilem laudat filius patrem
Mirabilis facta est scientia tua, alleluia alleluia.

THE SUNDAY OF HOLY EASTER
Whom do you seek in the sepulchre, O Christians?
Jesus the Nazarene, O heavenly one.
He his not here, he has risen as he predicted; go and announce it, for he has risen.
Alleluia, the Lord is risen.

Today – let the just rejoice – has risen the strong lion, say you all, "Thanks be to God."
I have arisen and I am with you, alleluia.
The light of the world, the Lord, has risen today.
You have laid your hand upon me, alleluia.
Your hand, O Lord, has saved the world today, and therefore
Your knowledge has become wonderful.
The Lord's knowledge has become wonderful today.
Alleluia alleluia.
V. *Lord, you have tested me and known me; you have known my sitting down and my rising up.*

To the women who had come to the tomb the angel said "Now the Lord has risen."
I have arisen and I am with you, alleluia.
"Go quickly, tell the disciples, for the Lord has risen as he said."
You have laid your hand upon me, alleluia.
Woe to you, Judas, who did betray the Lord and did receive the price from the Jews.
Your knowledge has become wonderful, alleluia alleluia.
V. *As the son of God arose from the dead on the third day, exulting he said to the Father:*

Today the strong lion, Christ, the son of God, has risen; say to him "Thanks be to God, yea."
I have arisen and I am with you, alleluia.
The victor, rising, remains God forever.
You have laid your hand upon me, alleluia.
Breaking all hellish bonds the conqueror rises forth to heaven.
Your knowledge has become wonderful, alleluia alleluia.
All you brethren, say "Glory be to God on high."
V. *Glory to the Father and to the Son and to the Holy Spirit; as it was in the beginning, and is now, and will be for ages of ages. Amen.*

Yea, dearly beloved, sing the words of Christ, yea:
I have arisen and I am with you, alleluia.
Who said to the Father in the voice of the prophet,
You have laid your hand upon me, alleluia.
The Son praises the wonderful Father:
Your knowledge has become wonderful, alleluia alleluia.

(translation adapted from Alejandro Planchart and John Boe, *Beneventanum troporum corpus* (hereafter *BTC*), part 1, Tropes of the proper of the mass from southern Italy, A.D. 1000–1250 (2 v.). Madison, Wis.: A-R Editions, 1989).

Beneventan versions of imported repertories

Tropes and sequences were imported from the North, perhaps at the same time as the Gregorian chant, but more likely at a somewhat later stage since there is no evidence of eighth-century troping in the North. There is thus a repertory of imported tropes in the Beneventan manuscripts, alongside further tropes composed at Benevento for elaborating the now standard Gregorian chant.

It is worth noting that the Beneventan chant itself does not bear tropes. This is true for other local repertories as well: the Milanese, Old Spanish, and Old Roman chants do not undergo a stage of trope composition. This is in some cases owing to the fact that the phenomenon of troping grew up at a time when some of these repertories had fallen into disuse; but equally important is the fact that troping is a Frankish phenomenon at its origin, and was seen everywhere as an adjunct of the Franco-Roman Gregorian chant.

The oldest layer of tropes in the Beneventan manuscripts, then, is of northern manufacture; these appear in Benevento 40 and Benevento 38 (the same manuscripts which preserve the bulk of the surviving Beneventan chant), attached to Gregorian chants for the proper and the ordinary of the mass. How many earlier manuscripts containing tropes may once have been written in southern Italy must remain unknown. Already by the time of our earliest graduals from Benevento tropes are a part of the Gregorian scene. (In missals, some of which – notably Benevento 33 and Vat. lat. 10673 – are earlier than these graduals, it seems always to have been usual to exclude tropes).

But already in these earliest sources there is a second layer of locally-made tropes, appearing nowhere else in Europe, and with a textual and melodic style that sets them apart in many ways from the imported tropes that served as their models.

Beneventan and Frankish styles

Frankish tropes, like the chants which they accompany, are sometimes brilliantly melodic, featuring large leaps, clear melodic outlines with striking beginnings, arched shapes, clear cadences. Elsewhere they are more modest, matching the reserved style of the chants they accompany. They are designed to fit in with the melodies they decorate, often borrowing aspects of range or melody from an adjoining chant phrase. In the case of interpolated tropes like those for introits, their texts tend to be related to the text of the chant, so that when trope and chant are sung in alternation the resulting text makes some sort of sense as a whole. An example is the trope-set *Hodie exultent iusti* for the Easter introit, Example 7.

Example 7: Trope Hodie exultent, BTC p. 153

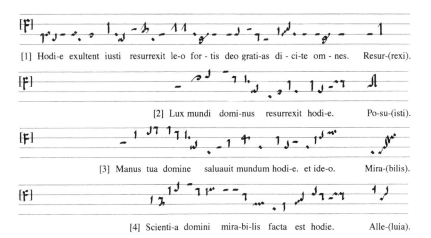

[1] Hodi-e exultent iusti resurrexit le-o for - tis deo grati-as di - ci-te om - nes. Resur-(rexi).

[2] Lux mundi domi-nus resurrexit hodi-e. Po-su-(isti).

[3] Manus tua domine saluauit mundum hodi-e. et ide-o. Mira-(bilis).

[4] Scienti-a domini mira-bi-lis facta est hodie. Alle-(luia).

This trope appears in groups of tropes for Easter in all five graduals of Benevento; we have seen it above in the context of Benevento 40. Its first phrase is widely known and probably of German origin. The subsequent verses, composed in Italy, perhaps at Benevento, show the tendency toward melodic repetition characteristic of Beneventan tropes. Note that each trope text serves as introduction to the portion of chant text that follows.

When local singers added tropes to the imported repertory, they reflected the esthetic tendencies of the south. Melodies are smoother, more stepwise, generally without jaggedness or dramatic leaps; multiple interpolations tend to be made as successive repetitions of a single melody, much like the fashioning of the Beneventan ingressae. The texts of Beneventan interpolated tropes – those with several trope elements sung at successive points in a single piece – are, as Alejandro Planchart says, "entirely self-referential." They are independent compositions, which in order to make sense must be read together, and not alternating with the chant's text. Thus the performance of an introit with a Beneventan trope seem more like alternating performances of two compositions, in two musical styles, than a single continuous performance. Such a trope is *Mulieres que ad sepulchrum* (Example 8), used in four of the Beneventan graduals (including the earliest) for Easter, and which is probably a Beneventan composition. As Planchart comments: "Like other Beneventan tropes, this trope merely co-exists with the introit text. Its three verses relate only to each other and, when read as such, present a coherent dramatic progression."

Example 8: Trope Mulieres que, BTC p. 165

[1] Muli-e-res que ad sepulcrum ue-nerant   ange-lus di-xit iam surrexit do-mi-nus. Resur-(rexi).

[2] Cito e-un-tes dicite disci-pu-li   quia surre-xit sicut di-xit do-mi-nus. Po-(suisti).

[3] Ve ti-bi iu-da qui tradi-disti do-mi-num et a iude - is   ac-cepi-sti pre-ti-um. Mira-(bilis).

Changing styles at Benevento

At Benevento, tropes for the introit far outnumber all other proper tropes; whereas elsewhere in Europe tropes to the offertory and the communion were relatively often used, they are extremely rare at Benevento. Instead, offertories were often decorated with prosulas, as were Alleluias. The art of the prosula, quite different from that of the trope in that it is the art of fitting words to pre-existing music, seems to have been a favorite procedure at Benevento.

About half the tropes surviving in south Italian manuscripts are found nowhere else; this is a large local repertory. Many of the remaining tropes are found only in other Italian manuscripts (where in some cases they might have been borrowed from Benevento), so that the importance of the local repertory must be emphasized.

The style of trope cultivated at Montecassino was very often cast in classicising hexameters. Many pieces from the Montecassino repertory were adopted at Benevento, particularly in the course of the twelfth century, when Cassinese influence was felt strongly in the monasteries of the city. Nevertheless, Beneventan musicians felt free to adapt the tropes of Montecassino to the style of Benevento, particularly in the case of tropes to the ordinary of the mass, much as Cassinese adapters sometimes corrected and amplified tropes borrowed from Benevento.

Alejandro Planchart, in the introduction to his edition of proper tropes from Beneventan manuscripts, writes on the situation at Benevento:

> To sum up, the proper trope repertory of the south Italian manuscripts seems to consist of an old layer of imported pieces, some of which may have reached Italy quite early on, and a second layer of pieces written locally to expand or complement the tropes received from abroad. These two layers make up almost the entire repertory that survives.

Trope repertories in Beneventan manuscripts

The manuscripts now at Benevento which contain tropes are the five graduals which transmit the Gregorian chant. In them we can see the changing attitude to tropes and repertories.

Already by the time of Benevent 38 and Benevento 40, tropes are present in graduals. These manuscripts present an array of proper and ordinary tropes, principally for the introit, the Kyrie, and the Gloria. These reflect the importation of an international repertory of northern manufacture, along with a few tropes made for local usage.

By the end of the eleventh century, Benevento 39 provides the richest south Italian repertory of tropes and sequences; its collection of ordinary tropes, presumably at the end of the manuscript, is now lost. Proper tropes, however, are spread throughout the volume; the five unica among proper tropes all seem to be local products or adaptations like the St Gall trope *Hodie sanctissimi patroni* adapted for St Peter.

Benevento 35, a gradual of the early twelfth century, has a repertory of proper tropes that shows what Planchart calls "an anthologizing bent" on the part of its scribe. There is a core of Beneventan works combined with works from Montecassino (1 trope), San Vincenzo, and elsewhere; eleven proper tropes are found here among the Benevento manuscripts. John Boe has shown that the collected Kyries were copied in groups: four well-known Italian Kyries are followed by a group borrowed from Rome; local Kyries follow, one having been inserted into the Roman group.

Benevento 34, of the first half of the twelfth century, has a number of proper tropes unique to Benevento, but they are almost all products of Montecassino, as is demonstrated by the deciphering of the palimpsest Vat. Urb. lat. 602 reported by Planchart. The manuscript represents a drastic departure from the traditional trope repertory of Benevento. The received tropes of Montecassino are sometimes altered, not always expertly. Kyries without verses appear for the first time here, no doubt in imitation of Montecassino custom. The complete standard Cassinese repertory of Gloria tropes is included. The presence of Cassinese influence at Benevento in the twelfth century is to be seen in many areas, notably the copying of the Montecassino ordinal for monastic churches in Benevento. Clearly the scribe of Benevento 34, who was trained in Montecassino scribal practices, intended his manuscript to reflect a strong influence from the great abbey to the north.

John Boe's study of the *Amen* which closes the Kyrie in manuscripts of Benevento is a fascinating example of changing patterns of adoption and adaptation. Roman Kyries, when they address the worshipper, end with a long melismatic Amen. Italian Kyries, including those of Benevento, which are arranged in trinitarian paragraphs and structured like a collect, end with a very brief Amen. At Montecassino Amens are used for Italian Kyries, but omitted for those borrowed from the Normans.

In Benevento 38 and Benevento 40, trinitarian Kyries known also at Rome or Montecassino have an Amen. Those borrowed from the North, and some local pieces, do not. In Benevento 35, however, all fourteen collected Kyries have Amen: a melismatic Amen if from Rome, a brief Amen if the Kyrie is local or at least non-Roman; the practice, current in Rome, of ending Kyrie with Amen, was the practice also of Benevento. But in Benevento 34, all the Kyries have their Amen removed (with a few telling exceptions noted by Boe); this perhaps reflects the practice of the most modern pieces at Montecassino, and perhaps also documents a change in the practices at Benevento itself, bringing it into line with the usage of Kyries in the North and, ultimately, of the universal Roman church.

The Persistence of Tradition

The gradual changes in the practices of the cathedral of Benevento resulted ultimately in the adoption of the Roman liturgy, and in increasingly faithful adherence to practices generally regarded as universal. Thus the later liturgical books now in the cathedral represent a more or less standard Roman liturgy resulting from the adoption of Franciscan books as models for the Roman church in the thirteenth century. Liturgial books made for local use may have a Beneventan calendar at their beginning, but the contents are generally those found in almost any book.

Despite this growing uniformity, it is possibly to detect elements of conservatism, of persistent local practice, in which we can hear echoes of a long-departed musical and liturgical practice. Three examples can give an idea of this tenacity of tradition.

1. Placement of the Exultet

The Beneventan rite, as we have seen, had almost completely disappeared by the twelfth century. And yet there persisted certain elements from the old rite, details of ceremony which do not match standard Roman practice, and which are traditional vestiges of a ceremonial which otherwise left little trace. An example of this is the practice of singing the Exultet, known in Benevento from early times through the beautiful Exultet rolls.

In the Roman liturgy the Exultet is the first public ceremony of Holy Saturday, preceding a long series of lections and prayers, but in the old Beneventan liturgy, the Exultet is sung after the lessons, as a sort of transition between the lections and the baptismal rites. So when we see, as we often do, the Exultet presented in this position after the lections, even where the Exultet itself and all other details of the ceremonial are Roman, we can presume that this church once practiced the old Beneventan liturgy, and has preserved at least one small element of this vanished tradition.

Benevento remained traditional: the placement of the Exultet remained unchanged even when a new text was adopted. The Benevento pontifical of the early twelfth century (now Macerata, Biblioteca comunale Ms. 378) gives a clear presentation of the overall order of the Beneventan liturgy for Holy Saturday. It preserves many details of the older ordo (and indeed quotes its language); although it retains almost nothing of the old Beneventan chant, the Exultet is placed in its Beneventan position, after the lections. The missal of St Peter's convent intra muros (London, Br. Lib. Eg. 3511) shows also that the shape of the rite remains Beneventan. Elsewhere in Benevento, the twelfth-century ordinals of the monastery of Santa Sofia (Naples, VI E 43, Vat. lat 4928) make it clear that Exultet comes after the lections; this is particularly interesting since the ordinals otherwise use exactly the language of Montecassino, but stop short of full revision by retaining the Beneventan placement.

This placement of the Exultet in its Beneventan position can be detected in rubrics from churches that have otherwise almost entirely adopted the Franco-Roman liturgy. These continue through the fifteenth century, and add information to that preserved in the Exultets themselves about the distribution and chronology of the Beneventan use of the Exultet. Examples of these include a Neapolitan ordo probably reflecting twelfth-century practice (the seventeenth-century transcription of the lost original is Naples, Bibl. Naz., Bibl. Brancacciana I.F.2); the thirteenth-century ordinal of Salerno (Salerno, Archivio capitolare); a fourteenth-century missal of Capua (Paris, Bibl. nat. lat. 829); a fifteenth-century missal of Montevergine (Rome, Biblioteca Casanatense MS 1103).

2. Local office music

Music from the old Beneventan liturgy survives for a long time in places where the liturgy is flexible (rogations, processions, and so on), or where the liturgy is otherwise lacking. In the latter case, it was found necessary or useful to supply music for important local feasts. Two of these local feasts, the Holy Twelve Brothers and Bishop Saint Barbatus of Benevento, have music in old Beneventan style that survives for a long time.

The Holy Twelve Brothers, martyrs in Santa Sofia, have not only an old Beneventan mass, but also a series of antiphons preserved in the missal-breviary Benevento 20 of the twelfth century. These antiphons survive also in fragments of an eleventh-century antiphoner now at Melk Abbey (Melk, Stiftsbibliothek MS 1012), in the late eleventh-century breviary fragments of

Montecassino Compactiones V, and in the late twelfth-century antiphoner Benevento 21. The cult of these saints was evidently not limited to Benevento, but spread throughout the region as part of a Lombard heritage deriving from the capital city of Benevento.

Saint Barbatus, bishop of Benevento, also has a series of antiphons in Beneventan style, surviving in Benevento 21, and also in the twelfth-century breviary Benevento 22 and in Vat. lat. 14446, a thirteenth-century breviary from Caiazzo.

These antiphons entered the local Gregorian repertory at a relatively early date; though their style is purely Beneventan, they provide music where none was received, and they survive precisely because they are not identified as music from the older liturgy, and because they are presented in the regular round of Gregorian office music. They survive in disguise.

And they survive for a long time. The antiphons for Saint Barbatus – without their music – are written in the book of offices for local saints now in the cathedral as manuscript 61, of the late fourteenth or early fifteenth century. And both series of antiphons, complete with music, continue to be copied into books for Beneventan use.

An antiphoner of the fourteenth century (manuscript 848) in the cathedral includes music for local saints, including both series of antiphons: the Holy Twelve Brothers and Saint Barbatus. In this case, at least, the old Beneventan musical style invaded the received Roman liturgy, and in the guise of Gregorian antiphons continued to be sung at Benevento at least until the time of the Council of Trent.

3. Rolls

There was a long and tenacious tradition of liturgical scrolls in the city of Benevento. Three rolls survive from the tenth century, an Exultet from the twelfth, and five devotional or liturgical roll from later centuries; the fifteenth-century inventory indicates regular use of rolls in the liturgy of the city. The long use of rolls at Benevento, and the particular uses to which they are put, contribute to what we know about liturgical scrolls in south Italy, and at the same time reflects a persistent tradition at Benevento.

This practice has often been linked to imitation of the use of scrolls in the Byzantine liturgy. Byzantine influence there undoubtedly was, and scrolls were indeed used in the Byzantine liturgy – though not usually for the same functions as in the West. And since Byzantine scrolls begin in the eleventh century, we must look elsewhere for the origins of the Beneventan tradition of liturgical scrolls.

There is clearly a tradition in Lombard lands, north and south, of using rolls in the liturgy. These traditions are related in their practices, and they reflect the link of the northern and southern Lombards before the fall of the northern Lombard capital of Pavia to Charlemagne in 774 and the consequent establishment of an independent Lombard state ruled from Benevento. The ultimate origin of such a practice might well go back to a time when rolls were much more common; there might well be Greek influences in the tradition; but the phenomenon is not so much south Italian as it is Lombard.

The use of the rotulus in southern Italy has many similarities to its use at Milan. In both rites rolls have a regular place in the liturgy. The use of many rolls is focused on the bishop or archbishop. Rolls are regularly used in processions. Nowhere else in Europe is the Exultet regularly sung from a roll, so far as we know, except for Milan and southern Italy: that is to say, in the two related liturgies of the Lombards. At Milan it is the custom to place the roll on the altar, whence it is taken by the priest or the the rotularius; the similar practice of laying the Exultet on the altar at Montecassino and related churches (including Santa Sofia at Benevento) may well be more than coincidence.

The Exultets in the Vatican and the Casanatense, along with the Casanantense pontifical rolls, are among the chief glories of Beneventan production; but the use of the liturgical roll at Benevento evidently continued for a long time. The fifteenth-century inventory of the Cathedral library shows the presence of a large number of rolls, some of which survive to this day. (They are numbers 33, 35–41, 44–47 in Richard Gyug's edition of the inventory in *La Cathédrale de Bénévent*, ed. Thomas Forrest Kelly, Ghent: Ludion, 1999).

This collection of rolls is extensive, but it does not seem to include any of the early illustrated rolls now in the Vatican and the Casanatense libraries. In this inventory the documents in Beneventan script are listed separately, and the portion transcribed here is from the list of books in modern, Frankish, writing. Thus no. 46, "carta ubi est *exultet iam angelica*," is clearly an Exultet roll, but equally clearly is neither of the surviving Beneventan-script rolls.

The cathedral of Benevento in the fifteenth century evidently continued the use of liturgical rolls as it had used them in the tenth century. From this list it appears that rolls were used for special liturgical occasions, for events taking place outside the choir, and especially for processions.

A paper envelope kept in the locked manuscript cabinet of the Biblioteca capitolare contains eight small scrolls, each of which is labeled on its dorse. Five of these are liturgical scrolls, standing at the end of a long tradition of the use of such scrolls at Benevento and in southern Italy.

One contains a Beneventan collection of prayers, including collects for major saints in the Beneventan calendar: St Barbatus (here promoted to archbishop); the translation of St Bartholomew from Lipari to Benevento; and St Mercurius. An added membrane includes materials that may have been intended for use in processions in time of war: a series of antiphon texts (now mostly illegible), versicles and responses, and a prayer for the protection of this city ("ut ponas in omnes fines istius ciuitatis pacem"). The rewriting of one of the prayers (for Saint Sebastian) indicates that the roll was still in use as late as the seventeenth century. It is possible that this roll is identical with the prayer roll listed in the fifteenth-century inventory and cited as no. 3 above ("Rotus unus cum orationibus pro letaniis"); we do not know that litanies were sung in procession on all these feast-days, nor that these particular prayers were said as part of the litanies; but this roll, and the one listed in the inventory, both contain collects, and perhaps the inventory gives us an idea of the function of a roll containing a single prayer for each feast.

Further rolls include the sequence *Stabat mater dolorosa* and two rolls with hymns (perhaps among those inventoried in the fifteenth century). A further scroll contains the hymn *Signum salutis*, regularly used for Sunday processions, which implores God's protection for our dwellings and for our city. The scroll seems to be written in a very late hand, perhaps of the seventeenth or eighteenth century, in imitation of earlier writing. This is a remarkably late persistence of the tradition of using scrolls.

That the cathedral of Benevento should preserve this tradition actively, elegantly, and prolongedly, is a mark of the conservatism of this ancient Lombard capital. The same city that preserved the older Beneventan liturgy (itself related to Lombard practices) made beautiful pontifical and Exultet rolls in the earlier middle ages, and continued the use of rolls for litanies, prayers, hymns, and the Exultet, for a longer time than we had previously imagined.

PALIMPSEST EVIDENCE OF AN OLD-BENEVENTAN GRADUAL

Since the pioneering studies of Dom Hesbert and his colleagues almost half a century ago, the music of the Old-Beneventan liturgy has received little attention from scholars until recently. There is now, however, a growing awareness that this liturgy and its music are important as a predecessor of the Gregorian chant which ultimately supplanted it, and as the survival of a musical and liturgical system which is among the earliest examples of Western Christian art[1]. But despite this renewed interest, many important questions remain unresolved.

For one thing, the repertory is evidently incomplete. Two Gregorian graduals in the Biblioteca capitolare of Benevento preserve almost all the surviving music. These two manuscripts (Benevento VI 38 and VI 40[2]) append to their Gregorian counterparts the propers of twenty-one Old-Beneventan masses, together with music for the special rites of Holy Week. But although most of the major feasts of the liturgical calendar are represented, there are substantial lacunae: Advent; the feasts after Christmas; Epiphany; Lent (except for Holy Week); and certain principal saints.

There is also the question of chronology. The creative period of Beneventan chant may have ended in the eighth century[3], though much of the music survives into the period of music-writing; the repertory as we have it comes almost entirely from manuscripts of no earlier than the eleventh century. There are at least sixteen sources that preserve Old-Beneventan music, some from the twelfth century and later; but none of the later sources preserves any piece not already known in the eleventh century. And with the exception of one fragment (the final flyleaf, folio 202, of Benevento Ms. VI 35, which preserves the end of the Christmas mass and the beginning

---

1 There is no recent study of the repertory beyond the brief notices by K. Schlager, Beneventan rite, in: The New Grove 2 (London 1980), p. 482-484; B. Baroffio, Benevent, in: MGG 15 (1973), p. 653-656; —, Liturgie im beneventarischen Raum, in: Geschichte der katholischen Kirchenmusik, Vol. 1, ed. K. G. Fellerer, Kassel 1972, p. 204-208. The repertory was first described by Dom R. Andoyer, in: Revue du chant Grégorien 20 (1911-12), p. 176-183; 21 (1912-13), p. 14-20, 44-51, 81-85, 112-115, 144-148, 169-174; 22 (1913-14), p. 8-11, 41-44, 80-83, 106-111, 141-145, 170-172; 23 (1919-20), p. 42-44, 116-118, 151-153, 182-183; 24 (1920-21), p. 48-50, 87-89, 146-148, 182-185. Dom René-Jean Hesbert published two substantial liturgical and musical studies focusing on the rites of Holy Week. The first deals with the musical tradition: La tradition bénéventaine dans la tradition manuscrite, in: Paléographie musicale 14 (1931), especially p. 263-465. Hesbert's second study focuses on liturgical questions with particular attention to Holy Week: L'Antiphonale missarum de l'ancien rite bénéventain, in: Ephemerides liturgicae 52 (1938), p. 28-66, 141-158; 53 (1939), p. 168-190; 59 (1945), p. 69-95; 60 (1946), p. 103-141; 61 (1947), p. 153-210. Two recent studies by John Boe of new sources are listed in subsequent footnotes.

2 Hereafter VI 38 and VI 40. These are the principal sources of Old-Beneventan chant. In the catalogue by J. Mallet and A. Thibaut (Les manuscrits en écriture bénéventaine de la bibliothèque capitulaire de Benevent, Tome I: manuscrits 1-18, Paris 1984), the Roman numerals will not be used, but they are included here in accordance with the form of all bibliography to date.

3 The Beneventan mass for the Holy Twelve Brothers, whose relics came to Benevento in 760, is a collection of pure Old-Beneventan music (Benevento VI. 40, f. 121ᵛ-122). But the Beneventan mass of Saint Bartholomew, whose remains came to Benevento in 838, and whose translation entered the calendar the following year, is modeled on Gregorian chant. See St. Borgia, Memorie istoriche della pontificia Città di Benevento, Vol. 1, Rome 1763, p. 237, 336-337. The date of Bartholomew's translation is often given as 808 (cf. Paléographie musicale 14, p. 450-451; Baroffio, Liturgie im beneventanischen Raum, above, note 1).

of that for Saint Stephen), all the sources known heretofore are books dedicated to Gregorian chant, in which Old-Beneventan music is included, as it were on sufferance, in books dedicated to the very chant whose imposition caused the suppresion of the local music.

And the geographical boundaries of this repertory have yet to be determined. The sources center on Benevento, and are generally written in the characteristic Beneventan script of South Italy; there is Old-Beneventan chant also from Montecassino[4], Farfa[5], Bari[6], and elsewhere. But Old-Beneventan music also survives from as far North as Lucca[7].

A new source of Old-Beneventan music has recently come to light which will add to the growing body of evidence needed to understand the significance of this South Italian repertory. This new document, however, important as it is for our understanding of this music, unfortunately neither adds significantly to our knowledge of the repertory, nor clarifies geographical or chronolgical problems. At the present stage of our knowledge it serves principally to caution us against underestimating the extent and importance of this early chant dialect.

***

The manuscript C 9 in the Biblioteca Vallicelliana, Rome, is a composite manuscript of unknown provenance[8]. It consists of 411 parchment folios with four paper flyleaves; the cover, of parchment over paper boards, has come loose to reveal the stitching. Although the binding may date only from the eighteenth century (when a title page and table of contents were written on the opening flyleaves), the order of the folios has not been disturbed.

The manuscript is composed of three distinct sections. The first part, consisting of 174 folios (presently numbered 1-173 bis) is written in Beneventan script. The second and third parts, in ordinary minuscule, will not concern us here[9].

Several hands can be distinguished in this first section:

I.   ff.   1-137:   (early 12th century[10])
                    Gregorius Magnus, Dialogi

---

4   See J. Boe, Old Beneventan Chant at Monte Cassino: Gloriosus Confessor Domini Benedictus, in: Acta Musicologica 55 (1983), p. 69-73.

5   Music for Holy Saturday survives on a single fragmentary leaf. See Paléographie musicale 14, plates XXVI and XXVII, there erroneously listed as „Cava".

6   A tract and an antiphon for the blessing of the font on Holy Saturday are preserved in a *benedictio ignis et fontis* in the Archivio del Duomo. Facsimiles in G. Cavallo, Rotoli di Exultet dell'Italia meridionale, Bari 1973, plates 13 and 14; and in M. Avery, The Exultet Rolls of South Italy, Vol. 2, Princeton 1936, plate XIII.

7   In Ms. 606 of the Biblioteca capitolare. A supplement to the main manuscript, in ordinary minuscule but with Beneventan notation, preserves Old-Beneventan music for Holy Week. See the facsimiles in Paléographie musicale 14, plates XXXIV-XLIII.

8   The manuscript is described, its contents inventoried, and relevant bibliography listed, in L. Avitabile, Fr. De Marco, M. Cl. Di Franco, and V. Jemolo, Censimento dei codici dei secoli X-XII, in: Studi medievali, 3rd Series, 11 (1970), p. 1037-1038; and in E. A. Loew, The Beneventan Script, second edition prepared and enlarged by V. Brown, Vol. 2: Hand List of Beneventan Mss., Rome 1980, p. 127-128. The first volume of a modern catalogue has appeared, but is does not include this manuscript: A. M. G. Vichi and S. Mottironi, Catologo dei manoscritti della Biblioteca Vallicelliana, Vol. 1, Rome 1961 (= Ministero della pubblica istruzione, Indici e cataloghi, Nuova serie 7). The three-volume handwritten catalogue available in the library contains a table of contents for the manuscript: Vincenzo Vettori, Inventarium Omnium Codicum Manuscriptorum Graecorum et Latinorum Bibliotecae Vallicellanae Digestum Anno Domini MDCCXLIV. Pars. I. Continet priores XXVI Tomos Itemque alios codices a litera A. ad F. inclusive.

9   For their contents, see the bibliography in the previous note.

10 Dates are those given in Loew, The Beneventan Script.

II. ff. 138-152:   (late 12th-early 13th century)
                              attributed to St. Jerome, letter to Heliodorus and Chromatius on the Nativity of the Blessed Virgin; Sermon and Miracles of Conception BVM; Poems to St. Mary Magdalen; Johannes Osareus, commentary on Matthew

III. ff. 153-166:   (late 12th-early 13th century)
                              Johannes Osareus, continued

IV. ff. 167-168:   (late 12th-early 13th century)
                              Sequence (*Stans a longe*[11]) in honor of the Blessed Virgin Mary

V. ff. 169-173 bis:(late 12th-early 13th century)
                              anonymous letter on the marriage of priests

The manuscript's structure shows that sections I-III are formed as a single unit. Section II is joined to Section I, despite the change of hand, by the fact that the text of pseudo-Jerome begins in the middle of a fascicle. And Section III continues directly from Section II in the middle of Johannes Osaureus' text, even though it begins a new fascicle with a new hand, and the entire section is written over the erased text of Priscianus, *Institutiones Grammaticae*[12].

Sections IV and V are likewise a single unit: they are palimpsest on pages from an Old-Beneventan liturgical manuscript; and we shall show that folios 168 and 169 (which join sections IV and V) are consecutive folios from the same manuscript.

Both of these larger sections (I-III, IV-V) have a further connection, in that both sections contain palimpsest page from this Old-Beneventan manuscript.

It is to these pages that we now turn.

***

The palimpsest Old-Beneventan pages are in two groups: (I) two single leaves and three bifolia used individually in fascicles 2 through 5 of the present manuscript; and (II) a complete fascicle reused in its original order.

I. Fascicles 2 through 5 of Vallicelliana C 9 contain Old-Beneventan leaves, arranged in the following fashion (the Old-Beneventan leaves are indicated by asterisks):

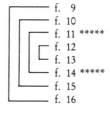

Fascicle 2

           f. 9
           f. 10
           f. 11 *****
           f. 12
           f. 13
           f. 14 *****
           f. 15
           f. 16

---

11 This is the only musical notation in the Beneventan portion of Vallicelliana C 9. On this sequence see R. Crocker, The Early Medieval Sequence, Berkeley 1977, p, 398-399. A version of the peace is edited in N. de Goede, The Utrecht Prosarium, Amsterdam 1965, p. 115 (= Monumenta musica Neelandica).

12 Jemolo, Censimento, p. 1038 (above, note 8); Loew and Brown, p. 127-128 (above, note 8); M. De Nonno, Contributo alla tradizione di Prisciano in area beneventano-cassinese: il „Vallicell. C. 9", in: Revue d'histoire des textes 9 (1979), p. 123-139.

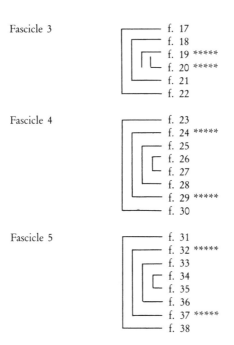

Fascicle 3
- f. 17
- f. 18
- f. 19 *****
- f. 20 *****
- f. 21
- f. 22

Fascicle 4
- f. 23
- f. 24 *****
- f. 25
- f. 26
- f. 27
- f. 28
- f. 29 *****
- f. 30

Fascicle 5
- f. 31
- f. 32 *****
- f. 33
- f. 34
- f. 35
- f. 36
- f. 37 *****
- f. 38

Hence there are 8 folios of palimpsest Old-Beneventan music, including three bifolia and two single leaves.

II. Folios 167-173bis are all Old-Beneventan palimpsests, and, as we shall see, are preserved in Vallicelliana C 9 as a fascicle arranged as it was in the original manuscript:

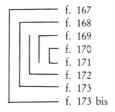

- f. 167
- f. 168
- f. 169
- f. 170
- f. 171
- f. 172
- f. 173
- f. 173 bis

The arrangement of the original pages shows that these palimpsest leaves were all taken from the same dismantled Old-Beneventan liturgical book.

The present page size is approximately 29.3 cm high by 20.5 cm wide. The Old-Beneventan writing area was 14 cm wide, and probably 29.9 cm high (through the present cropping of the leaves makes this determination difficult). The systems of text and music, thirteen to a page, were spaced about 2.3 cm apart.

The original ruling can occasionally be seen (for example on folio 24); there is one dry-point line for each line of text in the original manuscript, no line being drawn to align the musical notation. The upper script uses the original ruling — and the erased lines of text — as a guide, writing two lines of text over each original system of text and music. As a result, the upper script deliberately obscures the Old-Beneventan verbal text. The present visible vertical ruling (two parallel scored lines at the outer margin) may not be original: the upper text follows this margin almost more closely than the lower.

Some of the Old-Beneventan leaves (ff. 19, 20, 32/37 and 24/29) have been reversed, the new text being entered from bottom to top of the original page.

The most accessible portions of the lower text, naturally, are those not covered by the upper script; these occur most often in the generous lower margins of the present manuscript. Although the original text has been scrupulously erased, the effect of the vanished ink, making the parchment almost transparent, preserves much of the music and some of the text.

In most cases, the hair side, where it has not been directly covered with new writing, can be read with some success, especially with the aid of ultraviolet light; but the flesh side is almost invariably indecipherable: what may appear to be neumes and text is actually the transparent mirror-image of the hair side. All that can be seen on the flesh side is occasional bits of ink — a letter of text, or occasionally the shape of a decorated initial.

The text of the lower script is a typical eleventh-century Beneventan liturgical hand written in a brown ink. An orange-red ink is used for rubrics (but not between separated syllables of words), and decorates some of the smaller initials. Green, orange, brown and yellow inks are used for the larger initials. The music is written in partially diastematic Beneventan notation with a custos; the quilisma is regularly used.

***

The contents of these palimpsest pages, so far as we can tell, consist entirely of Old-Beneventan chant. This can be determined both by the musical style in general, which is highly characteristic, and by the fact that many pieces here are found elsewhere in the repertory, all of them used in the mass[13]. It would appear, then, that these leaves are pages from a Gradual of the Old-Beneventan rite.

For the pieces which also appear in other manuscripts there is no question of transcribing an additional reading. So little text and music are visible that, without the existence of other witnesses, it would be difficult to reproduce even a single word of the text. But for each piece every visible detail matches the other versions so exactly that we can be sure that they are virtually identical, varying from the Beneventan readings no more than they vary from each other.

We begin our musical and liturgical consideration of these leaves with folios 167-173bis, a complete fascicle, taken over intact into Vallicelliana C 9. These leaves have the same orientation for both scripts, and we will consider them in their bound order.

Folio 167 recto (=hair side)

> Thirteen lines (the whole page) are discernible here. The first three and a half lines show only neumes, spaced as in a relatively syllabic setting.
>
> In the middle of line 4 begins the Easter Offertory *Angelus domini* (VI 38, f. 53; VI 40, f. 27); this is followed immediately (line 7) by the Easter Communion *Qui manducaverit* (VI 38, f. 52; VI 40, f. 28), with its verses *Gloria et honor* and *Et nunc*. This second verse begins on line 13, and is incomplete on this page.

Folio 167 verso (= flesh side)

> Almost nothing is visible on this side; it is impossible to verify that the Easter Communion concludes on this side of the leaf. Small initials begin lines 2 and 12; line 12 concludes with a short rubric.

---

13 This is not surprising, since the extant sources preserve mainly music for the Mass.

IV

Folio 168 recto (= flesh side)

An almost entire unreadable flesh side. Line 13 begins with a small initial.

Folio 168 verso (= hair side)

This is perhaps the most legible of all these folios, because the upper script covers only five lines of the lower. Indeed, much of the music can be transcribed, but the texts are very difficult to decipher.

Lines 1-3 conclude a melismatic Old-Beneventan piece which ends with a double *Alleluia* followed by what appears to be a psalmodic ending.

Lines 4-8 contain another melismatic Old-Beneventan melody, whose text is almost indecipherable: line six appears to contain the words *cherubim et seraph[im]*.

On lines 9-12 is written *Michi autem absit gloriari* (VI 40, f. 124 v, there presented as an Ingressa in connection with the feast of the Exaltation of the Holy Cross[14]). The version presented here concludes with a twofold *Alleluia* with musical material drawn from the body of the melody, whereas the version in VI 40 concludes with Alleluias used elsewhere in the repertory[15]. After these Alleluias is written a psalmodic ending.

Line 12 begins *Dum sacra misteria* (VI 38, f. 83; VI 40, f. 61; both as Ingressa for St. Michael *in monte Gargano* — May 8); this piece continues on the top of folio 169 recto.

Folio 169 recto (= hair side)

The first two lines conclude *Dum sacra misteria* (thus linking two seperate sections of the upper script of Vallicelliana C 9.

Lines 3-11 record *Ecce sedet* (Ingressa for the Ascension in VI 38, f. 93 and VI 40, f. 71), here concluding with two Alleluias. The Beneventan version of this Ingressa includes only the first Alleluia; but the second is used elswhere in the repertory as a conclusion for two Communions[16].

Lines 12-13: *Factus est repente* (Ingressa for Pentecost in VI 40, f. 79 v, and VI 38, f. 99: but there erased and written over). This piece is incomplete on this page; undoubtedly it continued on f. 169 verso, but this can no longer be verified.

Folio 169 verso (= flesh side)

Little is visible on this side.

Line 5 begins with an initial.
Line 7 concludes with a rubric apparently referring to St. John the Baptist, though only a few letters are visible ([I] oh [anne] bap [tiste]).

The following piece, beginning on line 8, is *Lumen quod animus cernit* (Ingressa for St. John the Baptist in VI 38, f. 110, and VI 40, f. 89).

Line 12 begins another piece, possibly *Petrus dormiebat* (Ingressa for Saint Peter and Paul in VI 38, f. 115 v, and VI 40, f. 99), though so little remains that identification is uncertain.

Folio 170 recto (= flesh side)

Except for tiny flecks of colored ink for initials, none of the lower script is visible.

---

14 See below, p. 13.
15 These *alleluia* are attached to the Ingressae of Easter (VI 38, f. 52ᵛ; VI 40, f. 159ᵛ); Pentecost (VI 40, f. 79ᵛ); and the Exaltation of the Holy Cross (VI 40, f. 124ᵛ).
16 For the Communion of Saints Peter and Paul (VI 40, f. 99ᵛ), and for the Easter Communion, where it is cued VI 38, f. 47, but entirely absent in VI 40.

Folio 170 verso (= hair side)

Very little is visible on this side.

A few neumes can be seen on lines 11 and 12.
Line 12 contains the beginning of a short threefold *Kyrie eleison* which continues on the beginning
of line 13 (but which is not followed by *Christe eleison*). The remainder of line 13 preserves a few
neumes, but almost no text.

Folio 171 recto (= hair side)

Fragments of Old-Beneventan melodic formulas are visible throughout the page, but no text can
be read.

Lines 12 and 13 have neumes in what is apparently a syllabic musical setting.

Folio 171 verso (= flesh side)

No music or text is visible.

Folio 172 recto (= flesh side)

No music or text is visible.

Folio 172 verso (= hair side)

Line 2 begins with an initial, possibly a P.

Line 7 begins with a larger initial.

Line 10 concludes a piece, whose text is illegible, in clear Old-Beneventan style. Probably a rubric
occupied the end of this line.

Line 11 begins *Prima predicationis* (Ingressa for Saint Andrew in VI 38, f. 140 and VI 40, f. 142).
The piece is complete here except for the final two syllables; but the continuation is not visible
on f. 173 recto.

Folio 173 recto (= hair side)

It is unfortunately impossible to show that *Prima predicationis* continues from f. 172 verso. Only
the lower part of this page reveals any neumes or text.

Line 6 begins with a large initial of uncertain shape.

Lines 7-13 preserve sequences of neumes, and fragments of text. Although Old-Beneventan melodic
shapes are apparent, the fragments do not permit meaningful transcription or the recognition of
any existing piece.

Line 8 includes the word *alleluia*.

Line 10 includes the words *orbis terre*.

Line 13: the middle of the line contains a round initial (O? Q? D?).

Folio 173 verso (= flesh side)

No music or text is visible.

Folio 173bis

This leaf, which concludes section 1 of Vallicelliana C 9, is far darker than all the others, and is
worn on the edges. For many years it must have been the final, outside page of a manuscript —
thought ist was not meant for this purpose: it ends incomplete, with a catchword for the next
gathering at the bottom of the verso. Additional sections now follow folio 173bis, but do not continue from it. Though folio 167 — the other half of this bifolium — makes it clear that folio 173bis
was indeed part of the original Old-Beneventan manuscript, the palimpsest remains on this folio
are almost invisible.

***

After a rather laborious excursion through this palimpsest fascicle, we can now stand back and consider those elements that are clearly identifiable, and their liturgical order.

The following condensed diagram will assist (broken lines indicate individual liturgical items which cannot be recovered):

f. 167r	---- (syllabic)
	Angelus domini (Easter Offertory)
	Qui manducaverit (Easter Communion)
f. 167v	
f. 168r	
f. 168v	---- . . . *alleluia*

	Michi autem absit (Exaltation[17] Ingressa)
	Dum sacra misteria (St. Michael Ingressa [May 8])
f. 169r	*Dum sacra, continued*
	Ecce sedet (Ascension Ingressa)
	Factus est repente (Pentecost Ingressa)
f. 169v	----
	Lumen quod (J. Baptist Ingressa)
	Petrus dormiebat? (Peter & Paul Ingressa)
f. 170r	
f. 170v	*[Kyrie eleison]*
f. 171r	
f. 171v	
f. 172r	
f. 172v	----

	Prima predicationis (Andrew Ingressa)
f. 173r	
f. 173v	
f. 173bis^r	
f. 173bis^v	

Of primary importance here is that all the music is in the Old-Beneventan style. In one single stretch of three pages (ff. 168v - 169v) we can place all the liturgical items in succession (except for one unidentified piece before *Lumen quod*) in the Old-Beneventan liturgy. And the unidentified music is characteristically Old-Beneventan.

With the exception of the final flyleaf (f. 202) of Benevento VI 35 (which contains music for Christmas followed immediately by music for Saint Stephen) this is our only surviving evidence that Old-Beneventan chant ever existed in separate books. In all the other sources of Old-Beneventan music the older liturgy clearly plays a secondary role. In these books Old-Beneventan offices or masses are included as ,doublets' following their Gregorian

---

17 See below, p. 13.

counterparts[18]; as occasional antiphons[19]; or as integral parts of Gregorian-Beneventan Holy Week rites[20].

The pieces we can identify in Vallicelliana C 9 are in liturgical order; and with one exception, they appear in this same order in both VI 38 and VI 40.

The exception is *Mitchi autem absit gloriari*, which in VI 40 is the Ingressa for the first of two Old-Beneventan masses of the Holy Cross. These two masses are attached, without identifying rubrics, to the Gregorian mass for the Exaltation of the Holy Cross (September 14). The curious presence of two masses at this place suggests that one of them belongs elsewhere. The first of the Old-Beneventan masses in VI 40 has texts that glorify the Cross[21], while the second records the recovery of the True Cross by Heraclius[22]. It appears that the first mass (using texts familiar in the Gregorian liturgy), celebrates the Roman feast of the Exaltation (September 14) while the second is for the Gallican feast of the Invention (May 3)[23].

One of these feasts (probably the Invention[24]) was possibly not originally a part of the Old-Beneventan liturgy. As the newer feast of the Invention came to be celebrated in Italy, a new mass was made for it at Benevento. Clearly there is some confusion in the transmission of these two masses by the eleventh century.

The feast of the Invention is indeed present earlier in VI 40[25], but it is not followed by an Old-Beneventan mass. Why was not the second of these masses placed there?

We cannot be certain. But we do know that the first mass, at least, was copied from another book (and not from memory or dictation). The Offertory and Communion are cued only, without musical notation: a common practice when the pieces in question are notated in full elsewhere in the same book. But the notated versions are nowhere present in VI 40; clearly the music of this first Old-Beneventan mass of the Holy Cross was copied from a book which did contain these pieces: possibly an Old-Beneventan gradual. Some additional scribal confusion has evidently occurred in the rearrangement required to accomodate Old-Beneventan music in a Gregorian gradual.

---

18 In VI 38 and VI 40; in the „Solesmes flyleaves" (see my forthcoming article in Études grégoriennes); and in the Montecassino Compactiones (see Boe, Old Beneventan Chant at Monte Cassino, above, note 4).

19 See J. Boe, A New Source for Old Beneventan Chant. The Santa Sophia Maundy in MS Ottoboni lat. 145, in: Acta Musicologica 52 (1980), p. 122-133.

20 See Paléographie musicale 14.

21 Ingressa: *Michi autem absit gloriari*; Alleluia V.: *Dicite in gentibus quia dominus regnavit a ligno;* Off. *Adoramus crucem;* Comm. *Crucem tuam.*

22 Ingressa: *Venite omnes veneremur lignum sancte crucis per quos nos christus sacro redemit sanguine suo.* V. *Defuncto chosroe eraclius suscepit gloriosissimum lignum sancte et vivifice crucis quod cum ingenti honore hierusolimam detulit.* V. *Gaudentes itaque omnes populi cum ymnis et canticis victorie regi obviam exierunt cernere desiderantes.* Alleluia *Dicite in gentibus.* Off.: *Miraculo de tam miro cum omnes terrerentur respicientes in altum viderunt signum sancte crucis in celo flamme fulgore resplendere.* Comm.: *Tunc imperator eraclius offerens hierusolimis multa donaria ecclesias reparari iussit ex ipsius sumptibus et constantinopolim rediit divina fretus potentia.*

23 See H. Leclercq, Croix (Invention et Exaltation de la vraie), in: Dictionnaire d'archéologie chrétienne et de liturgie, Paris 1907-1953, Vol. 3, 2me partie, p. 3131-3139. See also J. H. Miller, Cross, in: New Catholic Encyclopedia 4, Washington 1967, p. 479.

24. The Invention was a Gallican feast of the first half of the eighth century, only later brought to Italy. However, a seventh-century cartulary of Naples mentions the Invention, but not the Exaltation (see the articles by Leclercq and Miller cited in the previous note); perhaps the Invention was known in Southern Italy earlier than we think.

25 Both Gregorian feasts of the Holy Cross are present in VI 38 as well.

Michi autem absit, then, is the Ingressa for the Exaltation of the Holy Cross. In Vallicelliana C 9, however, it appears at the place assigned to the Invention. With this exception, all the liturgical items identified so far are in their proper order, arranged as follows:

> Easter: Offertory
> Easter: Communion
>
> [a gap of three pages]
> Invention [Exaltation] of the Holy Cross: Ingressa
> St. Michael (May 8): Ingressa
> Ascension: Ingressa
> Pentecost: Ingressa
>
> [a single unidentified piece]
> John the Baptist: Ingressa
> Saints Peter and Paul: Ingressa
>
> [a gap of almost six pages]
> Saint Andrew: Ingressa
>
> [an additional four pages]

But even though these leaves contain mass chants in liturgical order, they are not part of a normal gradual: the masses are far from complete.

It is true that we have successive elements for a single mass in the case of Easter. But the other pieces we can identify are all Ingressae, and they are placed directly in succession, without the accompanying Alleluia, Offertory and Communion which are indispensible to an Old-Beneventan mass. There is not even room between pieces to cue the incipits of the other elements of a mass.

What is the function of such a series of entrance chants? It is regrettable that no visible rubrics label these pieces, for perhaps they do not function here as entrance chants at all. We know of several Offertories and Communions in the repertory that survive with a variety of liturgical functions[26], but nowhere else do Ingressae serve also for occasional use as processional antiphons or the like.

There is also the matter of gaps. In VI 38 and VI 40, the next Old-Beneventan music after Easter is that for St. Michael (May 8); but here there are three pages of music before the Ingressa of the Invention of the Holy Cross. What liturgical functions could intervene? Masses for Easter Week, Sundays after Easter, Rogation, and Saints Tiburtius and Valerianus, George, Mark, and Vitalis, are all present in both VI 38 and VI 40-- although not accompanied by Old-Beneventan ,doublets'. We could add substanially to our knowledge of the Old-Beneventan rite and its music if these pages were recoverable.

A longer gap (almost six pages) occurs between *Petrus dormiebat* for Saints Peter and Paul and *Prima predicationis* for St. Andrew. In the Old-Beneventan repertory of VI 40 there are eight Ingressae (each accompanying a complete mass) which fill this gap[27]. But by even a generous estimate these eight pieces would occupy no more than three and a half pages here. The eight

---

26 See my forthcoming study in Études grégoriennes.
27 Actually there are nine Ingressae, but one is *Michi autem absit,* which appears earlier in Vallicelliana C 9. They are:

Lawrence:	*Gratias ago deo meo*	Simon & Jude:	*Michi autem nimis*
Assumption:	*Surge propera*	All Saints I:	*Gaudeamus omnes*
XII Fratrum:	*Sancti videntes*	All Saints II:	*Isti sunt sancti*
[Invention:	*Michi autem absit*]	Martin:	*Stolam iocunditatis*
Exaltation:	*Venite omnes*		

complete masses would fill this space comfortably: but I can find no correspondence among the neumes and syllables that are occasionally visible; and such a change of format — from a series of Ingressae to a series of whole masses — seems unlikely.

Here again, then, is a space amounting to something less than three pages, some thirty-five lines, filled with irretrievable Old-Beneventan liturgical music[28].

And there is a final space of some four pages following the Ingressa for Saint Andrew; fragments of music and text remain, but not enough to reconstruct a piece or a phrase.

Indeed, what could follow Saint Andrew? If this book followed the liturgical order of VI 38 and VI 40, there would follow masses for the Sundays after Pentecost and a series of votive masses.

***

We can now return to the three bifolia and two single leaves from this Old-Beneventan manuscript which are found in fascicles 2 through 5 of Vallicelliana C 9. The order in which these leaves now appear could be generated from an Old-Beneventan fascicle arranged as diagrammed below, whose leaves were removed one by one, starting from the center, and erased for use in what is now Vallicellianan C 9 (leaves maked with an asterisk were reversed before receiving the upper script):

---

28 The feasts that occur in VI 38 and VI 40 between the feast of Saints Peter and Paul and that of Saint Andrew are the following (those with Old-Beneventan masses are marked with asterisks; names of Saints are left in the genitive as they appear in the MSS):
SS. Processi et Martiniani (VI 38 only)
S. Felicitatis and daughters
S. Praxedis (VI 40 only)
S. Apollinaris (VI 38 only)
SS. Nazari et Celsi (VI 38 only)
SS. Simplicii, Faustini, et Beatricis (VI 38 only)
Transfiguration (VI 38 only)
Holy Trinity (VI 38 only)
S. Ciriaci (VI 38 only)
S. Laurentii*
S. Tiburtii (VI 40 only)
S. Yppoliti (VI 40 only)
Assumption*
SS. Eremeti et Augustini (VI 38 only)
S. Sabini
Beheading of John the Baptist
S. Felicis (VI 38: Felicis et Audacti)
Holy Twelve Brothers*
Nativity of the Virgin
S. Gorgoni
SS. Prothi and Jacinthi (VI 40 only)
Exaltation of the Holy Cross*
SS. Cornelii and Cypriani
S. Nicomedis (VI 40 only)
SS. Cosme and Damiani
Dedicatio S. Michahelis
SS. Simonis and Iude*
All Saints*
Quatuor coronati (VI 40 only)
S. Martini*
S. Cecilie
S. Clementis

Folio in Vall. C 9	Folio in hypothetical fascile
f. 37ᵛ	A
f. 29ᵛ	B
f. 20	C
f. 11	D
f. 14	E
f. 19ᵛ	F
f. 24ᵛ	G
f. 32ᵛ	H

These leaves contain music used elsewhere for Holy Week; and arranging them in this fashion places the known music in liturgical order. Happy as we would be, however, to have another complete Old-Beneventan fascicle, we shall see that there are too many problems to leave this arrangement unchallenged.

Nevertheless, it will be convenient to refer to these leaves by their location in this hypothetical gathering, since the reversing of some leaves in Vallicelliana C 9 makes former versos into rectos, and folios which formerly preceded others now follow them.

Folio A opens with a large initial, probably a P; most of the characteristic Old-Beneventan music of this piece can be deciphered for lines 2 and 3; the word *Johannes* appears twice. The text and music are unknown elsewhere in the repertory. The rest of the folio and its verso are not readable.

Folio B contains no recognized pieces. The music for the first three lines (but not the text) is partly legible, and is characteristically Old-Beneventan. At the end of line 2 is a rubric which seems to conclude „. . . *esima Ingsa.*" Thus the neumes which can be seen on line 3 may be part of a Lenten Ingressa. These few neumes, without their text, are all the evidence we presently have for the existence of Old-Beneventan music for the first five weeks of Lent.

Folios C, D, and E preserve only isolated fragments of neumes or letters. The neumes are sufficient, however, to demonstrate that the music is in the Old-Beneventan style. Folio D begins with an initial letter S; most of the music of the first line of this piece (but not its text) can be read: the music is not that of any known Old-Beneventan piece.

Folio E has a top line of music in syllabic style, evidently part of a Credo: though the text here cannot be read, that of the third line reads *[consub] stantialem patri per quem omnia fa[cta] s[unt qui] propter nos homines*[29].

Folio F is best considered by beginning on the verso.

This side begins with the end of the Ingressa *Postquam surrexit* for Maunday Thursday (VI 40, f. 4v): *vos debetis alter alterius pedes lavare dicit dominus*. The Ingressa concludes on line 2, leaving a space for a now-illegible rubric. Line 3, which we should expect to continue with music for the Maundy Thursday mass and *mandatum*, does not do so. It begins with three initials, spaced about 2 cm apart so as to allow the first two to serve as cues to pieces which are not noted here in full. The initials and text are not legible, and the cues (if that is what they are) are not noted. The third initial is the beginning of a piece whose opening music (only the music of this line can be read) is not that of any known Old-Beneventan piece. The remainder of this side is illegible, and no further music for Maunday Thursday is to be found on any other folio.

---

29 A fragment of another Old-Beneventan noted Credo is found on the flyleaf (f. 202ʳ) of Benevento VI. 35, preceding the Christmas Offertory. Unfortunately these two cannot be compared; all that remains in VI 35 is *vitam futuri seculi. Amen.* In a forthcoming study I shall discuss fragments of a third Old-Beneventan Credo in a palimpsest manuscript at Montecassino.

The recto of this folio, preceding the Maunday Thursday Ingressa, preserves only two initial letters: a T beginning line 4, and what may be the P of *Postquam surrexit* on line 10. This letter T possibly marks the beginning of the Ingressa *Testificatur* for Palm Sunday (VI. 38, f. 37v), but if so there is room only for the Ingressa, and not for the rest of the mass. Or perhaps there was music in the Old-Beneventan rite for the days of Holy Week between Palm Sunday and Maunday Thursday; but the presence of lacunae in both VI 38 (after Palm Sunday) and VI 40 (before Maunday Thursday) prevent our knowing whether some piece beginning with the letter T was a feature of the mass of Wednesday in Holy Week.

Folio G contains no music that we know. At its place in this hypothetical fascicle we should expect to find music for Good Friday, but none of these fragmentary remains can be identified with Old-Beneventan music for that day. All we have, in fact, is a few fragments on the recto. Line 1 shows the conclusion of a piece that ends *libera nos*, with a strongly-characteristic Old-Beneventan cadence. There follows a rubric that reads *of.*, and the beginning of a piece whose text is not readable, though almost one complete line of music remains. If this latter piece is an Offertory, then the preceding music may be that of a Gradual or Ingressa. (It is probably not an Alleluia, since its music is not the melody used for almost every Old-Beneventan Alleluia-verse.)

Folio H begins on its recto (the present f. 32v) with two lines which conclude the Old-Beneventan tract *Domine audivi* for Holy Saturday (Benevento 38, f. 44; VI 40, f. 15v)[30]. The text preserved is *superexcelsa mea deducit me victor in psalmis canentem.* At the end of line 2 is a short, illegible rubric.

Line 3 begins the Old-Beneventan tract *Cantabo nunc dilecto* (VI 38, f. 45; VI 40, f. 17v)[31]. Two lines of this tract are partially visible; nothing more can be seen on this page.

On the verso of folio H, about halfway down the page, is a large initial M. This may be the opening of the Easter Ingressa *Maria vidit angelum*; none of the remaining Old-Beneventan pieces for Holy Saturday begins with this letter.

At first glance we might think that folio H, with the end of Holy Saturday and the beginning of Easter, is followed immediately by the first folio of the Old-Beneventan fascicle already discussed, which shows the Easter Offertory halfway down the first page (f. 167).

But there are difficulties on both sides of this possible Easter Ingressa. The space between the Ingressa and the end of the preceding Tract *Cantabo* — some twelve or thirteen lines — is not nearly sufficient for all the remaining music for Holy Saturday. We should expect two more tracts, two antiphons, and the music for the Midnight Mass[32].

Likewise the space between the initial M on folio H and the beginning of the Easter Offertory on folio 167 is insufficient even for the Easter Ingressa. This is a space of some nine or ten lines. In VI 38 (where the Easter mass appears to be complete, and line lengths are approximately equal to those here) the Easter pieces are as follows:

Ingressa	10 1/2 lines
Acclamation	1/2 line
Gloria (cued)	1/4 line
Alleluia	2 1/4 lines
	13 1/2 lines

Of the nine- or ten-line space in Vallicelliana C 9, the last three lines, preceding the Easter Offertory, have syllabic music which is not otherwise known. Possibly these are the neumes for the end of the *Gloria in excelsis* (cued in VI 38), but if so, what of the Alleluia? If we could read clearly the text and music in these intervening spaces we could come much closer to resolving these difficulties; but for the moment we must content ourselves with the observation that, even though folio H concludes with music for Holy Saturday and folio 167 begins with music for Easter, the two are not

---

30 Facsimiles in Paléographie musicale 14, plates XVIII (VI40) and XXIV (VI 38).
31 Facsimiles in Paléographie musicale 14, plates XX (VI 40) and XXIV (VI 38).
32 These are the pieces provided in VI 40. But even the Holy Saturday music of VI 38, which now is shorter by two erased Tracts and an antiphon, is far too large for this space.

joined in the way we expect. Either one or more intervening leaves are missing, or both the Holy Saturday and Easter rites here are different from, and substantially shorter than, the version we find in VI 40.

***

After a possibly tiresome and repetitive survey, what can we learn from these palimpsest leaves?

First, we have discovered extensive portions of a book that contained only Old-Beneventan music. This in itself is of primary importance, for it suggests that the Old-Beneventan rite was used in its entirety at least into the period of written musical-liturgical documents. In all our other sources we see the Benventan repertory included piecemaeal in books devoted to the „official" Gregorian chant (exepting, always, the Old-Beneventan flyleaf from VI 35). It is particulary unfortunate that we cannot determine the provenance of this manuscript; the likeliest origin seems to Benevento itself[33].

We have identified in this document eleven (and possibly thirteen) pieces which are known elsewhere in the Old-Beneventan repertory:

Testificatur (?)	PalmS	Ingressa	fol. Fv (= 19r)
Postquam surrexit	MThurs	Ingressa	fol. Fr (= 19v)
Domine audivi	HSat	Tract	fol. Hr (= 32r)
Cantabo	HSat	Tract	fol. Hr (= 32r)
Angelus domini	Easter	Offertory	fol. 167r
Qui manducaverit	Easter	Communion	fol. 167r
Michi autem absit	InvHCross	Ingressa	fol. 168v
Dum sacra misteria	Michael (8 May)	Ingressa	fol. 168v
Ecce sedet in medio	Ascension	Ingressa	fol. 169r
Factus est repente	Pentecost	Ingressa	fol. 169r
Lumen quod animus	John Bapt	Ingressa	fol. 169v
Petrus dormiebat (?)	Peter & Paul	Ingressa	fol. 169v
Prima predicationis	Andrew	Ingressa	fol. 172v

Most of these pieces are used as Ingressae in other sources, where they are at the head of complete masses. But a collection of Ingressae from their masses might not be designed for use at mass at all. A series of pieces for the major feasts of the year in fact could be used as processional, votive, or *mandatum* antiphons, like the Old-Beneventan pieces in the manuscript Vatican Ottoboni latinus 145[34]. But the presence here of other elements of the Easter mass and of Tracts for Holy Saturday show that this book is designed, at least in part, for the principal liturgy of the day.

If this book is a Gradual, however, many questions remain to be answered. Why are these Ingressae separated from their masses? What was the shape of the Old-Beneventan Lenten liturgy? What occupies the spaces before and after the feast of St. Andrew? Why do the Holy Week rites apparently differ from those described by Dom Hesbert[35]? These and many other questions must for the moment await further research.

---

33 M. De Nonno, Contributo (above, note 12), p. 129, argues for the Beneventan origin of a portion of the manuscript — though not the portion under consideration here. Mallet and Thibaut (Les manuscrits, p. 16, n. 3; above, note 1) note that the rich holdings of manuscripts in Beneventan script at the Biblioteca Vallicelliana may come in part from Baronius, who in 1599 received the benefice of Santa Maria in Venticano, some 20 kilometers southeast of Benevento. The musical notation is similar to that of Benevento VI 40.

34 See Boe, A New Source (above, note 19).

35 See the studies by Hesbert cited in note 1.

Particularly frustrating in studying this document is the difficulty faced by pre-Guidonian singers: instantly recognizing a piece one already knows, while being unable to bring to life an unknown melody. The problem here, however, is not notation but preservation. We cannot make a meaningful reconstruction of text and melody when the remains are so fragmentary.

But from this document there is ample evidence that the Old-Benventan repertory is significantly larger than was known heretofore; we are in the presence of many *unica* in these thirty-two pages. But the fragmentary nature of the remains can only tantalize us for the moment, and compel us to renew the search for a document which — we now can feel more certain — once existed: the Gradual of the Old-Beneventan rite.

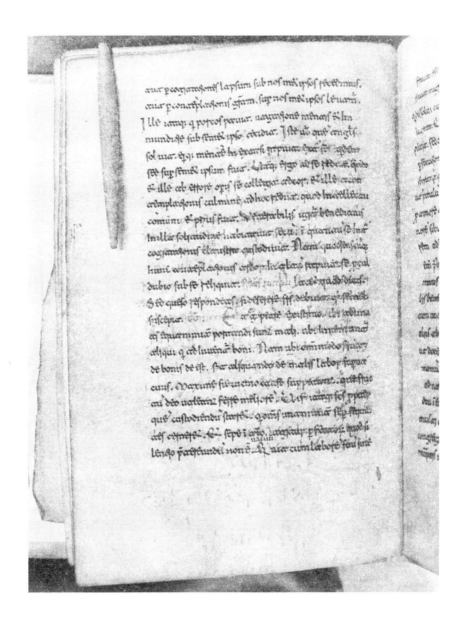

Plate 1:
Rome, Biblioteca Vallicelliana Ms. C 9, folio 32. The lower script (inverted in the present bottom margin) shows the end of the Old-Beneventan tract *Domine audivi*, and the beginning (on line 3) of the Old-Beneventan tract *Cantabo*.

Plate 2:
Rome, Biblioteca Vallicelliana Ms. C 9, folio 167. The lower script visible in the bottom margin shows the end of the Old-Beneventan Easter Communion verse *Gloria et honore*, and, on the bottom line, the beginning of the Communion verse *Et nunc*. The Communion itself, *Qui manducaverit*, begins under the fourth line of the upper script.

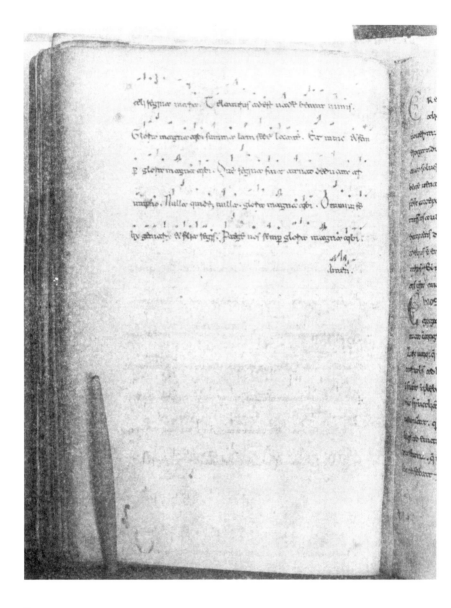

Plate 3:
Rome, Biblioteca Vallicelliana Ms. C 9, folio 168 verso. The lower script contains Old-Beneventan music; what appears in the photograph to be the text of the lower script is in many cases the reversed image of the upper script on the verso. The bottom line shows the beginning of the Old-Beneventan Ingressa *Dum sacra misteria.* The four lines preceding this show the Ingressa *Michi autem absit gloriari.*

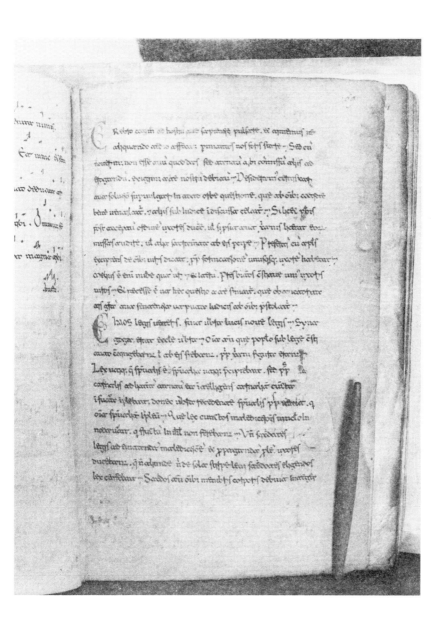

Plate 4:
Rome, Biblioteca Vallicelliana Ms. C 9, folio 169. At the top of the page, the lower script shows the end of the Old-Beneventan Ingressa *Dum sacra misteria* continued from the previous page. In the bottom margin can be seen the first two lines of the Old-Beneventan Ingressa *Factus est repente.*

V

MONTECASSINO AND THE
OLD BENEVENTAN CHANT

The term 'Old Beneventan' describes the archaic non-Gregorian chant found chiefly in two eleventh-century Graduals in the chapter library at Benevento.[1] This is perhaps in part a translation of Dom Hesbert's 'Ancien rit bénéventain',[2] with a hint of analogy to the 'Old Roman'[3] chant. The term means that this chant is 'Old', that is, that it pre-dates the introduction of Gregorian chant into southern Italy; and that it is 'Beneventan'. But both words need to be evaluated carefully.

What is 'Old' about the Old Beneventan chant? And what is 'Beneventan'? As to its age, the visible history of the Old Beneventan chant takes place almost entirely within the first half of the eleventh century. The music is not written down earlier than Gregorian chant; with rare exceptions[4] the repertory as we have it comes

---

[1] Benevento, Archivio Capitolare, MSS 38 and 40. Manuscripts of the chapter library of Benevento will be identified here without the Roman numerals which have been part of their shelf numbers in most of the literature to date. This accords with the practice of the new catalogue of Beneventan manuscripts: J. Mallet and A. Thibaut, *Les manuscrits en écriture bénéventaine de la Bibliothèque capitulaire de Bénévent*, i: *Manuscrits 1–18* (Paris, 1984).

[2] R.-J. Hesbert, 'L' "Antiphonale missarum" de l'ancien rit bénéventain', *Ephemerides Liturgicae*, 52 (1938), pp. 28–66, 141–58; 53 (1939), pp. 168–90; 59 (1945), pp. 69–95; 60 (1946), pp. 103–41; 61 (1947), pp. 153–210.

[3] The term 'Old Roman', coined by B. Stäblein ('Alt- und Neurömischer Choral', *Kongress-Bericht: Gesellschaft für Musikforschung Lüneburg 1950*, ed. H. Albrecht, H. Osthoff and W. Wiora, Kassel and Basle, n.d., pp. 53–6), refers to an archaic non-Gregorian musical repertory found in certain Roman manuscripts of the eleventh century and later. See H. Hucke, 'Gregorian and Old Roman Chant', *The New Grove Dictionary of Music and Musicians*, ed. S. Sadie, 20 vols. (London, 1980), vii, pp. 693–7.

[4] The final flyleaf, fol. 202, of Benevento, Archivio Capitolare, MS 35, which preserves the end of the Christmas Mass and the beginning of one for St Stephen, may be a page from a lost Old Beneventan Gradual. A benedictional roll in the Archivio del Duomo of Bari may also be representative of the uncontaminated Old Beneventan liturgy; it preserves a Tract and an antiphon for the blessing of the font on Holy Saturday. Facsimiles in G. Cavallo, *Rotoli di Exultet dell'Italia meridionale* (Bari, 1973), plates 13 and 14; and in M. Avery, *The Exultet Rolls of South Italy* (Princeton, 1936), ii, plate xiii.

V

entirely from books of Gregorian chant, in which Old Beneventan music is either supplementary or disguised among the very chants whose imposition caused the suppression of the local music.

The antiquity of this chant, then, is established by an understanding of its textual, liturgical and musical archaisms, and from other historical evidence. Hesbert argued that the creative period of Beneventan chant had ended in the early eighth century with the coming of Gregorian chant,[5] and perhaps he was right. But despite whatever pressure there may have been to the contrary – pressure which may well, of course, have affected the transmission of the chant itself – somehow the remains of this archaic local repertory survived into the early eleventh century, when musical manuscripts began to be written in southern Italy.[6] The very act of writing down music, of course, has much to tell us about stability of transmission, about moments of change in tradition.[7] And in the case of the Old Beneventan chant, the moment of writing precedes by only a few years the moment of almost complete suppression.

And what is 'Beneventan' about the Old Beneventan chant? The term is used in E. A. Lowe's classic *The Beneventan Script*[8] to describe the characteristic writing of a large area of southern Italy and Dalmatia, centred on the medieval duchy of Benevento. The

---

[5] See the studies by Hesbert cited in note 2, and his essay in Paléographie Musicale, ser. I, 14 (Tournai, 1931), pp. 248–465. The Beneventan Mass for the Holy Twelve Brothers, whose relics came to Benevento in 760, is a collection of pure Old Beneventan music (Benevento 40, fols. 121^v–122). But the Beneventan Mass of St Bartholomew, whose remains came to Benevento in 838, and whose translation entered the calendar the following year, is modelled on Gregorian chant. See S. Borgia, *Memorie istoriche della pontificia Città di Benevento*, I (Rome, 1763), pp. 237, 336–7. The date of Bartholomew's translation is often given as 808 (cf. Paléographie Musicale, ser. I, 14, pp. 450–1; B. Baroffio, 'Liturgie im beneventanischen Raum', *Geschichte der katholischen Kirchenmusik*, ed. K. G. Fellerer, 2 vols., Kassel, 1972–6, I, pp. 204–8).

[6] The gradual MS Benevento, Archivio Capitolare 33, contains very little Old Beneventan chant, though thought by some to date from as early as the tenth century (Lowe/Brown – see below, note 8 – II, p. 21), and hence to antedate the main Beneventan sources of this chant. Recent opinion is that the manuscript is not demonstrably from Benevento (Mallet and Thibaut, *Les manuscrits*, pp. 76, n. 5, 90), and probably dates from the eleventh century; see the introduction, by J. Hourlier, to Paléographie Musicale, ser. I, 20 (Berne and Frankfurt, 1983), pp. 17*–18*.

[7] Some recent studies dealing with the relationship of music writing to oral tradition include H. Hucke, 'Toward a New Historical View of Gregorian Chant', *Journal of the American Musicological Society*, 33 (1980), pp. 437–67; L. Treitler, 'Homer and Gregory: the Transmission of Epic Poetry and Plainchant', *The Musical Quarterly*, 60 (1974), pp. 333–72.

[8] Published as E. A. Loew (*sic*), *The Beneventan Script: a History of the South Italian Minuscule* (Oxford, 1914); 2nd, enlarged edition (= Lowe/Brown) by V. Brown, 2 vols. (Rome, 1980). The use of the word 'Beneventan' for south Italian writing is, of course, much older. See Lowe/Brown, I, pp. 37–40, 338.

Montecassino and the Old Beneventan chant

geographical boundaries of this musical repertory have yet to be determined; but the sources of Old Beneventan chant are written practically without exception in the characteristic Beneventan script and notation.[9] The chief surviving sources are probably from Benevento itself: the two eleventh-century graduals Benevento 38 and 40;[10] but Old Beneventan chant survives also from Montecassino,[11] Farfa,[12] Bari[13] and as far north as Lucca.[14]

The term 'Old Beneventan', useful as it is, must not be understood as fixing a time or place, given the fragmentary nature of the repertory and the span of time that separates the surviving sources from the active period of the chant. But if we identify lines of transmission and locate influential centres for the cultivation of this music, we contribute substantially to our understanding of the importance of this rite and its chant.

There are reasons for focusing on Benevento itself as an important centre of this chant: (1) Our largest sources of Old Beneventan chant are Benevento 38 and 40, which are also among the earliest. (2) Much Old Beneventan Holy Week music survives in many later sources in Benevento.[15] (3) A significant item in the repertory is a mass for the Holy Twelve Brothers, whose relics were interred by Prince Arichis of Benevento in his newly established church of Santa Sofia in 760.[16] (4) Six Old Beneventan antiphons survive in a manuscript (Vatican City, Biblioteca Apostolica Vaticana, Ottob. lat. 145) written for use at Santa Sofia, though modelled on a source from Montecassino.[17]

---

[9] An exception is the supplement to Lucca, Biblioteca Capitolare, MS 606 (fols. 150ᵛ–156ᵛ), containing a series of Holy Week pieces which includes Old Beneventan chants; the manuscript is written in ordinary minuscule, though the musical notation is Beneventan. See the facsimiles in Paléographie Musicale, ser. I, 14, plates XXXIV–XLIII.

[10] Their provenance is unfortunately far from certain; see Mallet and Thibaut, Les manuscrits, introduction, pp. 7–104, especially pp. 67–94.

[11] See J. Boe, 'Old Beneventan Chant at Monte Cassino: Gloriosus Confessor Domini Benedictus', Acta Musicologica, 55 (1983), pp. 69–73.

[12] Music for Holy Saturday survives on a single fragmentary leaf (Farfa, Biblioteca dell'Abbazia, MS AB. F. Musica XI). See Paléographie Musicale, ser. I, 14, plates XXVI and XXVII, there erroneously listed as 'Cava'.

[13] See above, note 4.

[14] In MS 606 of the Biblioteca Capitolare. See above, note 9.

[15] The music for Holy Week is studied, and some of the sources identified, in Hesbert's introduction to Paléographie Musicale, ser. I, 14, pp. 248–446.

[16] See note 33 and the discussion on pp. 72–4.

[17] See J. Boe, 'A New Source for Old Beneventan Chant: the Santa Sophia Maundy in MS Ottoboni lat. 145', Acta Musicologica, 52 (1980), pp. 122–33.

This last document makes a connection between Benevento and the great mountaintop abbey founded by St Benedict. It is almost inevitable that Montecassino should figure prominently in any discussion of medieval southern Italy. Montecassino in the eleventh and twelfth centuries was a monastic and ecclesiastical centre of primary importance and a significant political power. An active and influential centre of learning, it was by far the most important centre for Beneventan writing.[18] And so an important and inevitable question is whether the Old Beneventan chant was ever in regular use at Montecassino. We already have hints of its use there. In addition to the Vatican manuscript just mentioned, there is an Old Beneventan Communion for St Benedict preserved in a fragmentary Gradual at Montecassino.[19]

In order to give fuller treatment to this question, I should like to introduce three new eleventh-century sources of Old Beneventan chant, for these, in addition to increasing our basic materials, suggest that the Old Beneventan chant was used at Montecassino, and strengthen the notion of a strong Benevento–Montecassino link. All three are palimpsests, only partly recoverable, but each is the remnant of a book devoted to Old Beneventan chant, and they are thus witnesses to an earlier stage in transmission than that represented by the piecemeal retention of the repertory in Gregorian books.

I. The manuscript Rome, Biblioteca Vallicelliana, c 9,[20] includes sixteen palimpsest folios from an Old Beneventan musical manu-

---

[18] In the absence of the long-awaited publication of H. Bloch's *Montecassino in the Middle Ages*, discussions of the history of Montecassino during this period may be found in Lowe, *The Beneventan Script*, pp. 1–21; H. Bloch, 'Monte Cassino, Byzantium, and the West in the Earlier Middle Ages', *Dumbarton Oaks Papers*, 3 (1946), pp. 163–224 and plates 217–58; E. Caspar, *Petrus diaconus und die Monte Cassineser Fälschungen* (Berlin, 1909), pp. 1–18. The standard work is E. Gattola, *Historia abbatiae Casinensis*, 2 vols. (Venice, 1733), with his *Ad historiam abbatiae Casinensis accessiones*, 2 vols. (Venice, 1734). There is also a history by L. Tosti, *Storia della badia di Monte-Cassino* (Naples, 1842; 2nd edn, Rome, 1891). The earlier history of Montecassino is studied in G. Falco, 'Lineamenti di storia cassinese nei secoli VIII e IX', *Casinensia*, 1 (Montecassino, 1929), pp. 457–548; and in A. Citarella and H. Willard, *The Ninth-century Treasure of Monte Cassino in the Context of Political and Economic Developments in South Italy*, Miscellanea Cassinese 50 (Montecassino, 1983), esp. pp. 51–82.

[19] See Boe, 'Old Beneventan Chant at Monte Cassino'.

[20] The manuscript is described, its contents inventoried and relevant bibliography listed, in L. Avitabile, F. De Marco, M. C. Di Franco and V. Jemolo, 'Censimento dei codici dei secoli X–XII', *Studi Medievali*, ser. III, 12 (1970), pp. 1037–8; and in Lowe/Brown, II, pp. 127–8. The first volume of a modern catalogue has appeared, but it does not include this

script.[21] These palimpsest pages are written in characteristic Beneventan script and notation of the earlier eleventh century. We cannot read new pieces in this manuscript; indeed, in such fragmentary form it is difficult to recognise familiar ones. But all the pieces we can recognise here are known only from the Old Beneventan repertory, all of them used in the Mass. The musical details that remain match the other known readings with that surprising faithfulness that seems to characterise the Old Beneventan transmission. Even where only a few neumes are recoverable there is no music that is not highly characteristic of Old Beneventan chant; and often there are long sections of clearly Old Beneventan, but not quite legible, music. It would appear, then, that these leaves are pages from a Gradual of the Old Beneventan rite.

A number of pieces in this document which are known elsewhere in the Old Beneventan repertory are listed in Table 1. It is possible to identify the contents of three successive pages (fols. 168^v–169^v) and a portion of a fourth (fol. 168^r). This in itself is of prime importance, for it suggests that a distinct Old Beneventan repertory was copied into separate books (and was presumably sung) at least into the period of written musical-liturgical documents. The presence of several successive elements for the Easter Mass, and of two Tracts for Holy Saturday, are features characteristic of a Gradual. But elsewhere in these pages at least five Ingressae (beginning with *Michi autem absit*) are placed directly in succession, without the accompanying Alleluia, Offertory and Communion which are indispensable to an Old Beneventan Mass. There is not even room between pieces to cue the incipits of the other elements of a Mass.

What is the function of such a series of entrance chants? It is regrettable that no visible rubrics label these pieces, for perhaps they do not function here as entrance chants at all, but as some sort of

manuscript: A. M. Giorgetti Vichi and S. Mottironi, *Catalogo dei manoscritti della Biblioteca Vallicelliana*, I, Ministero della Pubblica Istruzione, Indici e Cataloghi, nuova serie, 7 (Rome, 1961). The three-volume handwritten catalogue available in the library contains a table of contents for the manuscript: (Vincenzo Vettori), 'Inventarium Omnium Codicum Manuscriptorum Graecorum et Latinorum Bibliothecae Vallicellanae Digestum Anno Domini MDCCXLIV. Pars I. Continet priores XXVI Tomos Itemque alios codices a litera A. ad F. inclusive.'

[21] The manuscript and its Old Beneventan contents have been considered and described in detail in T. F. Kelly, 'Palimpsest Evidence of an Old-Beneventan Gradual', *Kirchenmusikalisches Jahrbuch*, 67 (1983), forthcoming.

Table 1 *Palimpsest Old Beneventan music in Rome, Vallicelliana MS* c 9

Folio	Incipit	Feast	Function	Benevento MS
14ᵛ	Credo (fragment)[a]	?		
19ʳ	Testificatur (?)	Palm Sunday	Ingressa	38, fol. 37ᵛ
19ᵛ	Postquam surrexit	Maundy Thursday	Ingressa	40, fol. 4ᵛ
32ʳ	Domine audivi	Holy Saturday	Tract	38, fol. 44
				40, fol. 15ᵛ
32ʳ	Cantabo	Holy Saturday	Tract	38, fol. 45
				40, fol. 17ᵛ
167ʳ	Credo (fragment)[b]	Easter		
167ʳ	Angelus Domini	Easter	Offertory	38, fol. 53
				40, fol. 27
167ʳ	Qui manducaverit	Easter	Communion	38, fol. 53
				40, fol. 28
168ᵛ	Michi autem absit	Invention of Holy Cross	Ingressa	40, fol. 124ᵛ
168ᵛ	Dum sacra misteria	St Michael (8 May)	Ingressa	38, fol. 83
				40, fol. 61
169ʳ	Ecce sedet in medio	Ascension	Ingressa	38, fol. 93
				40, fol. 71
169ʳ	Factus est repente	Pentecost	Ingressa	38, fol. 99
				40, fol. 79ᵛ
169ᵛ	Lumen quod animus	St John the Baptist	Ingressa	38, fol. 110
				40, fol. 89

Table 1 – *continued*

Folio	Incipit	Feast	Function	Benevento MS
169^v	Petrus dormiebat (?)	SS Peter and Paul	Ingressa	38, fol. 115^v 38, fol. 99
170^v	Kyrie^c	?	?	
172^v	Prima predicationis	St Andrew	Ingressa	38, fol. 140 40, fol. 142

Notes:

[a] One line of music (whose text cannot be read) and, two lines below, the text '[consub]stantialem patri per quem omnia facta sunt qui propter nos homines' are all that can be read of a Credo here. A fragment of another Old Beneventan noted Credo is found on the flyleaf (fol. 202^v) of Benevento 35, preceding the Christmas Offertory. That fragment's music is found also later in this manuscript (see below, note b). Unfortunately these two cannot be compared; all that remains in MS 35 is 'et vitam futuri seculi. Amen'. A third Old Beneventan Credo is discussed below (see Table 2).

[b] Portions of four lines of music are visible on this page, immediately preceding the Easter Offertory; the concluding notes match exactly those found as the end of a Credo in Benevento 35, fol. 202. See above, note a.

[c] This threefold Kyrieleison, about half of whose relatively simple music is legible, is clearly not part of a larger nine-part structure. I shall not speculate on its function.

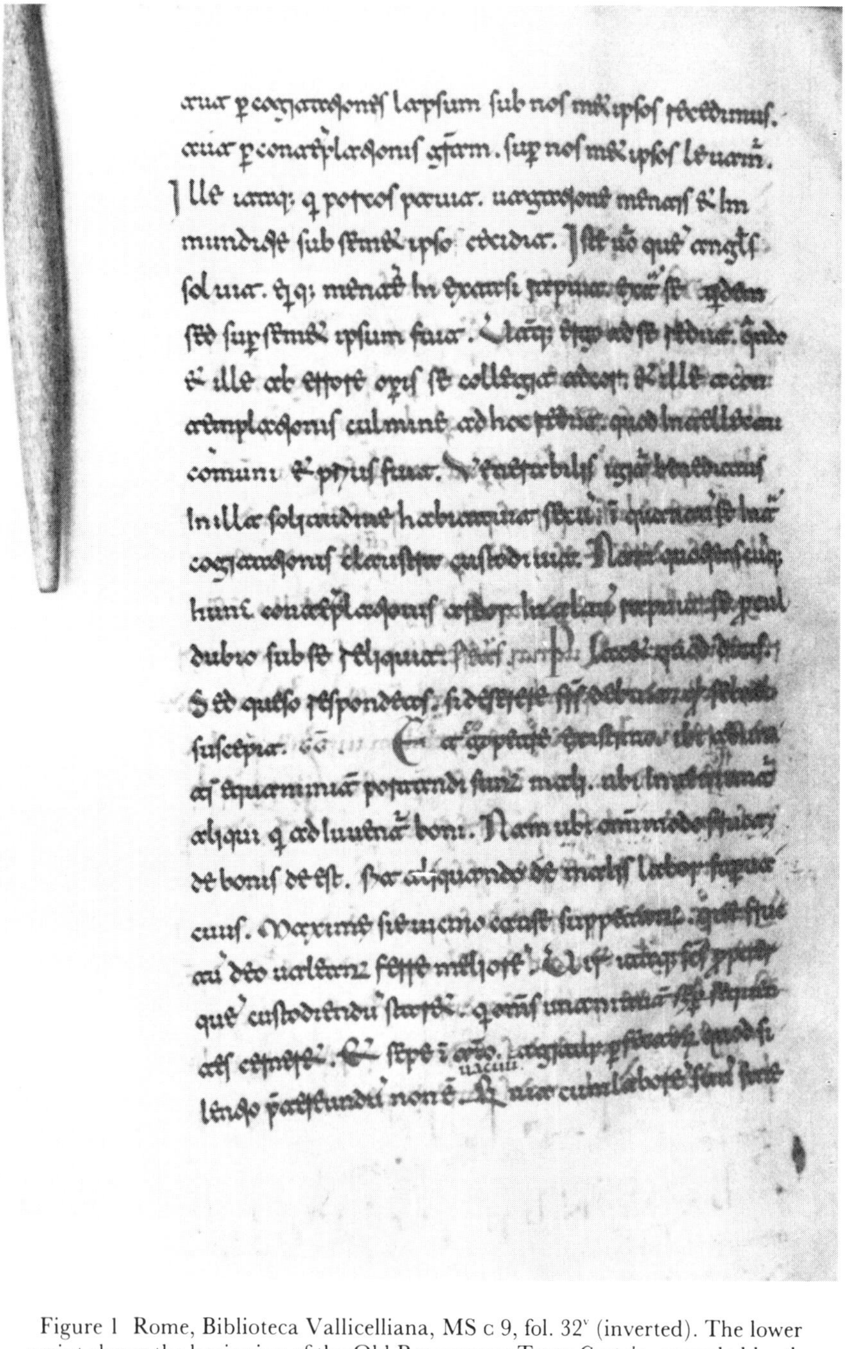

Figure 1 Rome, Biblioteca Vallicelliana, MS c 9, fol. 32ᵛ (inverted). The lower script shows the beginning of the Old Beneventan Tract *Cantabo*, preceded by the end of the Tract *Domine audivi*.

votive, processional or *mandatum* antiphon, like the Old Beneventan pieces in the Vatican manuscript Ottob. lat. 145.[22]

This book, whether it is a Gradual or not, raises many questions, including some not touched on here.[23] One of the most important, of course, is that of the manuscript's provenance. For the moment we can only say that the likeliest place of origin, perhaps not surprisingly, seems to be Benevento itself.[24]

II. A thirteenth-century cartulary of the abbey of Santa Maria de Mare in the Tremiti Islands (22 kilometres north of the Gargano peninsula) is now Vatican City, Biblioteca Apostolica Vaticana, MS Vat. lat. 10657.[25] Several Beneventan hands have recorded charters and diplomas relating to Santa Maria and to nearby Sancti Jacobi from the early eleventh century onwards.

Four bifolia in this manuscript are recycled leaves of another eleventh-century Old Beneventan Gradual, arranged as in Figure 2. There are two complete gatherings in the present manuscript, but, in the case at least of the first of them, they are not in their original arrangements. Table 2 lists the Old Beneventan pieces which have so far been identified in these leaves. I have examined these pages in

---

[22] See Boe, 'A New Source for Old Beneventan Chant'. We know of several Offertories and Communions in the repertory that survive with a variety of liturgical functions; a list is in T. F. Kelly, 'Une nouvelle source pour l'office vieux-bénéventain', *Études Grégoriennes* (in press). But nowhere else do Ingressae serve also for occasional use as processional antiphons or the like.

[23] These problems, along with matters relating to Beneventan Lenten and Holy Week practices, and questions of content raised by the manuscript's layout, are considered more fully in Kelly, 'Palimpsest Evidence' (forthcoming: see note 21).

[24] The musical notation is similar to that of Benevento 40. M. De Nonno ('Contributo alla tradizione di Prisciano in area beneventano-cassinese: il "Vallicell. C. 9"', *Revue d'Histoire des Textes*, 9 (1979), p. 129) argues for the Beneventan origin of a portion of the manuscript – though not the portion under consideration here. Mallet and Thibaut (*Les manuscrits*, p. 16, n. 3) note that the rich holdings of manuscripts in Beneventan script at the Biblioteca Vallicelliana may come in part from Baronio, who in 1599 received the benefice of Santa Maria in Venticano, some 20 km south-east of Benevento. Historian and hagiographer, Baronio was a member (and later *praepositus generalis*) of the Congregation of the Oratorio. The hagiographical *tomi* of the Biblioteca Vallicelliana, many of them in Beneventan script (see Lowe/Brown, II, pp. 130–2), may have been collected by him for his *Annales ecclesiastici*. On Baronio see *A Cesare Baronio: scritti cari* (Sora, 1963), esp. E. Vaccaro, 'Vita di Cesare Baronio', pp. 11–29.

[25] The manuscript is described in M. Vatasso and H. Carusi, *Bibliothecae Apostolicae Vaticanae codices manu scripti recensiti: Codices Vaticani latini, Codices 10301–10700* (Rome, 1920), pp. 614–29. The upper script is edited in A. Petrucci, *Codice diplomatico del monastero benedettino di S. Maria di Tremiti (1005–1237)*, 3 vols. (Rome, 1960).

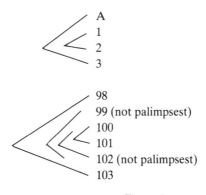

Figure 2

a forthcoming study, and should like to summarise here some conclusions:

(1) In the first fascicle, which contains music for Holy Week, one or more leaves must have intervened after folio A. Although a rearrangement of the bifolia to make folio A follow folio 2 puts the feasts in their proper order, there is not room here for the Tracts *Cantabo* and *Attende* which normally follow *Domine audivi* in the Beneventan rite.

(2) The music on folio 2^r, so close to the beginning of Holy Saturday on the back of the same sheet, can hardly be intended for Maundy Thursday (despite the evidence of Benevento 40), unless all of Good Friday was omitted. More likely is that these pieces are intended for Good Friday itself.[26]

(3) This manuscript presents multiple sections of three masses: (a) The Paschal Vigil (Alleluia and Offertory). (b) A mass, identified only by its rubrics, preceding the Beneventan Ingressa for St John the Baptist. (c) The Mass for SS Peter and Paul – or rather, two items from the mass in Benevento 40; if the Communion *Ut cognosceris* is part of the same mass as the Ingressa *Petrus dormiebat* beginning

---

[26] *Vadit propitiator*, which is used as the Gradual of the Beneventan Maundy Thursday Mass in Benevento 40, is a translation from the Greek of Romanos; versions of this text are used in the Ambrosian, Old Roman and Gregorian liturgies, almost always on Good Friday. (See Hesbert, 'L' "Antiphonale missarum" de l'ancien rit bénéventain', *Ephemerides Liturgicae*, 59, 1945, pp. 73–8).

Quis te supplantavit, clearly a movable piece, is used for both Palm Sunday and Maundy Thursday in Benevento 38 and 40; it is an address to Judas, who has already received the punishment for his betrayal of Jesus – a text more suited to Good Friday than to either of the preceding days.

Table 2 Palimpsest Old Beneventan music in MS Vatican lat. 1065)

Folio	Incipit	Feast	Function	Benevento MS
A^r	Sicut cervus	Holy Saturday	Tract	38, fol. 46^v 40, fol. 18
A^r	Omnes sitientes	Holy Saturday	Antiphon	38, fol. 46^v 40, fol. 18^v
A^r	Doxa en ips./Gloria	Holy Saturday	Antiphon	38, fol. 46^v 40, fol. 19
A^r	Alleluia V Resurrexit	Holy Saturday	Alleluia	38, fol. 46^v 40, fol. 19^v
A^r	Omnes qui in Christo	Holy Saturday	Offertory	38, fol. 47
2^r	Vadit propitiator	Maundy Thursday	Gradual	40, fol. 5
2^r	Quis te supplantavit (cued without notation)	Maundy Thursday	Communion	40, fol. 5
	Accipiens (antiphon?)	Good Friday	Communion	38, fol. 38
2^v	Ad vesperum	Holy Saturday	Antiphon	38, fol. 43^v 40, fol. 15^v
2^v	Domine audivi	Holy Saturday	Tract	38, fol. 44 40, fol. 15^v
100	Petrus dormiebat	SS Peter and Paul	Ingressa	38, fol. 115^v 40, fol. 99
100^v	[Petrus dormiebat, continued]			
100^v	R [a rubric indicating the start of a Gradual?]			
101	Ut cognosceret	SS Peter and Paul	Communion	40, fol. 99^v
103	The following rubrics are faintly visible in succession in the right margin: V [Alleluia-verse?] of [Offertory] co [Communion]			
103	Lumen quod animus	St John the Baptist	Ingressa	38, fol. 110 40, fol. 89
103^v	R [a rubric indicating the start of a Gradual?]			

two pages earlier, then the intervening parts of the mass must be exceptionally long.

(4) Graduals seem to be a more regular feature of masses in this manuscript than they are in Benevento 38 and 40.

III. The manuscript Montecassino, Archivio della Badia, 361, is a volume of 222 pages mostly in the hand of Petrus Diaconus, who was appointed librarian of Montecassino in 1131 or 1132.[27] In his untrained ordinary minuscule – unusual for Montecassino at the time[28] – Peter the Deacon copied works of classical authors: Vegetius (*De re militari*) and Frontinus (*De aquaeductu urbis Romae*) and fragments of Varro and Cicero. To this he added a series of his own works: sermons, *Liber de locis sanctis*, *Ortus et vita iustorum cenobi casinensis*, *Rhythmum Petri Diaconi casinensis de novissimis diebus*.[29]

This manuscript is important as the unique source of Frontinus's treatise, as a palaeographical document, and as the autograph of a fascinating personality whose complex fantasies and falsifications sought to increase the growing power and renown of his abbey.[30] But our interest here is not so much in Peter the Deacon's writings themselves as in what they cover, for in making this book the Cassinese librarian has preserved pages of a discarded volume of music for the Old Beneventan liturgy.

At least twenty-four of these palimpsest leaves once contained Old Beneventan chant.[31] I have identified thirteen further leaves from

27 See P. Meyvaert, 'The Autographs of Peter the Deacon', *Bulletin of The John Rylands Library*, 38 (Manchester, 1955), pp. 114–38.

28 V. Brown, in her *Handlist of Beneventan Mss.* which appears as vol. II of her second edition of E. A. Loew (*recte* Lowe), *The Beneventan Script* (Rome, 1980), says that this writing 'is by a Beneventan scribe trying to write ordinary minuscule' (p. 84).

29 For a full list of the contents, with other palaeographic information and bibliography, see D. M. Inguanez, *Codicum Casinensium manuscriptorum catalogus*, II, Pars II (Montecassino, 1934), pp. 208–12. The volume in its present form represents only about a third of the original manuscript, whose structure has been largely reconstructed in H. Bloch, 'Der Autor der "Graphia aureae urbis Romae" ', *Deutsches Archiv für Erforschung des Mittelalters*, 40 (1984), pp. 105–27.

30 On the subject of Peter the Deacon and his falsifications, see Bloch, 'Der Autor', pp. 61–6; Meyvaert, *op. cit.*; Caspar, *Petrus diaconus*, esp. pp. 19–21; and the introduction to R. H. Rodgers, *Petri Diaconi Ortus et vita iustorum cenobii casinensis* (Berkeley, 1972).

31 Montecassino 361 has recently been restored and rebound, making the physical make-up difficult to determine. The leaves measure approximately 24.3 cm high by 16.5 cm wide. Single pages from an earlier manuscript were detached and (usually) turned sideways and folded to form bifolia for the newer and smaller book. The older book was written in two columns each about 9 cm wide, with a separation of about 1 cm between columns: the writing space was thus about 19 cm wide. Side margins were generous, with the result that the complete writing width is nowhere visible within the 24.3 cm height of the new

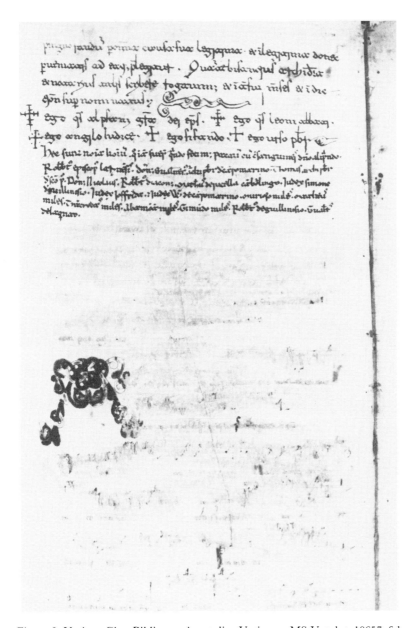

V

Figure 3 Vatican City, Biblioteca Apostolica Vaticana, MS Vat. lat. 10657, fol. 2ᵛ. The lower script shows the initial *A* of the Old Beneventan antiphon *Ad vesperum*. Below is the beginning of the Tract *Domine audivi* for Holy Saturday. A portion of fol. 3 shows the initial letters of two Old Beneventan pieces as yet unidentified.

V

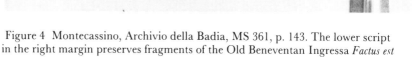

Figure 4 Montecassino, Archivio della Badia, MS 361, p. 143. The lower script in the right margin preserves fragments of the Old Beneventan Ingressa *Factus est repente*.

Montecassino and the Old Beneventan chant

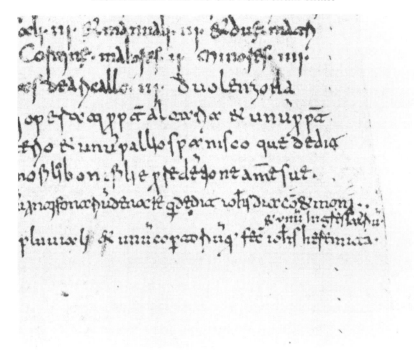

Figure 5 Montecassino, Archivio della Badia, Aula II, capsula CI, fasc. 1, no. 1:
Commemoratorium of Theobald (detail)

the older manuscript;[32] but in these the damage of passing time, and
the assiduity of fervent erasure, have left nothing visible but touches
of ink and the general layout of the original music manuscript. We
cannot say what they contained. These pages are written in rather
typical eleventh-century Beneventan liturgical and musical hands.

Where enough music and text remain to be identified, we can
recognise pieces known only in the Old Beneventan liturgy; no
Gregorian music is discernible now, and probably none was ever

manuscript. Lines in the older book were scored about 2 cm apart; there were at least
fourteen lines per page (as can be seen on the present pages 105–6).

Twelve single folios from the earlier manuscript, folded to receive new text, can be
identified as bifolia in Montecassino 361 (pp. 103–6; 125–6 with 135–6; 143–4 with 149–50;
157–8 with 167–8; 159–60 with 165–6; 161–4; 175–6 with 189–90; 177–8 with 187–8; 179–
80 with 185–6; 197–8 with 207–8; 199–200 with 205–6; 201–4); all of them contained Old
Beneventan chant, of which sometimes only fragments can still be read. Two other
palimpsest leaves also contain fragmentary remains of Old Beneventan music (pp. 139–
40; 193–4).

[32] Pages 115–16; 119–20; 123–4; 129–32 (a bifolium); 137–8; 141–2; 145–8 (a bifolium); 151–
2; 153–4 with 169–70; 174–5.

present in this older manuscript. Only a few pages reveal enough of text or music for an identification to be made. And even where we can recognise a piece, we can do so only by the very fragmentary remains. Even so, we can say that these pieces preserve precisely the melodic and textual tradition of the Benevento manuscripts.

The pieces that can now be identified in the lower script of Montecassino 361 are listed in Table 3. In two cases we can identify two pieces from the same mass – a typical feature of a Gradual; but we cannot decipher enough music and text to put it beyond doubt that the original book is entirely Old Beneventan: to show, for example, a Communion followed immediately by the Ingressa of the next Old Beneventan mass. But of the many fragments of neumes scattered throughout these palimpsest pages, many are clearly parts of standard Old Beneventan melodies, while there are no characteristic 'Gregorian' turns of phrase. If we could decipher more, and if we had more pages of the original book, we would doubtless confirm that it is an Old Beneventan Gradual.

The presence of the feast of the Holy Twelve Brothers in this Cassinese manuscript makes a connection with Benevento, for these are the saints whose relics were interred in Santa Sofia.[33] These well-known Beneventan saints were venerated throughout southern Italy, and their cult at Montecassino is no surprise,[34] but the presence of their Old Beneventan mass is perhaps more than we might have expected.

Until now, only two 'uncontaminated' sources of Old Beneventan chant were known: the single page now used as a flyleaf for Benevento 35, and a decorated benedictional roll at Bari.[35] Now we have three additional sources, all of them originally pure Old Beneventan books. The last is undoubtedly related to Montecassino; the other two are also related, as we shall see, but more indirectly.

---

[33] See the *Chronica monasterii casinensis* (abbreviated *Chron. mon. cas.*), of Leo Marsicanus and others, ed. H. Hoffmann, Monumenta Germaniae Historica (abbreviated MGH), Scriptores 34 (Hanover, 1980), I, 9. See also H. Belting, 'Studien zum beneventanischen Hof im 8. Jahrhundert', *Dumbarton Oaks Papers*, 16 (1962), pp. 156–7.

[34] Alfanus I, monk of Montecassino and later archbishop of Salerno in the Desiderian period, is the author of a thousand-line 'Metrum heroicum domni Alfani Salernitani arciepiscopi in honore sanctorum duodecim fratrum', edited from Cassinese manuscripts in A. Lentini and F. Avagliano, eds., *I carmi di Alfano I, arcivescovo di Salerno*, Miscellanea Cassinese 38 (Montecassino, 1974), pp. 97–126.

[35] See above, note 4.

Table 3 *Palimpsest Old Beneventan music in Montecassino 361*

Page	Text	Feast	Function	Benevento MS
126	Credo[a]	?		
143	Factus est repente	Pentecost	Ingressa	40, fol. 79
				38, fol. 99 (erased)
149	All. Tu es Petrus	SS Peter and Paul	Alleluia	40, fol. 99ᵛ
150	Ut cognosceris	SS Peter and Paul	Communion	40, fol. 99ᵛ
162	Ad honorem	All Saints	Communion	40, fol. 134
			Offertory	40, fol. 134ᵛ
166	Circui erunt	XII Fratrum	Offertory	40, fol. 122
166	Hos duodecim	XII Fratrum	Communion	40, fol. 122

Note:

[a] Yet another fragment of a Credo, this portion does not duplicate any portion of the other three fragments of Old Beneventan *Credos* (see Table 1, notes a and b). Here only short portions of several lines of text are visible in the present left margin: 'terum venturus/iudicare vivos et/regni non er/sanctum dominum/dit qui cum/adoratur & c/qui locutus est per'. The very few isolated fragments of notation make comparison difficult.

Musical sources have already hinted at the use of Old Beneventan chant at Montecassino; but these are Gregorian books, in which the Old Beneventan chant is included as extra material. Montecassino 361, however, preserves parts of a whole book of this chant, probably designed for use at Montecassino itself, and certainly present there when, as late as the twelfth century, Peter the Deacon re-used portions of it. When and why was such a book created? Further information on the Old Beneventan chant books at Montecassino is given by the monk Theobald, who became abbot of Montecassino in 1022. For much of his life Theobald was associated with the Cassinese dependency of San Liberatore at the foot of Mount Maiella in his native Abruzzi. When he was appointed to San Liberatore as·provost (*praepositus*) about 1007, Theobald found it poor and dark, the buildings in bad repair.[36] He set about making improvements and furnishing the church with books, ornaments and vestments. In his partly autograph *Commemoratorium*,[37] begun in 1019 and continued in subsequent years, Theobald details the objects that have been provided at his behest for San Liberatore.[38]

From the *Commemoratorium*, a rich source of detailed information, I want to concentrate on the last three words from a tiny entry at the end of a 'codicil' added to the original document after Theobald's election as abbot in 1022; this item, added in a contemporaneous hand, is at the extreme bottom right of the document, and reads: 'Et unum antifonarium de nocte qui dedit Iohannes diaconus et monachus, et unum ingressarium'.[39] (See Figure 5.) These last three words are intriguing. In a document full of references to books by

36 See E. Carusi, 'Intorno al *Commemoratorium* dell'abate Teobaldo (a. 1019–22)', *Bullettino dell'Istituto Storico Italiano*, 47 (1932), p. 182.

37 The document is Montecassino, Archivio della Badia, Aula II, capsula CI, fasc. 1, no. 1. It will receive a new number when it is catalogued by Dom Faustino Avagliano for *I regesti dell'archivio* (see note 54). A complete facsimile and transcription are provided in Carusi, 'Intorno al *Commemoratorium* dell'abate Teobaldo', pp. 173–90, with plate.

38 These aspects of Theobald's life are described in *Chron. mon. cas.*, II, 12, 42, 52, 56–8. See also Bloch, 'Monte Cassino, Byzantium, and the West', pp. 166–77; *idem*, 'Monte Cassino's Teachers and Library in the High Middle Ages', in *La scuola nell'occidente latino dell'alto medioevo*, Settimane di Studio del Centro Italiano di Studi sull'Alto Medioevo 19, II (Spoleto, 1972), pp. 577–8; and J. Gay, *L'Italie méridionale et l'empire byzantin*, Bibliothèque des Écoles Françaises d'Athènes et de Rome 90 (Paris, 1904), pp. 423–5, 438–41.

39 The order of these lines is not entirely clear. It appears, from the ink of the lowest line, which is now darker than those above it, and from the capital D aligned not only with the lines above but also with a line to the left, that the bottom line, 'Duo pluviali . . .', comes first, moving up to '& unum antifonarium . . .', with, last of all, the words '& unum ingressarium' squeezed between the two lines. See Carusi, p. 187.

type – ymnuarium, antiphonarium, psalterium, passionarium, etc. – it seems that an 'ingressarium' is a book, and that it is the book that contains Ingressae. Now the Ingressa is the entrance chant of the Old Beneventan mass; the term is also used in Milan, but Ambrosian books, to my knowledge, are never called Ingressaria.[40] An Ingressarium might be like a Graduale: a book of Ingressae and other pieces necessary for the principal liturgy of the day; models for such a book have just been reviewed – the palimpsest pages of Montecassino 361, or the more complete fragments from Vatican City, Biblioteca Apostolica Vaticana, MS Vat. lat. 10673. It is not impossible that one of these is the very book ordered by Abbot Theobald.[41] On the other hand, an Ingressarium might be just what it says: a book of Ingressae. And we have a model for that also: the palimpsest pages of Vallicelliana c 9 include a substantial series of Ingressae, presented without their masses. Such a collection might well be called an Ingressarium – though it is still difficult to imagine its purpose.

Whatever the exact nature of Theobald's volume, it seems that the future abbot of Montecassino caused a book of Old Beneventan chant to be copied for San Liberatore in the early years of the eleventh century; and the music used at a dependent abbey was surely not unfamiliar at the mother house.

As we begin to think of Montecassino as an important centre of Old Beneventan chant, it is natural to look for links between Montecassino and Benevento, another centre for this chant. There is, of course, a connection in Vatican, Ottob. lat. 145, a book evidently made from a Montecassino exemplar for the use of the abbey of Santa Sofia in Benevento.[42] It contains, among much else, six Old Beneventan antiphons for use in a monastic foot-washing ceremony.

---

[40] We should not forget the curious page of Ambrosian chant preserved in an eleventh-century hand from Montecassino: the flyleaf from Vatican City, Biblioteca Apostolica Vaticana, MS Ottob. lat. 3, which contains music for the Ambrosian office of the Tuesday and Wednesday of the second week of Lent. It is reproduced in Paléographie Musicale, ser. I, 14, plates xxxii–xxxiii, and in H. M. Bannister, *Monumenta vaticana di paleografia musicale latina*, II (Leipzig, 1913), plate 72. It is not inconceivable that Theobald's 'Ingressarium' was in fact a book of Milanese chant.

[41] On the Cassinese connection of Vat. lat. 10673, see below. For the survival of books prepared under Theobald's direction, see Bloch, 'Monte Cassino's Teachers and Library', pp. 577–8; Lowe/Brown, p. 50; E. A. Lowe, *Scriptura beneventana*, 2 vols. (Oxford, 1929), plates 56–62.

[42] See Boe, 'A New Source for Old Beneventan Chant'.

Five of these are known from Benevento 38 and 40; the sixth appears only at Montecassino, as a Communion for St Benedict.[43] And we have the connection of the Old Beneventan Mass of the Holy Twelve Brothers of Santa Sofia in Montecassino 361.

Naturally there is a continuing relationship between Benevento and Montecassino – between the capital of a powerful duchy ruled by independent Lombard princes from the eighth century until the coming of the Normans in the eleventh, and the neighbouring monastic foundation whose influence led it to play an ever larger role in the politics of southern Italy in those same years.[44] There are constant cultural, political and ecclesiastical exchanges between Montecassino and Benevento in that period. To name only a few well-known figures, the exchange includes Paul the Deacon, the eighth-century Lombard historian who was a teacher at the court of Benevento before entering Montecassino;[45] John of Benevento, abbot of Montecassino and friend of Theobald; and the great abbot Desiderius, a native of Benevento and monk of Santa Sofia.

Ecclesiastical relations are perhaps most important for our purposes; and surviving chronicles and other historical documents give us a glimpse of an important continuing relationship between Montecassino and the monastery of Santa Sofia. The church of Santa Sofia, established and dedicated by Prince Arichis II of Benevento, was named for Christ, the Holy Wisdom of God, after the example of the great basilica of Constantinople. The importance of the church to the princely aspirations of Arichis has been convincingly demonstrated by Hans Belting.[46] Arichis assembled relics of saints to glorify and embellish his court church, and to exemplify in ecclesiastical terms the virtues of his reign. The scattered remains of twelve martyrs (whom tradition later made into brothers) were gathered from throughout the region and interred in Santa Sofia, with great ceremony, in 760.[47] From that date, and no earlier, comes

[43] See Boe, 'Old Beneventan Chant at Monte Cassino'.
[44] For general histories of Montecassino and Benevento in this period, see the works cited in note 18; also C. Wickham, *Early Medieval Italy* (London and Totowa, N.J., 1981), pp. 146–67, and the extensive bibliography; still important is Gay, *L'Italie méridionale*.
[45] On Paul the Deacon's activities at Benevento, see *Chron. mon. cas.*, I, 15; U. Westerbergh, ed., *Chronicon salernitanum*, Studia Latina Stockholmensia 3 (Lund, 1956), pp. 10–13, 22, 24–5; Belting, 'Studien zum beneventanischen Hof', pp. 164–9; Bloch, 'Monte Cassino's Teachers', pp. 567–72.
[46] 'Studien zum beneventanischen Hof', pp. 182–8.
[47] See *Chron. mon. cas.*, I, 9; the *Translatio duodecim martyrum* in MGH, *Scriptores rerum*

the office of the Twelve Brother Martyrs, whose cult is celebrated also, as we have seen, at Montecassino. To the church of Santa Sofia Arichis attached a convent of nuns; and it is this community which forms a principal link with Montecassino.

But there are two versions of this relationship. Montecassino argues that Santa Sofia was, from its founding, subject to Cassinese authority, whereas the surviving Beneventan materials argue the continuing independence of the local monastery. Among the first to refer to Santa Sofia is the Cassinese monk Erchempertus, whose *Historia Longobardorum Beneventanorum* was written about 890 while the monks of Montecassino were in exile in Capua: 'And within the walls of Benevento Arichis founded a most seemly and sumptuous temple to God, which he called by the Greek name Agian Sophian, that is, Holy Wisdom; and, establishing a convent of nuns supplied with very ample estates and various resources, he placed it to remain forever under the authority of blessed Benedict.'[48]

When, around 1100, Leo Marsicanus came to quote this passage in his Chronicle of Montecassino,[49] he was careful to make particular the dependency of the new nunnery, and he added the words 'in monte Casino':

Of this Arichis master Erchempertus refers thus, in the history of the Lombard people which he composed after Paul the Deacon . . . Within the walls of Benevento he founded a most seemly and sumptuous temple to God, which he called by the Greek name ΑΓΗΑΝ CΩΦΗΑΝ, that is, Holy Wisdom. And enriched with very ample estates and various resources, and establishing a convent of nuns, he conveyed it to continue forever under the authority of blessed Benedict in Montecassino.[50]

Langobardicarum et Italicarum saec. VI–IX (abbreviated MGH *SS Lang*) (Hanover, 1878), pp. 574–6; Belting, 'Studien zum beneventanischen Hof', pp. 156–7.

[48] '[Arichis] Infra Beneventi autem moeniam templum Domino opulentissimum ac decentissimum condidit, quod Greco vocabulo Agian Sophian, id est sanctam sapientiam, nominavit; dotatumque amplissimis prediis et variis opibus sanctimoniale coenobium statuens, idque sub iure beati Benedicti in perpetuum reddidit permanendum.' MGH *SS Lang*, p. 236.

[49] The passage is quoted, in fact, through intermediary – an addition to the *Chronica sancti Benedicti Casinensis* in Montecassino, Archivio della Badia, MS 363, printed in MGH *SS Lang*, p. 488.

[50] 'De isto Arichis, ita refert domnus Herchempertus, in historia quam de Langobardorum gente post Paulum diaconum composuit. . . . Hic intra menia Beneventi templum Domino opulentissimum ac decentissimum condidit, quod Greco vocabulo ΑΓΗΑΝ CΩΦΗΑΝ, idest sanctam sapientiam nominavit. Ditatumque amplissimis prediis, et variis opibus, ac sanctimonialium cenobium statuens, id sub iure beati Benedicti in monte Casino tradidit inperpetuum permansuram.' *Chron. mon. cas.*, I, 9. Quoted here is the version of Munich, Bayerische Staatsbibliothek, MS Clm 4623 (Hoffmann's MS A), a manuscript prepared

Santa Sofia is also mentioned by Leo in an earlier passage, in which the chronicler seems aware of a controversial point: 'This same Gisulf began to build the church of Santa Sofia in Benevento. When, prevented by death, he was not able to complete it, Arichis, who succeeded him, wonderfully brought it to completion, and there establishing a convent of nuns, conceded it to the monastery of St Benedict, as we shall show in what follows.'[51] Leo goes on to assert that Charlemagne confirmed to Montecassino the possession of Santa Sofia in 787.[52] And Peter the Deacon, the notorious falsifier, fabricated such a document in his mid-twelfth-century *Registrum*.[53] Peter also includes copies of papal privileges confirming Santa Sofia as a possession of Montecassino from Nicholas I (*c.* 860, spurious?)[54] and John VIII (882, genuine?).[55] In the ninth century, the convent at Santa Sofia was governed by provosts (*praepositi*) appointed by Montecassino; the Chronicle and other documents give us the names of some of them.[56]

under the supervision of Leo and preserving the earliest version of the chronicle. A marginal addition in this manuscript, inserted after the word 'statuens', reads: 'german-amque suam ibidem abbatissam efficiens, cum omnibus omnino pertinentiis et possession-ibus eius' ('establishing his sister there as abbess, with all of its appurtenances and possessions').

[51] 'Iste Gisulfus cepit edificare ecclesiam sancte Sophie in Benevento. Quam cum morte preventus explere non posset, Arichis qui ei successit mirifice illam perfecit, ibique sanctimonialium cenobium statuens, monasterio sancti Benedicti hic in Casino concessit, sicut in sequentibus ostendemus.' *Chron. mon. cas.*, I, 6. The founding of Santa Sofia by Gisulph, and its completion by Arichis, are chronicled also in the *Annales Beneventani*; see O. Bertolini, 'Gli *Annales Beneventani*', *Bullettino dell'Istituto Storico Italiano*, 42 (1923), pp. 110, 111. Belting argues that the church was built entirely by Arichis; see 'Studien zum beneventanischen Hof', pp. 180–2; this article is of primary importance for Santa Sofia in the context of eighth-century Benevento.

[52] *Chron. mon. cas.*, I, 12.

[53] MGH, Diplomata Karolinorum 1 (Berlin, 1956), no. 158, pp. 213–16. On the falsifications in this diploma see E. Caspar, 'Echte und gefälschte Karolingerurkunde für Montecas-sino', *Neues Archiv*, 33 (1908), pp. 53–73. See also H. Hoffmann, 'Chronik und Urkunde in Montecassino' (abbreviated *PDR*), *Quellen und Forschungen aus italienischen Archiven und Bibliotheken*, 51 (1971), no. 108, p. 105; and p. 174.

[54] See P. F. Kehr, *Italia pontificia* (abbreviated *IP*), VIII (Berlin, 1935), p. 125, no. 33. An eleventh-century copy of such a document is in Montecassino, Archivio della Badia, Aula III, capsula VII, no. 6; see T. Leccisotti, *Abbazia di Montecassino: i regesti dell'archivio*, I, Ministero dell'Interno, Pubblicazioni degli Archivi di Stato 54 (Rome, 1964), pp. 223–4.

[55] *IP*, VIII, p. 126, no. 37.

[56] A document of 923 (Benevento, Archivio Storico Provinciale, Fondo Santa Sofia VIII. 33) mentions 'Antipertus presbiter et prepositus monasterii aecclesiae vocabulo Sanctae Sophiae' (see E. Galasso, 'Caratteri paleografici e diplomatici dell'atto privato a Capua e a Benevento prima del secolo XI', *Il contributo dell'archidiocesi di Capua alla vita religiosa e culturale del Meridione: atti del Convegno nazionale dalla Società di storia patria di Terra di Lavoro, 26–31 ottobre 1966* (Rome, 1967), p. 308); *Chron. mon. cas.*, I, 39, names Pergolfus and Criscio. An early twelfth-century hand, now very faint, has added the names of several abbesses,

Montecassino and the Old Beneventan chant

The later ninth century brought invaders to both monasteries. Montecassino was sacked and destroyed by the Saracens in 883,[57] and the monks lived in exile in Teano and Capua until 949. During the subsequent Byzantine reconquest of the area, Benevento was besieged and occupied for three years (891–4). And the monks of Montecassino, accepting the protection of the Byzantine empire, in June 892 obtained from Simbaticius, the imperial *protospatarius*, a privilege confirming their domains, including Santa Sofia in Benevento.[58]

A clear rupture comes in the mid-tenth century. For one thing, the nuns of Santa Sofia are replaced by monks. Rodelgarda, abbess in 938,[59] had by 953 been replaced by abbot Leo.[60] And we hear no more of provosts from Montecassino after a certain Iohannes in 945.[61] At the same time the Beneventan monastery begins to assert its independence. A document of 945, when the monks of Montecassino were still in exile, is the oldest of many which chronicle a continuing conflict between the two monasteries. It details a legal battle between the two abbots in the presence of Prince Landolf of Benevento; in the end Magelpotus, abbot of Montecassino, was required to relinquish all control of Santa Sofia.[62] This liberty was renewed later in the century by abbot John III of Montecassino (998–1011) to Gregory of Santa Sofia.[63]

abbots and *praepositi* to the *annales* in Vatican City, Biblioteca Apostolica Vaticana, MS Vat. lat. 4939. Among these are 'Criscius prepositus erat' (868) and 'Hoc tempore erat Criscius prepositus' (878), both on fol. 11; 'Iohannes prepositus' (945), fol. 11ᵛ. See Bertolini, 'Gli *Annales Beneventani*', pp. 116, 117, 121.

[57] *Chron. mon. cas.*, I, 44.

[58] *Chron. mon. cas.*, I, 49; *PDR*, no. 136, p. 106; ed. in T. Leccisotti, 'Le colonie cassinese in Capitanata, 3', *Miscellanea Cassinese*, 19 (1940), pp. 31–3; and in F. Trinchera, *Syllabus graecarum membranarum* (Naples, 1865), no. III, pp. 2–3. See Gay, *L'Italie méridionale*, pp. 147–9.

[59] Rodelgarda is mentioned in documents of 923 (see O. Bertolini, 'I documenti trascritti nel "Liber preceptorum beneventani monasterii s. Sophiae" ("Chronicon s. Sophiae")', *Studie di storia napoletana in onore di Michelangelo Schipa* (Naples, 1926), p. 36, no. 139), and in the *Annales beneventani* for the year 938 (Vat. lat. 4939, fol. 11ᵛ; Bertolini, 'Gli *Annales Beneventani*', p. 121).

[60] 'Leo abbas' is added to that year in Vat. lat. 4939, fol. 12; see Bertolini, 'Gli *Annales Beneventani*', p. 122.

[61] See note 56.

[62] 'Iudicabimus . . . ut amodo et deinceps perpetuis temporibus partem prephati cenovii sancte Sofie semper libera consistat cum suis pertinentiis et rebus hab omni condicione et subiectione atque dominatione a parte iamdicti monasterii sancti Benedicti. . . .' The document is transcribed (with a facsimile as plates 5 and 6) in Galasso, 'Caratteri paleografici', pp. 309–12.

[63] We know of Abbot John's renewal from the charters of popes Benedict VIII in 1022 and Leo IX in 1052 (see notes 72 and 74).

V

Abbot Azzo of Santa Sofia received charters from the emperors Otto I (972)[64] and Otto II (981)[65] confirming the abbey's independence. Otto III (999) confirmed the same privileges to abbot Gregory.[66] With Montecassino under the influence of the Byzantine empire through the princes of Capua,[67] these imperial charters are perhaps more an indication of political strategy than of ecclesiastical equity, more an affirmation of imperial supremacy than of historical fact. In any case they are general confirmations of rights and possessions, with no specific reference to Montecassino.

But Montecassino was far from accepting Santa Sofia's independence. According to the Chronicle of Montecassino, abbot Balduin was disturbed that the monastery of Santa Sofia had been 'drawn away from this monastery by violence' ('violentia ab hac coenobio subtractum'), and at his urging Pope Agapitus II in 946 warned Atenulf, Prince of Benevento–Capua, against keeping Santa Sofia;[68] a spurious document to this effect is recorded by Peter the Deacon.[69] Atenulf's donation of Santa Sofia to Montecassino, also recorded in Peter's *Registrum*, is likewise a forgery.[70] In her efforts to regain a lost child, Montecassino was not above creating documents useful in establishing her claims.

The earlier eleventh century shows an intensification of the controversy. In 1022 the Emperor Henry II invaded southern Italy to repulse the growing Byzantine influence, to which both Prince Pandulf of Capua and his brother Atenulf, abbot of Montecassino, had submitted.[71] Having re-established imperial authority at Benevento, both the emperor and his ally Pope Benedict VIII provided diplomas of protection and independence to abbot Gregory of Santa Sofia[72] – acts surely displeasing to the pro-Byzantine Atenulf of

---

[64] The original document, in Benevento, Archivio Storico Provinciale, Fondo Santa Sofia II. 1, is reproduced and transcribed in Galasso, 'Caratteri paleografici', plate 10 and pp. 126–8. From the copy in Vat. lat. 4939, fols. 126ʳ–128, it is printed in MGH, *Diplomatum regum et imperatorum Germaniae* (Hanover, 1879–84), I, no. 408, pp. 554–6.

[65] MGH, *Diplomatum regum et imperatorum Germaniae*, II (Hanover, 1888), no. 264, pp. 306–7.

[66] *Ibid.*, no. 310, pp. 736–7.

[67] Bloch, 'Monte Cassino, Byzantium, and the West', pp. 170–3.

[68] *Chron. mon. cas.*, I, 58.

[69] See *IP*, VIII, pp. 128–9; *PDR*, no. 11, p. 98, and, on its forgery, p. 194; see also J. F. Böhmer, *Regesta imperii*, II: *Sächsische Zeit, 5. Abteilung: Papstregesten 911–1024*, ed. H. Zimmermann, no. 203, p. 76.

[70] *PDR*, no. 207, p. 114.

[71] Gay, *L'Italie méridionale*, pp. 417–20; *Chron. mon. cas.*, II, 38.

[72] Benedict VIII: Vat. lat. 4939, fol. 139ʳ; see *IP*, IX (Berlin, 1962), p. 82, no. 2. Henry II: Vat. lat. 4939, fol. 132; MGH, Diplomata 3, no. 468, pp. 596–7; see Bertolini, 'Gli *Annales Beneventani*', pp. 136–8.

76

Montecassino and the Old Beneventan chant

Montecassino. After completing the siege of Capua, the emperor proceeded to Montecassino. Abbot Atenulf had already fled the approaching imperial army of the Archbishop of Cologne and perished at sea; and Henry persuaded the monks to elect as abbot a suitable non-Capuan candidate, one of those who, many years before, had left the monastery rather than live under abbot Manso of the house of Capua: Theobald, provost of San Liberatore.[73]

Thirty years later Santa Sofia's independence is confirmed by Pope Leo IX. A hostile Benevento had been excommunicated by Pope Clement II in 1051, and Leo IX received the submission of the city the following year and confirmed by charter that Santa Sofia owed no allegiance except to the papacy, specifying that it should remain 'free and immune from any subjection or yoke of the monastery of Cassino'.[74] A year later (July 1053) the papal and imperial forces lost the crucial battle of Civitate to the Normans, bringing the duchy of Benevento to an end after almost five centuries of Lombard rule.[75]

At the end of the century, reaching the apex of its power and influence, Montecassino continued its attempts to regain control of Santa Sofia, which it regarded as 'taken from the dominion of this place by violence'.[76] Leo Marsicanus, the great Cassinese chronicler, was himself involved in seeking justice in 1078 from Pope Gregory VII[77] and wrote a history of the case ('Breviatio de monasterio sanctae Sophiae in Beneventum et iudicium papae Urbani ex eo') which is preserved in the *Registrum* of Peter the Deacon.[78] Repeated appeals by Montecassino to Pope Urban II,[79] and to Pope Pascal II in 1113[80] and 1116,[81] failed to resolve the dispute; and indeed, although Santa Sofia continued to be listed as a dependency, Montecassino never

---

[73] Gay, *L'Italie méridionale*, p. 424; *Chron. mon. cas.*, II, 42; on Henry's intervention at Montecassino and Theobald's election, see Bloch, 'Monte Cassino, Byzantium, and the West', pp. 173–5; S. Hirsch, *Jahrbücher des deutschen Reichs unter Heinrich II.*, III, ed. H. Bresslau (Leipzig, 1875, repr. Berlin, 1975), pp. 198–210. Henry's charter to Montecassino is in MGH, Diplomata 3, pp. 603–4, no. 474.

[74] 'liberum et immune ab omni subiectione ac iugo Casinensis monasterii'; Vat. lat. 4939, fol. 141ᵛ; *IP*, IX, p. 83, no. 5.

[75] *Chron. mon. cas.*, II, 81–2, 84; Gay, pp. 477–90.

[76] 'violenter a dicione huius loci subducta'; *Chron. mon. cas.*, IV, 48.

[77] *Chron. mon. cas.*, III, 42; *IP*, VIII, p. 147, no. 112. Gregory VII himself confirmed Santa Sofia's independence in 1084 (Vat. lat. 4939, fols. 142ᵛ–145; *IP*, IX, p. 85, no. 12).

[78] *PDR*, no. 37, p. 100; ed. Gattola, *Historia*, p. 54.

[79] These appeals are detailed by Leo in his *breviatio*; see *Chron. mon. cas.*, IV, 7.

[80] *Chron. mon. cas.*, IV, 48.

[81] *Chron. mon. cas.*, IV, 60.

regained control of her erstwhile Beneventan daughter house. But this is all far beyond the period under discussion here.

What is of interest is the recognition on both sides of some historical relationship. Although by the eleventh century Santa Sofia's original subjection to Montecassino was either forgotten or overlooked at Benevento, we can perceive, in the period of our surviving Old Beneventan documents, a clear awareness of the long history of connection, dependent or antagonistic, between Montecassino and Santa Sofia.

Santa Sofia was not the only monastery to dispute its independence with Montecassino in the eleventh century. There is a similar connection between Montecassino and the distant monastery of Santa Maria in the Tremiti Islands, the source of one of our palimpsest Old Beneventan graduals. The story sounds familiar: Montecassino claimed Tremiti as a dependency, while the latter protested its long-standing independence.[82] Leo Marsicanus in the *Chronicle* makes a case for possession of Tremiti: he writes of 'The cloister of Tremiti, which a great many papal privileges show to have belonged to us from earliest times',[83] and notes that Paul the Deacon, who had been a court teacher at Pavia and at Benevento before entering Montecassino, had been exiled to Tremiti by the Lombard king Desiderius.[84]

But Montecassino's position in this case seems to be a weak one: the earliest genuine papal document asserting Cassinese authority at Tremiti is one from Urban II, as late as 1097.[85] The abbey of Santa Maria, however, in the eleventh century procured its own charters (which are copied into the very cartulary which obliterates our Old Beneventan chant) affirming the monastery's liberty. Tremiti was taken under imperial protection by Conrad II in 1038;[86] the privilege

---

[82] On relations of Montecassino with Tremiti, see T. Leccisotti, 'Le relazioni fra Montecassino e Tremiti e i possedimenti cassinesi a Foggia e Lucera', *Benedictina*, 9 (1949), pp. 203–15; J. Gay, 'Le monastère de Trémiti au XIᵉ siècle d'après un cartulaire inédit', *Mélanges d'Archéologie et d'Histoire*, 17 (1897), pp. 387–407; on confusion between Santa Maria and Sancti Jacobi see Leccisotti, 'Le relazioni', p. 207, and Caspar, *Petrus diaconus*, pp. 11–14.

[83] 'Tremitensis coenobii, quod nobis antiquitus pertinuisse Romanorum quoque privilegia pleraque testantur'; *Chron. mon. cas.*, III, 25.

[84] *Chron. mon. cas.*, I, 15.

[85] *IP*, VIII, p. 154, no. 141. See Caspar, *Petrus diaconus*, p. 13; Leccisotti, 'Le relazioni', pp. 206–7.

[86] MGH, Diplomata 5, p. 377, no. 272; Petrucci, *Codice diplomatico*, II, p. 68, no. 20.

was renewed by Henry III in 1054.[87] Pope Leo IX in 1053[88] likewise confirms the monastery's independence.

We know also of significant exchanges of personnel in the eleventh century between Tremiti and Montecassino. One eminent visitor was Frederick of Lorraine, papal chancellor, envoy to Constantinople, future abbot of Montecassino and later Pope Stephen IX;[89] and Frederick's successor as abbot of Montecassino, the great Desiderius, sojourned at Tremiti in the early years of his monastic life. Originally a monk of Santa Sofia in Benevento, Desiderius remained at Tremiti for a substantial time, departing only to avoid impending administrative duties.[90] In the later eleventh century, at about the time that Montecassino was making her strongest efforts to regain Santa Sofia, this conflict too came to a crisis; and it was Desiderius who, with toilsome and repeated efforts, brought the dispute to a conclusion in which Tremiti ultimately gained its autonomy.[91]

These two eleventh-century conflicts, in which Montecassino attempted to control Santa Sofia and Tremiti, are characteristic of a

---

[87] MGH, Diplomata 5, p. 441, no. 323; Petrucci, *Codice diplomatico*, II, p. 163, no. 52.

[88] *IP*, IX, p. 181, no. 1; Petrucci, *Codice diplomatico*, II, p. 156, no. 49.

[89] *Chron. mon. cas.*, II, 86; see below, pp. 80–1 and note 95.

[90] *Chron. mon. cas.*, III, 6.

[91] In his capacity as apostolic vicar for all of southern Italy under Nicholas II, Desiderius was ultimately charged by Alexander II in 1071 (*IP*, IX, p. 185, no. 5) to proceed to the reform of the monastery at Tremiti. He deposed abbot Adam and appointed the Cassinese monk Trasmundus; against this outsider the monks revolted, and were repressed with ruthless violence; Desiderius was forced to recall and depose his appointee. For some time relations were suspended between Desiderius and Ferro, whom Trasmundus had left in charge at Tremiti. Finally an appeal by Desiderius to the Norman Robert Guiscard resulted in a military occupation that sent Ferro away and turned the monastery over to Desiderius. Guiscard was willing to accept the fealty of the monks, but would not guarantee their independence from Montecassino; to rule Tremiti he appointed first three monks of Montecassino, later replaced by a single overseer. This last also rebelled against Desiderius, and he too was ultimately deposed and returned to his abbot. An attempt to make Tremiti subject to the abbot of Terra Maggiora (Torremaggiore) failed at the latter's death. The ultimate solution, approved by Pope Gregory VII, who recognised Desiderius as 'tutor et defensor' of Tremiti (*IP*, IX, pp. 183–4, no. 6), was to entrust the government of Tremiti to Ferro, who in turn would be responsible to Desiderius during the latter's lifetime, but thereafter only to the Pope (see *Chron. mon. cas.*, III, 25; Gay, 'Le monastère de Trémiti', pp. 387–405; Petrucci, *Codice diplomatico*, I, pp. XI–XLIX).

Thus Montecassino ultimately failed to gain control of Tremiti. Indeed, in 1081 (or 1082: see Petrucci, *Codice diplomatico*, II, p. 251), Desiderius himself relinquished all authority over Tremiti, giving full liberty to the monastery and to its abbot Ungrellus. The document detailing this event is copied onto fol. 9 of Vat. lat. 10657, the cartulary made in part from an Old Beneventan gradual. The document is printed in Petrucci, *Codice diplomatico*, II, pp. 250–3; from Naples, Biblioteca Nazionale Centrale, MS XIV A 3, it is printed in Gay, 'Le monastère de Trémiti', pp. 406–7; see Leccisotti, 'Le relazioni', p. 206.

period of great expansion in all areas of Cassinese life. But they also link three localities which used books of Old Beneventan chant; and the central link is Montecassino.

The three musical documents we have considered here come from the earliest layer of sources, for surely a whole manuscript of this chant precedes sources like Benevento 38 and 40, where Old Beneventan is supplementary to Gregorian. But these three early sources, important as they are, were short-lived: they are all palimpsests, pages newly written in the eleventh century but already useless in the twelfth, except as parchment. In discussing sources of Old Beneventan chant, we inevitably deal with the eleventh century – the period in which this music is first written, and also that in which it is suppressed.

The question of when Gregorian chant came to southern Italy is beyond the scope of this study, but we can point to the later eleventh century as the time of its ultimate victory over the local chant. And in the case of Montecassino we can point to a well-known specific moment for the suppression of the Old Beneventan chant.

In 1058 Pope Stephen IX visited Montecassino and strictly forbade the singing of 'Ambrosianus cantus'.[92] Old Beneventan chant is frequently called 'Ambrosian', particularly when it is found alongside Gregorian chant[93] – possibly out of a mistaken belief that it is identical with the liturgical chant of Milan, but more probably as a means of legitimising an endangered local repertory. The Ambrosian label is used at Montecassino for this music in the rubric

---

[92] 'Tunc etiam et Ambrosianum cantum in ecclesia ista cantari penitus interdixit.' *Chron. mon. cas.*, II, 94.

[93] Among the manuscript descriptions of Beneventan chant as 'Ambrosian' are the following:
 Vat. lat. 10673: 'officium sexta feria in Parasceben secundum Ambrosianum' (fol. 33); 'antifonas grecas latinasque ante crucem sicut in ambrosiano scripte sunt' (fol. 33).
 Lucca 606: 'Deinde Responsorium ambrosianum' (fol. 153).
 Benevento 33: 'Officium in parasceve secundum ambrosianum' (fol. 68).
 Benevento 38: 'Tractus ambrosianus' is used four times for the Beneventan Tracts *Domine audivi*, *Cantabo*, *Attende* and *Sicut cervus* (fols. 44–6; the last is palimpsest).
 Vatican, Ottob. lat. 145: 'Item quando non canimus ipse antiphone secundum romano quo modo supra scripte sunt canimus secundum ambrosiano hoc modo.' See Boe, 'A New Source for Old Beneventan Chant'.
 'Solesmes flyleaves', eight anonymously owned eleventh-century leaves from an antiphoner mixing Gregorian and Old Beneventan chant: 'vig. s. iohis bapt. [ant.] ambro. ad vesp'. See Kelly, 'Une nouvelle source pour l'office vieux-bénéventain'.

Montecassino and the Old Beneventan chant

('Ali. cō ambrō') of a Communion for St Benedict.[94] What Pope Stephen forbade was the singing of the local Ambrosian chant – the music we now call Old Beneventan. And when the Pope forbade Ambrosian chant he spoke from experience. Pope Stephen IX was Frederick of Lorraine (or Friedrich von Lothringen), a northerner educated at Liège; he had been chancellor to Pope Leo IX, the first great papal representative of the Cluniac reform. Leo, detained for almost a year in Benevento after his defeat by the Normans, sent Frederick as one of the famous legation to Byzantium that produced the great schism of 1054; in 1055, fleeing the wrath of the Emperor Henry III, Frederick took refuge at Montecassino. He subsequently retired to Tremiti, probably seeking greater security from imperial prosecution. He remained only a short time,[95] but doubtless long enough to hear the singing of some 'Ambrosianus cantus'.

After the death in 1055 of Montecassino's first German abbot, Richerius of Niederaltaich,[96] the election of one of the oldest monks was overturned by Leo IX's legate, cardinal Humbert, who oversaw the election as abbot of Frederick, his fellow ambassador to Constantinople.[97] Only a few weeks later Frederick himself was elected Pope, taking the name of Stephen IX.[98] It is this German Pope Stephen IX, the second northerner among the abbots of Montecassino, who forbade the singing of 'Ambrosianus cantus' at Montecassino in 1058. Frederick had opportunities to hear the Ambrosian chant as it was sung at Montecassino, at Benevento, and indeed at Tremiti. Raised and trained in the north, an ecclesiastical reformer like his master Leo IX, and now Pope, it is easy to imagine how unsuitable, even barbaric, he found the singing of this local chant.

---

[94] See Boe, 'Old Beneventan Chant at Monte Cassino'. Remember also the Cassinese connection of the 'Ambrosian' antiphons in Ottob. lat. 145. See above, p. 80 and note 93.

[95] Chron. mon. cas., II, 86; Leccisotti, 'Le relazioni', p. 204.

[96] Richerius was appointed by the Emperor Conrad II at the request of the community to re-establish imperial protection from Pandulf of Capua who, supported by the Byzantine empire, had imprisoned Theobald and imposed his own servant as abbot of Montecassino. See Chron. mon. cas., II, 56–65; Amatus of Montecassino, Storia de' Normanni, ed. V. de Bartholomaeis, Fonti per la Storia d'Italia 76 (Rome, 1935), II, p. 5; Desiderius, Dialogi de miraculis sancti Benedicti, MGH, Scriptores 30, I, p. 9; Bloch, 'Monte Cassino, Byzantium, and the West', pp. 187–8.

[97] The dramatic story of this election is told in Chron. mon. cas., II, 88–93.

[98] Fuller discussions of Frederick's career and the events leading to his election as abbot and Pope can be found in Bloch, 'Monte Cassino, Byzantium, and the West', pp. 189–93; Gay, L'Italie méridionale, pp. 509–51.

V

And, from the point of view of an abbot of Montecassino, forbidding the chant at the mother house ought to silence the daughters as well.

Frederick's successor as abbot was his friend, and the future Pope Victor III, the great Desiderius (1058–87). For students of art and architecture, for palaeographers and historians, the age of Desiderius marks the summit of Montecassino's fame and power, and her greatest artistic, literary and cultural flowering. It was this same Desiderius who presided over the suppression of the Old Beneventan chant, for as abbot of Montecassino in 1058 he was responsible for enforcing the papal decree.

Desiderius, like Frederick of Lorraine, links the three places discussed here: Montecassino, Benevento and Tremiti. Born at Benevento of noble parents, at an early age he became a monk of Santa Sofia, and had travelled to Tremiti as a youth[99] before entering Montecassino, like his friend Frederick, in 1055. We can imagine that Desiderius might have been less inclined to thoroughness than his northern predecessor in suppressing the local chant, which may, in fact, have been more familiar to him than Gregorian chant. Desiderius was, after all, a child of the region; he may well have had the opportunity to hear and sing the Old Beneventan chant, as a young monk of Santa Sofia, in his early travels to Tremiti, and indeed in his early years at Montecassino. Whatever his personal inclinations, however, by the height of Desiderius's abbacy the Old Beneventan chant had disappeared.

And so the Old Beneventan manuscripts of Montecassino became obsolete. Montecassino 361, and the relatively new *ingressarium* of abbot Theobald, and perhaps other manuscripts – these were no longer tolerated; their best use was to serve as raw material for more modern matters. An occasional piece might be saved: a favourite Communion for the founder, or a few votive antiphons. Many new liturgical books were made, and the old swept away: the Desiderian reform was so successful that no complete Gradual or antiphoner survives from pre-Desiderian Montecassino.

Only the accidental survival of fragments gives us a hint of what music may have been like at Montecassino before the tumultuous events of the eleventh century effected their changes. In fact, the written history of the Old Beneventan chant begins so shortly

[99] *Chron. mon. cas.*, III, 6.

82

Montecassino and the Old Beneventan chant

before its suppression that, were the history of events only slightly rearranged, its existence might not even have been suspected. But the evidence does survive, and we may be sure that Montecassino sang this chant, and played an important role both in its dissemination and in its suppression.

VI

BENEVENTAN FRAGMENTS AT ALTAMURA*

Thomas Forrest Kelly and Herman F. Holbrook

T‍HE Archivio Capitolare of the cathedral of Santa Maria Assunta in Altamura (province of Bari) has many records contained in *registri di amministrazione* ordered by the years they record and in many cases protected by parchment covers. Three of these *copertine* are fragments of liturgical manuscripts in Beneventan writing. The texts contained in the Beneventan fragments are of special interest for the liturgy of the Beneventan zone and will be analyzed and discussed below. It should be noted that two of the fragments have now been removed from the volumes they covered and are kept in a drawer in the Archivio Capitolare; shelf marks given here, therefore, are provisional. Herman F. Holbrook has generously undertaken the study and transcription of Fragment 1.

FRAGMENT 1

(Copertina del registro di amministrazione S. N. for 1563-64)

Herman F. Holbrook

Bound into the paper volume is a bifolium, originally the innermost of the quire, measuring 225 × 155 (170 × 95) mm., with 21 lines, and containing a tract on Septuagesima and calendric material. The color of the ink used for the text varies from light to dark brown. A large *S* partially infilled with red and preceded by a title in red signals the commencement of a new work on fol. 1r2; also edged or partially infilled with red are numerals and slightly smaller majuscules at the beginning of new sentences or clauses. The script displays the lozenges and shading characteristic of the general 'Cassinese' type of Beneventan (cf. pls. 7-10). Its overall aspect suggests a date of s. XI/XII as do such specific palaeographical features as the use of long final *r*, 2-sign for *tur*, and suprascript letters in abbreviations (e.g., *X* on fol. 2r5). An oblique stroke over *i* is used frequently to

In honor of Michel Huglo on his sixty-fifth birthday.

* These fragments first came to light during a visit to the Archivio Capitolare, Altamura in the summer of 1983. I am grateful to the archivist, don Oronzo Simone, for his kind assistance and for permission to publish the facsimiles, to dott. Giuseppe Pupillo of Altamura for much expert and technical help, and to the National Endowment for the Humanities and the American Academy in Rome for their support.

Reprinted from Thomas Forrest Kelly and Herman F. Holbrook, "Beneventan Fragments at Altamura," *Mediaeval Studies* 49 (1987): 466–79, by permission of the publisher. © 1987 by the Pontifical Institute of Mediaeval Studies, Toronto.

distinguish the letter rather than to mark accented syllables. Occasionally double parallel strokes indicate the suspension of several letters in what may be considered 'liturgical' words; cf. fols. 1r1, 3, 9 and 2v21 (*Sept\<uagesime>*, *termi\<nis>*, *Sexag\<esima>*, *Termi\<norum>* respectively). The 2-shaped inflection sign above *cur* (f. 1r8) is not answered by an interrogation mark at the end of the sentence. Other punctuation is limited to the point or comma preceded (or followed) by a single point except for what appears to be a single instance of the point surmounted by a hook (after *pascha* on fol. 1r8).

The anonymous tract, presently unidentified, concerning Septuagesima and various prepaschal fasting customs occupies fols. 1r-2r.[1] Another and in some respects textually better version is found in a manuscript with a Catalan provenance.[2] Our fragment commences with the statement that there are sixty-four days in the paschal season ('In Pascha sunt dies lxiiij'), by which presumably is meant the combined total for the periods of pre-Lent and Lent; this sentence appears to be the conclusion of another text, not preserved (?), which immediately preceded the tract on Septuagesima.[3] Next, there occurs the title *Ratio Septuagesime* which is followed by the text itself.

Modern scholars, as well as their medieval counterparts, have often asked why the three Sundays preceding Lent are named Septuagesima, Sexagesima, and Quinquagesima—respectively, the Seventieth, the Sixtieth, and the Fiftieth. There are fifty days from Quinquagesima up to, and including, Easter Sunday; but simple arithmetic quickly shows that there are neither sixty days from Sexagesima nor seventy from Septuagesima. It is generally assumed that these three Sundays were given their names merely by analogy with Quadragesima, the first Sunday in Lent, which falls on the fortieth day before the Sacred Triduum of Good Friday-Holy Saturday-Easter Sunday.[4] The author of this document, however, at the beginning of his work, adopts a numerological explanation with the phrase *pro vii terminis numerorum* (l. 2).[5] The text of the Altamura fragment is corrupt, and the strange

---

[1] Grateful acknowledgement is due to Pierre-Marie Gy, O.P. and Eric Palazzo for their investigation of possible incipits at the Institut de Recherche et d'Histoire des Textes, Paris. I have searched for this text in the published works of the ancient and medieval liturgical commentators named in the following surveys: Cyrille Vogel, *Introduction aux sources de l'histoire du culte chrétien au moyen âge*, 2nd edition (Spoleto, 1975), pp. 10-14 ('Liturgistes'); Douglas L. Mosey, *Allegorical Liturgical Interpretation in the West from 800 A.D. to 1200 A.D.* (Diss. Toronto, 1985); Roger E. Reynolds, 'Liturgy, Treatises on' in *Dictionary of the Middle Ages* 7 (New York, 1986), pp. 624-33.

[2] Roger E. Reynolds has edited and commented on the version of this text found in a manuscript of the Hispanic Society of America; see pp. 481-83 below in the present volume of *Mediaeval Studies*.

[3] This supposition is corroborated by the fact that, in the Catalan version of the text, the tract begins without the statement 'In Pascha sunt dies lxiiij'.

[4] F. L. Cross and E. A. Livingstone, eds., *The Oxford Dictionary of the Christian Church*, 2nd rev. edition (London, 1983), p. 1259 ('Septuagesima').

[5] References to the text are given by means of line numbers from the edition on pp. 470-71 below.

sequence of numbers next cited is intelligible only by comparison with the Catalan witness where it is clearly the number one, doubled seven times: i, ii, iiii, viii, xvi, xxxii, lxiiii.[6] Hence the sixty-four days of the paschal season.

Having explained the names of these three Sundays before Lent (ll. 1-4), the author then attempts to set forth the historical origins of their observance. The pre-Lenten period arose, he claims, as the conflation of the several penitential customs which were characteristic of the four ancient patriarchal sees (ll. 4-21). At Jerusalem, the Lenten fast is begun on Septuagesima and maintained throughout the ensuing weeks until Easter, except on Sundays, Thursdays, and Saturdays. At Alexandria, the fast opens on Sexagesima and is maintained except on Sundays and Thursdays. In Antioch it begins on Quinquagesima and in Rome on Quadragesima, and in both places only Sunday is exempt from the penitential discipline.

Jacques Froger has traced the rise and spread throughout the West of these amplifications of Lenten observance, and he attributed the practices to popular devotion.[7] Nevertheless, as the document under consideration here suggests, popular devotion in the West may have been informed by some consciousness of the variety and apparently greater rigour of the period of penitential fasting which preceded Easter in the East. Cassiodorus provides early evidence that such customs were known in the West.[8] Furthermore, Alcuin explicitly connects the various Eastern customs with the establishment in the West of the three pre-Lenten Sundays, and he claims to have heard this explanation from certain teachers while he was at Rome.[9] From Alcuin, the information passed into the works of subsequent liturgical commentators.[10]

It should be noted, however, that explanations other than historical abound in medieval liturgical commentary as well. Alcuin, in the work just mentioned, also adduces typological, mystical and numerological reasons for the origins and names of the pre-Lenten Sundays. Seventy is a number that may represent the seven weeks after which the Holy Spirit descended on the Apostles at Pentecost, or the seven gifts of the Holy Spirit. Sexagesima is fitting because in six days God completed the work of creation, and because six is a number 'perfect in its parts' ($1 \times 2 \times 3 = 6$). Quinquagesima is the fiftieth day before Easter, and therefore it signifies the remission of all our sins and the justification of life in Christ.[11]

[6] See Reynolds' edition, p. 482.3 below.

[7] Jacques Froger, 'Les anticipations du jeûne quadragésimal', Mélanges de science religieuse 3 (1946) 207-34.

[8] Cassiodorus, Historia ecclesiastica tripartita 9.38.18-19 (CSEL 71.561).

[9] Alcuin, Epistola 143 ad domnum regem de ratione Septuagesimae, Sexagesimae, et Quinquagesimae (MGH Epp. 4 [Berlin, 1895], pp. 225-26).

[10] e.g., Amalarius of Metz, 'Epistula ad Hilduinum abbatem de diebus ordinationis et quattuor temporum' in Opera liturgica omnia 3, ed. Jean Michel Hanssens (Studi e testi 140; Vatican City, 1950), pp. 343-44.

[11] Alcuin, Ep. 143 (MGH Epp. 4.226).

Beneventan Fragments at Altamura.

7. Altamura, Archivio Capitolare,
Copertina del registro di amministrazione S. N.
for 1563-64 (fol. 1r).

Beneventan Fragments at Altamura.

8. Altamura, Archivio Capitolare,
Copertina del registro di amministrazione S. N.
for 1563-64 (fol. 1v).

Beneventan Fragments at Altamura.

9. Altamura, Archivio Capitolare,
Copertina del registro di amministrazione S. N.
for 1563-64 (fol. 2r).

Beneventan Fragments at Altamura.

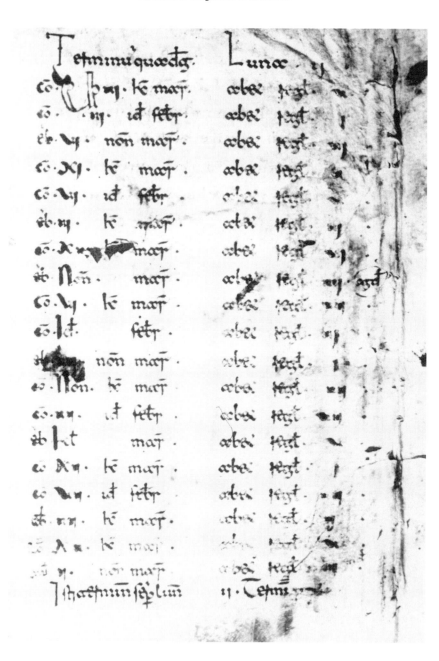

10. Altamura, Archivio Capitolare,
Copertina del registro di amministrazione S. N.
for 1563-64 (fol. 2v).

Beneventan Fragments at Altamura.

11. Altamura, Archivio Capitolare,
Copertina del registro di amministrazione 3
for 1521 (recto).

Beneventan Fragments at Altamura.

12. Altamura, Archivio Capitolare,
Copertina del registro di amministrazione 3
for 1521 (verso).

Beneventan Fragments at Altamura.

13. Altamura, Archivio Capitolare,
Copertina del registro di amministrazione 10
for 1526 (fol. xxx^r).

Beneventan Fragments at Altamura.

14. Altamura, Archivio Capitolare,
Copertina del registro di amministrazione 10
for 1526 (fol. xxx').

Beneventan Fragments at Altamura.

15. Altamura, Archivio Capitolare,
Copertina del registro di amministrazione 10
for 1526 (fol. XXXI^r).

Beneventan Fragments at Altamura.

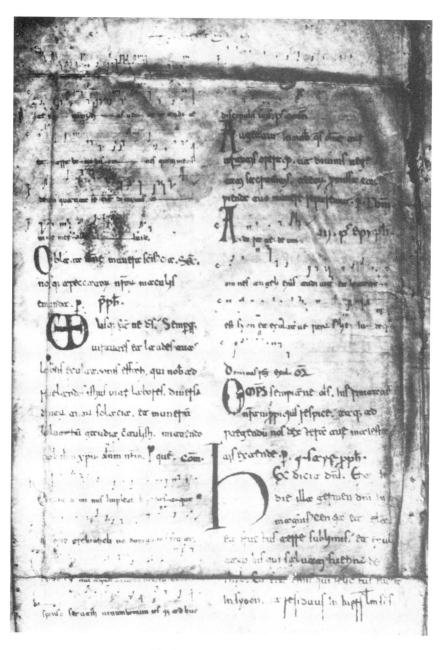

16. Altamura, Archivio Capitolare,
Copertina del registro di amministrazione 10
for 1526 (fol. xxxi ˅).

Since the anonymous author of our exposition speaks of the Lenten fast as beginning at Rome on Quadragesima (ll. 19-20), it may at first appear that he is unfamiliar with the practice of beginning the Lenten fast on the Wednesday after Quinquagesima (later to be known as Ash Wednesday). Chavasse, however, has demonstrated that, while Septuagesima cannot be older than the mid-sixth century (and is perhaps more recent than that), the Wednesday after Quinquagesima was accorded liturgical observance at Rome by mid-fifth century although it was not initially regarded as the formal beginning of Lent.[12] Hence a commentator writing of Septuagesima must also have been aware of Ash Wednesday. The solution to the apparent difficulty may be that, when our author refers to Quadragesima, he means the season which opens with Ash Wednesday. The earliest documentary evidence for this usage is the Gelasian Sacramentary (Vatican Library Reg. lat. 316), which contains a brief ordo identifying the Wednesday as '*IV feria ... in capite quadragesimae* (I, xvi)'.[13]

A substantial proportion of our Beneventan text is occupied by the author's account of those days of the week which are exempt from the fast according to the various customs of the patriarchates (ll. 22-28). Sunday, naturally, is not a day appropriate for fasting because, on the first day of the week, God created the world, the Saviour was announced to the Virgin Mary, and the Lord rose from the dead. Thursday is exempt from the fast for, on Thursday, the Lord washed the feet of his disciples at the Last Supper and committed to them his body and blood; also on Thursday, the Church blesses the holy chrism, and the Saviour ascended into heaven. Saturday is devoted to the veneration of the everlasting rest the saints have been promised in the heavenly Jerusalem.[14]

This tract concludes by reiterating the point that the Sundays of Septuagesima, Sexagesima, Quinquagesima, and Quadragesima reflect the respective traditions of the four ancient patriarchal sees.

The verso of the second folio is occupied by a calendric table or lunar guide to the *Termini quadragesimales*, the beginning of Lent, and is derived, at least ultimately, from two such tables compiled by Rabanus Maurus in his *De computo*, written in A.D. 820.[15] Our author, or perhaps some intermediate compiler, has

[12] Antoine Chavasse, 'Le Carême romain et les scrutins prébaptismaux avant le IXe siècle', *Recherches de science religieuse* 35 (1948) 337-38.

[13] Leo Cunibert Mohlberg-Leo Eizenhöfer-Petrus Siffrin, eds., *Liber sacramentorum romanae aeclesiae ordinis anni circuli*, 3rd edition (Rerum ecclesiarum documenta, Series maior, Fontes 4; Rome, 1981), p. 18. The text of this ordo is probably not as old as the mass texts of the Sacramentary (Chavasse, ibid., 336).

[14] Significance attributed to days of the week according to events of salvation history is common in medieval liturgical commentary. For an early example, pertinent to Sunday, see *Dies dominica* in Robert E. McNally, ed., *Scriptores Hiberniae minores* 1 (CCL 108B.173-86).

[15] Rabanus Maurus, *De computo*, ed. Wesley M. Stevens (CCM 44.303-304). Major works of Rabanus Maurus extant in Beneventan script are, for example, Monte Cassino, Archivio della Badia

extracted from Rabanus' first table two columns of information: *Termini quadrage-simales* and *Regulares*; from Rabanus' second table is drawn the column entitled *De communibus et embolismis annis.*

The logical juxtaposition of the text on Septuagesima and the calendric table suggests that the bifolium originally formed part of a computistical anthology. The presence of the calendric material in this form, if it is original to Rabanus Maurus, establishes that the compilation of such an anthology took place in the ninth century or later (after A.D. 820).

* * *

In transcribing the text given below, I have adopted modern principles of punctuation and capitalization while retaining the orthography of the manuscript. Erroneous or difficult readings are followed by (*sic*), (*ut vid.*) or (?).

(f. 1r) In Pascha sunt dies lxiiij. Ratio Septuagesime. Septuagesima non pro vii ebdomadibus vel pro lx (*sic*) diebus dicitur sed pro vii terminis numerorum, id est i, ii, xii, vxii (*sic*), vi, xiiij, et sic colliguntur ut ebdomada non summulis sed summule dis-partiantur per arbitrio (*sic*) dierum qui lxiiij sunt usque in Pascha. Solent (*sic*) queri a
5 nonnullis cur Septuagesima, Sexagesima, Quinquagesima, sive Quadragesima in sacris codicibus certis temporibus pretitulentur. Quibus ut quantum (?) possit occurrere quod volebant non debet hoc onerosum videri, si paulatim responsionis sermo modo (*ut vid.*) longum processerit, cum satis melium (*ut vid.*) sit fructum hoc (*sic*) laboris viam veritatis percurrere quam odio torpentis fallacie verba proferre. Cunctis namque legentibus libet
10 (*sic*) universum orbem iiij aecclesias (*sic*) ordinibus esse distributam (*sic*), videlicet Romanorum, Alexandrinorum, Hierusolimitanorum et Anthiocaene; que generaliter (f. 1v) uno vocabulo sancta aecclesia nuncupatur. Hee namque singulae aecclesie cum unam tenent catholicam sanctione fidei diversis utuntur officiorum ieiuniorumque moribus. Unde fit ut Hierusolimorum aecclesia inchoet ieiunium a Septuagesima usque in Pascha,
15 sublatis tribus diebus de unaquaque ebdomada, id est diem (*sic*) dominico et v feria et sabbato. Alexandrinorum vero aecclesia inchoet ieiunium a Sexagesima usque in Pascha, auferentes (*sic*) de singulis ebdomadibus diem dominicum et v feriam. Anthiocaena quoque aecclesia inchoat ieiunium a Quinquagesima usque in Pascha, subtrahens de unaquaque ebdomada diem dominicum sicuti faciunt (*sic*) et Romana ecclesia que a
20 Quadragesima inchoare consuevit ieiunium. Quamquam in hoc tempore variis utentes

---

5 quaestio *in marg.*   6 responsio *in marg.*   9 quaestio *in marg.*

---

132 *De origine rerum* and 133 *Commentarius in libros Regum,* and Vatican City, Biblioteca Apostolica Vaticana Vat. lat. 4955 *Commentarius in libros Regum* (listed in E. A. Loew, *The Beneventan Script. A History of the South Italian Minuscule* 2, 2nd edition prepared by Virginia Brown [Sussidi eruditi 34; Rome, 1980], pp. 70-71, 151). For another connection between the work of Rabanus Maurus and Beneventan script see Raymund Kottje, 'Beneventana-Fragmente liturgischer Bücher im Stadtarchiv Augsburg', *Mediaeval Studies* 47 (1985) 432-37.

doctrinis singule provincie et regiones diversos sibi mores usurpent prout queque voluntas duxerit. (f. 2r) Dies (*sic*) vero de ieiunio ista est ratio. A die dominico pro eo quod ipsa die conditus est mundus et ipso die est annuntiatus Salvator noster ab angelo Virginis (*sic*) Marie, et ipso die resurrectio Domini nostri Iesu Christi celebratur. Quinta feria propter
5 quia in ipso die lavit Dominus pedes discipulorum et tradidit corpus et sanguinem suum discipulis suis, ut (?) ipso (?) die conficitur chrisma, et ipso die Salvator noster ascendit ad celos. Sabbato propter veneratio (*sic*) aeterne quietis que promissa est sanctis in celesti Hierusalem. Cum hoc vero unum sit ieiunii tempus, iiij illis vocabulis distinguendo prodidit antiquitam (*sic*) iuxta morem iiij aecclesiarum memoratarum, idest Septuagesima, Sexa-
10 gesima, Quinquagesima, Quadragesima. Pro Hierusolimorum aecclesia accepto vocabulo Septuagesima, similitudo (*sic*) et pro Alexandrinorum ecclesia Sexagesima, necnon et pro Anthiocena aecclesia Quinquagesima, et Romanorum aecclesia vocavit antiquitas Quadragesima.

(f. 2v)	Termini quadragesimales	Luna ij
Communis	viij Kal. Martii	abet regularem v
Communis	iij Idus Februarii	abet regularem j
Embolismus	vj Nonas Martii	abet regularem vj
5 Communis	xj Kal. Martii	abet regularem ij
Communis	vj Idus Februarii	abet regularem v
Embolismus	iij Kal. Martii	abet regularem iij
Communis	xiiij Kal. Martii	abet regularem vj
Embolismus	Nonas Martii	abet regularem iiij
10 Communis	vj Kal. Martii	abet regularem vij
Communis	Idus Februarii	abet regularem iij
Embolismus	[ ] Nonas Martii	abet regularem j
Communis	Novem Kal. Martii	abet regularem iiij
Communis	iiij Idus Februarii	abet regularem vij
15 Embolismus	Kalendas Martii	abet regularem v
Communis	xij Kal. Martii	abet regularem j
Communis	vij Idus Februarii	abet regularem iiij
Embolismus	iiij Kal. Martii	abet regularem ij
Communis	xv Kal. Martii	abet regularem v
20 Embolismus	ij Nonas Martii	abet regularem iiij
	Isti termini semper lunae	ij. Terminorum...

1 Termini *corr. s.s. ex* Terminu   9 ogdoas *in marg.*

472

Fragment 2

(Copertina del registro di amministrazione 3 for 1521)

One leaf from a noted breviary has been removed from the *registro* and is kept separately. Trimmed on three sides, the folio now measures 330 × 200 (250 × 125) mm., with 32 long lines. The scribe, using a rich brown ink with traces of black, has produced an expert twelfth-century specimen of the 'Bari-type' of Beneventan (cf. pls. 11-12). Indeed, the script displays most of the features of this regional adaptation:[1] its appearance is generally round; *s* and *f* rest on the base-line; two nearly equal curves make up large *e*; *i* in the *fi* ligature rests on or above the base-line, forming a broad curve which turns inward; the shoulder of medial *r* is straight. Contrary, however, to the 'Bari-type' canon is the final *r* which goes slightly below the line (1r9, 14 and 1v3, 9), and the copyist prefers, for omitted *m* and *est*, the 3-shaped *m* sign and *ē* to the line surmounted by a dot and ÷. Abbreviations comprise the Nomina Sacra, the usual Beneventan forms for *autem, eius,* etc., and both the 'old' and 'new' systems for forms of *omnis* (1r22 *om̄s*, 1r28 and 1v22 *omīa*; 1v18 *oīpotentis*). Initial majuscule letters at the beginning of new sections are written in red and infilled or edged with green; somewhat smaller initial letters at the beginning of sentences are written in ink and then edged or infilled (wholly or partially) with red and/or green. A single point on the base-line serves for punctuation. Questions are marked with a sign resembling a modern check-mark; in two cases on the recto (ll. 11 and 12) the sign is placed over the interrogative word and final word in the sentence, while on the verso (l. 3) the check-mark appears over the interrogative word only.

The musical notation is not that of the Beneventan scribes of the region in the twelfth century or earlier, consisting instead of an early form of square notation with something of a French aspect.[2] It is diastematic relative to the scored line for the text, and uses a clef and custos.

---

[1] E. A. Loew, *The Beneventan Script. A History of the South Italian Minuscule,* 2 vols., 2nd edition prepared by Virginia Brown (Sussidi eruditi 33-34; Rome, 1980), 1.150.

[2] Beneventan musical notation appears rather frequently with ordinary minuscule, especially in codices of the twelfth and thirteenth centuries. Some examples are: Lucca, Biblioteca Capitolare Feliniana 606, fols. 150v-156r (*Paléographie musicale* 14 [Solesmes, 1931; rpt. Berne, 1971], pls. 34-43); Subiaco, Biblioteca del Protocenobio di Santa Scolastica xxii (24); Vatican City, Biblioteca Apostolica Vaticana Vat. lat. 10645, fols. 10-11, 12-15, 16-19, 20-21, 23a, 24-25, 26-27, 28-29, 38, 38*, 39, 40-41, 42-43, 44-45, 48-49, 65-67, 68. The reverse (Beneventan script with non-Beneventan notation) is much rarer; the only other example I know is Chieti, Biblioteca Capitolare 2, whose two initial fly-leaves are from an eleventh-century gradual in Beneventan script but with northern Italian notation (see *Paléographie musicale* 14, pls. 44-45). That scribes of different traditions should meet on the periphery of the Beneventan zone (Subiaco, Chieti) is not particularly surprising; nor is the survival of a Beneventan-derived musical notation after a change in writing style. The Altamura music-scribe, however, seems clearly to be a foreigner somehow transported (through Norman influence?) far from home.

The contents of this leaf concern the second and third nocturns of matins (according to the 'Roman' or 'secular' cursus) of Quinquagesima and are listed below, with italics denoting rubrics:

(recto)

1. [Lection] populi mei. ... spatiosus ad manendum. Tu autem domine. [Gen 23:11-15, 24:22-25; a composite text with a gap in continuity[3]]

2. ℟ Vocavit angelus domini Abraham. ℣ Et benedicentur [= CAO[4] 7911]

3a. *Lectio.* Inclinavit se homo et adoravit. ... locutus est mihi homo [Gen 24:26-30; continued on verso]

(verso)

3b. Venit ad virum. ... sermones meos. Tu autem domine. [Gen 24:30-33]

4. ℟ Credidit Abraham deo. ℣ Fuit autem iustus [= CAO 6346, used in Benevento, Biblioteca Capitolare VI 21 only, for Quinquagesima]

5. *a*[*ntiphona*] Sponsus [ut e thalamo]. *Ps* Celi enarrunt. [= CAO 5011]

6. *a*[*ntiphona*] Auxilium [nobis Salvator]. *Ps* Exaudiat. [= CAO 1537]

7. *a*[*ntiphona*] Rex sine fine. *Ps* Domine in virtute. [= CAO 4652]

8. *v*[*e*]*r*[*sus*] Exultare domine. [= CAO 2758 or 2759]

9. Pater noster. Et ne nos. Set.

10. [Blessing of the lector] Jube domne ben[edicere]. Evangelii documentis nos repleat virtus omnipotentis.

11a. [*Lectio*] *Secundum Lucam.* In illo tempore assumpsit Iesus duodecim discipulos. ... scripta sunt per prophetas de filio hominis. Et reliqua. [Lc 18:31 ff.]

11b. Redemptor noster previdens. ... verba non caperent eos [Gregory the Great, *Homiliae* XL *in evangelia* 1.2 (for Quinquagesima) (PL 76.1082B)]

That this leaf is a fragment of a Roman breviary can be deduced from the antiphon series cued on the verso, for these are drawn from a nine-part series of distichs. They are used in Ivrea, Biblioteca Capitolare 33 (CVI) for Sundays after Epiphany; the Sunday nocturns have three antiphons each, and to each nocturn is added an alternative group (*Item aliae antiphonae*) from this series of distichs.[5] The series is used, in the same order, in a number of Spanish manuscripts.[6]

The antiphons cited here are seventh, eighth and ninth in the series; evidently, therefore, they are used for the third nocturn of a secular office. A monastic third nocturn, of course, would have a single antiphon for canticles.

---

[3] The text skips from Gen 23:15 ('... istud est pretium inter me et te; sed quantum est hoc? sepeli mortuum tuum') to Gen 24:22 ('Postquam ergo biberunt cameli, protulit vir inaures aureas...') in this fashion: '... hoc est pretium inter me et te. Set quantum cameli. protulit vir inaures....'

[4] René-Jean Hesbert, *Corpus antiphonalium officii* (=CAO), 6 vols. (Rerum ecclesiasticarum documenta, Series maior, Fontes 7-12; Rome, 1963-79).

[5] See CAO 1, pp. 87, 89.

[6] The texts are edited in Guido Maria Dreves, *Analecta hymnica medii aevi* 17 (Leipzig, 1894), p. 19. See Amédée Gastoué, 'Le chant gallican', *Revue du chant grégorien* 41 (1937) 104 and n. 4.

We can be certain that the feast in question is Quinquagesima, not only from the homily of Gregory the Great for that day which is read at the third nocturn but also from the liturgical assignment of the chant pieces in other manuscripts. One of the responsories (*Credidit Abraham deo*, no. 4 above) is known only from south Italy, where it is used for Quinquagesima in Benevento VI 21.[7]

FRAGMENT 3

(Copertina del registro di amministrazione 10 for 1526)

A bifolium from a noted missal has been removed from the *registro* and is kept separately. Present measurements are 380 × 310 (250 × 160) mm., with 2 columns of 27 lines, and the first folio is stained from moisture. Originally forming the central bifolium of a quire, the leaves exhibit at the top of each recto a late foliation in the form of Roman numerals 'XXX' and 'XXXI' (traces of 'XXXI' are seen on our pl. 15); there are a few marginal additions in later hands. The script is an elongated version of the 'Bari-type' of Beneventan (cf. pls. 13-16): height and length of ascenders and descenders is exaggerated; broken *c* is frequently used; *f* and *s* do not go below the base-line, nor does *i* in the *fi* ligature; final *r* is short; notable is the breadth of the curve in the *ct* and *sp* ligatures (e.g., fol. xxx^{r}a10, 15, 24). The usual abbreviations designate the Nomina Sacra, and those for various cases of *omnis* follow the 'old' system (fols. xxx^{v}b8 *omīa*, xxxi^{r}b18 *omīs*); however, the use of a horizontal stroke for omitted *m* rather than the line surmounted by a dot or the 3-shaped symbol, together with the occasional appearance of *aūt* (fol. xxxi^{r}b16, 21) instead of *aū* for *autem*, suggests that the scribe was writing in an area exposed to the influence of Caroline minuscule. Letters which begin a section are in red and occupy from two to four lines; those beginning new sentences within a section are smaller and also in red, with the text in a brownish-black ink. Medial stops are indicated by the point or point combined with hook, and final stops by the point alone. A point surmounted by an oblique line flagged on both ends (see fol. xxxi^{r}b5) terminates a question. Neumes are occasionally added above the texts of readings and the preface (e.g., fol. xxx^{r}a18).

The notation of the chant pieces is written with clefs on dry-point lines. Though the style of notation is essentially Beneventan, especially as regards the shapes and linking of neumes, it has an attenuated quality, rather like the script, which sets it apart from most later Beneventan notations. Missing here is the rich variety of Beneventan liquescent neumes, as is the quilisma, which generally disappears from Beneventan notation in the twelfth century. Thus the fragment is surely not earlier than the twelfth century.

---

[7] See the references in CAO under the catalogue numbers listed.

Contents of the bifolium are as follows (italics indicate rubrics):

(fol. xxx^r)

1. [Alleluia. Benedictus qui] venit.
2. *Secundum Matheum.* In illo tempore venit dominus Iesus a Galileam (*sic*). ... in quo michi complacuit. [Mt 3:13-17]
3. *Secundum Lucam.* In illo tempore vidit Iohannes Iesum. ... hic est filius dei. [Jo 1:29-34]
4. *Off.* Timebunt gentes nomen tuum et omnes reges terre domine gloriam tuam.
5. *Sec.* Hostias tibi domine pro nati filii.
6. *Com.* Regi autem seculorum inmortali invisibili soli deo honor et gloria in secula seculorum.
7a. *Postcom.* Celesti lumine. [continued on verso]

(fol. xxx^v)

7b. [*Postcom.* concluded]
8. *Dom. II. post Epyphaniae. Intr.* Omnis terra.
9. *Or.* Omnipotens sempiterne deus qui celestia.
10. [*Lectio*] *Sapientiae.* Diligite iustitiam. ... habet vocis. [Sap 1:1-7]
11. *Gr.* Misit dominus.
12a. *Ad Romanos.* Fratres habentes donationes ... sive qui [Rom 12:6-7; continued on fol. xxxi^r]

(fol. xxxi^r)

12b. docet in doctrina. ... humilibus consentientes. [Rom 12:7-16]
13a. *All.* Omnis terra adoret te deus et psallat tibi; psalmum dicat nomini tuo domine.
13b. *All.* Laudate deum omnes angeli eius, laudate eum omnes virtutes eius. [added in lower margin by the same music-scribe]
14. *Secundum Iohannem.* In illo tempore nuptiae factae sunt. ... discipuli eius. [Jo 2:1-11]
15a. *Off.* Jubila deo.

(fol. xxxi^v)

15b. [*Off.* concluded]
16. *Sec.* Oblata domine munera sanctifica.
17. *Preph.* Vere dignum *usque* aeterne deus. Semperque virtutes.
18. *Com.* Dicit dominus implete hydrias.
19. *Postcom.* Augeatur in nobis.
20. *Dom. III. post Epyph.* [*Intr.*] Adorate deum.
21. *Or.* Omnipotens sempiterne deus infirmitatem nostram.
22. [*Lectio*] *Ysaye proph.* Haec dicit dominus. Erit in die illa germen. ... et residuus in Hierusalem sanctus [Is 4:2-3]

The missal contains parts of three masses for the season after Epiphany, and it has some noteworthy features. First, it uses three lections for the mass: Old Testament, Epistle and Gospel; this is a characteristic also seen in the archaic missal preserved in Benevento, Biblioteca Capitolare VI 33 (s. x/xi), where readings from the prophets precede the Epistle for a number of Sundays after Pentecost. Klaus Gamber has suggested that this may represent an early Roman usage.[8] Michel Huglo, however, has observed that these Old Testament lessons must have been included in the old Beneventan liturgy; they are in part drawn from pre-Vulgate texts, and one of the pre-Vulgate lessons from Jeremiah is found in the same manuscript in a Vulgate version among the Roman pericopes for Thursday of the fourth week of Lent.[9]

The surviving Old Testament lessons in this fragment are two: Sap 1:1-7 for the second Sunday after Epiphany and Is 4:2-? for the third Sunday after Epiphany. They display essentially Vulgate readings.

The missal in Benevento VI 33 has triple readings only for Sundays after Pentecost, not for the Epiphany season. The Altamura missal evidently provided a larger number of masses with three lessons: in its present form we cannot be sure that it did not contain Old Testament lessons for all Sundays. Still, using the evidence of Benevento VI 33, we can establish that there existed in south Italy a system of three lections at least for the 'green' Sundays of the liturgical year.

Except for this third lesson, the second and third masses of Altamura (for the second and third Sundays after Epiphany) are basically those of the Roman Missal prior to Vatican II. The surviving prayers for the masses at Altamura are found in later recensions of the Gelasian and Gregorian sacramentaries,[10] and the lessons

---

[8] 'Die Sonntagsmessen nach Pfingsten im Cod. VI 33 von Benevent', *Ephemerides liturgicae* 74 (1960) 428-31. The entire manuscript is reproduced in facsimile in *Paléographie musicale* 20 (Berne-Frankfurt, 1983); it is edited (though texts and music are not given *in extenso*) by Sieghild Rehle, 'Missale Beneventanum (Codex VI 33 des Erzbischöflichen Archivs von Benevent)', *Sacris erudiri* 21 (1972-73) 323-405.

[9] 'Fragments de Jérémie selon la Vetus Latina', *Vigiliae christianae* 8 (1954) 83-86.

[10] There are no formularies for Sundays after Epiphany in the earlier sacramentary of Hadrian; see Jean Deshusses, ed., *Le sacramentaire grégorien. Ses principales formes d'après les plus anciens manuscrits*, 3 vols. (Spicilegium friburgense 16, 24, 28; Fribourg, 1971-82), 1.83-348 (Hadrianum from Cambrai, Bibliothèque Municipale 164), and also Hans Lietzmann, ed., *Das Sacramentarium Gregorianum nach dem Aachener Urexemplar* (Liturgiegeschichtliche Quellen 3; Münster i. W., 1921). The Leonine Sacramentary of Verona likewise contains none of these prayers (Leo Cunibert Mohlberg-Leo Eizenhöfer-Petrus Siffrin, eds., *Sacramentarium Veronense (Cod. Bibl. Capit. Veron. LXXXV [80])* [Rerum ecclesiasticarum documenta, Series maior, Fontes 1; Rome, 1956]). They are found, however, in the supplement to the sacramentary of Hadrian (Deshusses 1.382-83, nos. 349-605).

The Altamura prayers for the second and third Sundays are not found in the Gelasian Sacramentary in Vatican City, Biblioteca Apostolica Vaticana Reg. lat. 316 (Leo Cunibert Mohlberg-Leo Eizenhöfer-Petrus Siffrin, eds., *Liber sacramentorum romanae aeclesiae ordinis anni circuli*, 3rd edition [Rerum ecclesiasticarum documenta, Series maior, Fontes 4; Rome, 1981]), but they appear in the eighth-century Frankish Gelasian sacramentaries (Kunibert Mohlberg, ed., *Das fränkische Sacramentarium Gelasianum in alamannischer Überlieferung (Codex Sangall. No. 348)*, 3rd edition [Liturgiegeschichtliche Quellen und Forschungen 1.2; Münster i. W., 1971], pp. 18-19, 23, and see also A. Dumas, ed., *Liber sacramentorum Gellonensis: Textus* [CCL 159; Turnhout, 1981], pp. 16, 22). A useful comparative table is found in J. Deshusses, ed., *Liber sacramentorum Gellonensis: introductio, tabulae et indices* (CCL 159A; Turnhout, 1981), pp. 12-15.

and chants are standard except for the two Alleluias in the second mass, which are nevertheless widely known pieces.[11]

In addition, the second mass includes the proper preface *Semperque virtutes*,[12] which is found in Gelasian sacramentaries[13] and among the appended prefaces in the supplement to the Gregorian Sacramentary.[14]

The first mass is more complex. As it is incomplete at its beginning we have no rubric labeling the feast; apparently it is a mass assembled for the octave of Epiphany.

This mass has two Gospel pericopes. It uses rare chant pieces, and its prayers are an assemblage of collects used elsewhere in various ways. Probably it too had an Old Testament lesson. The presence of two Gospel readings is unusual, perhaps unique; it seems to fuse two traditions in order to focus on the baptism of Christ. The pericopes, two accounts of the baptism written one after another, are two Gospels, and not a single composite reading, since they are labeled respectively *secundum Matheum* (Mt 3:13-17) and *secundum Lucam* (the passage is actually Jo 1:29-34) and each has the standard Gospel incipit *In illo tempore*.

The Matthew pericope, while rare elsewhere, is a regular feature of Beneventan books. It is used for the octave of Epiphany in Benevento VI 33, and for the same feast in the combined missal-breviary Benevento, Biblioteca Capitolare V 19 and in the missals London, British Library Egerton 3511 and Vatican City, Biblioteca Apostolica Vaticana Ottob. lat. 576, all of the twelfth century.[15]

The more usual Gospel series does not normally include the Matthew reading at all, although the passage from John is found for the Wednesday after Epiphany

---

[11] The Alleluia *Omnis terra* appears in Benevento, Biblioteca Capitolare VI 34, fols. 37v-38r for the second Sunday after Epiphany; it is an adaptation of the Alleluia *Amavit eum* and is widely used in medieval manuscripts (see Karl-Heinz Schlager, *Thematischer Katalog der ältesten Alleluia-Melodien aus Handschriften des 10. und 11. Jahrhunderts* [Munich, 1965], p. 147, no. 174). The Alleluia added in the lower margin, *Laudate deum* (adapted from the Alleluia *Excita domine*), is used in Benevento VI 34 for the feast of the Invention of the archangel Michael (8 May), but it is more widely found for the second Sunday after Epiphany; see Schlager, pp. 163-64, no. 205. This marginal addition, then, is designed to bring the Altamura missal into line with the more usual Roman practice.

[12] Edmond (Eugène) Moeller, ed., *Corpus praefationum*, 4 vols. (CCL 161A-D; Turnhout, 1980), no. 1439.

[13] In Gellone (Dumas, ed., *Liber sacramentorum Gellonensis*, p. 17), St. Gall (Mohlberg, ed., *Das fränkische Sacramentarium*, p. 19) and elsewhere (see the table in Deshusses, ed., *Liber sacramentorum Gellonensis*, p. 13).

[14] Deshusses, ed., *Le sacramentaire grégorien* 1.500, no. 1528.

[15] The same reading is used for the octave in an eleventh-century German Gospel-book, namely, Manchester, John Rylands University Library Lat. 159; see Walter Howard Frere, *Studies in Early Roman Liturgy* 2 (Alcuin Club Collections 30; Oxford, 1934), p. 82. This manuscript also includes Gospels for the three ferias after Epiphany; the octave interrupts the series, which continues with 'Dies iii' (i.e., the second feria after Epiphany), whose Gospel is *Vidit Iohannes Iesum*, the second pericope of Altamura. In this series, then, the two Gospels occur in the same order as at Altamura, but the series itself in the Rylands codex is not in proper liturgical order.

in both the early Gospel series in Rheims, Bibliothèque Municipale 10 and in the 'standard' series of London, British Library Harley 2788.[16]

This same Wednesday, however, is provided with another Gospel in an alternate arrangement attested by a number of sources; and this alternative Gospel is Mt 3:13-17 (the first of the two Altamura Gospels).[17]

The Altamura missal evidently fuses two traditions which use Gospels referring to the baptism: that of the south Italian manuscripts (Matthew) and the John pericope more usual elsewhere. It presents the two together for a feast that is evidently the octave of Epiphany (and not the Wednesday, for in that case the first Sunday would have to follow this mass). Both Gospels are present, but it seems unlikely that both were intended to be read; the scribe leaves the choice to the lector.[18]

The Collects for this mass, too, are a collection of 'wandering' prayers assembled for the octave at a stage later than the arrangement of Sundays after Epiphany (which are themselves later additions to the sacramentary).[19] Though they came to be associated with the octave, they are originally separate prayers, to judge from some early sources. They are both used for Epiphany itself in the Reginensis Gelasian Sacramentary.[20]

The Secret (*Hostias tibi domine pro nati filii*, no. 5 above) is used for the first Sunday in Gellone[21] and in other Gelasian sacramentaries;[22] while the Postcommunion (*Celesti lumine*) is used for the octave in the same manuscripts.[23] This latter prayer serves also for the vigil of Epiphany in several sources,[24] and as one of the prayers 'ad completum diebus festis' in the sacramentary of Hadrian.[25]

---

[16] Frere, ibid. 2.2, 30.

[17] ibid. 2.119. The Matthew reading is used for the same Wednesday in the central Italian missal fragments of Munich, Bayerische Staatsbibliothek Clm 29164; see Klaus Gamber, 'Die mittel-italienisch-beneventanischen Plenarmissalien. Der Meßbuchtypus des Metropolitangebiets von Rom im 9./10. Jahrhundert', *Sacris erudiri* 9 (1957) 269-70.

[18] The 'Martina' group of Gospels is characterized by its inclusion of readings for weekdays after Epiphany, and that series also brings the two Altamura Gospels into proximity. The Tuesday Gospel is Jo 1:29-34 (= Altamura no. 3), and Wednesday's Gospel is Mt 3:1-17, which includes the portion read at Altamura (see Frere, ibid. 2.91). But it seems unlikely that the Altamura double Gospel derives from this series since the texts would have to be shortened and their order reversed.

[19] Some of the prayers for the second and third Sundays are also to be found among the 'general' prayers in earlier sacramentaries containing no feasts in the Epiphany cycle. *Augeatur* (Altamura no. 19) is used in the Reginensis Gelasian sacramentary (Mohlberg, ed., *Liber sacramentorum romanae aeclesiae*, p. 187, no. 1263) in a series of eleven postcommunion prayers for Sundays; and *Omnipotens sempiterne deus qui celestia* (Altamura no. 9) is one of many 'orationes cottidianae' in the sacramentary of Hadrian (Lietzmann, ed., *Das Sacramentarium Gregorianum*, p. 63, no. 97.2 and Deshusses, ed., *Le sacramentaire grégorien* 1.325, no. 922).

[20] Mohlberg, ibid., p. 15.

[21] Dumas, ed., *Liber sacramentorum Gellonensis*, p. 15.

[22] Deshusses, *Liber sacramentorum Gellonensis*, p. 12.

[23] Dumas, ed., *Liber sacramentorum Gellonensis*, p. 16; Deshusses, ibid., p. 13.

[24] Deshusses, ed., *Le sacramentaire grégorien* 1.689.

[25] Deshusses, ibid. 1.209; Lietzmann, ed., *Das Sacramentarium Gregorianum*, p. 63.

Fairly early on, however, these two prayers were adopted into a new mass for the octave of Epiphany, as is evident from their use in the Gelasian sacramentaries of St. Gall and Angoulême,[26] and in the additions to the Gregorian Sacramentary of Cambrai, Bibliothèque Municipale 162-163.[27]

Hence the development of the octave as a feast celebrating the baptism of Christ is a somewhat later phenomenon, but the focus is clear by the earlier ninth century when Amalarius speaks about it:

> Sicut certavit scola cantorum in epiphania frequentare adventum magorum, simili modo certat in octavis epiphaniae frequentare baptismum Christi, quasi ipsa die baptizatus esset.[28]

Although their melodies are Gregorian in style, the chants of the Altamura mass are generally absent from the earliest Gregorian repertory.[29] They are not unknown, however, in south Italian graduals and missals. In Benevento VI 33 (fol. 8v) the Alleluia *Benedictus qui venit*[30] appears in the mass for the octave of Epiphany which begins with the Introit *In columbe specie*; the mass is incomplete owing to a lacuna, and so we cannot verify the presence of the Offertory and Communion of Altamura. However, the twelfth-century gradual Benevento VI 35 contains a full set of chants for the octave which match the surviving Altamura mass.[31]

This mass, then, is a uniquely south Italian formulary for the octave of Epiphany, a mass of relatively late development, in which the fusion of tradition is visible in the double Gospel and the local character attested by the regional chant.

---

[26] Mohlberg, ed., *Das fränkische Sacramentarium*, p. 17; Deshusses, ed., *Liber sacramentorum Gellonensis*, pp. 12-13 (table).

[27] Deshusses, ed., *Le sacramentaire grégorien* 1.689.

[28] *Liber de ordine antiphonarii* 25 in Jean Michel Hanssens, ed., *Amalarii episcopi Opera liturgica omnia* 3 (Studi e testi 140; Vatican City, 1950), p. 61.

[29] They are not found in the six Graduals edited by René-Jean Hesbert in *Antiphonale missarum sextuplex* (Brussels, 1935; rpt. Rome, 1985), none of which contains a mass for the octave of Epiphany.

[30] The Alleluia, based on the widely used *Dies sanctificatus*, is an adaptation hitherto known only in Benevento VI 33 and VI 35; see Schlager, *Thematischer Katalog*, pp. 78-81, no. 27.

[31] Int. *In columbe*; Gr. *Benedictus deus Israhel*; ℣ *Suscipiant*; All. ℣ *Benedictus qui venit*; Of. *Timebunt gentes*; Co. *Regi autem seculorum* (fols. 7v-8r). The Offertory in Benevento VI 35 varies from Altamura in the placement of the word *domine* (*Timebunt gentes nomen tuum domine et omnes reges terre gloriam tuam*); but the music is the same in both pieces, though for part of its length adapted to different syllables. Beneventan manuscripts do not agree completely with Altamura for this mass: Benevento V 19 includes a mass for the octave which differs from Altamura in its Alleluia (*Hodie baptizatus*); the Beneventan missals Egerton 3511 and Ottob. lat. 576 repeat the Epiphany chants (Int. *Ecce advenit*), and use a different Collect (*Deus cuius unigenitus*). Other Beneventan Graduals either have no mass for the octave (Benevento VI 34) or are lacking their Epiphany sections (Benevento VI 38, VI 39, VI 40).

A MUSICAL FRAGMENT AT BISCEGLIE
CONTAINING AN UNKNOWN BENEVENTAN OFFICE

In a private collection in Bisceglie (province of Bari) is a small paper volume of records for the year 1486 from the parish church of San Matteo in Bisceglie. Wrapped around the book as a cover, and still attached, is a bifolium from a noted antiphoner of the late eleventh or early twelfth century.[1]

The front folio of the wrapper (folio A) measures approximately 300 × 228 mm., and the original writing surface measures 270 × 161 mm., in fourteen long lines. Each folio is ruled with four dry-point lines for each system of text and music; prickings for this ruling can be seen on the outer edge of folio A.

The parchment is of medium thickness and yellowish, the exposed sides (folios A recto, Z verso) being much darkened. There is some damage, including missing parchment, at the bottom of both folios, and there are moisture stains and generally much evidence of wear. An original hole in the bottom of folio Z is obscured now by the absence of parchment above the hole, and of all the parchment below to the bottom of the folio.[2]

A blackish-brown ink, now somewhat faded, is used for both text and music; rubrics are in an orange-red ink. The two large initials are colored with the orange-red ink of the rubrics as well as with yellow (now faded), green, blue, and a much-tarnished silver. Smaller initials are infilled or touched with red, green, or yellow.

---

[1] The fragment was called to my attention by Professor Virginia Brown; Professor Francesco Magistrale, whose researches first brought the fragment to light, kindly arranged for me to examine and photograph it (see plates). The fragment was described for the first time by Clelia Gattagrisi at the congress *Scrittura e produzione documentaria nel mezzogiorno longobardo* (Badia di Cava, 3–5 ottobre 1990), in whose forthcoming acts her report will appear.

[2] The penultimate lines of both sides of folio Z seem to be complete, skipping over what must be the original hole; on folio Zv, the direct after "esse" shows the relative position of the next visible neume.

Reprinted from Thomas Forrest Kelly, "A Musical Fragment at Bisceglie Containing an Unknown Beneventan Office," *Mediaeval Studies* 55 (1993): 347–56, by permission of the publisher. © 1993 by the Pontifical Institute of Mediaeval Studies, Toronto.

348

The text is written in a clear and careful Beneventan script of the "Bari type." It does not, however, have the rounded appearance of many examples of this type; it has a strong vertical orientation typical of manuscripts written in Apulia outside of the immediate area of the Bari zone, though the ascenders and descenders are rather short. There is a general resemblance to the scripts of two liturgical Gospel books of the region: Bitonto, Biblioteca Comunale A 45, and the evangelistary without shelf-number in the Cathedral of Bisceglie.[3]

Many characteristics of the Bari-type script are to be seen in this document.[4] *S* and *F* do not descend below the base line;[5] broken *C* is used regularly except after *E*; two nearly equal curves make up large *E*; the *FI* ligature, not so large as is often found in Pugliese scripts, rests on the base line; final *R* is short; medial *R* in ligature with *E*, *A*, etc., is straight-shouldered. Uncharacteristic of this type, however, are the ligatures *GI* and *EI*, which are joined at a clear right angle.[6] An unusual form of the letter *A*, an uncial form with a partially detached loop extending well below the base line, occurs three times (fol. Av, line 4, "alleluia"; lines 9 and 13, "aurum").[7]

Abbreviations are infrequent, as is typical of texts written to be accompanied by musical notation, and they follow the Beneventan procedures, though they do not use the abbreviation-stroke with superscript point typical of many Puglian scribes. The Nomina Sacra appear (*dñs*, fol. Zr, line 7), as well as the standard signs for the syllables *pro*, *per* (fol. Ar, line 3), *pre* (fol. Zr, line 7); *qui* (fol. Zr, line 1), *bis* (fol. Ar, line 14). The word "omnes" is abbreviated in the older system (*om̄s*, fol. Zr, line 10).[8] Final *-us* is indicated both by a 3-shaped sign (fol. Zr, line 4) and by a sign resembling a semicolon (fol. Zv, line 1). Final *M* looks like a superscript 3 (fol. Av, line 5), except for the word "dum" (fol. Zr, line 10), which evidently

---

[3] A study with many facsimiles of the Bitonto evangelistary is Francesco Magistrale, *Il codice A 45 della Biblioteca Comunale "E. Rogadeo" di Bitonto* (Bari, 1984); on both manuscripts, see Giulia Orofino, "Gli evangeliari in Beneventana di Bisceglie e di Bitonto e la produzione miniaturistica in Puglia nel XII secolo," in *I codici liturgici in Puglia* (Bari, [1986]), 197–232.

[4] E. A. Loew, *The Beneventan Script: A History of the South Italian Minuscule* [= TBS], second edition prepared and enlarged by Virginia Brown, 2 vols., Sussidi eruditi 33–34 (Rome, 1980), 1:150.

[5] An exception is the *S* in "hierusalem," fol. Av, line 3.

[6] Loew cites a rounded form of these ligatures as typical of the Bari type. See TBS 1:143–44. Examples of *GI* here: "regis," fol. Ar, line 8; "magi," fol. Ar, lines 4, 5. *EI* is found on fol. Av, line 5.

[7] The same form is found in Bitonto A 45, fol. 68: see Magistrale, *Il codice A 45*, p. 22 and facsimile, p. 65.

[8] See TBS 1:210–13.

lacks an abbreviation-stroke; final superscript *S* is found in the Greek word "Thalas" (fol. Av, line 7); enclitic *-que* is indicated by a stroke added to the final letter; and the final letter of words ending in *-nt* takes its characteristic altered form.

Punctuation on these folios is limited to two signs: a point set slightly above the base line, and used for more important pauses and endings; and, rarely, a diagonal stroke to indicate subsidiary pauses (for example, the stroke preceding "alleluia," fol. Av, line 7).

The musical notation is fully diastematic, oriented on the three dry-point lines left blank between lines of text. C- and F-clefs are used, but, as will be seen, they are not used for the portions of the music in Beneventan chant on folio Z. As in all Beneventan notation, the direct appears at the end of each line, and is here often used as well in the course of a line to reposition the notation (e.g., fol. Av, line 12, after "letantur"), and after a psalmodic ending to show the pitch for the reprise of the antiphon (e.g., fol. Av, line 4, before "Magi").

The neumes are carefully written and follow the traditions of Beneventan notation. Of particular interest is the presence of the quilisma, an undulating neume that generally disappears from Beneventan notation at the beginning of the twelfth century (one such quilisma is on the first syllable of "celestis," fol. Av, line 10). A relatively rare sign is the Beneventan episema, a hairline stroke used here at the ends of groups of strophic neumes, and virtually invisible in the plates. This is a feature of some manuscripts of the later eleventh century, such as Benevento, Biblioteca Capitolare 40, and Vatican City, Biblioteca Apostolica Vaticana Ottob. lat. 145.

The two leaves of this bifolium are from an antiphoner of the Office; they are not consecutive, and hence not the innermost in their quire. It is not possible to determine whether the antiphoner is of monastic or secular use, as the responsories on folio Ar are not numbered, and the number of antiphons for Lauds and the day hours on folio Av is a series equally suitable for monastic or secular Lauds.[9]

The contents fall into two groups: folio A contains responsories and antiphons from the Roman office for Epiphany, using material generally known all over Europe, though there is the unusual feature of a Greek

---

[9] Of related Beneventan books (see below, p. 351 and notes 12–15), the one representative of what seems to be the secular Office, Benevento 19, is the most distant from the Bisceglie fragment in terms of the selection and order of chants for the Epiphany. The presence of a responsory before *Benedictus* at Lauds would be a characteristic sign of the monastic Office; but its absence here cannot be given much weight, since the responsory is often missing in other monastic books of the Beneventan zone.

version of one of the antiphons; folio Z, by contrast, contains unknown music in a style that makes clear that these pieces are part of the Beneventan liturgy, used in southern Italy before the coming of Gregorian chant. We will consider each of these groups in turn.

Folio A contains the following pieces:

Folio Ar [Matins of Epiphany]

1. "... puerum cum maria matre eius, et procidentes adoraverunt eum" (end of ℣. *Et intrantes* of ℟. *Stella quam viderunt;* CAO[10] 7701)
2. ℟. *Videntes stella* [*sic*] ℣. *Stella quam viderunt*[11] (CAO 7864)
3. ℟. *Tria sunt munera* ℣. *Salutis nostre* (CAO 7777)
4. ℟. *Hic est dies preclarus* ℣. *Dies sanctificatus* (CAO 6821)

Folio Av [Lauds of Epiphany]

5. a. *Ante luciferum* (CAO 1434)
6. a. *Venit lumen* (CAO 5344)
7. a. *Magi viderunt* (CAO 3654)
8. a. *Maria et flumina* (CAO 3700)
9. a. *Thalas ke potamie* (Greek version of *Maria et flumina*)
10. a. *Apertis thesauris* (CAO 1447)
11. a. [*ad Benedictus*] *Hodie celestis* [*sic*] *sponso* (CAO 3095)

[antiphons for the weekdays after Epiphany?]

12. a. *Tria sunt munera* (CAO 5181)
13. a. *Omnes de Saba venient* (incomplete; CAO 4119?)
14. "... cum ymnis in eternum domino. Deo gratias" (on an additional line in the bottom margin, but perhaps by the same hand, an incomplete troped *Benedicamus Domino*).

These antiphons and responsories are evidently a portion of the office for the Epiphany. Folio Ar includes the final responsories of Matins, and the large initial *A* on the verso marks the beginning of Lauds. The arrangement of these pieces is closely paralleled by the four surviving noted witnesses

---

[10] These numbers refer to the catalogue and editions of antiphons and responsories found in vols. 3–4 of René-Jean Hesbert, *Corpus antiphonalium officii* [= CAO], 6 vols., Rerum ecclesiasticarum documenta, series maior, fontes 7–12 (Rome, 1963–79).

[11] The verse *Stella* does not include the variant listed in CAO for manuscript *L* (Benevento 21; see next note).

of this office from southern Italy, although none of them has the remarkable Greek translation of *Maria et flumina*. The responsories and antiphons here are precisely those of Benevento 21[12] and Montecassino 542.[13] Benevento 22 lacks the responsory *Videntes stellam* but is otherwise entirely in accord.[14] Benevento 19, whose Matins have nine responsories, is the farthest removed from the Bisceglie fragment. Its office uses none of the responsories preserved here; it inverts the order of two Lauds antiphons; and the antiphon *Omnes de Saba* does not appear.[15]

Particularly remarkable in this otherwise normal Gregorian office is the presence of an evidently supernumerary antiphon in Greek. This is a transliteration in Latin letters of a text which is a Greek version of the antiphon *Maria et flumina* (fol Av, line 8). The text is derived from the first half-verses of Daniel 3:77–78, but in inverse order; the Greek text apparently has the same vocabulary as the Septuagint, though the transmission here is far from clear.[16] The transliteration is as follows:

Thalas ke potamie eblogite ton kyrion. ymnodi to pige ton kyrion alliluia.

[θάλασσαι καὶ ποταμοί εὐλογεῖτε τὸν κύριον· ὑμνεῖτε, αἱ πηγαί τὸν κύριον, ἀλληλούια.]

Its melody is the same in both versions, adapted only slightly for the needs of the two texts; on the basis of the somewhat unsatisfactory matching of melody to text in the Greek version, it appears that the Latin version may be the original.

---

[12] Benevento, Biblioteca Capitolare 21; in CAO this is siglum *L*, a late twelfth- or early thirteenth-century antiphoner of uncertain provenance, but almost certainly not from the Beneventan monastery of San Lupo. The manuscript was formerly called V.21; I follow the practice of dropping the Roman numerals, no longer useful, as adopted in the catalogue by Jean Mallet and André Thibaut, *Les manuscrits en écriture bénéventaine de la Bibliothèque capitulaire de Bénévent*, vol. 1 (Paris, 1984). The order of pieces for the Epiphany can be seen in CAO 2:103–9. The antiphon *Tria sunt* is one of two antiphons for the single nocturn of feria 2, and *Omnes de Saba* is one of two for feria 3.

[13] Montecassino, Archivio della Badia 542, an incomplete monastic antiphoner of the second half of the twelfth century; pages 34–41 contain the parallel portions for the Epiphany. *Tria sunt* is one of two antiphons marked *Fr ij ad noct*, while *Omnes de Saba* is the single antiphon for feria 3.

[14] Benevento, Biblioteca Capitolare 22, a noted monastic breviary of the twelfth century, fols. 88r–91r.

[15] Benevento, Biblioteca Capitolare 19, a twelfth-century mixed breviary-missal with notation, *pars hiemalis;* a companion volume is Benevento 20. The antiphons at Lauds (fols. 165v–166r) are *Ante luciferum, Venit lumen, Apertis, Maria et flumina, Magi*, and *Hodie celesti*. The antiphon for Terce is *Tria sunt munera* (fol. 166r).

[16] The Septuagint version of these verses reads εὐλογεῖτε, αἱ πηγαί, τὸν κύριον· ὑμνεῖτε καὶ ὑπερυψοῦτε αὐτὸν εἰς τοὺς αἰῶνας. εὐλογεῖτε, θάλασσαι καὶ ποταμοί, τὸν κύριον· ὑμνεῖτε καὶ ὑπερυψοῦτε αὐτὸν εἰς τοὺς αἰῶνας. I am grateful to Professor Nathan Greenberg of Oberlin College for advice on the Greek text.

This piece is not, to my knowledge, used in this form in the Byzantine liturgy.[17] The presence of a Greek text, however, in a Beneventan liturgical manuscript is not so rare as it might seem. Six other antiphons, all of them used in the rites of Holy Week, are found in double Latin/Greek forms in at least some manuscripts of the Beneventan zone. In addition the Greek sticheron *Pascha ieron* is found in manuscripts in Beneventan script in manuscripts at Benevento and at Florence.[18] That Greek music should be found in Puglia is surely no surprise in view of the long tradition of Byzantine involvement (though not always friendly) with the region of Bari. Latin scribes, however, seldom wrote down what they evidently regularly heard. There is little place in the official liturgy for music in Greek;[19] but our scribe evidently had heard this music, for he writes down the pronunciation, not the transliteration, of the antiphon.[20]

* * *

For the contents of folio Z we provide a transcription, as these texts are otherwise mostly unattested.

---

[17] See Henrica [Enrica] Follieri, *Initia hymnorum ecclesiae graecae*, 5 vols. in 6, Studi e testi 211–15bis (Vatican City, 1960–66).

[18] Details of these Greek pieces and their appearances are in Thomas Forrest Kelly, *The Beneventan Chant* [=TBC] (Cambridge, 1989), 206–17; not mentioned there is the appearance of *Pascha ieron* in Florence, Biblioteca Medicea Laurenziana MS 33.31, fol. 45r + MS 29.8, fol. 77v (the latter folio pasted over with paper); I am grateful to Professor Virginia Brown for calling my attention to this witness.

[19] This piece adds to the number of connections between the Greek language and the feast of the Epiphany in the West. The famous group of antiphons (the *Veterem hominem* series) reportedly translated from the Greek for Charlemagne serves for the Octave of the Epiphany: see Jacques Handschin, "Sur quelques tropaires grecs traduits en latin," *Annales musicologiques* 2 (1954): 27–60; Joseph Lemarié, "Les antiennes 'Veterem hominem' du jour octave de l'Épiphanie et les antiennes d'origine grecque de l'Épiphanie," *Ephemerides liturgicae* 72 (1958): 3–38; Oliver Strunk, "The Latin Antiphons for the Octave of the Epiphany," in *Recueil de travaux de l'Institut d'Études byzantines 7: Mélanges Georges Ostrogorsky* 2 (Belgrade, 1964), 417–26, reprinted in Strunk, *Essays on Music in the Byzantine World* (New York, 1977), 208–19; and one of the antiphons sung in Greek and Latin for the second adoration of the Cross on Good Friday in the old Beneventan liturgy is *Omnes gentes* / *Panta ta etni*, whose Latin form is used in the Gregorian liturgy for Epiphany: see Kelly, TBC, 214–15.

[20] Such words as "eblogite" suggest an aural process; indeed, the scribe seems to be writing heard (or remembered) Latin: he writes "Hodie celestis sponso" instead of "celesti"; in the antiphon *Venit lumen* he writes "illumine" instead of "in lumine"; and on fol. Av, line 8, he writes "alliluia." On the question of Latin music-scribes writing Greek, see Charles M. Atkinson, "The *Doxa*, the *Pisteuo*, and the *ellinici fratres*: Some Anomalies in the Transmission of the Chants of the 'Missa graeca,'" *The Journal of Musicology* 7 (1989): 81–106.

A Musical Fragment at Bisceglie Containing an Unknown Beneventan Office.

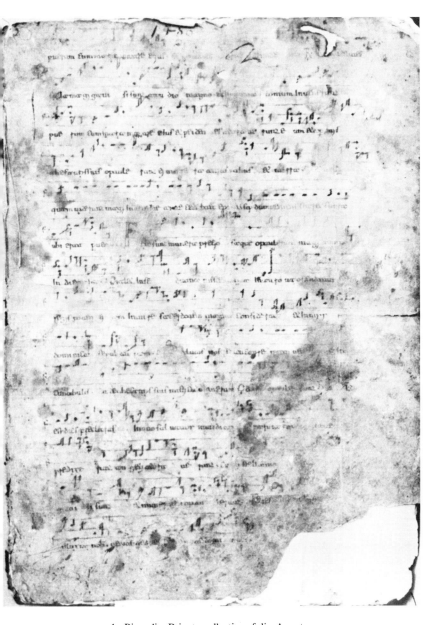

1. Bisceglie, Private collection, folio A recto.

A Musical Fragment at Bisceglie Containing an Unknown Beneventan Office.

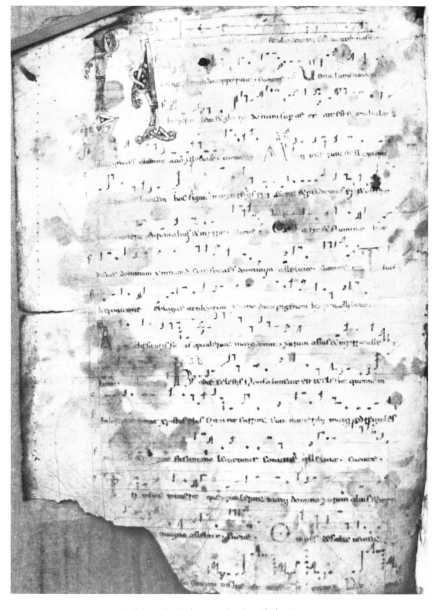

2. Bisceglie, Private collection, folio A verso.

A Musical Fragment at Bisceglie Containing an Unknown Beneventan Office.

3. Bisceglie, Private collection, folio Z recto.

A Musical Fragment at Bisceglie Containing an Unknown Beneventan Office.

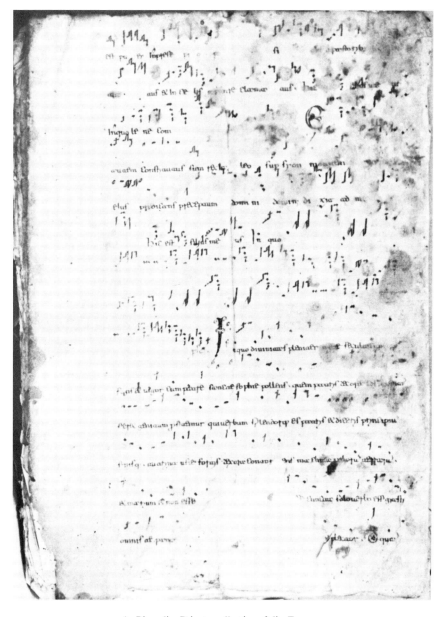

4. Bisceglie, Private collection, folio Z verso.

Folio Zr [Beneventan office of the Octave of Epiphany?]

15. (℣) ... cum letentur; quia statim ut ex virginem natus est xpistus.

16. <a.> Hodie celi letati sunt et mare dulce factum est quia a iohannes in iordane dominus baptizatus est. <Ps.> Benedicite dominum.[21]

℣. Celi apostolos et mare gentes designant; in quibus dulce xpistianum nomen destillat.

17. a. Baptiza me iohannes baptiza benedicam te et tu iordane gaudens suscipe me ego hodie sanctificabo fontes aquarum.[22] <Ps.> Dominus regit me.

℣. Filius dei altissimi quem preco ostendendo[23] predixit; pro inplenda iustitia adveniens dixit.

18. Iordanis fluvius se retenuit intrante domino aqua contremuit nova creatio surgit de flumine qui illuminat omne seculum. <Ps.> Omnes gentes.

℣. Du<m> nostra crimina baptismo suo lavisset; et suum dominum ac creatorem sensisset. Iordanis.[24]

19. <R.> Ecce completa sunt omnia que predicta sunt marie virginis; <...>-minus; Natus /folio Zv/ est puer in presepio; positus a pastoribus demonstratus et in celis a patre clamatus; hic est filius meus in quo bene com<placui>.

℣. Ego autem constitutus sum rex labeo super syon montem sanctum eius predicans preceptum domini dominus dixit ad me hic est filius meus in quo

20. Prosa. In quo

divinitas pleniter ante secula <...>

fons et vigor cum patre sancte sophie pollens

quem patris decora co<...>mam fieret genitum profitemur

qui verbum splendorque es patris et diceris principium finisque;

---

[21] Compare the text of the responsory *Hodie coeli aperti sunt* (CAO 6846), which appears in Benevento 21 for the Epiphany.

[22] Compare the text of the antiphon CAO 5062 ("Super ripam Jordanis stabat beatus Joannes; indutus est splendore, baptizans Salvatorem: Baptiza me, Joannes, baptiza, benedico te; et tu, Jordanis, congaudens suscipe me"), which appears in Benevento 19, fol. 272r, for the Octave of the Epiphany; see also Handschin, "Sur quelques tropaires," 30–31 and n. 2; Lemarié, "Les antiennes," 32–33, 37.

[23] The scribe has added the third syllable above the line.

[24] The texts of this antiphon and its verse are used in Benevento 21, fols. 43v–44r, as the third and fourth of four verses attached to the antiphon *Precursor Johannes* for the Octave of the Epiphany; see CAO 4358. The melody of *Jordanis fluvius* in Benevento 21 is the same as that found here, though the melodies of *Dum nostra crimina* are different. The melody of *Jordanis fluvius*, with its literal internal repetition and its little similarity to other melodies of the Beneventan rite, raises complex questions about the origin of these melodies and texts which must be saved for another occasion.

tu trina usie fortis dextra contor<qu>ens machina polorum terrarum
   et marium
et non esse <.....>-se cuncta solo verbo effigiasti omnis te pant<.....>
   plector.
O quam/ / / / / /

We do not have the beginning of this office, where an opening rubric might
have indicated the feast; but the office is probably a doublet—a Beneventan
office which would have followed the Gregorian office for the same feast.
But that feast is evidently not the Epiphany. Normally the Beneventan office
should follow immediately after the Gregorian office for the same feast.
Here, however, at least one folio, and more likely a bifolium, has intervened,
and the missing end of the Gregorian office together with the beginning
of the Beneventan could hardly occupy a full folio. Since there was intervening material, and since the Beneventan texts focus on the baptism of
Christ by John the Baptist, the likely feast is the Octave of the Epiphany,
which from at least the ninth century focusses on this biblical event.[25] The
lost rubric might also have indicated that the music to follow belongs to
the old Beneventan chant; such indications are used eight times in other
manuscripts that combine the two rites.[26] An example of such a rubric is
that attached to the Vespers for St. John the Baptist in the so-called Solesmes
Flyleaves, also in a private collection,[27] whose opening rubric reads *vig<ilia>
s. iohannis bapt. a<nt>. ambro. ad vesp.*, that is, Ambrosian antiphons
for Vespers, following the Gregorian antiphons that had preceded.[28] If the
now-incomplete Bisceglie manuscript included a normal Gregorian office
(of the Octave of the Epiphany?) followed by this special Beneventan office,
a warning rubric would probably have been needed.

   This Beneventan office resembles in many details the other two surviving
offices of the Beneventan liturgy. As is the case in the Vespers of the Solesmes
Flyleaves and in the Vespers of Good Friday surviving in several manuscripts,[29] each antiphon here is followed by a *versus ad repetendum*, a non-

---

[25] See Amalarius of Metz, *Liber de ordine antiphonarii* 25: "Sicut certavit scola cantorum
in epiphania frequentare adventum magorum, simili modo certat in octavis epiphaniae
frequentare baptismum Christi, quasi ipsa die baptizatus esset" (ed. Jean Michel Hanssens,
Amalarii episcopi Opera liturgica omnia 3, Studi e testi 140 [Vatican City, 1950], 61).

[26] See Kelly, TBC, 181–82.

[27] For a study of this fragment and a facsimile, see Thomas Kelly, "Une nouvelle source
pour l'office vieux-bénéventain," *Études grégoriennes* 22 (1988): 5–23; see also Kelly, TBC,
94–95, 312.

[28] Beneventan chant is regularly called Ambrosian by its scribes; see Kelly, TBC, 181–83.

[29] Benevento 38, fol. 43r–v; Benevento 39, fol. 25r–v; Benevento 40, fol. 43r–v; Lucca,
Biblioteca Capitolare Feliniana MS 606 (an eleventh-century missal in ordinary minuscule

psalmodic text set to the music of the psalm-tone and sung after the psalm as a prelude to the reprise of the antiphon.[30]

Folio Z begins with the end of a *versus ad repetendum*, to judge from its melodic shape. Since an antiphon must have preceded, the full office must consist of at least four antiphons followed by a great responsory. However, since both the other surviving Beneventan offices conclude with *Magnificat*, and since none of these antiphons is followed by a canticle (*Magnificat* or *Benedictus*), we can suppose that following the responsory there must have been at least one further antiphon, for the canticle.

* * *

That different patterns of transmission lie behind these two offices, Gregorian and Beneventan, is evident from the two ways of indicating psalmody at the ends of antiphons. Each Gregorian antiphon is followed by *euouae* (the vowels of *seculorum amen*) to serve as text for the neumes of the psalmodic ending; the Beneventan antiphons follow an equally familiar procedure giving the incipit of the psalm with the music of the psalm-tone ending written above it.[31]

The reponsory *Ecce completa sunt*, folio Zv, followed by a prosula, has a somewhat confusing layout. The respond ends on lines 2–3 with the text "hic est filius meus in quo bene complacui," followed by the verse *Ego autem constitutus.*[32] Near the end of the verse, the reprise of the respond is written out: "hic est filius meus in quo"; but the melody stops at "quo" for the enormous melisma that occupies lines 6 through 9. This melisma

---

but with Beneventan notation in this section), fol. 156r–v; three later manuscripts, all in non-Beneventan hands and all without musical notation for the texts in question, also transmit the Beneventan Vespers: Subiaco, Biblioteca del Protocenobio di Santa Scolastica XVIII (19), fol. 77r–v; Salerno, Archivio del Museo del Duomo, MS without shelf-number (no. 3 in Arturo Capone, *Il duomo di Salerno*, 2 vols. [Salerno, 1927]), fol. 130r; Salerno, MS without shelf-number (Capone 4), fols. 134v–135r.

[30] Such verses do exist outside the Beneventan liturgy, of course; see, for example, the office of St. Lawrence (CAO offices 50[3] and 103); on *versus ad repetendum* used with introits in Beneventan manuscripts, see *Paléographie musicale,* vol. 14 (Tournai, 1931; rpt. Berne, 1971), 207.

[31] This latter procedure is used for the Beneventan Vespers of Good Friday in Benevento 38, 39, and 40; the Solesmes Flyleaves give only the *versus ad repetendum* after the antiphons, with no psalm and no psalm-tone formula. The system of combining psalm-text with tone-ending is, however, not unique to the transmission of Beneventan chant; it is used, for example, in the (Gregorian) offices transmitted in Benevento 22, a noted breviary of the twelfth century.

[32] The beginning of this verse is melodically very similar to the verse *Ecce terremotus* of the Beneventan responsory *Tenebre.* See the trancription in Kelly, TBC, 136, and the facsimiles in *Paléographie musicale* 14, plates 61 (Vat. lat. 10673) and XVI–XVII (Benevento 40).

may be an addition to the original melody,[33] in order to accommodate the prosula *In quo divinitas* which follows immediately and which is set syllabically to the melody of the melisma. The prosula here is incomplete, finishing on the nonextant following folio.

The Bisceglie fragment provides new evidence concerning the relationship between the Old Beneventan and the Ambrosian liturgies which confirms many other musical and textual similarities between the Milanese and the Beneventan liturgies.[34] The text of the Bisceglie responsory *Ecce completa sunt* is used as a responsory *cum infantibus* in the Milanese liturgy at Second Vespers of the Epiphany.[35] And despite their many differences, the two melodies are so similar as to make clear the musical relationship between these two pieces, and to reinforce the growing awareness of the close relationship of these two "Lombard" liturgies.[36]

[33] This melisma does not have the appearance of a Beneventan melody; the frequent strophic neumes (appearing as groups of two or three lozenges) are not typical of Beneventan melody; the double cursus, which shapes the entire melody, and the repetition of brief figures are also unusual in Beneventan musical procedure.

[34] On musical and textual parallels between Milan and Benevento, see Kelly, TBC, 181–203; see also Thomas Forrest Kelly, "Beneventan and Milanese Chant," *Journal of the Royal Musical Association* 112 (1987): 173–95; idem, "Non-Gregorian Music in an Antiphoner of Benevento," *The Journal of Musicology* 5 (1987): 478–97; Terence Bailey, "Ambrosian Chant in Southern Italy," *Journal of the Plainsong and Mediaeval Music Society* 6 (1983): 1–7.

[35] It appears, for example, in London, British Library Add. 34209 (pp. 112–13), an Ambrosian *pars hiemalis* of the twelfth century. See the facsimile published as *Paléographie musicale*, vol. 5 (Solesmes, 1896); the piece is transcribed in *Paléographie musicale*, vol. 6 (Solesmes, 1900), 125–26.

[36] The reader who can compare our plate 4 with the facsimile in *Paléographie musicale* 5 will not need to be an expert to recognize very similar melodic contours in the neumes of such passage as "in quo bene," "constitutus sum," "predicans preceptum," and others. At the same time, the Bisceglie melody is closely related to the Beneventan chant by its regular use of standard melodic formulae.

VIII

A Beneventan Borrowing
in the Saint Cecilia Gradual

The publication by Max Lütolf of the gradual made in 1071 for the basilica of Saint Cecilia in Rome[1] has made available to scholars one of the most important documents of the so-called Old Roman chant.[2]

The Saint Cecilia gradual, now Cologny, Bibliotheca Bodmeriana ms. 74, is the oldest of the three sources of Old Roman music for the mass, but it is in some ways the least conservative of the three. In particular, it contains many sequences, mostly borrowed from elsewhere; of the other two Old Roman graduals, one has no sequences at all: this is the thirteenth-century book for St. Peter's, now Vatican, Biblioteca Apostolica Vaticana [BAV] San Pietro F. 22; and the other has sequences, but gathers them in an appendix: this is the gradual, probably only a little younger than the Saint Cecilia gradual, and probably made for the Lateran Basilica, now Vatican, Bibl. Vaticana Vat. lat. 5319.

The St. Cecilia gradual was written by John the Priest, who signed and dated the manuscript in a romanesca minuscule which is accompanied by musical notation showing a strong similarity to the Beneventan notation of southern Italy. In assembling the gradual, John sought to embellish the liturgy of Santa Cecilia with additional liturgical material, and he sought it in large measure in the repertories of southern Italy, among the books of Montecassino and Benevento.

His gradual contains three Alleluias whose melodies are drawn from the repertory of the Old Beneventan chant. (Although I had previously noted one of these Alleluias,[3] it was my friend Professor Alejandro Planchart who first pointed out two further adaptations, and credit goes to him in the first instance along with my thanks.) The third mass of Christmas (introit *Puer natus*), and the masses of Epiphany and Easter, each have a Beneventan Alleluia which follows the normal Alleluia of the Roman mass.

Christmas 3, f. 12v: Al. *Hodie natus est nobis dominus, gaudent omnes angeli in celo*, second verse *Gaudete in domino semper gaudete cum letitia quia natus est nobis saluator mundi* with sequence *Ecce annuntio celicole*
Epiphany, f. 19v: Al. *Hodie baptizatus est dominus in iordane ab Iohanne Baptista* with sequence *Gaudent omnes celicole*
Easter, f. 80v: Al. *Resurrexit tanquam dormiens dominus quasi potens crapulatus a uino* with sequence *Quem queritis mulieres*

All three of these Alleluias have the melody of the Old Beneventan Alleluia *Resurrexit*, which is used in the St. Cecilia gradual for Easter, though in the Old Beneventan liturgy it is used for Holy Saturday in the earlier sources. This unusual text, likening the risen Christ to a drunken man, is otherwise unattested in the Roman liturgy, although it is a regular feature of the Ambrosian rite.[4] The second verse *Gaudete* of the Alleluia *Hodie natus est* has the melody of the Beneventan verse *Laudate pueri*, which serves as a second verse to *Resurrexit* in five graduals of Benevento and in the palimpsests in Vat. lat. 10657; in the Farfa fragments *Laudate pueri* appears as the only verse. This second verse for Easter, as Kenneth Levy has pointed out, may be related to the process of admitting catechumens to baptism, and the double-verse complex reflects an amalgamation of the double significance of the day: resurrection and initiation.[5] This verse *Laudate pueri* itself is not found in the Saint Cecilia gradual; nevertheless, its melody, and the double-verse tradition of which it is a part, continue even where it is no longer related to the feast, as is seen in the Saint Cecilia gradual for Christmas. Evidently, though, the second verse of *Hodie natus est* was not made in Rome.

The Beneventan Hodie-complex of Alleluias

The sources in Beneventan script for *Resurrexit* are the following:

Benevento, Biblioteca Capitolare
    30 (gradual, s. 13), f. 75v   Easter Day
       verse 1 only
    33 (missal, s. 10/11), f. 79   Holy Saturday
       verse 1 only
    34 (gradual, s. 12 1/2), f. 126   Easter Day
       2 verses, the second marked ›non‹ in a later hand
    35 (gradual, s. 12 in.), f. 68   Holy Saturday
       2 verses
    38 (gradual, s. 11 1/2), f. 46v   Holy Saturday
       2 verses, second marked ›prosa‹

39 (gradual, s. I I ex.), f. 27v	Holy Saturday
2 verses	
40 (gradual, s. I I 1/2), f. I9v	Holy Saturday
2 verses	

Montecassino, Archivio della Badia
    Compactiones V (breviary, s. I 1/12)   Easter vespers
        Alleluia and verse I presented as a responsory

Farfa, Bibl. dell'Abbazia
    AF. 338 Musica XI (gradual, s. I I) Holy Saturday
        verse 2 only[6]

Baltimore, Walters Art Gallery
    W 6 (missal, s. I I 2/2), f. I24v   Holy Saturday
        verse I only

Rome, Biblioteca Apostolica Vaticana
    Vat. lat. 10657 (gradual, s. I I), f. A   Holy Saturday
        2 verse

Some of these manuscripts transmit adaptations of the Alleluia *Resurrexit*, all of which begin with the word *Hodie:*

Alleluia V. *Hodie natus est nobis* Baltimore, Walters W. 6, f. 86 Christmas
Alleluia V. *Hodie migravit ad Dominum* Benevento 39, f. 121 St. Peter
Alleluia V. *Hodie transfiguratus est Dominus* Benevento 39, f. 140v Transfiguration

To this list may now be added a second copy of *Hodie natus*, together with a new second verse, and a new member of the group, *Hodie baptizatus*, both from the Saint Cecilia gradual. This brings the number of Alleluia using this melody to five, three of them for the season before Easter: Christmas, Epiphany, and Holy Saturday. It may be that these are part of a larger series of Alleluias, now lost.

Given the lack of Beneventan sources for the period of the liturgical year that precedes Holy Week,[7] it is difficult to evaluate this phenomenon of *Hodie Alleluias*, with their Byzantine flavor.[8] For all that we know, this melody, with a variety of associated texts, might have been used for the entire year up to Easter in the Beneventan liturgy. For there is another melody, used for Easter Day and for almost all the feasts of the liturgical year which fall after Easter. Until now this other melody appeared to be essentially the only melody for the Beneventan Alleluia, with two exceptions: (1) *Resurrexit* for Holy Saturday and its adaptations, and (2) the Alleluia *Posuisti* for St. Stephen, found in the precious fragment of a pure Beneventan gradual which is now the final flyleaf,

f. 202, of Benevento 35. A change of melody between Holy Saturday and Easter reminds one of the Byzantine change of mode at the same point in the liturgical year;[9] and given the Byzantine flavor of the *Hodie* texts, a picture of the Beneventan liturgy as having two Alleluia-melodies is a possibility that ought to be considered.

The *Hodie* text for the Epiphany Alleluia matches very closely the theme of the Epiphany at Benevento. Despite the fact that no Epiphany mass survives in Beneventan chant (Benevento 38 and 40, which surely contained it, have lacunae for Epiphany), we know that at Benevento the Epiphany concentrated on the baptism of Christ, while the Roman rite centers on the visit of the Wise Men. The texts of the Beneventan vespers of the Epiphany in the Bisceglie fragment,[10] and a fragment in the palimpsest leaves of Rome, Biblioteca Vallicelliana C 9,[11] make the baptismal focus clear in the Beneventan rite. The Alleluia *Hodie baptizatus est Dominus in Iordane ab Iohanne Baptista* of the Bodmer manuscript is ill-suited to the theme of its adopted Roman mass, which in the Bodmer manuscript includes also the more appropriate Alleluia *Vidimus stellam*.

Other liturgical rites, especially ones thought to be relatively archaic, seem to have a limited number of Alleluia melodies which are adapted to a variety of verse-texts; there are essentially ten melodies at Milan;[12] the Old Roman rite shows a similar sort of adaptation;[13] and indeed the group of Gregorian Alleluias using the melody of the Christmas *Dies sanctificatus* is thought to represent a stage before the great medieval flowering of individual Alleluia-melodies.[14]

However, there is good reason to suggest that these Hodie-Alleluias are a later phenomenon, not part of the early layer of Beneventan chant.

That the *Resurrexit /Hodie* complex might be a melody serving for the first half of the liturgical year is somewhat confused by two issues: first, it appears in the second part of the year also, for St. Peter and for the Transfiguration. And there is another melody in the Beneventan liturgy, used for the Alleluia *Posuisti in capite eius* for St. Stephen, just mentioned; this same text is cued, but without music, as the Alleluia of the old Beneventan mass for St. Lawrence in Benevento 40. This melody, then, is apparently used in both halves of the liturgical year; and its presence for St. Stephen suggests that a Christmas cycle of Alleluias based on the *Resurrexit /Hodie* melody did not have exclusive application to all the masses in the cycle.

The second issue is that the *Hodie* adaptations appear to be relatively late. Although the Holy Saturday Alleluia *Resurrexit* is found in the earliest and central sources of Beneventan chant, the *Hodie* adaptations are found only in later (Benevento 39) or peripheral (Baltimore, Bodmer) manuscripts. Further, in the Bodmer manuscript the Alleluia *Resurrexit* is used for Easter, while in the early and central Beneventan sources it is the Alleluia for Holy Saturday;

the Bodmer borrowing, then, is relatively late, though of course that says nothing about the antiquity of its source or sources. But the *Hodie* text from Benevento 39 for the Gregorian mass of St. Peter, at least, must be a later creation, since if it were a regular and early part of the Beneventan liturgy it would surely be present also in the Beneventan masses for St. Peter which survive in the earlier Benevento 38 and Benevento 40.

How did these Alleluias come to Rome?

These Beneventan Alleluias in the Bodmer manuscript are not part of the central corpus of Roman chant. They appear as doublets in the Bodmer manuscript, each Beneventan Alleluia following another, usually Roman, Alleluia for the same mass; and these Beneventan pieces do not appear in either of the other Old Roman graduals. How then did they come to be included here?

Each of these Beneventan Alleluias in the Bodmer manuscript is accompanied by a sequence, and this doubtless explains the borrowing of Alleluias into a context where Alleluias are already provided: the scribe went in search of sequences to embellish and enrich his repertory, and he found them in a manuscript from southern Italy: in each of these cases he imported also the Alleluia that accompanied the sequence, even though the result was that these masses appeared to have two Alleluias.

This process of borrowing seems to apply to all twenty sequences in the Saint Cecilia gradual. They are not a part of the Roman liturgy as found in the other two Old Roman graduals: they have been incorporated into this book from elsewhere. This is not the place for a detailed study of the borrowed material in this manuscript, but a summary of some of the characteristics of these pieces makes it easier to consider the specifically Beneventan portions of this borrowed repertory.[15]

Sequences are evidently not a part of the Old Roman liturgy. Of the other two surviving Old Roman graduals, as we have seen, one has no sequences at all: this is the thirteenth-century Vatican, San Pietro F. 22. The other, Vat. lat. 5319, has no sequences in the main body of the gradual, but appends eight sequences, each with a (Gregorian) Alleluia, along with two other Alleluias for the Easter season. The Beneventan Alleluias of the St. Cecilia gradual do not appear in 5319. The 5319 arrangement seems to be an intermediate stage between San Pietro F. 22 and the situation in the Saint Cecilia gradual, where twenty sequences are incorporated into the main liturgical sequence of the gradual, without direct indication that they are not an original part of the liturgy.

In the Saint Cecilia gradual, all the sequences of 5319 are included among the twenty, except for *Epyphaniam domino canamus*, whose place is taken by *Gaudent omnes caelicolae*, which in turn is preceded by one of the Beneventan Alleluias. Did the scribe John replace one Alleluia/sequence pair in a received repertory with another? If so, he chose a different process on another occasion; for one of the 5319 sequences is not replaced when John has another sequence in mind for the same feast: *Rex omnipotens die hodierna*, one of the sequences of 5319, is the second sequence for the Ascension in Bodmer 74, preceded by no Alleluia but by the sequence *Ascendit deus in iubilo*. This is the only case where John provides two sequences for the same feast.

And if John is borrowing the 5319 repertory directly, he is evidently interested in the sequences only, and not in the Alleluias which accompany them in 5319: none of the Alleluias which precede the other seven sequences in 5319 is used with these (or any other) sequences in St. Cecilia.

Perhaps John took over the 5319 repertory wholesale and added to it, replacing all its Alleluias but only one of its sequences. He did not of course work from 5319 itself, which did not yet exist. But more likely is that he went himself to the well, and drew from the same waters as the scribe of 5319 using a larger vessel; that he chose most of the same sequences probably depends on the well itself. Among its contents were Beneventan Alleluias.

John the priest, like the scribe of 5319, attaches sequences to Alleluias. A sequence does not stand alone, except for the special cases of *Rex omnipotens* just mentioned, and the sequence *Lux de luce* for Holy Saturday, a sequence borrowed from Benevento and sung on a special day with a special Alleluia intoned by the celebrant.[16]

The sequences in the St. Cecilia gradual are preceded by Alleluias that appear nowhere else in the Old Roman manuscripts.[17] These unique Alleluias, of which our Beneventan examples are a small part, usually appear as doublets, as second Alleluias, following a more normal piece. Indeed, there is a considerable number of Alleluias evidently imported into the manuscript without sequences: at least twenty additional Alleluias (that is, in addition to Alleluias followed by sequences) in Bodmer 74 appear in none of the other Roman manuscripts, and may result from external borrowing. Most of these Alleluias are unusual; the Alleluias borrowed in 5319 are drawn mostly from what we now know as the Gregorian repertory; but the Alleluias in the Saint Cecilia gradual are generally unique or very little known.

Where did John go for his material? Alejandro Planchart's forthcoming study of the prosulas and proses at Rome will suggest that the material comes from a variety of sources, with large numbers of pieces from Beneventan, and especially Cassinese, repertories, but with many items from a more widespread Italian repertory, and others from northern Frankish repertories.[18] It seems clear that this is not a wholesale adaptation from the repertory of a single manuscript; certainly no manuscript survives which contains all of John's additions to the Roman liturgy. Our question here must be a simpler one: where did he get the Beneventan Alleluias?

Even though the scribe of Bodmer 74 has selected three versions of an Old Beneventan Alleluia-melody, his source was certainly not a manuscript of the Old Beneventan liturgy: he would not have found sequences in such a manuscript.[19] His source, at least for these Alleluias, was probably a ›Gregorian‹ gradual with tropes and sequences like those found at Benevento. The sequences that he imported with them are certainly ones known in Italy, and used in Beneventan manuscripts.[20] Unfortunately his hypothetical source manuscript seems no longer to exist: or at least, the portion he used has not survived.

One manuscript that might have served as a source for the Bodmer gradual is Benevento 39; this manuscript has the Alleluia *Resurrexit*, and two adaptations of its melody, both beginning with the word *Hodie* (*Hodie migravit* and *Hodie transfiguratus*), as we have seen. It could also have contained the other two *Hodie* Alleluias known in Bodmer; but the manuscript is now incomplete, beginning with the Monday before Palm Sunday: we cannot know what the Alleluias were for Christmas and the Epiphany.

The source may well have been a manuscript much like Benevento 39: but it was not Benevento 39 itself. Bodmer's version of the Alleluia *Resurrexit* is not that of Benevento 39: Bodmer omits the prosula *Laudes ordo* present in Benevento 39 (and in Benevento 38), and omits the second verse *Laudate*. This selective borrowing would of course have been possible for the scribe; but in Benevento 39 the Alleluia is not accompanied by the sequence *Quem queritis mulieres*, which was surely the reason for the borrowing in the first place; the sequence is used instead for Easter Thursday. The Bodmer scribe's Beneventan manuscript doubtless contained the Alleluia *Resurrexit* followed by *Quem queritis mulieres;* but there is now no surviving manuscript in Beneventan script that provides this combination.

But it seems entirely possible that such a manuscript existed. Although there are only seven graduals in Beneventan script that survive more or less complete, there are surviving fragments of fifty-one additional graduals, and the estimate of additional manuscripts of which no trace remains might range around five hundred.

The manuscript might well have traveled to Rome, to the important scriptorium of Santa Cecilia,[21] from the monastery of Montecassino. It should be remembered that the cardinal priest of Santa Cecilia at the time of the copying of the Saint Cecilia gradual was Desiderius, abbot of Montecassino, cardinal priest of Santa Cecilia since 1058 and elevated to the Papacy as Victor III in 1086. Desiderius is Montecassino's greatest abbot, who presided over the renewal of the buildings, the books, and the liturgy of his monastery.[22] That Desiderius should have had some influence on the important activities of eleventh-century

Santa Cecilia has often been supposed, but remains to be demonstrated in detail.[23]

Nevertheless, a few facts may help to suggest further avenues of exploration. It has been demonstrated that the Beneventan chant was used at Montecassino and was probably well known to Desiderius, who had been a monk of the monastery of Santa Sofia at Benevento, once the center of Beneventan chant.[24] It is known, as well, despite the evident eradication of the Beneventan chant at Montecassino,[25] that the Alleluia melody of interest to us, namely *Resurrexit*, was known there: it survives, albeit in the form of a Responsory, in a fragment in the Compactiones mentioned above. It appears that this melody, despite the suppression of the Beneventan chant, survived as an Alleluia among the Gregorian repertory (much as it does in Benevento 39, with its additional *Hodie* adaptations). As such, it should have been included among the many books produced under Desiderius at Montecassino as part of the process of renewing the liturgy of the abbey and its books.[26] That such books made their way to Rome is evident from the inclusion of the Alleluias in the Bodmer gradual, and also, no doubt, from the Beneventan look of the musical notation itself used in the city from the eleventh century onward. Further attention to repertories on the one hand, and to matters of historical connections and book-production on the other, may lead us towards a clearer view of the complex and poorly understood history of book-production in medieval Rome.

---

[1] *Das Graduale von Santa Cecilia in Trastevere*, ed. Max Lütolf, 2 vols., Coligny-Genève 1987 (= *Bibliotheca Bodmeriana* 2).

[2] Access to the manuscript was for a long time considerably restricted; nevertheless, its existence and general outlines have been noted: see Jacques Hourlier and Michel Huglo, *Un important témoin du chant ›vieux-romain‹: Le Graduel de Sainte-Cécile du Trastévère*, in: *Revue grégorienne* 31 (1952), pp. 36–37; Thomas Connolly, *The Graduale of S. Cecilia in Trastevere and the Old Roman Tradition*, in: *JAMS* 28 (1975), pp. 413–58; for the relation of the manuscript to other old-Roman sources see Michel Huglo, *Le Chant ›vieux-romain‹: Liste des sources et témoins* indirects, in: *Sacris erudiri* 6 (1954), pp. 96–124.

[3] See Thomas Forrest Kelly, *The Beneventan Chant*, Cambridge 1989, p. 288.

[4] At Milan the text is used, as at Benevento, as the Alleluia for Holy Saturday; the text regularly has »Resurrexit tamquam dormiens dominus, quasi *potans* crapulatus a uino«, whereas the Beneventan text has *potens*, with the sole exception of Benevento 35 (*potans*); see Kelly, *Beneventan Chant*, p. 288.

[5] Kenneth Levy, *The Italian Neophytes' Chants*, in: *JAMS* 23 (1970), pp. 181–227, especially pp. 183, 219–220.

[6] This source is a fragmentary bifolium. The neumes of the second verse follow the Alleluia, but their text has been cut off at the

bottom of the page; whether anything followed this verse is now impossible to determine.

[7] Four of the five graduals in the Chapter Library at Benevento are now lacking their Advent and Christmas sections: see Kelly, *Beneventan Chant*, pp. 300–303.

[8] See Anton Baumstark, *Die Hodie-Antiphonen*, in: *Die Kirchenmusik* 10 (1910), pp. 153–60.

[9] See Levy, *Neophytes' Chants*, pp. 218–220.

[10] See Thomas Forrest Kelly, *A Musical Fragment at Bisceglie Containing an Unknown Beneventan Office*, in: *Mediaeval Studies* 55 (1993), forthcoming.

[11] See Kelly, *Beneventan Chant*, p. 67; the palimpsest is described in idem, *Palimpsest Evidence of an Old Beneventan Gradual*, in: *KJb* 67 (1983), pp. 5–23.

[12] Terence Bailey, *The Ambrosian Alleluias*, Egham: The Plainsong and Mediaeval Music Society 1983, pp. 46–52 and 88–91.

[13] The Old Roman melodies are transcribed from Vatican MS Vat. lat. 5319 in Margareta Landwehr-Melnicki and Bruno Stäblein, *Die Gesänge des altrömischen Graduale Vat. lat. 5319*, Kassel and elsewhere 1970 (= *Monumenta monodica medii aevi* 2), facsimiles are in Lütolf, *Das Graduale*. Another view of the Old Roman Alleluias, with a suggestion that there may actually be a large number of old melodies, is Philippe Bernard, *Les alléluias mélismatiques dans le chant roman: recherches sur la genèse de l'alléluia de la messe romaine*, in: *Rivista internazionale di musica sacra* 12 (1991), pp. 287–362.

[14] The *Dies sanctificatus* group includes melodies for a part of the year around Christmas, including St. Stephen, St. John, and the Epiphany; see Karlheinz Schlager, *Alleluia-Melodien I.*, Kassel and elsewhere 1968 (= *Monumenta monodica medii aevi* 7), p. 564; idem, *Thematischer Katalog der ältesten Alleluia-Melodien*, München 1965 (= *Erlanger Arbeiten zur Musikwissenschaft* 2), no. 27, pp. 78–81; David G. Hughes, *Evidence for the Traditional View of the Transmission of Gregorian Chant*, in: *JAMS* 40 (1987), p. 378 note 3.

[15] A detailed study of the proses and prosulas of the Roman manuscripts is in preparation by Alejandro Planchart; it is to appear in a forthcoming volume in honor of Kenneth Levy; Professor Planchart with characteristic kindness has provided me a preliminary version of his study.

[16] On this sequence see Kenneth Levy, *Lux de luce: The Origin of an Italian Sequence*, in: *MQ* 57 (1971), pp. 40–61.

[17] In addition to the exception of *Rex omnipotens* and *Lux de luce* just mentioned, qualifications and exceptions include the sequence *Gaude eia* for St. Lucy, preceded by the All. v. *Specie tua* with second v. *Diffusa*, also found in 5319; the sequence *Clara gaudia festa* for Easter Monday is preceded by the Alleluia *Angelus domini*, which appears in the supplement of 5319, f. 156v, but not attached to this or any other sequence; sequence *Dic nobis quibus* for Easter Tuesday follows the usual Old Roman All. *Venite*, which however here has a unique second verse *Oportebat;* the sequence *Summa sollempnitas*, for the Octave of Easter, is preceded by a doublet Alleluia *Post dies octo*, which appears in the supplement of 5319, f. 156v, but not attached to this or any other sequence. Details can readily be seen in the synoptical liturgical tables in Lütolf, *Das Graduale*, vol. 1.

[18] See above, note 14.

[19] No complete Beneventan chant-book for the mass survives; but there are at least four fragmentary remains, and considerable other evidence about the nature of such books. See Kelly, *Beneventan Chant*, pp. 41–42.

[20] Information on the use in Italy of these sequences can be found in Lance W. Brunner, *Catalogo delle sequenze in manoscritti di origine italiana anteriori al 1200*, in: *RIM* 20 (1985), pp. 191–276; see also the forthcoming study by Planchart (above, note 15).

[21] On books of Santa Cecilia see Paola Supino Martini, *Roma e l'area grafica romanesca (secoli X–XII)*, Alessandria 1987, pp. 108–117.

[22] For an assessment of Desiderius' importance and his effect on the arts, the reader is referred to Herbert Bloch's classic study *Montecassino, Byzantium, and the West in the Earlier Middle Ages*, as revised in his *Monte Cassino in the Middle Ages*, 3 vols., Cambridge, Mass. 1986, vol. I, pp. 1–136. For

Desiderius' elevation to the cardinalate, see ed. Hartmut Hoffmann, *Die Chronik von Montecassino (Chronica Monasterii Casinensis)*, Hannover 1980 (= *Monumenta Germaniae Historica, Scriptores* 34), p. 374.

[23] See the discussion in Connolly, *The Graduale of S. Cecilia in Trastevere*, especially pp. 436–438; Levy, *Lux de luce*, p. 44.

[24] See Thomas Forrest Kelly, *Montecassino and the Old Beneventan Chant*, in: *Early Music History* 5 (1985), pp. 53–83.

[25] Pope Stephen IX, Desiderius' predecessor as abbot and as pope, visited Montecassino in 1058, and forbade the singing of what he, and all the scribes who refer to the local liturgy, called »Ambrosian« chant; according to the chronicle of Montecassino, »Ambrosianum cantum in ecclesia ista cantari penitus interdixit«; ed. Hoffmann, *Die Chronik von Montecassino*, p. 353.

[26] On the scriptorium of Montecassino and the renewal of books under Desiderius see Bloch, *Monte Cassino in the Middle Ages*, I, 71–82; Kelly, *Beneventan Chant*, p. 15 note 66; Francis Newton, *The Desiderian Scriptorium at Monte Cassino. The Chronicle and some Surviving Manuscripts*, in: *Dumbarton Oaks Papers* 30 (1976), pp. 35–54 plus 4 plates.

NEW BENEVENTAN LITURGICAL FRAGMENTS
IN LANCIANO, LUCERA, AND PENNE
CONTAINING FURTHER EVIDENCE OF THE
OLD BENEVENTAN CHANT*

THREE new liturgical fragments in Beneventan script and musical notation are described here. The fragments, dating from the eleventh and twelfth centuries, are evidence of books of music for use in the liturgy: two graduals with tropes and sequences, and one antiphoner. In southern Italy complete books of these types survive in very small numbers, so any new discovery is valuable in what it teaches us about the number and distribution of books for the liturgy. These fragments, however, are of particular interest. Two of the three contain liturgical material (parts of two masses) from the Old Beneventan liturgy, practiced in southern Italy before the adoption there of the chant now called Gregorian. The remaining fragment has a distinctive south-Italian repertory for the Roman mass and includes material from this repertory found in no other source: a lost south Italian trope from Montecassino and a mass for St. Amicus that is otherwise unknown.

In what follows, each fragment will be described physically, its contents inventoried and analyzed, and a transcription made of the surviving texts. The paleographical descriptions of the fragments depend on the advice of Virginia Brown.

As new sources in Beneventan script continue to turn up, it becomes increasingly clear that close attention to fragments has much to teach us. Although we continue to wish that more complete documents had survived, there is a great deal to be learned from the close observation of what remains. Not only do fragments contribute to the larger picture of writing and usage, but even in fragmentary form they may preserve—as these documents do—texts, music, and other information that only they can provide.

* The discovery of the fragments described here is owing to the continuing efforts of the Monumenta Liturgica Beneventana group at the Pontifical Institute of Mediaeval Studies at the University of Toronto. I am grateful to Professor Virginia Brown and her colleagues for calling these fragments to my attention.

Reprinted from Thomas Forrest Kelly, "New Beneventan Liturgical Fragments in Lanciano, Lucera, and Penne Containing Further Evidence of the Old Beneventan Chant," *Mediaeval Studies* 62 (2000): 293–332, by permission of the publisher. © 2000 by the Pontifical Institute of Mediaeval Studies, Toronto.

294

LANCIANO, ARCHIVIO DI STATO DI CHIETI, SEZIONE LANCIANO,
FONDO NOTARILE GIOVANNI CAMILLO GIRELLI 1632–1638

A bifolium from a gradual of the twelfth century. The manuscript, probably designed for use at San Pietro Avellana, contains music for the feasts of late October and for parts of November. It preserves a trope for All Saints, probably from Montecassino, that is otherwise unrecoverable, and the beginning of a unique mass for St. Amicus.

Description.

The volume of notarial records once covered by this fragment was from the Fondo Notarile Giovanni Camillo Girelli, 1632–1638. It consists of 119 numbered paper folios; on the top of the first page is written "1632 al 1638," and the name "Giovanni Camillo Girelli" is found many times in the volume. The bifolium has been detached and is now kept in a folder with the pencil indications "1632/38" and "12." On the flesh side of the fragment, upside down with respect to the original Beneventan script, is written "Camillo Girelli," and the series of years between 1632 and 1638. The volume was restored in 1994–95 by the firm Restauro "San Giorgio" di Pandimuglio Massimiliano, located at Soriano nel Cimino (Viterbo). Camillo was a notary active at Roio del Sangro, a modest-sized town on a promontory overlooking the Sangro, a short distance downstream from San Pietro Avellana.

Each folio of the fragment measures about 332×225 mm., with a writing area measuring 255×133 mm. containing ten long lines of music and text. The fragment is dark and stained on the flesh side, which served as the outside of the notarial document. The fragment is slightly mutilated at its outer edges and at the bottom; of three holes in the parchment, only one deprives us of text or music.

The parchment was ruled on the hair side after being folded and pricked. Prickings visible in the outer margin guided the ruling of four drypoint lines for each system, one line serving as the base for the text and the other three as a musical staff. Double vertical bounding lines define the inner and outer margins.

The script is written in a brownish-black ink; a darker black ink was used for the neumes. Orange-red ink was used for rubrics, initial letters, and the colored staff-line that indicates the musical pitch F.

Decorated letters include three drawn in black ink for the beginnings of three masses. These occupy the space of one line of text and music, and have space provided for them inside the left margin. They are either intricate interlace patterns terminating in an animal's head (the letter *D* used for both St. Clement and the Vigil of St. Andrew) or the composition of intertwined animals used for the letter *G* of All Saints. These letters look as though they were meant to be filled in with colored inks. The mass of St. Amicus begins with a letter *D* in red ink, consisting of a loop decorated with curved flourishes. A red initial *I* of smaller dimensions begins the trope for All Saints. Other initial letters, used at the beginning of individual chants, consist of black letters infilled or decorated with the orange-red ink of the rubrics. Orange-red ink is used in the texts of chants to indicated places where a reprise is to begin (as after an introit-verse) or where a chant resumes after an interruption (as with the introit of All Saints, in which the trope-verses are to be intercalated).

The musical notation is elegant without being fussy, clearly the work of an experienced notator. As in most notations of the twelfth century, the quilisma is not used.

The script exhibits an interesting mix of features.[1] Characteristic of the Bari type: the slight leftward lean; a roundish aspect achieved in part by the circular bowls of *a* and *d*; the round upper loop of *e* that is noticeably large, and the absence of sharply defined lozenges; straight-shouldered *r* in ligature (*ri* excepted). From the Montecassino variety of Beneventan the script takes *s* and final *r* that descend below the base-line, straight *i* in ligature, and the style of decoration used for majuscules beginning a new text. This Bari-Cassinese blend suggests, of course, that the fragment was copied in an area subject to dual palaeographical influence. The closure of the lower loop of *e* when the letter is written by itself, i.e., in final position or isolated from the remainder of the word, supports the twelfth-century date proposed above for the musical notation. Since the use of crenellated majuscule *Q* ("*Quos*") as late as the twelfth century points to the Abruzzo, it is likely that the scribe was working in a center located in a southern area of that region, i.e., near Puglia. As we shall see shortly, this surmise in confirmed by some distinctive textual features.

This was probably the next to innermost bifolium of the quire. Musical materials between the two folios of this fragment would probably have included the rest of the mass of St. Amicus; the mass of St. Martin (11 Nov.), which might have included tropes; in addition, a number of other masses would have been indicated with cues to chants found earlier in the manuscript or in the common of saints.[2]

---

[1] This paragraph is based on the suggestions and descriptions of Virginia Brown.

[2] Masses which would mostly consist of cued materials include SS. Valentine and Hilarius (2 Nov.), the Quattuor Coronati (8 Nov.), St. Theodore (9 Nov.), St. Martin I, pope (10 Nov.), St. Menna (10 or 11 Nov.), the Vigil of St. Martin, confessor (Nov. 10), St. John Chrysostom (13 Nov.), and St. Gregory Thaumaturgi (17 Nov.). This list is based on the masses found in the "Breviarium" in London, British Library Egerton 3511 (formerly Benevento 29), the closest source to our fragment (on this source, see p. 301 and n. 28 below). The amount of

Contents.

This handsome gradual has features of particular interest for musical and liturgical scholars. It regularly contains certain liturgical elements that elsewhere were already disappearing in the twelfth century. The verses for the offertory, which were beginning to disappear in twelfth-century manuscripts, are regularly present in southern Italian manuscripts, and it is characteristic to find them here. Psalm-verses for the communion are regularly recorded here, as they are in other graduals in the orbit of Montecassino (Montecassino, Archivio della Badia 546, an incomplete gradual of the end of the twelfth century or the beginning of the thirteenth; Vatican City, Biblioteca Apostolica Vaticana Vat. lat. 6082, a notated missal of the twelfth century closely derived from Montecassino usage), though they are not used in the graduals of Benevento of the eleventh and twelfth century.[3]

The *versus ad repetendum* appears regularly with introits and communions in this fragment. Such verses are generally thought to be sung after the psalmody and doxology, and they imply a further repetition of the introit or communion antiphon.[4] They occur in early manuscripts and *ordines* but are quite rare in the twelfth century. They do, however, appear regularly for introits and communions in Vat. lat. 6082 for Sundays and the feasts of saints.[5] It may be that this tradition of *versus ad repetendum* survived in the Cassinese orbit, if not at Montecassino itself, in an area represented by our fragment and by Vat. lat. 6082. At Montecassino the practice of using *versus ad repetendum* was in decline after the twelfth century, to judge from the incomplete gradual Monte-

space required between these two surviving folios depends greatly, of course, on the extent of the mass of St. Martin.

[3] The five graduals in Beneventan script in the Biblioteca capitolare of Benevento, MSS 34, 35, 38, 39, 40, all present the communion generally without psalmody. For some manuscripts from elsewhere that contain communion verses, see Michel Huglo, *Les tonaires: Inventaire, analyse, comparaison* (Paris, 1971), 401–2.

[4] For further information on the communion psalmody and the *versus ad repetendum,* see David Hiley, *Western Planchant* (Oxford, 1993), 496–99. While *versus ad repetendum* are occasionally found in later manuscripts for the introit (see *Paléographie musicale* 15 [Solesmes, 1937; rpt. Berne, 1971], 165–66), they are extremely rare for the communion. A few such verses for the introit are noted by Alejandro Enrique Planchart in *Beneventanum troporum corpus I: Tropes of the Proper of the Mass from Southern Italy, A.D. 1000–1250,* 2 vols., Recent Researches in the Music of the Middle Ages and Early Renaissance 16 and 17–18 (Madison, 1994), 1:xxii–xxxiii (Table 1).

[5] In cases where the chant in question is indicated only by its incipit no psalm-verse or *versus ad repetendum* is given. The psalmody and *versus ad repetendum* in our fragment for the introit and communion of All Saints and the communion of St. Andrew appear in Vat. lat. 6082; the other such verses in our fragment are not given in Vat. lat. 6082 since there the chants are given as incipits.

cassino 546, whose *versus ad repetendum* for introits of a few major feasts have subsequently been eradicated from the manuscript.[6]

The verses for introits and communions in the Lanciano fragment are cited according to the Roman Psalter; even though the newer Gallican Psalter was widely used from Carolingian times, the Roman Psalter persisted in southern Italy.[7]

The fragment contains a trope for use with the introit for All Saints which appears to be unique.[8] This trope consists of four Latin hexameters, with cues for their interpolation in the performance of the introit *Gaudeamus,* as shown below with the full text of the introit written out in italics and the cues in small capitals (see plate 1; for a musical transcription of the trope, see Appendix 1).

Iunior atque senex, gradus omnis sexus uterque	*GAUDEAMUS* *omnes in domino*
Dentur manus plausum, dent lingue carmina laudum	*DIEM festum celebrantes sub honorem sanctorum omnium*
Quos aquilo zephirus genuit quos auster et eurus	*DE QUORUM sollemnitate gaudent angeli*
Et laudant patrem laudant spiramen et almum	*ET COLLAUDANT filium dei.*

The classicizing aspects of this trope point to the orbit of Montecassino. Though many tropes of southern Italian origin survive in tropers of Montecassino and Benevento, the regular use of hexameters is typical of the tropes of Montecassino, and the references here to the winds suggest an interest in classical literature typical of the Cassinese poets.[9] Although several sets of trope-verses for this introit survive in manuscripts from Benevento,[10] the only source

---

[6] The third mass of Christmas (this mass also has a *versus ad repetendum* for the communion: both verses have been erased); Epiphany (erased); St. Benedict (not erased).

[7] The Roman Psalter is edited—based in part on two Cassinese manuscripts—in Robert Weber, *Le psautier romain et les autres anciens psautiers latins,* Collectanea biblica latina 10 (Rome, 1953); the Gallican Psalter is conveniently consulted in *Biblia sacra iuxta vulgatam versionem,* ed. R. Weber, 2 vols. (Stuttgart, 1975). On the various versions of the Psalter and their use as texts for chants, see Joseph Dyer, "Latin Psalters, Old Roman and Gregorian Chants," *Kirchenmusikalisches Jahrbuch* 68 (1984): 11–30; on the Roman Psalter in south Italian liturgical manuscripts, see *Paléographie musicale* 14 (Solesmes, 1931; rpt. Berne, 1971), 145–51.

[8] Surviving tropes from southern Italy are edited in *Beneventanum troporum corpus,* ed. John Boe and Alejandro Enrique Planchart, Recent Researches in the Music of the Middle Ages and Early Renaissance 16–28 (Madison, 1989–). I am grateful to Professor Planchart for his confirmation of the uniqueness of this trope, and of its Cassinese aspect.

[9] On the literary style of Cassinese tropes, see Planchart, *Beneventanum troporum corpus I* 1:xv, xlv.

[10] Ibid. 1:25–28, 2:63–74.

from Montecassino is palimpsest at this point. The Cassinese troper Vatican, Urb. lat. 602 does contain a trope for All Saints, of which only a few initial letters are now visible on fols. 12v–13r. The opening letter *I*, along with a *D* beginning the second portion of the trope, suggest that the trope in Vatican, Urb. lat. 602 is *Iunior atque senex* as preserved in our fragment.[11]

The Lanciano fragment preserves the beginning of a unique mass for St. Amicus, who died in the middle of the eleventh century as a recluse at the monastery of San Pietro Avellana,[12] after having spent much of his life in a hermitage on the confines of the Marche and Abruzzo. A *vita* of St. Amicus was composed in San Pietro Avellana while those who knew the saint were still alive.[13] San Pietro was a foundation of St. Dominic of Sora; it was given to Montecassino in 1069,[14] and the Cassinese possession of the monastery provides the tenuous connection that allowed Montecassino to claim Amicus for her own.[15] The present comune of San Pietro Avellana is named for the site of the monastery.

Despite Montecassino's possession of the monastery and her pride in Amicus, the saint seems not to have had a liturgical celebration at Montecassino. Relevant Cassinese sources, admittedly few, do not give a proper mass for his feast on November 3;[16] the Cassinese "breviarium sive ordo officio-

[11] Ibid. 1:93. Professor Planchart in a private communication concurs in the identification of this Lanciano trope with the lost trope for All Saints in Urb. lat. 602.

[12] On this monastery and its relation to Montecassino, see Herbert Bloch, *Monte Cassino in the Middle Ages,* 3 vols. (Cambridge, 1986), 1:362–64.

[13] The two surviving *vitae* of St. Amicus are edited by Charles De Smedt, *AA SS* Nov. 2 (Brussels, 1894), 92–99, with introduction on 89–92. De Smedt (90–91) attributes the longer *vita* to that "Bernardus Casinensis monachus" who, according to Peter the Deacon, "descripsit miracula sancti confessoris Christi Amici Casinensis monachi" (see Peter the Deacon, *De viris illustribus casinensibus* 37 [PL 173:1043B]); this life is edited from the fourteenth-century manuscript Montecassino, Archivio della Badia 34, pp. 156–192 (see M. Inguanez, *Codicum casinensium manuscriptorum catalogus,* 3 vols. [Montecassino, 1915–41], 1:47); it was edited also, but with errors, in vol. 1 of *Bibliotheca casinense: Florilegium casinense* (Montecassino, 1874), 244–54. The shorter *vita,* later in date and divided into twelve liturgical lections, seems to be incomplete and derivative of the earlier one; it is edited by De Smedt after a transcription in Brussels, Bibliothèque Royale 8299, from a lectionary of Spoleto cathedral.

[14] Bloch, *Monte Cassino in the Middle Ages* 1:364.

[15] See the previous note. On Amicus, see Jean-Marie Sansterre, "Recherches sur les ermites du Mont-Cassin et l'érémitisme dans l'hagiographie cassinienne," *Hagiographica* 2 (1995): 57–92 at 79–80.

[16] These include the missal Vat. lat 6082 (see below); the missal Montecassino 540 (s. XI/XII) and the gradual Montecassino 546 (s. XII/XIII) do not contain this portion of the year (on Montecassino 546, see Thomas Forrest Kelly in *I fiori e' Frutti santi: S. Benedetto, la Regola, la santità nelle testimonianze dei manoscritti cassinesi,* ed. Mariano Dell'Omo [Mi-

rum," which details the offices for days with proper material, gives nothing for his feast.[17] Calendars of Montecassino (where his name might indicate a mass drawn from the common) do not cite him,[18] though he is cited in Cassinese martyrologies.[19] An origin at Montecassino of the mass in our fragment seems unlikely, since no musical materials for Amicus are known in sources from Montecassino (nor from any place except the origin of this fragment, which appears from other liturgical evidence to be seen below not to be Cassinese). The presence in our manuscript of a mass for St. Amicus suggests an origin at or near San Pietro Avellana. This was an important monastery which, at least in the thirteenth century, had an impressive library of liturgical and other manuscripts.[20] Eight antiphoners for the night office, seven for the day office, and sixteen psalters are listed in an inventory of 1271. The monastery also possessed "liber unus de vita Sancti Amici."[21] Curiously, the list makes no reference to a gradual, unless the "liber Missalis unus" is such a book.[22] No

lan, 1998], 163–64, with bibliography). For an overview of surviving sources of music for the Mass in southern Italy, see Klaus Gamber, *Codices liturgici latini antiquiores*. Spicilegii Friburgensis subsidia 1, 2d ed., 1 vol. in 2 (Freiburg, 1968), *pars prima*, 239–48, 250–54; see also the *Supplementum*, Spicilegii Friburgensis subsidia 1a (Freiburg, 1988), 53–57.

[17] The mass would of course not appear in this ordinal for the Office, but the absence of his feast in this very Cassinese document is significant. The manuscripts containing this ordinal include five in the Montecassino tradition: Vatican, Urb. lat. 585 (ca. 1100); Paris, Bibliothèque Mazarine 364 (ca. 1100); Los Angeles, J. Paul Getty Museum 83.ML.97 (formerly Montecassino 199, then Ludwig IX.1; ca. 1100); Montecassino 198 (s. XII/XIII); Montecassino 562 (s. XIII). Three further twelfth-century versions, based on the Montecassino ordinal, were made for churches in Benevento: Naples, Biblioteca Nazionale VI E 43 (for a church dedicated to St. Mary); Vatican, Vat. lat. 4928 (Santa Sofia); Benevento, Biblioteca capitolare 66 (St. Peter's *intra muros*). An edition of these sources is in preparation.

[18] A convenient list of Cassinese calendars is in Virginia Brown, "A New Beneventan Calendar from Naples: The Lost 'Kalendarium Tutinianum' Rediscovered," *Mediaeval Studies* 46 (1984): 385–449 at 393–95. Of the calendars listed there I have examined those associated with the ordinal of Montecassino (Vat. lat. 4928 [Santa Sofia, Benevento, s. XII]; Naples, Biblioteca Nazionale VI E 43 [Benevento, s. XI/XII]; Vatican, Urb. lat. 585 [Montecassino, s. XI/XII]; Los Angeles, J. Paul Getty Museum 83.ML.97 [Montecassino, s. XI/XII]; Paris, Bibliothèque Mazarine 364 [Montecassino, s. XI/XII]) and with liturgical books of relevant date related to Montecassino (Montecassino 127 [s. XIII]; Montecassino 540 [s. XI/XII]; Montecassino 546 [s. XII/XIII]; Vatican, Vat. lat. 6082 [s. XII]).

[19] De Smedt (see n. 13 above), 89.

[20] An inventory of 1271 is published in M. Inguanez, *Catalogi codicum casinensium antiqui (saec. VIII-XV)*, Miscellanea cassinese 21 (Montecassino, 1941), 68–69 (Inguanez had previously published this list in 1931).

[21] Ibid., 69.

[22] This "liber Missalis" is probably not a sacramentary, since there is listed an "Ordo sacramentorum liber unus." It may of course be a missal. Perhaps the antiphoners for the day office ("Antiphonaria de die") included one or more graduals.

monastery of this importance would have been without a gradual, and our fragment is likely to have served the monastery where the cult of St. Amicus was strongest.

Half a century ago Mauro Inguanez surmised that the script used at San Pietro Avellana was that of Bari. This was based on two eleventh-century fragments gathered in the *compactiones* of Montecassino which had served as covers of documents from San Pietro Avellana: four folios of Gregory, *Moralia in Iob* and one folio from a homiliarium.[23] Inguanez also identified Montecassino, Archivio della Badia manuscript 465 (John the Deacon, *Vita Gregorii Magni,* also in Bari-type script of the eleventh century) with San Pietro Avellana on the basis of documents written on p. 322 of that codex which name the monastery.[24] This new fragment from Lanciano points to San Pietro Avellana through its mass for St. Amicus, and its script does contain some definite Bari-type features. Hence it does seem very probably that the Bari type of Beneventan script played a definite role at San Pietro Avellana at least during the eleventh and twelfth centuries, and this fragment is important as an early and almost certain witness of this.[25]

It is highly regrettable that the fragment includes only the first three words of the introit of St. Amicus; its words do not correspond with any text in either of the two lives of the saint. Its melody (perhaps in mode 1 or mode 6) does not seem to be an adaptation of a preexistent Gregorian introit-melody, and we can surmise that this mass was composed at Montecassino or at San Pietro Avellana in honor of the local saint. Although St. Amicus was evidently remembered in Cassinese martyrologies,[26] I know of no musical materials from Montecassino for the saint's mass or office.

Comparison with other manuscripts of music for the mass from southern Italy makes clear that the Lanciano fragment is closest in its liturgical usage to two sources. One of these is the twelfth-century missal Vat. lat. 6082, whose

---

[23] Mauro Inguanez, "Frammenti di codici abruzzesi," in *Miscellanea Giovanni Mercati,* vol. 6, Studi e Testi 126 (Vatican City, 1946), 272–81 at 274–75. The fragments are now missing from the *compactiones,* according to information supplied by Virginia Brown, though Inguanez does provide facsimiles. Inguanez identified these fragments with items in the catalogue of S. Pietro mentioned above (n. 20). Although such volumes are named in the 1271 list ("Omelie quinque"; "moralia Iob libri tres" [Inguanez, *Catalogi codicum,* 69]), they are not cited as being in Beneventan, a distinction not made in that catalogue.

[24] Inguanez, *Codicum casinensium manuscriptorum catalogus* 3:104–5, with a facsimile at Tab. 2.

[25] I am grateful to Virginia Brown for pointing out Inguanez's attributions of other manuscripts to San Pietro de Avellana.

[26] De Smedt (see n. 13 above), 89.

origin is generally cited as being Montecassino or the Cassinese orbit.[27] The other source closely related liturgically to our fragment is the "Breviarium de die qualiter missa debetur celebrari" written on a separate bifolium in a twelfth-century Beneventan hand and now bound as fols. 10–11v of London, British Library Egerton 3511.[28] This is a list of 156 masses, indicated by the incipits of their chants and lections; it is not a summary of the Beneventan missal in which it is now bound[29] but represents a somewhat different liturgical tradition, to which we can now relate the fragment under examination here.

A comparison with the manuscripts of Benevento indicates that the Lanciano fragment, while adhering to the the widespread tradition of Roman liturgy and "Gregorian" chant, varies in many details from the sources now at and related to Benevento, while it shares many of those same details with the two manuscripts just mentioned. A more detailed comparison of these manuscripts follows below. What it shows is that a liturgical tradition, typical of southern Italy but varying from the uses of Benevento and Montecassino, links the Lanciano fragments with the missal Vat. lat. 6082 and the "Breviarium de die." That usage, closely related to the practice of Montecassino, may be associated with the area around San Pietro Avellana, for which the Lanciano fragment seems to have been intended.

In the material that follows, the masses of the Lanciano fragment are compared with those found in other south Italian manuscripts. These manuscripts, and their abbreviations, are as follows:[30]

B29 London, British Library Egerton 3511 (formerly Benevento 29). Missal, s. XII, of St. Peter's *intra muros,* Benevento.

B29br London, British Library Egerton 3511 (formerly Benevento 29), fols. 10r–11v, "Breviarium de die qualiter missa debetur celebrari," s. XII.

B30 Benevento, Biblioteca capitolare 30. Notated missal, s. XIII.

---

[27] See E. A. Loew, *The Beneventan Script: A History of the South Italian Minuscule,* vol. 2: *Hand List of Beneventan MSS.,* 2d edition prepared and enlarged by Virginia Brown (Rome, 1980), 152 and the literature cited there.

[28] Formerly Benevento, Biblioteca capitolare 29, a partially-notated missal of the twelfth century made for the convent of St. Peter's *intra muros* of Benevento (Jean Mallet and André Thibaut, *Les manuscrits en écriture bénéventaine de la Bibliothèque capitulaire de Bénévent* [hereafter Mallet-Thibaut], 3 vols. [vol. 1: Paris, 1984; vols. 2–3: Paris and Turnhout, 1997] 1:76–77; 2:137–45). This convent had close connections with Montecassino, to judge from their use of a late-twelfth-century ordinal copied from that of Montecassino, now Benevento, Biblioteca capitolare 66 (see Mallet-Thibaut, 2:288–97).

[29] Mallet-Thibaut, 2:339 n 1.

[30] Detailed descriptions of all the manuscripts now or formerly at Benevento may be found in Mallet-Thibaut. On Vat. lat. 6082, see n. 27 above.

B33   Benevento, Biblioteca capitolare 33. Notated missal, s. X/XI.
B34   Benevento, Biblioteca capitolare 34. Gradual with tropes, s. XII².
B35   Benevento, Biblioteca capitolare 35. Gradual with tropes, s. XII¹.
B38   Benevento, Biblioteca capitolare 38. Gradual with tropes, s. XI¹.
B39   Benevento, Biblioteca capitolare 39. Gradual with tropes, s. XI ex.
B40   Benevento, Biblioteca capitolare 40. Gradual with tropes, s. XI¹.
V6082 Vatican City, Biblioteca Apostolica Vaticana Vat. lat. 6082. Notated missal, s. XII.

Simonis et Iude: All sources have this offertory, except B29br (which mentions only the introit); offertory verses are not used in B29, B30, and V6082. The communion is present in all sources (except B29br as above), though the verses are not present; V6082, which does use such verses, gives only an incipit for the communion; these verses do appear where V6082 gives the communion in full in the common of apostles).

Maximi: This mass is indicated in V6082 and B29br by giving incipits for the introit and communion as in our fragment (in V6082 full versions appear in the common of one martyr). The mass appears in none of the Benevento sources.

Germani: This mass is found in this form in V6082, B29br, and B29 (in all three cases the gradual is *Iuravit*). Only two further sources have liturgical material for this feast; B33 provides collects only; and B39 has a different introit (*Statuit*) and communion (*Beatus servus*), and adds a second gradual, *Inveni David*.

Vig. Omnium Sanctorum: Our fragment preserves the same mass as is found in V6082 and B29; there is nothing for this feast in B30, B33, B38, or B40. Other regional manuscripts have a variety of differences, as follows. In B35 and B39, the offertory is *Letamini in domino*. The communion is *Iustorum anime* in B39 and *Signa eos* both in B35 and as a second communion in B39.

Omnium Sanctorum: Our fragment preserves the same mass as is found in V6082; no mass is present in B29br; other regional manuscripts have a variety of differences. The introit verse is found in all manuscripts except B33, which has a different verse. The versus ad repetendum is found only here and in V6082. The gradual *Gloriosus* is found in B29, B35, V6082; elsewhere (B30, B34, B38, B39, B40) the gradual is *Iustorum anime*. The Alleluia *Iusti fulgebunt* is found only in B29 and V6082; other manuscripts have a variety of Alleluias (see Mallet-Thibaut, 2:639). The offertory *Letamini* is found only in B29 and V6082; other manuscripts (B30, B33, B34, B38, B39, B40) have *Exsultabunt sancti*. The communion is universal; the psalm-verse and *versus ad repetendum* are present in V6082.

New Beneventan Liturgical Fragments.

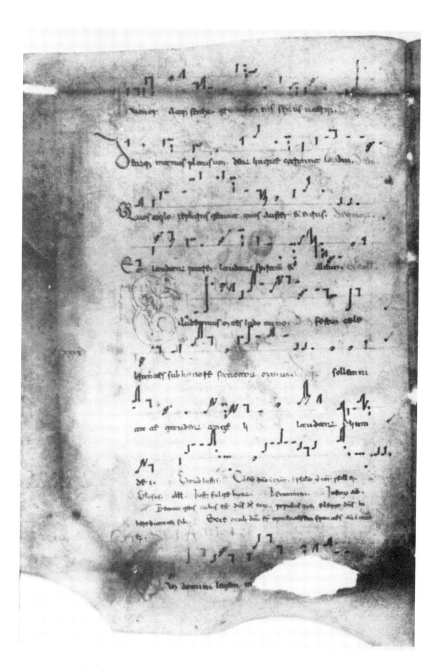

1. Lanciano, Archivio di Stato di Chieti, Sezione Lanciano,
fondo notarile Giovanni Camillo Girelli 1632–1638, fol. A verso.

New Beneventan Liturgical Fragments.

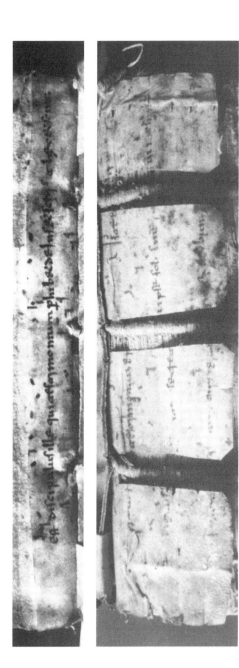

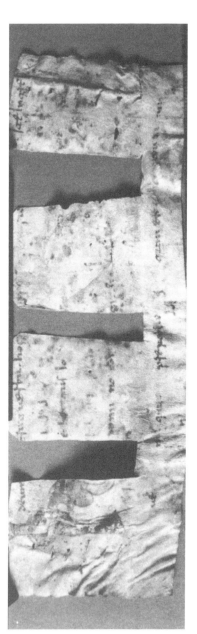

2. Lucera, Biblioteca comunale, Cinquecentina 658,

New Beneventan Liturgical Fragments.

3. Penne, Archivio Storico dell'Archidiocesi di Pescara-Penne,
leaf A recto (fragment 6v) and verso (fragment 6r)

New Beneventan Liturgical Fragments.

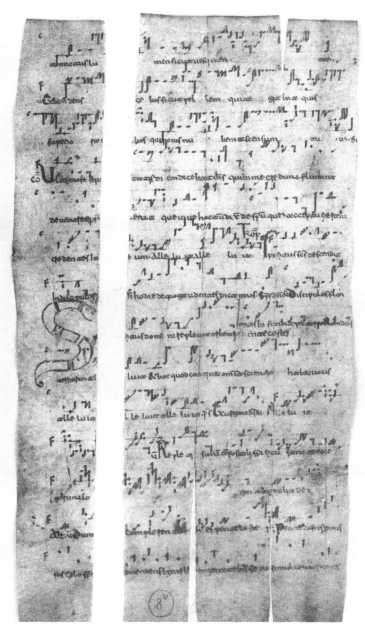

4. Penne, Archivio Storico dell'Archidiocesi di Pescara-Penne,
leaf D recto (fragment 8v)

Cecilie: The communion of our fragment is found in all the sources, except for B29br (which indicates only introit and gospel) and B30 (which does not contain this portion of the calendar). The communion is given in incipit in V6082, but the full version, with verses as here, is found in the common of virgins.

Clementis: The introit verse *Misericordias* is found only in V6082, B29br and B29; elsewhere (B34, B35, B38, B39, B40) the verse is *Domine exaudi.* The gradual *Iuravit* is found in V6082, B29, B29br, B40; elsewhere (B34, B35, B38, B39) the gradual is *Exaltent eum.* The Alleluia *Iustus germinabit* is found in V6082, B29, B29br; elsewhere the Alleluia is *Ora pro nobis* (B34, B35, B38, B39) or *Inveni David* (B40). The communion *Domine quinque* is found in V6082, B29, B29br; elsewhere (B34, B35, B38, B39, B40) the communion is *Beatus servus.*

Grisochoni: Most manuscripts of Benevento do not contain this mass; it is found in B29 and B29br, in which the only chant pieces are those named in our fragment; and in V6082, which in addition cues the other chant pieces.

Catherine: In V6082 and B29br this mass is given after that of St. Mercurius. V6082 has the two pieces given here (though their placement is confused in the manuscript); B29br cues the introit with the indication "per ordinem"; B29 gives only collects in a second hand. Other manuscripts do not have this mass.

Mercurii: B29br and V6082 give the same mass as our fragment; B29 gives a different mass, which has only the offertory in common (In. *Letabitur iustus.* Gr. *Posuisti domine.* Al. *Iustum deduxit.* Of. *Posuisti.* Co. *Posuisti.*); it also includes prayers and lections (owing to the fact that Mercurius is a significant saint at Benevento); other manuscripts omit this mass or do not contain this portion of the sanctoral.

Petri Alexandrini: B29br and V6082 give the mass as here; other manuscripts omit it or do not contain this portion of the sanctoral.

Vigilia Sancti Andree: The introit verse is given as *Celi enarrant* in V6082, and is confirmed by all sources (B29, B29br, B34, B38, B39, B40) except B35, which gives the verse *Domine probasti me.* The gradual *In omnem terram* is found only in V6082, B29 and B29br; elsewhere (B34, B35, B38, B39, B40) the gradual is *Nimis honorati sunt.* Several manuscripts (6082, B34, B38, B39, B40—but not B29 or B29br) give an Alleluia, *Nimis honorati.*

Saturnini et Sisinnii: Both V6082 and B29br indicate this mass, on the same day as the Vigil of Andrew, by indicating the introit *Iudicant sancti* (B29br also cues the communion *Quod dico*). This mass may well have been indicated also in our fragment, in a now-illegible portion.

304

Andree: Three manuscripts (B35, B39, B40) give a different Alleluia (*Sancte Andrea apostole*), while the others (B29, B29br, B34, B35, B38, B39, B40, V6082) agree with our fragment. All manuscripts give the communion psalm-verse; V6082 also indicated the *versus ad repetendum*.

Transcription.

The transcription that follows supplies, in angle brackets (⟨ ⟩), missing or illegible portions of text from other south Italian manuscripts. This missing text is in some cases hypothetical, and is designed to provide a context for the fragmentary nature of the surviving texts. Editorial explanations are given in square brackets ([ ]).

/// indicates a lacuna in the manuscript.

* indicates a piece given only in incipit without musical notation. Such pieces presumably appeared elsewhere in the missal (sometimes the folio number is added), either in the common of saints or in an earlier mass; this is a standard practice.

[fol. Ar]

⟨Sanctorum Simonis et Iude [28 Oct.]⟩

⟨Of.⟩   In omnem terram exivit sonus eorum et in fines orbis terre verba eorum [Ps 18:5].

　　⟨v.⟩   Celi enarrant gloriam dei et opera manuum eius annuntiat ⟨firma⟩mentum [Ps 18:1].

　　⟨v.⟩   Dies diei eructuat verbum et nox ⟨nocti⟩ indicat scientiam [Ps 18:2].

⟨Co.⟩   Vos qui secuti estis me dicit dominus sedebitis super sedes iudicantes duodecim tribus Israhel alleluia alleluia.

　　⟨ps.⟩Mirabilis facta est scientia tua ex me confortata est nec potero ad eam [Ps 138:6].

　　⟨R.⟩   Dinumerabo eos et super arenam multiplicabuntur [Ps 138:18]. All⟨eluia⟩ [musical cue to the second *alleluia* of the communion].

⟨Sancti Maximi [30 Oct.]⟩

⟨In.⟩   Gloria et honore*

⟨Co.⟩   Posuisti domine*

⟨Sancti Germani [30 Oct.]⟩

⟨In.⟩   Sacerdotes dei*

　　/// [hole]

⟨All.⟩   Tu es sacerdos*

⟨Of.⟩   Inveni David*

⟨Co.⟩   Fidelis servus*

          /// [hole]

⟨Vigilia Omnium Sanctorum [31 Oct.]⟩

⟨Gr.   Timete⟩ dominum*

Of.   Exultabunt sancti*

Co.   Dico autem vobis*

  ⟨ps.?⟩ Venite fili* [Ps 33:12?]

                                    [fol. Av]

⟨Festivitate Omnium Sanctorum [1 Nov.]⟩

⟨Tropus⟩

          Iunior atque senex, gradus omnis sexus uterque. GAUDEAMUS
          Dentque manus plausum, dent lingue carmina laudum. DIEM
          Quos aquilo zephirus genuit quos auster et eurus. DE QUORUM
          Et laudant patrem laudant spiramen et almum. ET COLLAUDANT

⟨In.⟩   Gaudeamus omnes in domino diem festum celebrantes sub honore
          sanctorum omnium, de quorum sollemnitate gaudent angeli et
          collaudant filium dei.

    ps.   Gaudete iusti in. [Ps 32:1 (Roman Psalter)]

    R.   Confitemini domino in cythara, in psalterio decem cordarum psallite ei.
          [Ps 32:2, Roman Psalter] De quorum.

Gr.   Gloriosus.*

All.   Iusti fulgebunt.*

Of.   Letamini.*

Co.   Iustorum anime*.

    ps.   Beata gens cuius est dominus deus eorum, populus quem elegit dominus
          in hereditatem sibi [Ps 32:12 (Roman Psalter)].

    R.   Ecce oculi domini super timentes eum sperantes autem in misericordia
          eius [Ps. 32:18 (Roman Psalter)].

Sancti Amici conf. [3 Nov.]

⟨In.⟩   Dum domini legem m/// [hole, 3–4 words to end of line]

          /// [several folios missing]

[fol. Br]

[Sancte Cecilie (22 Nov.)]

⟨Co. Confundantur⟩

⟨ps.⟩Veniunt mihi miserationes tue et vivam, quia lex tua meditatio mea est [Ps 118:77].

R. Fiat domine [dom. omitted in Gallican and Roman psalters] cor meum immaculatum [Ps 118: 80]. In tuis [cue to communion *Confundantur*].

Sancti Clementis pape [23 Nov.]

⟨In.⟩ Dicit dominus sermones mei quos dedi in hos [=os] tuum non deficient de ore tuo, adest enim nomen tuum. Et munera tua accepta erunt super altarem meum.

ps. Misericordias tuas domine [Ps 88:1, Roman Psalter].

R. Disposui testamentum electis meis iuravi David servo meo [Ps. 88:4]. Et munera.

Gr. Iuravit dominus*

All. Iustus germinabit*

Of. Veritas mea.*

Co. Domine quinque*

Sancti Grisochoni [24 Nov.]

⟨In.⟩ In virtute tua* per ordinem.["xxxviii" added later above line]

All. Gloria et honore*

Sancte Caterine [25 Nov.]

⟨In.⟩ Me expectaverunt* ["xxxii" added later above line]

Co. Simile est*

Sancti Mercurii [25 Nov.]

⟨In.⟩ Iustus n⟨on⟩ c⟨onturbabitur⟩.*

Gr. Iustus non.*

All. Letabitur*

Of. Posuisti*

Co. Letabitur*

Sancti Petri Alexandri⟨ni⟩ [26 Nov.]

⟨In.⟩ Gloria et*

Gr.　Iustus ut palma*

All.　Posuisti domine*

Off.　Desiderium*

Co.　Posuisti.*

Vigilia Sancti Andree [29 Nov.]

⟨In.⟩　Dominus secus mare galilee vidit duos fratres Petrum et Andream, et vocauit eos. Venite post me, faciam vos fieri piscatores hominum. Ps.

[No text is given here, but the psalm-tone is written out; the incipit of the verse is given without notation on the next line. The following three elements are written one above the other, starting from the bottom.]

⟨ps.⟩Celi enarrant* [Ps 18: 1].

Gr.　In omnem terram*

Of.　Gloria et honore*

Co.　Dicit Andreas Simoni fratri suo

[fol. Bv]

invenimus messiam qui dicitur Christus, et addu⟨x⟩it eum ad Iesum.

⟨ps.⟩Dies diei eructat verbum, et nox nocti indicat scientiam [Ps 18: 2].

[An illegible area to the right of the beginning of the Alleluia following, containing three short lines, may well have given an indication of the mass of SS. Saturninus and Sisinnius; it surely must have indicated at least the feast of St. Andrew, its introit and the introit verse.]

⟨**Sancti Andree** [30 Nov.]⟩

In.　Mihi autem nimis honorati sunt.

Gr.　Constitues eos.⟩

All.　Dilexit Andream dominus in odorem suavitatis.

Of.　Mihi autem nimis*

Co.　Venite post me, faciam vos piscatores hominum. At illi relictis retibus et navi secuti sunt dominum.

　ps.　Celi enarrant gloriam dei, et opera manuum eius annuntiat firmamentum [Ps 18:1].

　R.　In omnem terram exivit sonus eorum et in fines orbis terre verba eorum [Ps 18:5]. At illi. [musical cue to communion].

　///

308

A single folio, almost complete, of a liturgical musical book, perhaps a combined antiphoner-gradual, of the eleventh century, including fragmentary remains of the Old Beneventan chant. The fragment was first discovered by Rosa Salvati of the University of Bari, and was brought to my attention by Virginia Brown. I am grateful to the Director of the Biblioteca comunale, Dottore Antonio Orsitto, and to Signor Michele Conte, for providing access to the fragment.

Description.

The fragment is now in two pieces from a single folio which was used to reinforce the binding of a book. This volume (Bede, *Commentarii in omni divi Pauli epistolas* [Venice: sub signo sancti Bernardini, 1543]) probably came to the library from one of the monastic libraries of the region of Lucera, according to the staff of the library.

The parchment leaf was wrapped around the inside of the spine, so that portions of the top and bottom of the leaf appear inside the inner and outer covers of the volume. Three slot-shaped holes were removed from the leaf to accommodate the cords of the binding and the leaf was subsequently cut in two, with the result that it now appears as two separate pieces each resembling a coarse four-toothed comb. One of these pieces is now detached from the binding; the other is still bound into the book, and thus a portion of its center is invisible (see plate 2 for a composite photograph of the pieces forming the verso).

Each piece measures about 55 mm. high by 150 mm. wide; almost nothing is lost between the two fragments, so that when they are reunited the leaf measures about 110×150 mm. There are eight systems of text and music visible; the full width of the writing area is visible, measuring about 130 mm.; each system occupies a vertical distance of about 14 mm. The original page probably had eleven such systems,[31] and would thus have had a writing area of ca. 130×154 mm.

Single bounding lines and base-lines for the script seem to have been ruled from the hair side, though they are now scarcely discernible. Perforations visible in the margins are related to the binding of the printed book and not to the manufacture of the manuscript.

The text is written in a dark brown ink, with a slightly lighter ink used for

---

[31] This estimate is based on the supposition that the series of Lauds and Vespers antiphons would have include five antiphons for psalms and one for the Gospel canticle. See the transcription of the contents below, where two complete antiphons are probably missing at the bottom of the recto side.

the musical notation. Rubrics (only one is visible) may have been written in an orange ink, which is now faded to a color almost as dark as that of the text. The musical notation is written *in campo aperto*, using the space above the text with no guidelines; the *custos* appears at the ends of musical lines, but there are no clefs or colored lines to indicate specific pitches.

Surviving decoration consists of two large (two-line) decorated initials. They are relatively simple, outlined in brown ink, using rather wide vegetal patterns divided into sections colored with blue, orange, yellow, and reddish-violet. They seem consistent with a date in the earlier part of the eleventh century. Smaller initial letters include one (beginning the responsory *Virgo est electus*) outlined in brown and infilled with blue and orange; of two letters at the beginning of antiphons, one is touched with orange and one is not.

The script is quite small and resembles in general aspect the writing of other neumed manuscripts copied in the first half of the eleventh century (e.g., Benevento, Biblioteca capitolare 40).[32] There is a noticeable inconsistency in the height of letters whether they consist solely of minims or involve a bow to which is attached an ascender or descender. The relatively large size of *e* is somewhat out or proportion to the other letters. When *e* is followed by *r,* the shoulder of the latter may be either straight or sloping. Final *s* usually rests on the base-line; at times the shaft may descend slightly below it. The headstroke of *t* in final position continues upwards to the right. Caudate *e,* i.e., *e* with cedilla, occurs in "c*ae*na" and "h*ae*c."

Contents.

The fragment shows a responsory, a series of antiphons, and an ingressa, all for the feast of St. John the Evangelist. The ingressa, a piece of the Old Beneventan repertory, has music and text which are otherwise unknown. The responsory and antiphons are well attested in manuscripts of the Gregorian tradition.

The arrangement of these pieces is in itself unusual. Were it not for the presence of the ingressa, the fragment would appear to be a leaf from an antiphoner of the office. The responsory *Virgo est electus* that begins our fragment is not universally used and is not obviously the last responsory of Matins; but since almost all antiphoners of southern Italy group all the responsories of the night office in a single series rather than separating them by the antiphons for each nocturn, and since the antiphons that follow are sung at Lauds in the south-

---

[32] This paragraph is based on the suggestions and descriptions of Virginia Brown. For a facsimile of Benevento 40, see *Benevento, Biblioteca Capitolare 40: Graduale,* ed. Nino Albarosa and Alberto Turco, Codices gregoriani 1 (Padua, 1991).

Italian tradition, we can presume that *Virgo est electus* is the last responsory of Matins.[33]

The fragment then presents a series of antiphons: though no rubric is visible, these are surely the antiphons for Lauds (and probably also for Vespers), and they are well attested in sources from southern Italy and elsewhere. However, this particular order of antiphons for Lauds or Vespers is found nowhere else in southern Italy (or elsewhere, so far as I am aware).[34] This manuscript represents a liturgical tradition not otherwise attested in the south.

So far so good. Next, in an antiphoner, should follow the music for the feast of the Holy Innocents.[35] Instead we have an ingressa, the opening chant of the mass in the Old Beneventan rite.

This ingressa is in itself an important addition to our knowledge, for it provides confirmation of a missing piece of the calendar of the Old Beneventan rite. Whereas the Beneventan masses preserved as doublets after their Gregorian counterparts in the eleventh-century graduals Benevento 38 and Benevento 40 provide music for most of the major feasts of the liturgical year, both manuscripts begin incomplete and thus deprive us of information about the practices in the Beneventan liturgy before the rites of Holy Week. This lacuna is partially filled by an eleventh-century fragment now the final flyleaf (fol. 202) of Benevento 35, which provides portions of masses of Christmas and St. Stephen.[36] A fragment at Bisceglie demonstrates the existence of Old Beneventan music for the Epiphany.[37] But we have no information about the Old

---

[33] Though it is rare, this responsory is known in southern Italy, being found for St. John the Evangelist in Benevento, Biblioteca capitolare 21. This manuscript is described in Mallet-Thibaut, 2:71–75; it is edited as manuscript L in R.-J. Hesbert. *Corpus antiphonalium officii* [CAO], 6 vols., Rerum ecclesiasticarum documenta, Series maior, Fontes 7–12 (Rome, 1963–79). The responsory *Virgo est electus* appears in an appendix of materials added to Benevento 21, fol. 304v.

[34] The traditions of Montecassino (Montecassino 542 and the eight witnesses of the Montecassino-based ordinal) and Benevento (Benevento 19, 21, 22, 23, etc.) uniformly call for the psalm-antiphons *Valde honorandus, Hic est discipulus ille, Hic est discipulus meus, Sic eum volo,* and *Ecce puer meus,* the *Benedictus*-antiphon *Iste est Iohannes,* and the *Magnificat*-antiphon *Iste est discipulus.* Though our fragment is incomplete, it is clear that the two *His est discipulus* antiphons do not appear in south-Italian order. For the Beneventan tradition, see Mallet-Thibaut, 3:703–4 (including one witness, Benevento 66, of the Montecassino ordinal). For the tradition of other places, see CAO, vols. 1 and 2.

[35] The Holy Innocents material might be preceded by some indication, probably by brief cues, of the antiphons to be used at the little hours of the feast for St. John the Evangelist.

[36] A summary of the masses known from these three sources is found in Thomas Forrest Kelly, *The Beneventan Chant* (Cambridge, 1989), 66.

[37] See Thomas Forrest Kelly, "A Musical Fragment at Bisceglie Containing an Unknown Beneventan Office," *Mediaeval Studies* 55 (1993): 347–56.

Beneventan liturgy in the time between St. Stephen and the Epiphany (nor, for that matter, for the time of Advent and Lent). If a mass for St. Stephen was sung, it is easy to imagine that ones must have existed, as in the Roman and Ambrosian liturgies, also for the two following days, St. John the Evangelist and for the Holy Innocents. The present fragment helps to fill that gap, indicating the existence of a mass for St. John, even though it is tantalizingly incomplete.

The text of the ingressa does not seem to have been used in the Roman liturgy nor in the Milanese.[38] It is a nonscriptural text, apparently beginning with the word *Hodie* as do a number of other Old Beneventan texts. Its melody, fragmentary as it is, is indisputably Old Beneventan. The melody begins with a syllabic recitation on a podatus (like the ingressa for Maundy Thursday),[39] and the surviving notation gives clear indication of the presence of the many invariable musical formulae which characterize the Old Beneventan chant.[40] It is a great disappointment that the remainder of this mass is not present, for it would add considerably to the repertory of surviving pieces of Old Beneventan chant.[41]

The presence of this ingressa raises questions about the nature of the manuscript from which our fragment survives. Although the Old Beneventan chant was once contained in separate books, most of these have been lost, and the chief surviving witnesses are books—like our fragment—which insert part of the older repertory in the context of a musical manuscript of the Gregorian chant. Thus Benevento 38 and Benevento 40 are both Gregorian graduals

---

[38] The presence of texts shared between the two "Lombard" liturgies, Beneventan and Ambrosian, has been remarked before. On musical and textual parallels between Milan and Benevento, see Kelly, *Beneventan Chant,* 181–203; see also idem, "Beneventan and Milanese Chant," *Journal of the Royal Musical Association* 112 (1987): 173–95, "Non-Gregorian Music in an Antiphoner of Benevento," *The Journal of Musicology* 5 (1987): 478–97, and *The Exultet in Southern Italy* (New York and Oxford, 1996), 208–11; and Terence Bailey, "Ambrosian Chant in Southern Italy," *Journal of the Plainsong and Mediaeval Music Society* 6 (1983): 1–7.

[39] Benevento 40, fols. 4v–5r; facsimiles in *Paléographie musicale* 21 (Solesmes, 1992), 165–66, and in color in *Benevento, Biblioteca Capitolare 40: Graduale* (see n. 32 above); transcription in *Paléographie musicale* 14:276. On this opening formula, see Kelly, *Beneventan Chant,* 100–104.

[40] On these formulae, see Kelly, *Beneventan Chant,* 97–108.

[41] It is possible that only the ingressa, and not the entire mass, was present in the manuscript. The flexibility of assignment of the further musical items in a mass, and the preservation (in the palimpsest Rome, Biblioteca Vallicelliana C 9) of a series of ingressae without their accompanying masses, suggest that ingressae may on occasion have been transmittied independently. See Kelly, *Beneventan Chant,* 80–84, 310–11; and idem, "Palimpsest Evidence of an Old-Beneventan Gradual," *Kirchenmusikalisches Jahrbuch* 67 (1983): 5–23.

which preserve some twenty-one Old Beneventan masses by recording them as doublets after the Gregorian mass for the same feast. Elsewhere there are Old Beneventan offices which survive as doublet offices in Gregorian antiphoners.[42] But nowhere so far has there been discovered a Beneventan *mass* preserved in a Gregorian book for the Office. This fragment does so, and it raises questions about the larger contents of its parent manuscript.

Can we be sure that the ingressa whose fragmentary beginning is recorded here is the beginning of a whole mass? Nothing but the discovery of the next folio will make this certain. Generally, however, an ingressa is followed by at least an Alleluia, offertory, and communion. Nowhere is a Beneventan ingressa presented in another function than as the opening chant of the Mass. (It does not, for example, do double duty as a responsory or an antiphon, where it might be found in an antiphoner of the Office.)

Thus our fragment, in addition to recording Gregorian and Beneventan chant for the same feast, contains both music for the Office and music for the Mass. We can imagine that it might have presented the full day's music for each feast in each rite: first the Gregorian music, with the Mass chants inserted after the music for Lauds; and then the Beneventan, beginning with the Mass and perhaps continuing with Office music.[43]

This is not the way music-manuscripts are organized in the Gregorian tradition, which normally separates Mass and Office. But the Ambrosian tradition does organize its musical manuscripts in precisely this way,[44] and there is a strong Ambrosian connection with the Old Beneventan chant. The Beneventan chant indeed called itself "Ambrosian," and there are liturgical and musical reasons for positing a kinship between the two rites and their music.[45]

Moreover, there is evidence in southern Italy of liturgical books with music which combine Mass and Office in "Ambrosian" fashion. At Benevento there is

---

[42] See the following note.

[43] Beneventan Office music is rare; what does survive is never more that a single office—called Vespers where it is labeled at all—for any feast; the offices consist of several antiphons, a responsory, and a concluding antiphon. Such offices survive for Good Friday, St. John the Baptist, and the Epiphany. On the Good Friday Vespers, see Kelly, *Beneventan Chant*, 55–58, esp. 56–57. Vespers for St. John the Baptist survives in the privately-owned "Solesmes Fragment"; see idem, "Une nouvelle source pour l'office vieux-bénéventain," *Études grégoriennes* 22 (1988): 5–23 with facsimile; facsimile in *Paléographie musicale* 21, plates 300–301. Office music for the Epiphany in a privately owned fragment is discussed in Kelly, "Musical Fragment at Bisceglie"; facsimile in *Paléographie musicale* 21, plates 222–23.

[44] See Kelly, *Beneventan Chant*, 184. For a survey of surviving books of the Ambrosian liturgy, see Michel Huglo, Luigi Agustoni, Eugène Cardine, and Ernesto Moneta Caglio, *Fonti e paleografia del canto ambrosiano*, Archivio ambrosiano 7 (Milan, 1956).

[45] See n. 38 above.

air of volumes which contain music for the Mass and the Office, divided
o two volumes at Easter; these are MSS 19 and 20,[46] and they suggest that
"Ambrosian" type of chant-book is not unknown in the south. A twelfth-
tury fragment now in the Vatican, containing texts and music from Mass
d Office of the time after Epiphany, may be further evidence of this kind of
ok.[47] Neither of these south Italian examples, however, gives any evidence of
shing to transmit both the Gregorian and the Old Beneventan repertories to-
ther in a single series; they are books of the Gregorian tradition.

Our fragment might possibly be extracted from a volume—more likely a set
volumes—incorporating in a single series the music for Office and Mass in
two Latin liturgical rites practiced in eleventh-century southern Italy. Such
compendium would be bulky, but the discovery of further portions of it
uld be of enormous historical and musical value.

anscription.

Missing or illegible text supplied from other south Italian manuscripts are in
gle brackets (⟨ ⟩). Editorial explanations are in square brackets ([ ]).
indicates the end of a line in the manuscript.
indicates the joint between pieces.

[recto]

Virgo est electus a domino atque inter ceteros | magis di⟨lect⟩us qui supra   CAO 7901
⟨pectus eius recum⟩bens | evangelii ⟨flu⟩enta de ips⟨o sacr⟩o dominici
⟨pecto⟩ris | fonte pota⟨vit et⟩ verbi dei ⟨gratiam in toto ter⟩rarum || orbe
diff⟨fu⟩dit. V. S⟨piritus sancti grati⟩a debriatus alti⟨us divini⟩tatis | pate-
f⟨ecit arca⟩num. De ipso. |

Va⟨lde h⟩onorandus est b⟨eat⟩us Iohannes qu⟨i sup⟩ra pectus | domini in   CAO 5309
cena recubuit. euouae.

Hic est discipulus ⟨meus sic eum volo manere donec veniam. euouae.⟩   CAO 3052?

[two further antiphons?]

Hic⟩   CAO 3051

[verso]

est discipulus ille qui testimonium perhibet de his et scripsit hec et scimus
| quia veru⟨m est⟩ testimonium ei⟨us. euouae.⟩

Iste e⟨st disc⟩ipulus qui | dignus f⟨uit esse⟩ inter secret⟨a de⟩i ipse solus   CAO 3421

---

[46] Mallet-Thibaut, 2:61–70.
[47] Vat. lat. 10645 (a collection of fragments), fol. 63.

meru⟨it di⟩vina inspira|tione ⟨dice⟩re: in princi⟨pio⟩ erat verbum ⟨et ver-
bum⟩ erat apud ‖ deum ⟨et deus⟩ erat verbum. hoc ⟨erat⟩ in principio
⟨apud deum. euouae.⟩

Item Ingressa.

H⟨odi?⟩e beatus Io⟨hannes⟩ . . . meruit | ⟨a?⟩ domino de⟨le?⟩gi sic eum
⟨volo manere donec?⟩ | veni⟨am⟩ quia preparatum est ⟨. . .⟩ gaudium |
⟨. . .⟩

PENNE, ARCHIVIO STORICO DELL'ARCHIDIOCESI DI PESCARA-PENNE

Fragments of four leaves from a twelfth-century gradual with tropes and sequences. There are fragmentary remains of an Old Beneventan mass for the feast of the Purification. I am grateful for the generosity and hospitality of the Archivista, don Giuseppe Di Bartolomeo.

Description.

Twelve vertical strips of parchment were used to strengthen the binding of a volume of notarial records dating between 1417 and 1575 labeled "Volume cartaceo manoscritto relativo al Capitolo de Penne." Along with other manuscript fragments, these were removed and restored at the Soprintendenza Archivistica per l'Abruzzo e Molise. Some of the strips have been joined together, evidently by the restorer, to form larger portions of the original folios. The resulting restored fragments (each of one or more strips) have been given numbers and the indications "recto" and "verso" in pencil on the fragments. These numbers are not related to the ordering of folios in the original manuscript.

The fragments from this manuscripts are those numbered 6, 7, 8, 9, and 10. They form portions of four leaves which, arranged in the order in which they appeared in the original manuscript, can be described as follows:

Leaf A = fragment 6: one strip, ca. 285×45 mm., the recto side in the manuscript here labeled as verso.

Leaf B = fragment 9: two strips joined, ca. 288×37 mm., representing the inner half of its folio.

Leaf C = fragments 10 and 7: fragment 7, ca. 285×43 mm., is one strip, the innermost of the folio; fragment 10 consists of the outermost two strips of the same folio, ca. 289×48 and 287×42 mm. A very small portion of the writing area is missing between fragments 7 and 10. The recto side of the folio is fragments 10v+7r; the verso is 10r+7v.

Leaf D = fragment 8: four strips, which provide almost the full written surface of the original folio, measuring about 286×144 mm.

The leaves of the original manuscript must have had outside dimensions roughly 290×145 mm., with a writing surface of about 235×125 mm. Folios are ruled on the flesh side with double bounding lines at right and left (those on the left are clearly visible on fragment 9v, those on the right on fragment 8v). The first line at the left is used to place the clef, the second to begin the text, though this second line is often disregarded; text and music often violate the boundaries on the right. Equally spaced drypoint lines are ruled to receive text and music; four lines are used for each system of text and music, the lowest for the text, and the three lines above it as a musical staff; each system of four lines is 18 mm. high. There are fourteen long lines of text and music per page.

Brown ink is used for the writing of text and music. The musical notation was written in a separate campaign; its ink appears darker than that of the text on leaf C, and lighter on leaf A. Orange ink is used for rubrics and decorated initial letters.

Decoration consists of large letters for the introits of masses, evidently to mark the beginning of the music for each feast. Two such letters survive (for *Gaudeamus,* leaf A verso, and *Spiritus domini,* leaf D recto), each the height of two systems of text and music. The letters are drawn rather roughly in out-line in orange ink; the *G* has interlaces and vegetable motifs; the *S,* divided into panels, has a bulbous shape at its top that may have been intended as an animal or human head. One initial, beginning the sequence *Advenit spiritus sanctus,* is the height of a single text-system, outlined in black and filled in with orange. Smaller letters (for the beginnings of liturgical chants other than introits) are the size of normal capitals but are highlighted with orange ink. Orange is also used for rubrics and to highlight letters of the internal lines of sequences and internal portions of liturgical chants (psalm, verse).

Like the script of the Lanciano bifolium discussed above, the small and well-formed script of the Penne strips was influenced by both the Montecassino and the Bari types of Beneventan.[48] Here the Bari type exerted the stronger force: this is evident in the generally broad aspect of the writing, slight leftward lean, roundness of the bows of letters like *d* and *q,* and usually straight shoulder of *r* in ligature (the *ri* ligature is the obvious exception) or connecting with a fol-lowing letter; the rubric *Ingressa* at the beginning of the feast of the Purifica-tion has an especially Bari-type look. Montecassino practice is reflected in the long shafts of *f* and *s* descending below the base-line and also in the use of straight *i* in ligature (although an occasional moderate swing to the left can sometimes be detected). The frequently pronounced length of straight *i* in liga-ture is remarkable in a neumed manuscript since descenders are usually only moderately long so as to avoid confusion with the subsequent notation. Another distinctive letter is the assibilated *ti*-ligature. Here the two curves representing the stem and cross-stroke of *t* are arranged in an almost horizontal position. As in other neumed manuscripts, the scribe permits himself abbreviations only in those places, like sequences, where the music is syllabic.

Musical notation is typical of Beneventan hands of the twelfth century. Clefs for F and C are used at the beginnings of musical lines; a red line indicating the position of F is used throughout where appropriate to the range of the music. A

---

[48] This paragraph is based on the suggestions and descriptions of Virginia Brown.

custos resembling a check-mark is used at the ends of lines to indicate the pitch of the first note of the next line, and is used occasionally elsewhere when a change of pitch-level is desired. The quilisma, which disappears from most Beneventan notations at the end of the eleventh century, is not used here.

These leaves are individual folios from four different locations in the same manuscript. The distance between the contents of leaves A and B in other surviving south Italian manuscripts is at least eighty folios; between C and D about ten folios. Although leaves B and C were near each other in the manuscript (their contents are one, two or three folios apart in other sources), they are not halves of a single bifolium, since the recto of each is the hair side of the parchment. It is conceivable, however, that leaves C and D formed a single bifolium with the hair side out; if so, they will have been probably the outermost bifolium in an unusually large quire.

It appears, though, that the manuscript must have been disassembled before being cut into strips. Strips from a bound manuscript might be expected to be taken from successive folios, or from the outer edges of available folios.[49] The result is that we have a selection from various places in the manuscript. It is to be hoped that further fragments (or folios, or quires!) of this very interesting manuscript may be recovered in the future.

Contents.

The contents of these fragments, with one exception, consist of musical materials known in southern Italy from the manuscripts of Benevento and Montecassino: liturgical chants from the Roman-Frankish "Gregorian" repertory for the Purification and St. Agatha (leaf A), the Invention of St. Michael and St. Gurdianus (leaf B), the dedication of a church (leaf C), and the vigil and feast of Pentecost (leaf D). There are sequences for Agatha, St. Michael, the Dedication of a Church; a widely known trope for Pentecost; and a prosula known also at Benevento. These materials will be considered in a moment.

The exceptional material is the fragmentary evidence of a mass in Old Beneventan chant for the feast of the Purification of the Virgin Mary. It is regrettable that we have only tiny fragments of this mass, but they are enough to provide further information about the shape of the Old Beneventan liturgy. Whereas there is surviving music in Old Beneventan style for the feast of the Purification among the antiphons for the procession and the blessing of candles, these are preserved in the repertory of Gregorian chants, and are thus not consciously transmitted as Beneventan.[50]

---

[49] Such a case is Benevento 40, which has many portions of blank outer margins cut away, evidently for re-use of the blank parchment.

[50] Two antiphons, *Lumen ad revelationem* and *Congregamini omnes*, are preserved on a

318

Except for the feast of St. John the Evangelist (see above in the discussion of the Lucera fragments), the surviving sources of the Old Beneventan chant give no evidence for masses between St. Stephen and Palm Sunday. There may have been a mass for the Purification among the many Old Beneventan masses preserved alongside their Gregorian counterparts in Benevento 38 and Benevento 40, but those portions of both manuscripts are now lacking. Thus the presence of this mass for the Purification in the Penne fragments, incomplete as it is, provides us with further liturgical information about the Old Beneventan liturgy.

The surviving music and text are unfortunately very incomplete. The rubric *Ingressa* is written in the right margin, even thought the ingressa itself begins at the beginning of the next line. We cannot be sure how large the ingressa's initial letter was, since the left portion of the page is missing; but the presence of the rubric to the right suggests that the Beneventan mass was considered part of the music for the feast of the Purification and not an entirely separate unit deserving a new beginning. This is how the Beneventan masses are presented in Benevento 38 and Benevento 40: the largest initials are for the beginning of a feast day (thus for the introit of that day); and the Beneventan mass which follows the Gregorian mass begins with a smaller initial.

The mass appears to consist of an ingressa and two further pieces, probably an offertory and a communion. Curiously, the ingressa never received musical notation. Small portions of three lines of text are visible (see plate 3):

-cepit virgo
-hel quod est
-is (*or* -us) misericor-

These do not correspond to any liturgical text known to me from the Roman or Milanese liturgies, though some texts include one or another of these excerpts.[51] The presence of nonscriptural composed texts for the ingressae of the

---

flyleaf from an eleventh-century gradual in Beneventan script in Bologna, Biblioteca Universitaria 2551 (the second antiphon is palimpsest) and in the early twelfth-century gradual Benevento 35; the second antiphon is found also in the twelfth-century Sora processional Vatican City, Biblioteca Apostolica Vaticana Reg. lat. 334. See Kelly, *Beneventan Chant*, 265, 279; facsimiles in *Paléographie musicale* 21, plates 225, 95, 311.

[51] The words "concepit virgo" appear, for example, in the responsories *Adorna thalamum* (CAO 6051) and *Videte miraculum* (CAO 7869), and in two Ambrosian responsories *Adorna thalamum* and *Senex puerum* (*Paléographie musicale* 6 [Solesmes, 1900; rpt. Berne, 1972], 149), but none of those texts includes any of the other portions of the ingressa. The second portion of text, "-hel quod est," may refer to Simeon's prophecy, "et gloria plebis tuae Israhel," but this configuration of words is unknown to me. The third portion, "-is (*or* -us) misericor-" can be found in the *Magnificat* antiphon "Qui fecit in me magna potens est, recordatus Dominus misericordiae suae" (CAO 4471).

Beneventan liturgy is no surprise,[52] and this ingressa is doubtless a paraphrase relating to Mary's virginity, the prophesy of Simeon, and the Song of Mary.

The second item in this Beneventan mass appears to be neither a gradual nor an Alleluia. Old-Beneventan graduals are rare in mixed Gregorian-Beneventan sources;[53] moreover, such a piece would have a substantial verse, not present here. An Alleluia would begin with a long melisma on the opening word, and would most likely be set to one of two melodies generally used in the Old Beneventan liturgy for this function. Even though the opening word with an abbreviated melisma might have appeared in the lost portion, the melody here does not correspond to any known melody for Alleluia in the Old Beneventan liturgy.

It appears, then, that the next piece is an offertory. In the Beneventan liturgy these are relatively simple antiphons without verses, similar in style to the Beneventan communions. The text of this piece is fragmentary, but it corresponds to the text *Senex puerum portabat* used in the Milanese liturgy as a psalmellus.[54] Although the Milanese melody is not that of the Penne fragments, the two liturgies share many liturgical texts.

The third and last item in the mass is presumably a communion. Its text, admittedly fragmentary, corresponds to the *Magnificat* antiphon *O dei genitrix* found, so far as I know, only in Benevento, Biblioteca capitolare 21.[55] In Benevento 21 the text is set to the melody of the well-known "O-antiphons" of Advent, whereas in the Penne fragments the same text appears in the context of a mass with a clearly Old Beneventan melody. It is easy to imagine that the antiphon may be a reworking of a text from the Old Beneventan liturgy, whose original is now partially recoverable in this fragment. The text is not known elsewhere with either melody, but there is evidence, in Benevento 21 and elsewhere, of Old Beneventan communions being preserved in Gregorian manuscripts as antiphons.[56] Although the Penne fragment preserves only a tiny

---

[52] See Kelly, *Beneventan Chant*, 73–74.

[53] See ibid., 75.

[54] A version of this piece may be consulted in London, British Library Add. 34209, p. 130 (facsimile in *Paléographie musicale* 5 [Solesmes, 1896]; transcription in *Paléographie musicale* 6:149); A slightly longer Milanese text is a responsory (on p. 131 in Add. 34209; transcription in *Paléographie musicale* 6:149), which also includes the fragmentary text from Penne.

[55] CAO 4022.

[56] Benevento 21, fol. 236 presents for the Holy Twelve Brothers of Benevento the *Magnificat* antiphon *Hos duodecim*, which is also used in Benevento 40, fol. 122, as the communion of the Old Beneventan mass. The Old Beneventan communion *Inter natos* of John the Baptist is found as a *Magnificat* antiphon in the so-called "Solesmes flyleaves" (see Kelly, "Une nouvelle source pour l'office vieux-bénéventain," facsimile, p. 6, and pp. 9, 10, 20, 23); the Old Beneventan communion *Sancta Maria exora*, for the Assumption, is found as an

portion of this text, it seems a reasonable supposition that the text as a whole is that preserved also in Benevento 21.[57]

The remaining contents of these leaves are what one might expect to find in a complete gradual-troper-sequentiary from southern Italy. As in other such manuscripts, tropes and sequences are integrated into the calendar rather than being gathered into separate sections of the manuscript, and the offertories are provided with verses. There is no evidence of psalmody for the communions.[58]

The repertory of tropes is this manuscript is unfortunately difficult to determine, since we have only one surviving example, a trope for Pentecost (see plate 4). With one exception there is no place in the surviving fragments where a trope is clearly absent; we do not have the beginning of the mass of the Invention of St. Michael or that of the Dedication, which might well have had tropes. The exception is the mass of St. Agatha, for which a trope is provided in Benevento 35; that trope, however, is unique among all the south Italian sources of tropes, and was likely a late (and somewhat corrupt) importation to the region.[59] The trope *Spiritus sanctus descendit* for Pentecost is found also in Benevento 34, 38, and 40, and different versions of it are found Benevento 35 and 39. These trope elements are importations from a widespread tradition.[60]

The use of prosulae for Alleluias is frequent in south Italian manuscripts, and one is found here as well. The Alleluia *Dum complerentur* for Pentecost provides a syllabic addition for the long melisma in the middle of the verse. This prosula is found also in Benevento 34, 35, 38 (added in a second hand), 39, and 40.[61]

antiphon in the fragment now Berkeley, University of California, Bancroft Library ff 2MS A2M2 1000:6 (facsimile in *Paléographie musicale* 21, pl. 221). In a related penomenon, a group of Old Beneventan communions is found together as antiphons for the weekly *mandatum* ceremony in Vatican City, Biblioteca Apostolica Vaticana Ottob. lat. 145; the difference in this latter case is that, whereas the pieces are used both as communions and as antiphons, they are transmitted in the Ottoboni manuscript as being Old Beneventan music, whereas in the cases of Benevento 21 and the Berkeley fragment, the Old Beneventan communions are presented as antiphons in a Gregorian context. On the Ottoboni manuscript, see John Boe, "A New Source for Old Beneventan Chant: The Santa Sophia Maundy in MS Ottoboni lat. 145," *Acta Musicologica* 52 (1980): 122–33.

[57] The text is relatively long, and its continuation occupied not only the first line of folio Av, but also much of its second line (which begins with only the first three syllables of the Introit *Gaudeamus*, placed to the right so that the initial G could extend into the left margin.

[58] The ends of two communions are clearly visible (*Ultimo* for the vigil of Pentecost and *Benedicite* for the Invention of St. Michael), and neither has either a verse or a psalmodic ending attached.

[59] See Planchart, *Beneventanum troporum corpus I* 1:26 (trope 24).

[60] See ibid. 1:66–67 (trope 71).

[61] See Mallet-Thibaut, 2:500; the text is edited from Benevento 34 and Paris, Bibliothèque nationale de France lat. 776 in Olof Marcusson, *Prosules de la messe 1: Tropes de*

Five sequences are present in these fragments, though none of them is complete. They are sequences generally found in southern Italy, and are representative of the repertory of sequences as known from the five gradual-tropers now at Benevento. These sequences are indicated in the table below.

SEQUENCES IN THE PENNE FRAGMENTS

The table refers to the following:

Lance Brunner, "Catalogo delle sequenze in manoscritti di origine italiana anteriori al 1200," *Rivista italiana di musicologia* 20 (1985): 191–276;

Mallet-Thibaut (see n. 1); page numbers are those of the index in volume 3, which refers to the various manuscripts in which the sequences appear;

Analecta hymnica medii aevi [AH], ed. Guido Marie Dreves, Clemens Blume, and Henry Marriott Bannister, 55 vols. (Leipzig, 1886–1922).

Incipit	Feast	Benevento MSS	Brunner	Mallet-Thibaut	AH
Eia organica	St. Agatha	35	228	3:1101	37:97
Rex nostras	Inv. St. Michael	38 39 40	258	3:1196	37:61
Ad templi . . . supra	Dedication	34 35 38 39 40	209	3:1041	53:402
Ad templi . . . fundata	Dedication	35 38 39 40	208	3:1041	7:243; 53:402
Advenit spiritus	Pentecost	34 35 38* 39 40	209	3:1043	37:34

* erased

With the exception of *Rex nostras,* which appears to be of West Frankish origin,[62] the sequences are of Italian origin. The two sequences beginning *Ad templi huius limina* are set to the same melody, and use much of the same language. They are often transmitted together in the Beneventan manuscripts, although the version *Ad templi . . . supra* is much less widespread in Italy than its sister, being found only in the manuscripts of Benevento and in the Penne fragments.

The liturgical materials from the Roman-Gregorian repertory in the Penne fragments are all familiar from their regular use in southern Italy and elsewhere. Appendix 2 shows the corresponding portions of the liturgical year from

l'alleluia, Corpus troporum II, Acta Universitatis Stockholmiensis, Studia Latina Stockholmiensia 22 (Stockholm, 1976). Marcusson's edition did not take other Beneventan manuscripts into account.

[62] See Richard L. Crocker, *The Early Medieval Sequence* (Berkeley, 1977), 12, 178–81, 438.

other south Italian manuscripts; it will be seen that the manuscript from which these fragments come does not exactly reproduce the repertory of any surviving manuscript.

Benevento 35 is closest in content to Penne, though it has a trope for Agatha not used here. It is the only manuscript to have the tract *Diffusa* for the Purification (although it includes it as an alternative); and it is the only manuscript with both of Penne's Alleluias for Pentecost (though they are in reverse order in a group of five Alleluias).

Transcription.

Missing or illegible text supplied from other south Italian manuscripts are in angle brackets (⟨ ⟩). Editorial insertions and comments are in square brackets ([ ]).
* indicates a piece given only in incipit without musical notation.

For leaf A, the transcription is arranged so as to show the surviving text line by line. The other leaves have been transcribed so as to show the structure of their contents, with line breaks shown by a vertical mark (|).

[Leaf A recto = fragment 6v (hair side)]

⟨**Purificatione beate Marie virginis**⟩

⟨Tr. Diffusa est gratia in labiis tuis propterea
benedixit te deus in eternum.⟩
  ⟨v. Specie tua et pulchritudine tua intende⟩   et prospere proce-
  ⟨de et regna. v. Propter veri-⟩   tatem et man-
  ⟨suetudinem et iustitiam et educes te⟩   mirabiliter dex-
  ⟨tera tua. v. Audi fili-⟩   a et vide et in-
  ⟨clina aurem tuam quia concupivit⟩   rex speciem tu-
  ⟨am.⟩

⟨Co. Responsum acce-⟩   pit Symeon
  ⟨a spiritu sancto; non visurum se mortem, nisi videret⟩ christum dominum.

                                                                   INGRES.
  ⟨. . .⟩   cepit virgo
  ⟨. . .⟩   hel quod est
  ⟨. . .⟩   is misericor-
  ⟨. . .⟩

⟨Of.? Senex puerum portabat,⟩   puer autem
  ⟨senem regebat, quem virgo concepit et pos-⟩   t par-
  ⟨tum quem genuit⟩   adoravit.

⟨Co.? O dei genitrix virgo ave gratia plena; ex te enim ort-⟩us est sol [verso = fragment 6r (flesh side)]

| iustitie quem Sym | ⟨-eon vidit, exclamavit dicens: |
| | Nunc dimittis, domine, servum tuum in pace.⟩ |

⟨In sancte Agathe⟩

⟨In.⟩ Gaudeamus om   ⟨-nes in⟩
      domino di   ⟨-em festum celebrantes sub honore Agathe⟩
      martires de cuius   ⟨passione gaudent angeli et collaudant filium⟩
      dei.

   ps. Eructav   ⟨-it cor meum [Ps 44:2].⟩
⟨Gr.⟩   ⟨Adjuvavit eam deus vultu⟩
      suo de   ⟨-us in medio eius non commovebitur.⟩
   v. F   ⟨-luminis impetus⟩
      letificat civ   ⟨-itatem dei, sanctifica-⟩
      vit taverna   ⟨-culum suum altissimum.⟩
Alleluia.   ⟨v. Mens mea so-⟩
      lidata est et   ⟨Christo domino in eter-⟩
      num fundat   ⟨-a permanet.⟩
⟨Seq. ⟩
                 ⟨Eia organica cantica.⟩
      Armonica c   ⟨-uncta genera ydropica musica dulcisona clan-⟩
      gant alle   ⟨-luia . . .⟩.[63]

[Leaf B = recto: fragment 9r (hair side)]

⟨Inventione sancti Michaelis⟩

⟨Seq.⟩[64]

      ⟨Rex nostra Christe laudes vultu nunc sereno sumito
      Impius ne nobis hostis ut optat noceat.
      Pectoras et casta spiritus almis conservet.
      Tu princeps populum pastorum hunc petre serva benigne.
      Laxando cui datum est nexus celo terraque solvere.
      Gressus que per cerulas vo⟩visti magistro presul ⟨tuo.⟩
      Optenti | ⟨iam pondere mereamur iniqui⟩ effice.
      Ave Maria ⟨vi⟩rgo virginum | ⟨valde colenda.
        Facta fulgida⟩ lucis omnia porta creantis nosque | ⟨redimentis potenter.
      Et nostri mem⟩or esto poscimus talia presta.
        Exuti | ⟨rebus inde corporis carminis no⟩vo odax revocantis ovanter.

[63]   As in Benevento 35, fol. 20r; AH 37:97.
[64]   Supplied here from Benevento 40, fols. 59v–60r.

Nam | ⟨Michahelis sunt suffragiam ma⟩gna nobis requirenda per evum.

Spiritus hac | ⟨hominis Christo famulantis in ar⟩ce polorum beate.

Pulsis iam torporibus | ⟨Christe sancte te poscimus hostem fugacem⟩ vincere posse dato desuper triumpho. |

⟨Debellans insidiantis maligni⟩ molimina dyra potenter protege clemens | ⟨tibi famulantes in evum.

Hiesu ter⟩ge cura medicinali vulnera adu- | ⟨nate plebis.

Pellens nubila tibi sup⟩plicantum atque canentum tuos | ⟨gloriosos triumphos.

Nunc gloria pa⟩tri natoque et spiritui almo sit per cunc- | ⟨ta secula. Amen.⟩

⟨Of. Stetit⟩ angelus iusta aram tem- | ⟨pli habens thuribulum au⟩reum in manu sua et da-

[verso = fragment 9v (flesh side)]

ta sunt ⟨ei⟩ incensa multa e⟨t ascendit fu-⟩ | mus aromatum in conspect⟨u dei alleluia. ⟩

⟨v. In con-⟩ | spectu a⟨ngelorum psallam tibi domine⟩ | et adorabo ad templum sanct⟨um tuum et confitebor tibi domine.⟩ |

Co. Benedicite omnes angeli domini d⟨omino; hymnum dicite et superexal-⟩ | tate eum in secula.

Sancti Gurdiani ⟨Cyrilli et Petri[?]⟩

⟨In. Sancti tui domine*[?]⟩

⟨Gr. Justorum anime⟩ | in manu dei sunt et n⟨on tanget illos⟩ tormentum malitie.

v. Visi su⟨nt oculis insipi-⟩ | entium mori illi autem ⟨sunt in pace.

⟨Alleluia. v. Sancti tui domine*?⟩ |

Of. Mirabilis deus in sancti su⟨is deus Israhel ipse dabit vir-⟩ | tute et fortitudinem pleb⟨i sue. Benedictus de-⟩ | us alleluia.

v. E⟨xurgat deus et dissipen-⟩ | tur inimici eius et fugian⟨t qui oderunt a faci-⟩ | e eius.

v. Pereant pecc⟨atores⟩ ////

[Leaf C recto = fragments 10v/7v (hair side)]

⟨In dedicatione ecclesie⟩

⟨Seq.⟩[65]

⟨Ad templi huius limina dedicata
gaudiorum laudes ovans pleps concrepent devota.

---

[65] As in Benevento 35, fol. 105–105v, with emendations from Benevento 40, fol. 64v; edited in AH 7:242–43 (no. 222).

Hodierna die qua adest festum annuum.
Supra cacumina montium fundata enim est domus ista.
Et exaltata est super omnes colles structura deifica.
Ex auro mundo circumtecta [-texta?] gemmis et rutilat muri per ampla.
Ubi adorant sanctam trinitatem populus omnes individuam.
Hec est enim illa celestis aula et angelorum patria.
Ecclesia firmaque petra dicta eternaque est regia.
Ex vivisque petris pacis visio urbs celsa Hierusalem etenim struitur bea-
    torum agmina.⟩
Qua deus quoque ⟨rex sum⟩mus super omnes unus ce⟨lsior⟩ in throno
    presi|de illo cui semper l⟨aus.⟩
Maiestate et virtu⟨te et⟩ angelorum sanc|ta agmina.
Inde⟨fessa(s)⟩ voce laudes personant⟨ur [Benevento 35: persolvatas] ce-⟩
    litus gloria.|
Adorandus me⟨tuen⟩dus est namque locus ⟨ubi a⟩dorandus atque | col-
    laudandus ⟨ide⟩m deus imperat cel⟨um et ⟩terra.
Beati sunt | qui habitant er⟨go in⟩ domo domini quia ab ⟨alto⟩ laudant regi
    mag|no personantur ⟨celi⟩tus gloria.
Adonay ⟨bene⟩dicte sapientie | claritas.
Fac ⟨nos⟩ ga[u]dere in evum in au⟨la s⟩ancta tua in seculorum | secula.
    Amen.

Seq.[66]

Ad templi huiu⟨s l⟩imina dedicata
ga|udiorum laude⟨s ov⟩ans plebs devota con⟨cre⟩pent.
Hodierna | ⟨die quia⟩ adest festa annuata.
Fun⟨d⟩ata enim est domus | ista supra cacumina montium.
Et exaltata est supra om⟨nes⟩ | colles structura ⟨deifica [? illegible]⟩.
⟨Nam hec est magna Hierusalem civitas scilicet illa superna.⟩[67]
Ex auro mundo circumcontex|ta gemmis⟨que rut⟩ilans muri per ampla.
⟨Ubi adorant⟩[68]

    [verso = fragments 7r/10r (flesh side)]

sancta[m] trini⟨tatem⟩ populus omnes ind⟨ividu⟩am.

---

[66] As in Benevento 35, fols. 105v–106v, with emendations from Benevento 40, fol. 65r–
66r; edited in AH 7:243–44 (no. 223); cf. AH 53:402–4 (no. 249); transcribed from Rome,
Biblioteca Casanatense 1741 in Lance W. Brunner, *Early Medieval Chants from Nonantola.
Part IV: Sequences*, Recent Researches in the Music of the Middle Ages and Early Renaissance 33 (Madison, 1999), lxv–lxvi, 69–71 (no. 35).
[67] This line, usually present, is omitted in the Penne fragment.
[68] This line, not present in the sources cited in n. 66 above, is completed from the preceding sequence.

Hec est illa | celestis aula ⟨ange⟩lorum patria.

Eccles⟨ia fir⟩maque petra eter|naque regia.

⟨Dictaque est pacis visio urbs celsa Hierusalem.⟩[69]

E⟨x v⟩ivisque petris struit⟨ur be⟩atorum agmina.|

Qua deus quoque ⟨summ⟩us rex super omnes u⟨nus c⟩elsiori in thro|no preside illo

⟨Sunt m⟩aiestates ⟨choros virtutes atque praestant⟩ angelorum sanctam | agmina.

Inde⟨fess⟩a voce laudes per- ⟨. . . [*Benevento 35:* persultant; *Benevento 40:* persultat]⟩ celitus.

Gloria[70] ⟨et regnum illi per secla depromunt.

Venerandus est ergo locus noscitus ubi preesse nomina talia.

Adorandus est idem deus imperans celum et terram cunctaque maria.

Denique omnis evum mortalis laudes ordo in excelsis decantant agmina sacra.

Gaudia celi poscat futura atque vita felicemque quietam munera plena.

Nosque pium flagitemus Christum semper esse nobiscum.

Paradysique ianua reseret ultimo spiritu ferentem vitam eternam. Amen.⟩

[Leaf D recto = fragment 8v (flesh side)]

⟨In vigilia pentecostes⟩

⟨Of. Emitte spiritum tuum et creabuntur, et renovabis faciem terre. Sit gloria domini in secula, alleluia.⟩

  ⟨v. Benedic anima mea . . . [?]⟩

  ⟨v. Confessionem et decorem induisti⟩ amictus lumen sicut vestimentum. |

  v. Extendens celus sicut pellem qui tegit in aquis | superiora ⟨e⟩ius qui ponis nubem ascensum tuum. Sit. |

Co. Ultimo festivitatis diem dicebat Ihesus qui in me credunt flumina | de ventre eius fl⟨u⟩ent aque vive; hoc autem dixit de spritu quem accepturi erant | credentes in eum, alleluia alleluia. |

Pentecostes

Tropus.

  Spiritus sanctus descendit | in discipulos ⟨Ch⟩r⟨ist⟩i hodie de quo gaudentes dicamus. SPIRITUS DOMINI. |

  v. Discipulos flammas infundit pectora blandas. |

---

[69] This line, usually present, is omitted in the Penne fragment.

[70] The remainder of the leaf is blank. The sequence is completed here from Benevento 35.

⟨In.⟩ Spiritus domini replevit orbem | terrarum, alleluia, et hoc quod continet
omnia scientia habet vocis | alleluia alleluia alleluia.

  ps. Exurgat deus et ⟨dissipentur⟩ [Ps 67:1].

Alleluia. | v. Repleti sunt apostoli spiritu sancto et ce|perunt loqui magnalia dei. |
All⟨eluia⟩* v. Dum complerentur dies pentecostes.

Prosa.

Pentecostes promis|sus celo spiritus adveniens ignis in enigmate bis senos
simul commorantes

[verso = fragment 8r (hair side)]

domini replevit pleniter discipulos linguis effantur omnibus Christi nec-
|non magnalia

[the Alleluia continues] erant omnes pariter sedentes.

Sequentia

Advenit spiritus sanctus hora die tertia.
Discipulis prebens charismatum dona. |
Omniumque linguarum eos loqui fecit genera.
Que prius in edificio turris con|fuderat superbia.
Et cunctis mirantibus dei non timent loqui magnalia. |
Quos ante Christi passio fugere fecit per compita.
Hos tamen compescere | procurabat iudeos
    plenos esse credens musti de crapula satis in|credula.
Quibus non metuit respondere petrus que noverat vera.
    Non | est abundantia vini clamans sed Iohelis prophetia.
Ecce cuius pri|mo negaverat fide predicat miracula.
Plenos eos iamque crediderat | linguarum gentibus munera.
Hodie sancta meri⟨ta que colenda.
Quibus spiritus sanctus | terram⟩[71] replet fluentem
    discipulis atque lingua⟨rum varia venit lingue⟩ | notitia.
In hac ergo die petimus tua sancta
mittere digneris ⟨ge⟩nitor alme | dona
    cordium atque nostrarum queque pelle tenebrosa.
Coop⟨er⟩ante nato ⟨tuo qui factus es mundi hostia.
Spiritus eiusdem sancti facienti quoque gratia.
Cuius est laus et gloria per secula. Amen.⟩[72]

---

[71] The illegible passages here and in the next line are supplied here from Benevento 40.
[72] The sequence is completed here from Benevento 40, fol. 79r.

APPENDIX 1

TRANSCRIPTION OF THE TROPE FOR ALL SAINTS IN THE LANCIANO FRAGMENT

Music typography by Alejandro Planchart

Lanciano, Archivio di Stato, fondo notarile Giovanni Camillo Girelli 1632–1638.

APPENDIX 2

LITURGICAL CONTENTS OF THE PENNE FRAGMENTS COMPARED WITH OTHER SOUTH ITALIAN MANUSCRIPTS

The contents of the Penne fragments are listed in the first column. Bracketed items in that column are not present in Penne but are found in other manuscripts in the table. Other manuscripts inventoried:

B33   Benevento, Biblioteca capitolare   33. Notated missal, s. X/XI.
B40   40. Gradual with tropes, s. XI¹.
B38   38. Gradual with tropes, s. XI¹.
B34   34. Gradual with tropes, s. XII².
B35   35. Gradual with tropes, s. XII¹.
B39   39. Gradual with tropes, s. XI ex.
MC 540   Montecassino, Archivio della Badia 540. Notated missal, s. XI/XII.
MC 546   546. Gradual, s. XII/XIII.
V6082   Vatican, Biblioteca Apostolica Vaticana Vat. lat. 6082. Notated missal, s. XII.

\\\ = lacuna   no = not present   * = indicated by an incipit   (2 of 2) = second of two   rep = *versus ad repetendum*

Penne	B33	B40	B38	B34	B35	B39	MC 540	MC 546	V6082
LEAF A **Purificatione**									
Tr. Diffusa	*Tr.* Lumen 14r	\\\	\\\	*Tr.* Nunc 49r	*Tr.* Nunc *Al. Tr.* Diffusa 18v	\\\	*Tr.* Nunc	*Tr.* Nunc 33r	*Tr.* Nunc 38r*
v. Specie									
v. Propter									
v. Audi									
⟨*Of.* Diffusa*⟩	14v	\\\	\\\	49r (verses)	19v (verses)	\\\	79r (no vv.)	33r*	38r*
Co. Responsum	14v	\\\	\\\	49v	19r	\\\	70r	33r	no

Penne	B33	B40	B38	B34	B35	B39	MC 540	MC 546	V6082
[OLD BENEVENTAN MASS]	no	≡	≡	no	no	≡	no	no	no
[S. Blasii]									
S. Agathe		no	no	no	no	≡	no	no	38v
In. Gaudeamus	14v	≡	≡	49v	19v (trope)	≡	80r?	34r	38v*
Gr. Adiuvavit	14v	≡	≡	50r	19v	≡	80r?	34r*	38v*
[*Tr.* Qui seminant]	15r	≡	≡	50r	no	≡	no	34r	38v*
All. v. Mens	no	≡	≡	no	20r	≡	81r (+prosula)	34r	38v
Seq. Eia organica	no	≡	≡	no	20r	≡	no	no	no
LEAF B									
Inv. S. Michaelis									
Seq. Rex nostra	no	59v (2 of 2)	81v (2 of 2)	no (2 others)	no (2 others)	77r (2 of 2)	≡	≡	no
Of. Stetit	95r (no v.)	60r (+prosula)	82v (+prosula)	170v (no pros.)	103r (+prosula)	79r (+prosula)	≡	≡	181r (no pros.)
v. In conspectu				171r*	103r	79r*	≡	≡	181r (+v. +v. ad R.)
Co. Benedicite	95v	61r	83r	no	no	no	≡	≡	no
[OLD BENEVENTAN MASS]	no	61r	83r	no	no	no	≡	≡	no
[S. Victoris]	no	no	no	no	no	no	≡	≡	181v

Penne	B33	B40	B38	B34	B35	B39	MC 540	MC 546	V6082
S. Gurdiani									
In. Sancti*	no	61v*	83v*	171r	103v*	79r	≡	≡	181v
Gr. Justorum	no	61v	83v	171r	103v	79r	≡	≡	181v*
v. Visi	no								no
[All. v. Sancti tui*]	no	61v*	83v*	171r*	no	79v*	≡	≡	no
[All. v. Pretiosa]	no	no	no	no	no	no	≡	≡	181v*
Of. Mirabilis	no	61v	83v	171r	104r	79v	≡	≡	181v*
v. Exurgat									
v. Pereant									
[Co. Justorum*]	no	62r*	84r*	171v*	104r*	79v*	≡	≡	181v*
LEAF C									
Dedic. ecclesie									
Seq. Ad templi . . . supra	no	64v	86r (1 of 3)	174v	105r	82v	≡	≡	no
Seq. Ad templi . . . fundata	no	65r	87r (2 of 3)	no	105v	83v	≡	≡	no
LEAF D									
Vig. Pentecostes									
⟨Of. Emitte	no	75v	96r	184r	111v	94r	≡	≡	168r (no vv.)
v. Benedic⟩									
v. Conf.									
v. Extendens									
Co. Ultimo festivitatis	no	75v	96v	184v	111v	94v	≡	≡	168r (+v.)

Penne	B33	B40	B38	B34	B35	B39	MC 540	MC 546	V6082
Pentecostes									
Tropus Spiritus s. v. Discipulis	no	76r (1 of 2)	96v (2 of 2)	184v (1 of 2)	112r	94r (1 of 2)†	≡	≡	no
In. Spiritus domini	99r	76r	97r	185r	112r (+rep)	94r	≡	≡	168v (+rep)
[Kyrie. Cunctipotens]	no	no	no	185v	no	no	≡	≡	no
[Kyrie. Christe clivis]	no	76	no	no	no	no	≡	≡	no
[Kyrie Supplices]	no	no	97r	186r	no	no	≡	≡	no
[Gloria*]	no	77r	no	no	no	no‡	≡	≡	no
[Gloria. Qui deus]	no	no	no	no	no	no	≡	≡	no
All. v. Repleti	no	no	no	no	115r (5 of 5 +prosula)	no	≡	≡	no
All. v. Dum com.	99r (1 of 2)	77r (3 of 3)	97v (2 of 2)	187r (2 of 3)	113r (3 of 5)	95v (2 of 2)	≡	≡	169r (2 of 2)
Prosula Pentecostes	no	77r	no	187r	113r	95v	≡	≡	no
Seq. Advenit spiritus sanctus	no	78r (2 of 2)	no (but a pal. seq)	188v (2 of 2)	113r (1 of 2)	97r (2 of 2)	≡	≡	no

† The trope has an additional verse between the two in our fragment: see Planchart, *Beneventanum troporum corpus I*, trope 71.
‡ The introductory trope *Sacerdos dei* appears on fol. 95v.

X

New evidence of the Old Beneventan chant

The material presented here summarizes information that has come to light in the last ten years regarding the repertory and practice of the Beneventan chant of southern Italy. The information itself is provided in tabular form; the commentary that precedes it gives some brief background and points out a few interesting details.

The Beneventan chant is one of those varieties of liturgical song that made the early medieval musical landscape so much more interesting than it later became, after the Carolingian urge to unity, combined with ecclesiastical reform, created a universal music that we now call Gregorian chant. Some of these early chant repertories have survived: the Ambrosian chant of Milan; the music of the Old Spanish liturgy. Others, like the Gallican chant, have disappeared.

The Beneventan chant falls somewhere between these two categories; there are no splendid complete books of Beneventan chant, as there are such books from the repertories of Spain and from Milan. The Beneventan chant, probably like others, was systematically suppressed, mostly in the course of the eleventh and twelfth centuries, in favour of the imported repertory we now call Gregorian. The result is that the Beneventan chant survives mostly in fragments and palimpsests, and in a few odd places in manuscripts of Gregorian chant where a scribe, out of some archaizing tendency, or some Beneventan *campanilismo*, has included a piece or two of the older repertory alongside the chant that ultimately replaced it.

This chant is called Beneventan because it was written by scribes who practised what Elias Avery Lowe called the Beneventan script,[1] a characteristic and calligraphic hand that was written in an area of Italy south of Rome that included Naples, Bari, and essentially every other place in Latin southern Italy and along the Dalmatian coast until at least the thirteenth century, and sometimes far longer. The chant itself is centred on Benevento, the capital of the Lombard

---

[1] See Lowe in the bibliography at the end of this article.

duchy of southern Italy, whose dukes in the eighth century asserted their independence at the fall of the northern Lombard kingdom to Charlemagne. They crowned themselves, struck coins, built the palace church of Santa Sofia, and they endowed and influenced many monasteries including Montecassino. The capital city of Benevento was until the eleventh century a stronghold of Lombard culture. The principal sources of the chant are there, and the repertory itself has a Beneventan cast, preserving music for feasts of special significance to the southern Lombards; the south Italian feast of St Michael on 8 May, commemorating an appearance by the archangel on Monte Gargano; Saint Barbatus, Bishop of Benevento; and the Holy Twelve Brothers, whose relics were entombed in the palace church of Santa Sofia.

But nobody in southern Italy called this music Beneventan chant; when they referred to it by name, they called it 'Ambrosian' chant. It was not, however, the Ambrosian chant which we know from manuscripts of the area around Milan: it was the southern Ambrosian chant. There are connections, however, liturgical and musical, between the northern and southern Ambrosian chants and they suggest that the Lombard kingdom, north and south, once shared a similar ('Old Lombard'?) liturgy and music, whose subsequent separate developments produced the repertories we now call Beneventan and Ambrosian. We will continue to call the southern Italian chant 'Beneventan'; more properly it should be called by the name its users gave it, but the result is just too confusing.

A word of background about the fragmentary aspect of this repertory is in order. Without it the information reported here will look very paltry, but in fact in its context it does contribute to our knowledge of this chant.

Three sources give us about 90 per cent of the surviving Beneventan music. Two of these, now Benevento, Biblioteca capitolare manuscripts 38 and 40, are eleventh-century Gregorian graduals in which the scribes have included duplicate Masses, in Beneventan chant, for a number of principal feasts. Each of these manuscripts is incomplete at the beginning, so we are deprived of any Beneventan music they may have contained for the time before Holy Week. This lacuna is filled to some extent by the third source, a single folio (now fol. 202 of Benevento, Biblioteca capitolare, MS 35) from a pure Beneventan gradual, containing portions of the Masses of Christmas and St Stephen. Altogether in these three sources there is music for twenty-two feasts, including much interesting music for Holy Week. The surviving repertory is not enormous, and these three sources preserve most of what we have.

And yet there are about a hundred sources that give some evidence of the Beneventan chant. For the most part they are fragments or palimpsests, or a piece or two included in another manuscript; most of them do not add to the known repertory, but they do tell us a great deal about the geographical and chronological extent of the Beneventan chant, and they confirm that the chant was widely copied and used.

Ten years ago, in *The Beneventan Chant* (from which the introduction here is summarized) I published a list of all the sources of Beneventan chant known at the time. It is inevitable that further searching should unearth a few more items, and my purpose here is to bring the record up to date, to enumerate the sources of and about Beneventan chant that have come to light since 1989.

It would be pleasant to report the long-awaited discovery of a complete book of Beneventan chant, filling in all the lacunae and revealing at last the many details of the Beneventan liturgy which remain undocumented. This is not that moment, alas, although that book may still exist somewhere in an unvisited cupboard in a distant library. What I can report is a number of small additions to what we know. Some of these new items are very modest indeed, but they add to the growing evidence that the Beneventan chant was widely practised, that it is not a curious phenomenon limited to a few odd manuscripts. They add also to our liturgical knowledge, documenting music for feasts of which we previously had no evidence, and they increase the known repertory of Beneventan pieces.

A number of the documents listed here have already been reported in the literature; I include them for the sake of completeness, so that this list, together with the one printed in 1989, will provide a complete conspectus of the known sources of Beneventan chant.

Let us turn to the sources themselves. I have divided them into categories according to the sort of information they supply, and numbered the entries for ease of reference.

In category A are three mentions in archival documents of books which are likely to have contained Beneventan chant. Two of these are 'antiphonaria' which are called 'ambrosianum': undoubtedly a reference to the local variety of Ambrosian chant. The documents date from late tenth-century Salerno and from Bari in the middle of the eleventh century. Whether the books were new when they were mentioned is impossible to tell. These two important cities are known from other sources to have practised the Beneventan chant, but no substantial source from either place has been found; now, however, we know at least that they existed. The third book mentioned is from Benevento, included in an inventory of books made in the 1370s. At that time the book in question was described as 'a missal in Lombard – that is to say, Beneventan – script, *secundum antiquatam consuetudinem'*. There are of course many things that might be meant by 'antiquatam consuetudinem'; but that ancient custom, whatever it was, was recognized as such at Benevento and needed no further explication. I include it in this list because it may well be a book of the Beneventan liturgy. If so, it is interesting that in the latter part of the fourteenth century a Beneventan bibliographer seems to have recognized it as part of a disused tradition. The lost Capuan manuscript, no. 4, surely contained the Exultet in its Beneventan form, but may or may not have been a book of the Beneventan liturgy.

In category B, I include two obscure, if fascinating, references to the monastic Office at Benevento being performed according to the 'old custom', or being an 'officium longobardum'. As late as the sixteenth century the nuns of San Vittorino, even if they no longer sang, performed this 'officium longobardum'. It may

X

have been performed according to the same 'antiquatam consuetudinem' mentioned in the fourteenth-century inventory. I wonder whether it was Beneventan chant.

Category C consists of sources that are further witnesses to elements of the Beneventan chant already known. They give evidence of the sheer numbers of written sources of the chant that once existed, and in some cases they show the remarkable persistence of the tradition.

Many of these sources preserve music for Holy Week and Easter. This is not surprising, given the archaizing nature of Holy Week on the one hand, and the fact that the sources known heretofore are also mostly sources of music for Holy Week and Easter. These pieces were the last to disappear.

The Beneventan Vespers of Good Friday, having only three psalm-antiphons and a fourth for *Magnificat*, each accompanied by a *versus ad repetendum*, are already known to have been widely disseminated, appearing as far north as Subiaco. The second of the two tonaries in the important music-theoretical manuscript Montecassino 318 (whose liturgical tradition is not that of Montecassino or of Benevento) includes the Beneventan antiphons of Good Friday Vespers among its many Gregorian examples sorted into differentiae, with no evidence that these antiphons are in any way remarkable to the scribe. Further sources (nos. 8 and 9) give the full text of the Vespers music, but without notation: these include a pontifical of Benevento, and a remarkable series of manuscripts from Salerno, dating from the thirteenth to the fifteenth century, but all stemming, it appears, from a liturgical reform operated in the twelfth.

Those Salerno manuscripts retain, well into the fifteenth century, a substantial amount of music for the Beneventan rites of Holy Saturday, including one piece, no. 12, that does not survive anywhere else.

The Beneventan Exultet has two elements: a text, which disappears early everywhere except at Salerno, where it survives in the two fifteenth-century missals (no. 13 in the list); and a melody, known from many other places in the Beneventan liturgy, which often survives even when the text of the Exultet has shifted to the now-universal Franco-Roman version. This melody has been identified in a further fragmentary source from Stroncone in central Italy, no. 14. The lost ordinal of Capua, no. 4, known only from eighteenth-century quotations, evidently contained the Beneventan Exultet, and probably much else besides.

The alleluia of the Beneventan Mass of the paschal vigil, with its remarkable text, shared by the Ambrosian liturgy, about arising like a drunken man from wine, is at the centre of a complex of melodic adaptations. The alleluia itself appears occasionally as a substitute for the responsory at Easter Vespers in the Roman rite (nos. 15 and 16); its text is prescribed in eight copies of the ordinal of Montecassino and in the Salerno breviary, suggesting its widespread use in southern Italy from the eleventh to at least the fifteenth century (a corroborating thirteenth-century witness is already known in the gradual Benevento 30).

The melody of this alleluia was adapted to new texts, usually beginning with the word 'Hodie', for a variety of other feasts. Beneventan Masses for these feasts do not survive, but the alleluias have passed into the Roman repertory in a few places. Such adaptations were already known for Christmas (*Hodie natus est nobis*, Baltimore, Walters Art Museum, MS W. 6, fol. 86), for Saint Peter (*Hodie migravit ad Dominum*, Benevento 39, fol. 121), and for the Transfiguration (*Hodie transfiguratus est Dominus*, Benevento 39, fol. 140v). The keen eye of Alejandro Planchart noticed three further examples of this melody, all appearing in the Old Roman gradual of Santa Cecilia. These include a further witness of *Resurrexit tamquam dormiens*; a second copy of *Hodie natus*, together with a new second verse; and a new member of the group, *Hodie baptizatus*, for Epiphany. These were evidently borrowed into the Roman manuscript from a south Italian gradual-troper; and since they were borrowed along with the sequences they accompanied, it is clear that the source for the Roman borrowings was not a book of old Beneventan chant. But these new pieces strengthen the idea that this melody may have been more widespread in the Beneventan liturgy than was hitherto supposed, and that there may have been a series of alleluias, like the *Dies sanctificatus* series in the Roman chant, of which these are the surviving fragments.

The translated Greek sticheron *Pascha ieron*, known to have been sung at the end of Easter Vespers in twelfth-century Rome, is found without notation at the end of the Beneventan Mass for Easter in Benevento 40. A second witness, perhaps erased personally by Boccaccio and certainly overwritten by him, contains this piece with its notation (see no. 19) in fragmentary form on two parts of a single folio now divided between two manuscripts in Florence (and one of these has paper pasted over it). Unfortunately, not much of the notation can be read with certainty, but the original manuscript was a late thirteenth-century Gregorian gradual. It also contained the Easter alleluia *Resurrexit*, no. 18.

At Benevento itself, certain items of purely local interest survived for quite a long time. The fourteenth-century antiphoner now in the Biblioteca capitolare, no. 22 on the list, continues to transmit the series of old Beneventan antiphons for two local feasts: Saint Barbatus (Bishop of Benevento in the sixth century) and the Holy Twelve Brothers, martyrs 'invented' and buried in the church of Santa Sofia in the eighth century. Indeed, one of the antiphons of Saint Barbatus, or at least its text, was converted into a alleluia-verse and appears in a group of local Masses published at Benevento in 1868. I wonder if it was ever sung, and to what melody?

So much for the new evidence of pieces already known from other sources – most of those discussed so far have been published in facsimile, as indicated in the list. Now we turn to new sources that extend the known repertory of Beneventan chant.

The first of these, no. 25, is not really a separate piece, but an *alleluia* added to the end of a Gregorian antiphon *Deus de celis qui es pius*. The alleluia, added in the margin, has a clearly Beneventan cast, even though it is incomplete. Perhaps it was a remnant of the old order used from time to time in festival seasons and applied to new music.

In a private collection in the Adriatic city of Bisceglie, near Bari, is a bifolium from an eleventh-century gradual now serving as a book-cover (no. 26). It contains, in addition to the Gregorian Office of the Epiphany, an almost complete Vespers for the Epiphany or its Octave in Beneventan chant. There are four antiphons, each with the characteristic Beneventan *versus ad repetendum*, and a great responsory with a prosula; this responsory bears a close kinship to a piece known at Milan. It is incomplete here, and presumably an antiphon followed for *Magnificat*, as in the other two surviving Beneventan Offices (for Good Friday and for St John the Baptist).

Number 27 is a fragment wrapped around the spine inside the cover of a sixteenth-century book in the Biblioteca comunale of Lucera (Province of Foggia); the parchment, shaped like two combs, comes from an eleventh-century manuscript and includes the beginning of a Beneventan Mass for Saint John the Evangelist. The fragment shows a Gregorian responsory and a series of antiphons, followed by an ingressa, all for the feast of St John the Evangelist.

The ingressa is the opening chant of the Beneventan Mass, and this fragment is in itself an important addition to our knowledge, for it provides confirmation of a missing piece of the calendar of the Old Beneventan rite. We know almost nothing of the time between St Stephen's Day and Holy Week (except for the Epiphany Office just mentioned), owing to the incomplete state of the two main manuscripts, Benevento 38 and Benevento 40. We do have part of a Mass for St Stephen in the fragmentary leaf in Benevento 35 mentioned earlier, and it is easy to suppose that the Beneventan liturgy, like the Roman and the Ambrosian, would have celebrations for all three days after Christmas: Stephen, John, the Holy Innocents. Now we have confirmation of one more.

The text of the ingressa, so far as I can tell, is not used in the Roman liturgy nor in the Milanese. It is a non-biblical text, apparently beginning with the word 'Hodie', as do a number of other Old Beneventan texts. Its melody, fragmentary as it is, is indisputably Old Beneventan.

How can we be sure that this fragmentary ingressa is the beginning of a whole Mass? Nothing but the discovery of the next folio will make this certain. Generally, though, an ingressa is followed by at least an alleluia, offertory and communion. Nowhere is a Beneventan ingressa presented in another function than as the opening chant of the Mass. But nowhere so far has there been discovered a Beneventan Mass preserved in a Gregorian book for the Office. This fragment does so, and it raises questions about the larger contents of its parent manuscript.

We can imagine that the manuscript might have presented the full day's music for each feast in each rite: first the Gregorian music, with the Mass chants inserted after the music for Lauds; and then the Beneventan, beginning with the Mass and perhaps continuing with Office music.

This is not the way music manuscripts are organized in the Gregorian tradition, which normally separates Mass and Office. But it is the way music books are organised in the Ambrosian liturgy, and in the Old Spanish. Moreover, there is evidence in southern Italy of liturgical books combining Mass and Office in what we might call 'Ambrosian' fashion. At Benevento there is a pair of volumes of this kind, MSS 19 and 20, and they suggest that the 'Ambrosian' type of chant-book is not unknown in the south. A twelfth-century fragment now in the Vatican (Vat. lat. 10645, fol. 63) may be further evidence of this kind of book. Neither of these south Italian examples, however, gives any evidence of wishing to transmit both the Gregorian and the Old Beneventan repertories together in a single series; they are books of the Gregorian tradition.

This tiny fragment might possibly be extracted from a volume – more likely a set of volumes – incorporating in a single series the music for Office and Mass in the two Latin liturgical rites practised in eleventh-century southern Italy. Such a compendium would be bulky, but the discovery of further portions of it would be of enormous historical and musical value.

A final item, no. 28, helps to fill the liturgical lacuna between Christmas and Lent, for it has a Beneventan Mass for the Purification of the Virgin, 2 February. Fragments of four twelfth-century leaves now in Penne were part of a gradual with tropes and sequences, a manuscript similar in repertory to the gradual Benevento 35. One of the leaves preserves portions of this Beneventan Mass coming after the Gregorian Mass for the Purification. The Mass seems to consist of an ingressa and two further pieces, probably an offertory and a communion. Curiously, the ingressa never received musical notation. We have only tiny fragments of this Mass, but they are enough to provide further information about the shape of the Old Beneventan liturgy. Although we already have two antiphons in Beneventan style for the feast of the Purification, these are preserved in the repertory of Gregorian chants, and are thus not consciously transmitted as Beneventan.

The texts here are fragmentary. The surviving portions of the ingressa do not correspond to any liturgical text known to me from the Roman or Milanese liturgies, though some texts include one or another of these excerpts. The presence of non-biblical composed texts for the ingressae is characteristic of the Beneventan liturgy; this ingressa is a paraphrase relating to Mary's virginity, the prophesy of Simeon, and the Song of Mary. The second piece of the Mass, probably an offertory, has a fragmentary text whose surviving portion matches the text of the psalmellus *Senex puerum portabat* in the Milanese liturgy. The third and last item in the Mass is presumably a communion. Its text, admittedly fragmentary, corresponds to the antiphon *O dei genitrix* found, so far as I know, only in the antiphoner Benevento 21, where it has the melody of the well-known 'O-antiphons' of Advent. But there is evidence, in Benevento 21 and elsewhere, of Old Beneventan communions appearing in Gregorian manuscripts as antiphons. Although the Penne fragment preserves only a tiny portion of this text, it seems a reasonable supposition that the text as a whole is that preserved in Benevento 21 with a Gregorian melody.

The items listed in this survey do not significantly alter our view of the Old Beneventan chant. They are distributed like the Beneventan chant already known:

Masses preserved as doublets in Gregorian graduals; a few treasured items for
Holy Week and for local saints, preserved persistently and often in places where
the Gregorian repertory had no substitute to offer; and a few tantalizing
reminders that this liturgy was once widely copied and disseminated in a purer
form.

I should like to acknowledge here the generosity of my colleagues. I am not
the discoverer of most of the items in this list, though I may have been the first
to recognise them for what they were. Were it not for colleagues like John Boe,
Virginia Brown, Carmelo Lepore, Alejandro Planchart, and many others, this list
could not have been assembled. There is a small but dedicated group of scholars
who work on Beneventan matters, and the information produced in the last few
years is astounding: Herbert Bloch's long-awaited book on Montecassino; Francis
Newton's study of the scriptorium of Montecassino; Jean Mallet and André Thibaut's staggeringly complete catalogue of the manuscripts of Benevento; John
Boe and Alejandro Planchart's edition of Beneventan tropes (*Beneventanum Troporum Corpus*); the continuing cataloguing and description of Beneventan sources
by the Monumenta Liturgica Beneventana project in Toronto, led by Virginia
Brown, Roger Reynolds and Richard Gyug. There never was a finer group of
collaborators, or of friends. I wish for all scholars the blessing of such splendid
colleagues.

A. References to lost books of the Beneventan rite

1. **Salerno 990**: From a document of donation of Prince John and Princess Sikel-
gaita to the church of Sancta Maria in Salerno.

'... sed et offeruimus ibidem unum calicem de argentum et due patene similiter de
argentum, et unum turibulum similiter de argentum seu et quadtuor circitoria cerica et
quadtuor copertoria similiter serica, quam et offeruimus ibidem codices quem inferius
declaramus: duobus liber comites, unum indifanario de die et unum de nocte, **et alium
ambrosianum**, una omelia quadragintam et alia feriale, et unum collectarium qui abet de
apocalipsin et de moralia iob, eptati-/p.200/cum unum et unum salomon, una moralia
iop et dua questionaria, et gestarulum unum, et unum manule serico ...' (Morcaldi *et
al.*, *Codex Diplomaticus Cavensis*, vol. 2 (1875), doc. 425, pp. 297–300 at 298.)

2. **Bari, April 1067**: from a document in which Iohannes, basilicos cliricos et
cubuclisius, gives under certain conditions to the monk Nicolaus presbiter et
monachus of Bari the church of Sanctus Priscus de loco Sao.

'De mobilibus vero [Iohannes] dedit mihi [Nicolao] omelia et feriale cum gestis de sanctis.
antifonarium de dia et alium de nocte, **unum ambrosianum**. et solomonem psalterium.
orationale. viginti tribus quaterni de gestis sanctorum. una cortina. sabano rosata ...' (G.
B. Nitto de Rossi, Francesco Nitti di Vito, *Codice diplomatico barese*, vol. 1, Le pergamene
del duomo di Bari (952–1264) Bari, n. p., 1897. No. 26, anno 1067, April.)

3. **Benevento, 1370s**: An inventory of the goods of fifty-three parish churches
under bishop Ugo Guidard of Benevento, made in the 1370s. Of the books listed,

forty-seven (24 per cent) are either *antiqui* or *de lictera longobarda*, four of these *cum notis*; from 'ecclesie sce Marie abbatis arnonis' is listed '**missale unum de lictera longobarda secundum antiquatam consuetudinem**'. (Benevento, Biblioteca capitolare, MS 295, fol. 60; Lepore, 'L'Eglise de Bénévent', 65, n.2; see also Lepore, 'Gli *scriptoria* beneventani'.)

4. **Capua, 11th century**: Natale, *Lettera*, pp. 65–6, mentions a lost 'Rituale o sia Messale Capuano', s. 11, from which he cites the Beneventan text of the Exultet. See Kelly, *The Exultet*, 142.

B. References to older (Beneventan?) practice

5. Benevento, Biblioteca capitolare, MS 71, fol. 2r Capitula constitutionum of bishop Ugo Guidard, 1371: 'Item statuimus et ordinamus ut officium semper et integraliter secundum usum et consuetudinem romane curie et hic approbatum, persolvatur et dicatur, abietta **consuetudine antiqua, que peius dicenda est corruptela**, circa laudum decantationem . . .' (Lepore, 'L'Eglise de Bénévent', 65, n.2; see also Lepore, 'Gli *scriptoria* beneventani')

6. Benevento, Biblioteca capitolare, MS 322, fol. 13v (Visitation of the monastery of S. Victorinus, 17 April 1542); the abbess, and others, say they perform the 'officium longobardum', but without music (by this time the number of nuns had been reduced to seven): 'Interrogata quomodo persolvunt divinum officium, dixit quod officium predictum dicunt tam diurnum quam nocturnum horis debitis, sed semper in verbis et non cantatum, et quod faciunt dicta domna abbatissa cum aliis sororibus et monialibus **officium longobardum secundum regulam sancti Benedicti**'. (Lepore, '*Monasticon*', 167n600)

C. New witness to known Beneventan music

a. Good Friday: Vespers

7. Good Friday Vespers antiphons are included in the second tonary of Montecassino, Archivio della Badia, MS 318 (11c.). On the tonary, see Brunner, 'A Perspective'; Merkley, *Italian Tonaries*, 120–8, 244–85; Huglo, *Les tonaires*, 193–7.

8. Rome, Biblioteca Casanatense, MS 614, pontifical of Benevento (12/13c.), has Good Friday Vespers, s. n., fols 150v–51.

9. Salerno, Museo Diocesano: five manuscripts have full text of Good Friday Vespers s. n. The manuscripts have no shelf numbers; they are described in Capone, *Il duomo*, vol. 2; sacramentary, Capone no. 5 (13c.); ordinal, Capone no. 7 (14c.); breviary, Capone no. 6 (15c.); two missals, Capone nos. 3 and 4 (15c.). Facsimile from Salerno 3 in PM 21, p. 279.

b. Holy Saturday

i. Pieces retained at Salerno (on all of these see PM 21, pp. 388–90; Kelly, 'La liturgia')

10. *Ad vesperum demorabitur fletus*: cited in sacramentary, notated in the ordinal and the two missals.

11. *Sicut cervus*: cited in sacramentary, notated in the two missals; in Capone 3 the melody has subsequently been simplified.

12. *Transivimus*: cited in sacramentary, notated in the ordinal and the two missals.

13. *Exultet*: Beneventan text of the Exultet cited in sacramentary and ordinal, and highly ornamented melody notated in the two missals (see Kelly, *The Exultet*, 111–12; Latil, 'Un Exultet inedito').

ii. Exultet
[13. Salerno manuscripts (above)]

14. Stroncone (near Terni), Archivio Storico Comunale Frammenti, Giudiziario 21-1, a single leaf from a notated missal of central Italy, 12 1/2c., shows the beginning of the Exultet with the Beneventan melody. The threefold *Lumen Christi* has the ornamented melody found also in the central Italian manuscripts New York, Morgan Library, M 379; Rome, Vall. F 29; Rome, Vall. B 32; Subiaco XVIII (on these see Kelly, *The Exultet*, 154–5). Facsimile of the fragment (but not showing *Lumen Christi*) in Baroffio, *Frammenti*, 81, description p. 18.)

[4. Capua, lost ordinal, cited Natale]

c. Easter:

i. Alleluia Resurrexit tamquam dormiens
15. The ordinals of Montecassino and related ordinals of Benevento, 11–13c., cite the text at Easter Vespers. ('ad uesp. ... *Alleluia*. v. *Resurrexit tamquam dormiens dominus*'.) The manuscripts containing this ordinal include five in the Montecassino tradition: Vatican MS Urb. lat. 585 (*c.* 1100); Paris, Bibl. Mazarine, MS 364 (*c.* 1100); Los Angeles, Getty, MS 83.ML.97 (ex Ludwig IX.1; ex Montecassino MS 199; *c.* 1100); Montecassino MS 198 (12/13c.); Montecassino MS 562 (13c.). Three further twelfth-century versions, based on the Montecassino ordinal, were made for churches in Benevento: Naples, Bib. naz., MS VI E 43 (for a church dedicated to St Mary); Vatican MS Vat. lat. 4928 (Santa Sofia); Benevento, Biblioteca capitolare, MS 66 (s. Petri *intra muros*). An edition of these sources is forthcoming.

16. Salerno, Museo Diocesano, breviary s. n. (Capone, *Il duomo*, no. 6). The full text is given s. n. at Easter Vespers.

17. Cologny-Genève, Bibliotheca Bodmeriana, MS 74, fol. 80v, at Easter Mass (Kelly, 'A Beneventan Borrowing'; facs. PM 21, p. 226)

18. Firenze, Biblioteca Medicea-Laurenziana, MS 33.31, fol. 41 (see the entry below), at Easter Mass (Brown, 'Bocaccio'; facs. PM 21, p. 231)

ii. Pascha yeron imin

19. This Greek sticheron, found without notation in Benevento 40 at the end of the Beneventan Easter Mass, is found with barely discernible notation on a palimpsest folio from a Neapolitan manuscript of the late thirteenth century now divided between two autograph manuscripts of Boccacio: Firenze, Biblioteca Medicea-Laurenziana, MS 29.8, fol. 77v and MS 33.31, fol. 45r (Brown, 'Bocaccio'; facs. PM 21, p. 232)

d. Adaptations of alleluia Resurrexit tamquam

20. *Hodie natus est nobis dominus, gaudent omnes angeli in celo,* second verse *Gaudete in domino semper gaudete cum letitia quia natus est nobis saluator mundi,* Christmas, third Mass, Bodmer 74, fol. 12v (Kelly, 'A Beneventan Borrowing'; PM 21, p. 226)

21. *Hodie baptizatus est dominus in iordane ab Iohanne Baptista,* Epiphany, Bodmer 74, fol. 19v (Kelly, 'A Beneventan Borrowing'; PM 21, p. 226)

e. Offices of local saints

i. Saint Barbatus (antiphon-series in Beneventan style: see Kelly, TBC, 257)
[15. Three Beneventan ordinals of the Montecassino group, 12–13c., cite these antiphons: Naples, Bib. naz., MS VI E 43 (for a church dedicated to St Mary); Vatican MS Vat. lat. 4928 (Santa Sofia); Benevento, Biblioteca capitolare, MS 66 (s. Petri *intra muros*)]

22. Benevento, Bibl. capitolare, MS 61 (Offices of Bartholomew, Januarius, Barbatus, 14/15c., non-Beneventan script, perhaps a copy of older material; a seventeenth-century copy is Vatican MS Vat. lat. 11800) contains the Office s.n.

23. Benevento, Biblioteca capitolare, MS without shelf-number, antiphoner 14c., the full Office notated.

24. *Missae propriae* (see bibl.) of Benevento (1868), p. 9 has an alleluia-verse whose text corresponds to one of the antiphons: *Vir domini Barbatus actionibus celeber et coruscus miraculis, sectam internecionis pellendo Beneventi effulsit.*

ii. The Holy Twelve Brothers (antiphon-series in Beneventan style: see Kelly, TBC, 258)
[15. Three Beneventan ordinals of the Montecassino group, 12–13c., cite these antiphons: Naples, Bib. naz., MS VI E 43 (for a church dedicated to St Mary); Vatican MS Vat. lat. 4928 (Santa Sofia); Benevento, Biblioteca capitolare, MS 66 (s. Petri *intra muros*)]

92

[23. Benevento, Biblioteca capitolare, MS without shelf-number, antiphoner s.n. 14c., the full Office notated]

D. Sources of hitherto-unknown Beneventan music

25. Vatican City, BAV Ottoboni lat. 145 (already noted for Beneventan communions used as antiphons of mandatum: see Boe, 'A New Source'); fol. 126v, an appended alleluia, partly cut off, for a. *Deus de celis qui es pius* (the antiphon itself does not look Beneventan). Also a. *Pater sanctus dum intenta*, fol. 123 (cf. this ant. in PM 21, see index p. 443)

26. Bisceglie, private collection without shelf number: fragmentary Office of the Epiphany or of its Octave (Kelly, 'A Musical Fragment at Bisceglie')

27. Lucera, Biblioteca comunale, Cinquecentina 658, binding fragments. Beginning of a Beneventan Mass (ingressa) of St John the Evangelistss, in a context that may be a *totum*. Transcription: 'Item Ingressa. H<odi?>e beatus Io<hannes> . . . meruit | <a?> domino de<le?>gi sic eum <volo manere donec> veni<am> quia preparatum est < . . . .> gaudium / / / /' (Kelly, 'New Beneventan Liturgical Fragments')

28. Penne, Archivio Storico dell'Archidiocesi di Pescara-Penne, frammenti 6-10. Fragments of four leaves from a twelfth-century gradual-troper, including portions of a Beneventan Mass for the Purification. Transcription: 'Ingressa: . . . -cepit virgo . . . -hel quod est . . . -is [or -us] misericor- . . . [Offertory? (text supplied from Ambrosian psalmellus] <Senex puerum portabat,> puer autem <senem regebat, quem virgo concepit et pos>t par-<tum quem genui->t adoravit. [Communion? (text supplied from antiphon in Benevento 21)] <O dei genitrix virgo ave gratia plena; ex te enim ort->us est sol iustitie quem Sym<-eon vidit, exclamavit dicens: Nunc dimittis, domine, servum tuum in pace.]' (Kelly, 'New Beneventan Liturgical Fragments')

Bibliography

Baroffio, Giacomo, Cristina Mastroianni and Fabrizio Mastroianni, *Frammenti di storia medioevale: Mostra di codici e frammenti di codici liturgici dei secoli XI–XIV dall'archivio storico del Comune di Stroncone*. Stroncone: Comune di Stroncone, Soprintendenza archivistica per l'Umbria [1998].

Beneventanum troporum corpus, ed. John Boe and Alejandro Enrique Planchart, Recent Researches in the Music of the Middle Ages and early Renaissance. 16–26, Madison: A-R Editions, 1989– .

Bloch, Herbert. *Monte Cassino in the Middle Ages*. 3 vols., Cambridge, MA: Harvard University Press, 1986.

Boe, John. 'A New Source for Old Beneventan Chant: the Santa Sophia Maundy in MS Ottoboni lat. 145', *Acta Musicologica*, 52 (1980), 122–33.

Brown, Virginia. 'Boccaccio in Naples: the Beneventan Liturgical Palimpsest of the Laurentian Autographs (MSS. 29.8 and 33.31)', *Italia medioevale e umanistica*, 34 (1991), 41–126.

Brunner, Lance W. 'A Perspective on the South Italian Sequence: the Second Tonary of the Manuscript Montecassino 318', *Early Music History*, 1 (1981), 117–64.

Capone, Arturo. *Il duomo di Salerno*. 2 vols., Salerno: F.lli Di Giacomo di Giov., 1927; Spadafora, 1929.

Huglo, Michel. *Les tonaires. Inventaire, Analyse, Comparaison*. Paris: Heugel, 1971.

Kelly, Thomas Forrest. 'A Beneventan Borrowing in the Saint Cecilia Gradual', in Bernhard Hangartner and Urs Fischer, eds., *Max Lütolf zum 60. Geburtstag. Festschrift*. Basel: Wiese, 1994, pp. 11–20.

Kelly, Thomas Forrest. 'A Musical Fragment at Bisceglie Containing an Unknown Beneventan Office', *Mediaeval Studies*, 55 (1993), 347–56.

Kelly, Thomas Forrest. 'New Beneventan Liturgical Fragments in Lanciano, Lucera, and Penne Containing Further Evidence of the Old Beneventan Chant', *Mediaeval Studies*, forthcoming.

Kelly, TBC = Thomas Forrest Kelly, *The Beneventan Chant*. Cambridge: Cambridge University Press, 1989.

Kelly, Thomas Forrest. 'La liturgia, la musica e la tradizione nella Salerno del dodicesimo secolo', forthcoming.

Kelly, Thomas Forrest. *The Exultet in Southern Italy*. New York: Oxford University Press, 1996.

Latil, Agostino. 'Un "Exultet" inedito', *Rassegna gregoriana*, 7 (1908), cols. 125–34.

Lepore, Carmelo. 'Gli *scriptoria* beneventani', forthcoming.

Lepore, Carmelo. '*Monasticon beneventanum*: Insediamenti monastici di regola benedettina in Benevento', *Studi beneventani*, 6 (1995), 25–168.

Lepore, Carmelo. 'L'Eglise de Bénévent et la puissance publique: relations et conflits', in *La cathédrale de Bénévent*, ed. Thomas Forrest Kelly. Ghent-Amsterdam: Ludion/Flammarion, 1999, 45–65.

Lowe, Elias Avery. *The Beneventan Script: A History of the South Italian Minuscule. Second Edition prepared and enlarged by Virginia Brown*. 2 vols. Sussidi eruditi, 33–4. Rome: Edizioni di storia e letteratura, 1980; an expanded version of the first edition, Oxford, 1914.

Mallet, Jean and André Thibaut. *Les manuscrits en écriture bénéventaine de la Bibliothèque capitulaire de Bénévent*, 3 vols. Vol. 1. Paris: CNRS, 1984; vols. 2–3 Paris: CNRS and Turnhout: Brepols, 1997.

Merkley, Paul. *Italian Tonaries*. Ottawa: The Institute of Mediaeval Music, 1988.

Missae propriae sanctorum quorum officia celebrantur in civitate dioecesi et provincia beneventana ... Naples: Typis Cajetani nobile equitis, 1868.

Morcaldi, Michele, Mauro Schiana and Sylvano de Stephano, *Codex Diplomaticus Cavensis*, 8 vols. Milan, Pisa, Naples: Hoepli, 1873–93.

Natale, Francescantonio. *Lettera dell'abate Francescantonio Natale intorno ad una sacra colonna de' bassi tempi eretta al presente dinanzi all'atrio del duomo de Capua*. Naples: Vincenzio Mazzola-Vocola, 1776.

Newton, Francis. *The Scriptorium and Library at Monte Cassino, 1058–1105*. Cambridge: Cambridge University Press, 1999.

PM 21 = *Paléographie musicale*, Vol. 21: *Les témoins manuscrits du chant bénéventain*, ed. Thomas Forrest Kelly. Solesmes: Abbaye Saint-Pierre, 1992.

THE OLDEST MUSICAL NOTATION
AT MONTECASSINO

The oldest example of musical notation preserved at Montecassino, and the oldest surviving datable example of Beneventan notation, occurs in the colophon of Montecassino manuscript 269 on page 351. The manuscript was written at Capua before the year 949 by a certain Iaquintus while his monastic community was in exile from Montecassino.[1]

Iaquintus identifies himself in a colophon at the bottom of the page reproduced here: «Qui libro legit in isto oret pro Iaquinti sacerdote et monacho scriptore ut Deum habeat adiutorem». Another scribe has transcribed Iaquintus' rustic capitals in the (to him) more legible Beneventan script.

The manuscript, recently restored at Grottaferrata, consists of 352 pages measuring 295 × 217 mm with a writing space of 238 × 168 in two columns of 31 lines; it is a copy of St. Gregory the Great's *Moralia in Iob*. The final words *Deo gratias Amen* are spread apart to receive the notation, and they have been decorated with green and red ink. The notation itself, undoubtedly provided by Iaquintus, is written in the same black ink used for the rest of the manuscript, and the notation is also heightened with green and red inks. Iaquintus took up another pen, a finer one than he had used for the text of St. Gregory, and wrote the Beneventan neumes which give life to his prayer of thanksgiving at the completion of his task.

The neumes, few as they are, are in many ways typical of the earliest Beneventan musical notation. They are written *in campo aperto* – with no line to guide the height of the neumes; they are finely drawn, much thinner than text written by the same scribe; and they are only partially diastematic. Note the two shapes of the Beneventan torculus (the first and last neumes) which vary according to the preceding pitch; the two typical scandicus (on *Amen*); the character-

---

1   The date is based on a scribal indication (p. 13): «... quem Aligernus venerabilis Benedicti monasterii abbas ipsius cenobii capuani fieri precepit». Aligern returned to Montecassino and became its abbot in 949. See ELIAS AVERY LOEW, *The Beneventan Script. A History of the South Italian Minuscule*. Second Edition prepared and enlarged by Virginia Brown, 2 vols, Rome, 1980 (Sussidi eruditi 33-4), hereafter *TBS2*, I: 324-5; FRANCIS L. NEWTON, *Beneventan Scribes and Subscriptions, with a List of Those Known at the Present Time*, «The Bookmark», XLIII 1973 pp. 17-18.

istic four-note climacus descending from an oriscus, one punctum written sideways and the last one a longer stroke.

This thin, spidery, early type of Beneventan notation gave way in the eleventh century to a style which, though still *in campo aperto*, is much more strictly diastematic and which matches the Beneventan script in many particulars: it includes many more strictly vertical strokes; it uses the contrasting thick and thin lines typical of the script; and it is written with a pen of generally the same breadth as that used for the text.[2]

Other examples of first-stage Beneventan notation are relatively rare, and they appear to date from no earlier than the end of the tenth century.[3] The most prominent examples are listed below, in roughly chronological order. Dates are those provided by Lowe in *The Beneventan Script*,[4] where bibliography on all these manuscripts may be found.

1. Vatican City, Biblioteca Apostolica Vaticana Ms. 9820; Exultet roll of St. Peter's, Benevento (Saec. x ex.).[5]

2. Benevento, Biblioteca Capitolare Ms. 33; missal (Saec. x/xi).[6]

---

2   Examples of this 'second-stage' Beneventan notation can be seen in Benevento, Biblioteca Capitolare Mss. 38 and 40; facsimiles in *Paleographie musicale*, 14, Solesmes, 1931, rpt. Berne, 1971, plates XXIV (Ms. 38, ff. 44v-45) and XII-XXII (Ms. 40, folios 9v-20); see also the facsimiles in *Paléographie musicale*, 21, Solesmes, 1992; a complete color facsimile of Benevento 40 is *Benevento Biblioteca Capitolare 40 Graduale*, ed. Nino Albarosa and Alberto Turco, La Linea Editrice, Padova 1991 (Codices gregoriani, 1).

3   Two examples should be mentioned that might be considered earlier sources of Beneventan notation than those named below: (1) Paris, Bibliothèque Nationale de France, Ms. lat. 2832, a ninth-century manuscript of Lyons not in Beneventan script, has neumes added to the sybilline prophecy on f. 123v, but these are probably substantially later additions; a facsimile is in HIGINI ANGLÈS, *La musica a Catalunya fins al segle XIII*, Publicacions del Departament de Musica 10, Biblioteca de Catalunya, amb la collaboracio de la Universitat Autonoma de Barcelona, Barcelona 988), p. 295, figure 77. (2) Naples, Biblioteca Nazionale Ms. Vindob. lat. 5, a commentary on Vergil from the early tenth century, includes some neumes which are not however in Beneventan notation. See the facsimile in RAFFAELE ARNESE, *I codici notati della Biblioteca Nazionale di Napoli*, Olschki, Firenze 1967, pl. 8 (Biblioteca di bibliografia italiana, 47); see also pp. 176-8.

4   Above, note 1; the *Hand List of Beneventan Mss.* which appears as Volume 2 includes Lowe's original dates along with a much-expanded bibliography by Brown.

5   For a probable date of 981-987 see See ELIAS AVERY LOWE, *Scriptura Beneventana: Facsimiles of South Italian and Dalmatian Manuscripts from the Sixth to the Fourteenth Century*, 2 vols., Clarendon Press, Oxford 1929, 2, commentary to Plate LI. Complete facsimile as *Exultet-Rolle. Vollständige Facsimile-Ausgabe in Originalgrösse des Codex Vaticanus latinus 9820 der Biblioteca Apostolica Vaticana* with commentary by H. Douteil and F. Vongrey, Graz, 1975; another facsimile in GUGLIELMO CAVALLO, with GIULIA OROFINO and ORONZO PECERE, *Exultet. Rotoli liturgici del medioevo meridionale*, Istituto Poligrafico e Zecca dello Stato, Roma 1994, commentary, pp. 101-106, facsimile pp. 107-118; for many other facsimiles see *TBS2*.

6   Complete facsimile as *Paléographie musicale*, 20, Bern and Frankfurt, 1983. On Virginia Brown's dating of the manuscript in the early 11th century see footnote 16 below.

3. Manchester, John Rylands University Library Ms. 2; Exultet roll (Saec. xi in.).[7]
4. Bari, Archivio del Duomo, Benedictional roll (Saec. xi[1] [ante a. 1067]).[8]
5. Bari, Archivio del Duomo, Exultet 1 (Saec. xi[1] [ante a. 1067]).[9]
6. Vatican City, Biblioteca Apostolica Vaticana Ms. Vat. lat. 10673; gradual (Saec. xi).[10]
7. Twenty-one folios of a notated missal now preserved in four Swiss libraries (Saec. xi).[11]
8. Lucca, Biblioteca Capitolare Feliniana Ms. 606; a missal, of the eleventh century as it seems to me, in ordinary minuscule. Folios 150-156v contain an appendix using early Beneventan notation.[12]
9. Baltimore, Walters Art Museum Ms. 6; a missal for the diocese of Canosa (post a. 1054).[13]

None of these sources can be dated so precisely as Montecassino 269 (the oldest and most precisely dated is Vat. lat. 9820), but paleographical evidence suggests that there is no notation in this list from before the end of the tenth century.

At Montecassino itself the same situation obtains. Although no complete musical manuscripts of Montecassino survive from before the age of Desiderius (abbot 1058-87), surviving examples of musical notation in the early Beneventan style can be dated, like the sources named above, from the late tenth through the middle of the eleventh century. These may be grouped into three categories according to the function of musical notation in the manuscript. They are listed below; dates in quotation marks are those of Lowe in *TBS2*, where further bibliography on each manuscript may be found.

---

7   Complete facsimile (pp. 123-127) and commentary (pp. 119-122) in CAVALLO, *Exultet*.
8   Complete facsimile (pp. 143-145) and commentary (pp. 147-150) in CAVALLO, *Exultet*; another facsimile in GUGLIELMO CAVALLO, *Rotoli di Exultet dell'Italia meridionale*, Adriatica, Bari 1973, plates 12-17.
9   Complete facsimile (pp. 129-134) and commentary (pp. 135-141) in CAVALLO, *Exultet*; another facsimile in CAVALLO, *Rotoli*, plates 1-11.
10   Complete facsimile in *Paléographie musicale*, 14.
11   Lucerne, Stiftsarchiv St. Leodegar Ms. 1912 (bifolium); Peterlingen, Stadtarchiv (without number; 5 folios); Zürich, Staatsarchiv Ms. W 3 AG 19 (fasc. III) (10 folios); Zürich, Zentralbibliothek Ms. Z XIV 4, nos. 1-4 (4 folios). For facsimiles and a study of these fragments see ALBAN DOLD, *Die Zürcher und Peterlinger Messbuch-Fragmente*, Texte und Arbeiten, 25, Beuron, 1934; see also *Paléographie musicale*, 14, plates X-XI.
12   Facsimiles in *Paléographie musicale*, 21, plates 232-241; *Paléographie musicale*, 13, plates XXXIV-XLIII. See also THOMAS FORREST KELLY, *Beneventan Liturgy and Music in Tuscany: Lucca, Biblioteca Capitolare Feliniana ms. 606*, «Ricerche di storia dell'arte», XLIX 1993, pp. 51-4.
13   Facsimiles of folios 124v-125 and folio 86 in *Paléographie musicale*, 21, plates 1-3.

A. Musical cues in a liturgical manuscript.

10. Montecassino 230 («a. 969-87» according to Lowe, but dated by Francis Newton 1058-1066[14]), pp. 157-168, contains a series of complete offices with lections for the common of saints. At first the scribe notates the beginning of each musical piece above its text; but in the course of p. 158 he changes his system (perhaps for lack of space in the format of the manuscript) and indicates thereafter for each piece only its mode using Roman numerals in red ink.

B. Surviving fragments of musical manuscripts.

11. Montecassino Compactiones VI contains a leaf (labeled 'Saec. x' in pencil) from a noted missal of the late tenth century.[15]

12. Montecassino 271 («saec. xi med.») contains the Dialogues of St. Gregory the Great; but it is palimpsest on portions of three manuscripts. One of these, in uncial («saec. vii/viii») contains texts of St. Augustine and portions of a Gregorian missal without notation. Other pages are palimpsest on portions of two missals in Beneventan script («saec. x/xi»), one of which (masses of Lent with lacunae) contains musical notation.[16]

13. Three fragmentary remains probably from a single gradual of the late tenth or early eleventh century: (1) an orange envelope in Montecassino Compactiones XXII contains a fragment (about 95 × 70 mm.) with Gregorian Alleluias and their verses;[17] (2) a leaf (marked '3' in pencil) also in Compactiones XXII shows in its margin the reversed offset impression (about 64 × 32 mm) of texts and neumes probably from the same manuscript; (3) in Compactiones VII, which contains some 217 folios of a missal «saec. xii»,[18] one of

---

14 The date is based on Paschal tables in the manuscript; see LOWE, *Scriptura Beneventana* 2, commentary to Plate LI. On the manuscript's origin at Montecassino rather than Capua, see *TBS2*, 1: 340. Francis Newton's extensive study has re-dated the manuscript to 1058-1066; it is the work of the master scribe Grimoald. See NEWTON, *The Scriptorium and Library at Monte Cassino, 1058-1105*, Cambridge University Press, Cambridge 1999, pp. 43-47, 89-95, 408 and plate. 136; see the index, p. 408.

15 Loose fragments recovered from bindings and elsewhere at Montecassino are kept in a series of numbered folders; within the folders the individual items are often not numbered or otherwise identified.

16 On the palimpsests see VIRGINIA BROWN, *Early Evidence for the Beneventan Missal: Palimpsest Texts (Saec. X/XI) in Montecassino 271*, «Mediaeval Studies», LX 1998, pp. 239-306. Brown (p. 241) considers these missals to be older than Benevento 33, which she dates in the early elevent century.

17 I was unable to locate this envelope on a visit to Montecassino in April 2002; I photographed the fragments in 1986.

18 Studied in ALBAN DOLD, *Umfangreiche Reste zweier Plenarmissalien des 11. und 12. Jhs. aus Monte Cassino*, «Ephemerides liturgicae», LIII 1939, pp. 114-144.

two leaves marked '7' is repaired with a fragment (58 × 40 mm) from the same gradual.

14. Montecassino 446 consists of two sections (the first is mentioned below at no. 16). The second (pp. 199-352), in ordinary minuscule «saec. xii», is palimpsest on pages of a musical manuscript, probably a Gregorian antiphoner, of the early eleventh century.

15. Montecassino 468, a volume of Lombard and canon law in ordinary minuscule «saec. xii/xiii» contains many palimpsest pages from an unidentified musical manuscript, probably a Gregorian gradual (cf. the rubric *co* on p. 9), of the early eleventh century.

C. Occasional neumes in non-musical manuscripts.

16. Montecassino 446, in its earlier portion (pp. 1-198, «saec. x/xi») includes on pp. 83-85 a series of three Alleluias with musical notation.

17. Montecassino 218, a glossary «a. 909», includes on p. 142 a line of textless neumes in a hand probably of the eleventh century.[19]

18. Montecassino 148, a homiliary «a. 1010»[20] has a few neumes added to the beginning of the *Carmen sanctorum Diodori et Mariniani*, p. 243.

19. Montecassino 103, a homiliary «saec. xi in.», contains neumes for the sybilline prophecy *Iudicii signum* on pp. 185-6; these are written over a still earlier erased notation.[21]

20. Montecassino 462, a homiliary «saec. xi in.», contains neumes for the sybilline prophecy *Iudicii signum* on pp. 272-3.

21. Montecassino 95 («saec. xi[1]») contains Eusebius (Rufinus), *Historia ecclesiastica*; at the end, much in the celebratory manner of Iaquintus in Montecas-

---

19 These neumes appear to be a short self-contained melody; although the presence of liquescence ought to make it possible to identify the original text, I have not been able to locate it. The neumes are written in a space between two lines near the end of an incomplete glossary (the glossary identified by G. Loewe as 'asbestos', and which is edited from the eighth-century St. Gall 912 in GEORGIUS GOETZ, *Corpus Glossariorum Latinorum*, 4, pp. 199-208, with variants from Montecassino 218). Neither the text of St. Gall 912, nor that of the tenth-century Vatican City, Biblioteca Apostolica Vaticana MS Vat. lat. 1469, which also contains a version of this glossary, corresponds to the Montecassino glossary at the end of Montecassino 218. It appears that the Cassinese scribe interrupted the glossary in the course of the letter 'u', continuing it later after leaving the space in which the neumes now appear. The page has a number of other later additions in space left blank. For a discussion of Montecassino 218, with a facsimile of folios 26v-27, see LOWE, *Scriptura beneventana*, pl. XXXIII. The manuscript is dated in the earlier tenth century in GUGLIELMO CAVALLO, *La trasmissione dei testi nell'area beneventano-cassinese*, «Settimane di studio del Centro italiano di studi sull'alto medioevo», XX 1975, pp. 357-424 at 363-64 note 35.

20 The date is given by the scribe Martinus on p. 505; see LOWE, *Scriptura beneventana*, 2, commentary to Plate LVII; NEWTON, *Beneventan Scribes*, pp. 27-28; NEWTON, *The Scriptorium*, p. 34 note 31 and index p. 408.

21 See NEWTON, *The Scriptorium*, index p. 407.

sino 269, the scribe writes a verse of the hymn *Gloria tibi trinitas* with musical notation (p. 372).

22. Montecassino 451, a pontifical «saec. xi», includes notation for a few musical pieces: the responsory *Responsum accepit*, p. 200, and *O redemptor sume carmen*, pp. 259-60.[22]

★ ★ ★

Evidently the renewal of liturgical books under abbot Desiderius resulted in the erasure or dismemberment of the older musical manuscripts of Montecassino. All the items in category B above are either fragments or they are palimpsests whose upper scripts were written beginning in the age of Desiderius. The older notation, less than precise as to absolute pitch, was rejected in favor of more modern (and more elegant) manuscripts with clefs and pitch-lines. Only in codices where musical notation is not essential to the function of the book does notation survive unaltered.

Like the non-Cassinese sources of early Beneventan notation, these Montecassino sources date only from the third quarter of the tenth century, extending to the first part of the eleventh, after which they are replaced by the second-stage Beneventan notation.

Thus the brief musical interjection of Iaquintus, written before 949, is by several decades the earliest datable source of Beneventan notation. It does not, however, appear to be tentative or experimental. There is little enough to judge by, but Iaquintus seems secure and relaxed in his notation, and his neumes look very much like those that survive from later in his century and from the next. He was perhaps an adept music-scribe; at least his habits of notation were already formed. What a pity that no complete music-book survives from his hand or that of his contemporaries!

The question of the beginnings of musical notation in South Italy naturally arises here. While this not the place for a full-dress study of this important issue, a few remarks may be in order. First, it seems evident that musical notation was not invented separately in the Beneventan zone, but that it was imported: this is suggested by the kinship that Beneventan notation has with (apparently) earlier northern notations. The style of the first-stage Beneventan notation is so unlike the well-developed Beneventan script then in use, and so rapidly adapts itself to the mannerisms of Beneventan scribes, that it seems at its origin foreign to the zone.

---

22 NEWTON, *The Scriptorium*, p. 380 and plate 79. Newton dates the manuscript to the first half of the Desiderian period, i. e., the third quarter of the eleventh century.

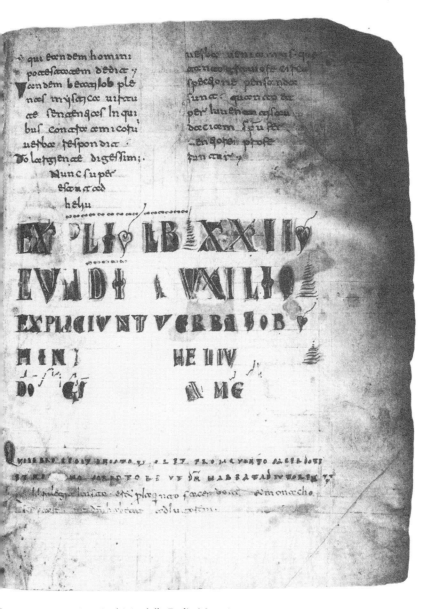

Tav. I: Montecassino, Archivio della Badia Ms. 269, p. 351

The very rapid development of musical notation in the Beneventan zone uggests its importation and assimilation to the Beneventan script. The thin, spi-

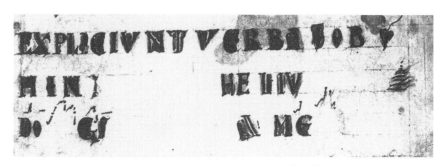

Tav. II: Montecassino, Archivio della Badia Ms. 269, p. 351 (detail)

dery early Beneventan notation gave way in the early eleventh century to a style which is more vertically oriented, and which matches the Beneventan script in many particulars: it includes many more strictly vertical strokes; it uses the contrasting thin and thick lines typical of the script; and it is written with a pen of generally the same breadth as that used for the text. By the eleventh century the music looks like the script; and from then onward, music and text go hand-in-hand, reaching a height of elegance and refinement in the twelfth century. The Beneventan notation looks foreign at its beginnings, and only at a second stage becomes assimilated to the style of the local script.

Kenneth Levy has argued, on the basis of graphic similarities, that Gregorian chant, *with neumes* (and the neumes are Levy's chief point) arrived in southern Italy in the late eighth century.[23] We have suggested reasons for agreement with Professor Levy about the date of the arrival of the liturgy itself,[24] but the question of musical notation is problematical. While the musical aspect of the liturgy might have been transmitted orally using books containing texts only (such as the uncial missal mentioned in number 12 above), it seems unlikely that a notational system imported in the eighth century would by the end of the tenth have changed so little in its paleographical aspect. Already in the first half of the eleventh century the notation has adapted itself to the norms of Beneventan writing, and makes further changes rapidly thereafter; that the notational style should have been static, the notation looking different from the script, from the late eighth century until the eleventh seems incompatible both with the later continuous changes and with the substantial developments in the Beneventan script itself during the same period. More consistent with the available evi-

---

23   KENNETH LEVY, *Charlemagne's Archetype of Gregorian Chant*, «Journal of the American Musicological Society», XL 1987, pp. 1-30.

24   THOMAS FORREST KELLY, *The Beneventan Chant*, Cambridge University Press, Cambridge 1989, pp. 18-25.

lence, it seems to me, is that musical notation was received only shortly before the time of Iaquintus; that it rapidly gained a foothold on account of its great utility; and that it changed, almost as rapidly, into the clearly Beneventan notation of the eleventh century that so well matches the idiosyncrasies of the local script. We cannot say that there was no musical notation in the eighth century: only that there is no evidence of its use in southern Italy until the middle of the tenth. Indeed, it may be the arrival of a useful system of notation that prompted the writing of the local chant in the same style of writing used to record the Gregorian melodies.

Montecassino 269 gives us a new date for the earliest Beneventan notation; by the middle of the tenth century musical notation was familiar in South Italy, and it was known at Montecassino as soon as anywhere else. The date of its arrival, however, must remain an open question.

XII

ABBOT DESIDERIUS
AND THE TWO LITURGICAL CHANTS OF MONTECASSINO *

Abbot Desiderius is remembered in many ways. In a fresco in the Lateran basilica he was depicted as a principal exponent of the papal reform of the eleventh century [1]; he was a consummate diplomat, succesfully bridging the transition from Lombard to Norman power; he cultivated the arts, creating the great basilica of Montecassino and incomparably enriching its library. Though my subject here is a small one in the illustrious career of Desiderius, it is of considerable importance in the musical history of south Italy; for it was Desiderius who presided over the demise at Montecassino of the liturgical chant which nowadays we call «Beneventan».

We know from the *Chronicle* that in 1058 Pope Stephen IX visited Montecassino, of which he had been made abbot shortly before his recent elevation to the papacy, and strictly forbade the singing of «Ambrosian» chant: *Tunc etiam et Ambrosianum cantum in ecclesia ista penitus interdixit* [2]. And as the pope's designated successor as abbot, it fell upon Desiderius to carry out the papal decree.

This *Ambrosianus cantus* is not the liturgical chant of Milan which is called by the name of St. Ambrose. It is the liturgical chant

* I acknowledge with thanks the support of the National Endowment for the Humanities, The American Academy in Rome, and the American Council of Learned Societies.

[1] See H.E.J. Cowdrey, *The Age of Abbot Desiderius. Montecassino, the Papacy, and the Normans in the Eleventh and Early Twelfth Centuries*, Oxford 1983, pp. xii-xiii.

[2] *Die Chronik von Montecassino*, ed. H. Hoffmann, in *Monumenta Germaniae historica* (=M.G.H.), *Scriptores* XXXIV, Hannover 1980 (= *Chron.*), II, 94.

of the Lombard South, entirely different from the Gregorian repertory, used from early days in the Beneventan zone [3]; the name «Ambrosian» is always used to identify the local chant, perhaps in the mistaken belief that it is identical with the music of Milan [4]. But the appeal to St. Ambrose is also a means of legitimizing an endangered local repertory; it recognizes a Lombard heritage from the North, and it provides the authenticity and authority the local music needed to compete for a place among the chants attributed to St. Gregory the Great.

Surviving musical sources to be discussed shortly make it clear that Beneventan chant was used at Montecassino. Indeed, Montecassino is an important center of Beneventan chant, at least in the period of music-writing. Montecassino is also, however, an important promoter of the Roman liturgy; that the abbey should play both roles simultaneously is a curious phenomenon related to her position between Rome and Benevento, between secular power and the church. This double tradition goes far back in the abbey's history, though it is not easy to trace it in detail.

The Beneventan chant is essentially a Lombard phenomenon, linked with the fortunes of those invaders who made in south Italy a cultural and political sphere of influence that lasted until the eleventh century. It has many Lombard characteristics: the chant seems to originate from Benevento, the capital of the southern Lombards; its liturgy gives importance to Lombard saints, such as the archangel Michael *in Monte Gargano* and the Holy Twelve Bro-

---

[3] For use of the term «Ambrosian» to signify Beneventan chant see TH. F. KELLY, *Beneventan and Milanese Chant*, «Journal of the Royal Musical Association», 92, 1987, 173-195.

[4] On the Beneventan chant and its sources see M. HUGLO, *L'ancien chant bénéventain*, «Ecclesia orans» 2, 1985, 265-293; K. H. SCHLAGER, *Beneventan Rite, Music of the*, in *The New Grove Dictionary of Music and Musicians*, ed. S. SADIE, 20 vols., London 1980, Vol. II, 482-484; B. BAROFFIO, *Liturgie in beneventanischen Raum*, in *Geschichte der katholischen Kirchenmusik*, ed. K. G. FELLERER, 2 vols., Kassel 1972-1976, Vol. I, 204-208; comprehensive studies of a portion of the Beneventan music and its liturgy were made by R. J. HESBERT, in *Paléographie musicale*, Vol. XIV (=*PM* 14), Solesmes 1931 (repr. Berne 1971), 248-465, and in *L'«Antiphonale missarum» de l'ancien rit bénéventain*, «Ephemerides liturgicae» 52, 1938, 28-66, 141-58; 53, 1939, 168-90; 59, 1945, 69-95; 60, 1946, 103-141; 61, 1947, 153-210. Recent studies on specific aspects of Beneventan chant by the author and by John Boe are cited in the notes to follow.

thers interred in the princely church of Santa Sofia of Benevento; the extent of the use of Beneventan chant matches that of the widest sphere of Lombard power, namely that of the duchy of Benevento in the eighth century; and its close kinship with the Ambrosian chant of Milan suggests the existence of an early Lombard musical tradition forced into separate channels by the division of the Lombards at the fall of Pavia to Charlemagne in 774.

The eighth century for the Lombards of the South marks a political and cultural high point; Benevento becomes the capital of a principality upholding Lombard culture and values, and its princes succeed, as the Lombard kings of the North do not, in avoiding entanglements with Popes, Franks, and Byzantines. Chroniclers of later ages remember the days of Arichis II with pride and nostalgia. This is doubtless the high point of the Beneventan chant as well; the period during which perhaps the last of it was composed, and during which, owing both to the power and influence of the southern Lombard capital and to the close allegiance which the church owed to the state, the chant spread throughout the Lombard South.

The church under the early Lombard princes was closely subjected to the ruler[5]. Lombard influence was thus strongly felt also at Montecassino. The rebuilding of Montecassino begun under Petronax (ca. 718) owes much to the support of the Beneventan dukes Romuald II (706-730) and Gisulf II (742-751)[6]. Gisulf's wife Scauniperga established, in a former pagan temple, the church of St. Peter *in Civitate* (or *in monastero*)[7]. Abbot Gisulf (796-817), who was re-

---

[5] See B. RUGGIERO, *Principi, nobiltà e Chiesa nel Mezzogiorno longobarda. L'esempio di s. Massimo di Salerno*, Naples 1973, 27-36; H. E. FEINE, *Studien zum langobardisch-italischen Eigenkirchenrecht. II. Teil*, «Zeitschrift der Savigny-Stiftung für Rechtsgeschichte», Kanonistische Abteilung, 31, 1942, 11-20.

[6] For Gisulf's extensive donation of territory to Montecassino see *Chron.* I, 5. See also T. LECCISOTTI, *Montecassino*, 10th ed., Montecassino 1983, 32; G. FALCO, *Lineamenti di storia cassinese nei secoli VIII e IX*, in *Casinensia*, Montecassino 1929, 476-477.

[7] See *Chron.*, I, 5, which reports information from the *Chronica sancti benedicti casinensis* edited in *M.G.H., Scriptores rerum langobardicarum et italicarum saec. VI-IX* (= *M.G.H., SS. Lang.*), Hannover 1878 (rep. 1964), 480. On the church of St. Peter see F. AVAGLIANO, *Monumenti del culto a San Pietro in Montecassino*, «Benedictina» 14, 1967, 79. The church was the site of a reunion of the monks from above (on the mountain) and those below

sponsible for a significant building campaign at Montecassino that included the basilica and monastery of San Salvatore below the mountain, as well as much extensive work above, was of «the noble family of the dukes of Benevento»[8], and had presumably therefore been close to the court of Arichis II and his successors. And the two great chroniclers of the Lombards, Paul the Deacon and Erchempert, were both monks of Montecassino. Erchempert, in particular, displays a fierce ninth-century pride in those of his Lombard ancestors who successfully resisted the encroachments of Carolingians or Byzantines.

The Beneventan chant probably originated from the southern Lombard capital. The political and cultural divisions between North and South that were a constant feature of Lombard relations were irrevocably fixed by the fall of Pavia to Charlemagne in 774 and the establishment of an independent principality centered at Benevento under Arichis II. By this time Beneventan chant was already securely in place. The Beneventan mass of the Holy Twelve Brothers points clearly to the Benevento of the second half of the eighth century[9]. These are martyrs whose relics were gathered by Arichis himself and interred by him in the ducal church of Santa Sofia in 769. Such a mass would not have originated elsewhere and been adopted later at Santa Sofia; and since the cult of these saints did not exist at all until their remains were collected by Arichis we can be certain that the mass was not composed before 760, nor, probably, much later. At that time what we call the Beneventan chant must have already been in use at Benevento, since the *ingressa* (the opening chant of the Beneventan mass) for the Holy Twelve Brothers is an adaptation of the *ingressa* of the Beneventan Easter mass[10].

---

for the special ceremonies of Easter Tuesday, which included singing in Greek. See A. CITARELLA and H. M. WILLARD, *The Ninth-Century Treasure of Montecassino in the Context of Political and Economic Developments in South Italy*, Montecassino 1983 (Miscellanea Cassinese, 12), 111-116.

[8] *Chron.* I, 17.

[9] See the metrical description in *M.G.H., SS. Lang.*, 574-576; on the date, see lines 74-78.

[10] At least the borrowing would appear to have been in this direction. The form of the Twelve Brothers *ingressa* is not so balanced as the Easter version, owing to its reversing the order of two internal phrases. The Easter *ingressa* itself uses a text known elsewhere; it is found, in a slightly different version and without notation, in the vast collection of processional an-

The extension of the cult of these martyrs — intended by Arichis as *patroni patriae* [11] — to Montecassino and throughout the region is evidence not only of the use of the Beneventan chant, but more directly, of the importance of Benevento as the political and cultural focus of the region, at least in the eighth century [12].

There is much evidence, albeit fragmentary, that the Beneventan chant was used at Montecassino.

1. An *ordo qualiter agatur in parasceben* added to Casin.175, pp. 587-588, in the late tenth or early eleventh century [13], describes a mixed Beneventan-Gregorian Good Friday rite, including the Latin versions of the three adoration antiphons used regularly at Benevento,

---

tiphons in the ninth-century antiphoner of Compiègne (R.J. HESBERT, *Antiphonale missarum sextuplex*, Brussels 1935 [repr. Rome 1985], 223), and with a non-Beneventan melody in Vat. Reg. lat. 334 and Oxford, Bodleian Ms. Douce 222; with three additional lines, it serves as a Kyrie-trope in Benevento, Bibl. Cap. Ms. 34 and Benevento 39. The Easter text itself thus may have been adopted at Benevento from a very old layer of hymnody; it is scarcely likely that the poem known in the north was modeled on a Beneventan text for the Twelve Brothers.

[11] *M.G.H., SS. Lang.*, 575, line 52.

[12] The Beneventan mass is found at Montecassino in the palimpsest gradual Ms. 361; see below. The feast itself is noted widely in South Italian calendars and martyrologies. Alfanus I, monk of Montecassino and later bishop of Salerno, is the author of a thousand-line *Metrum heroicum domni Alfani Salernitani archiepiscopi in honore sanctorum duodecim fratrum*, edited from Cassinese manuscripts in A. LENTINI AND F. AVAGLIANO, eds., *I carmi di Alfano I arcivescovo di Salerno*, Montecassino 1974 (Miscellanea Cassinese, 38).

[13] The literature on this famous manuscript, written in tenth-century Capua and including Paul the Deacon's commentary on the Rule of St. Benedict, is large; see the bibliography in E. A. LOEW, *The Beneventan Script. A History of the South Italian Minuscule*, Second Edition prepared and enlarged by V. BROWN, 2 vols., Rome 1980 (Sussidi eruditi, 33-34) [=*TBS2*], Vol. II, 74; the *ordo* is edited in *Bibliotheca casinensis seu codicum manuscriptorum qui in tabulario casinensi asservantur series*, 5 vols., Montecassino 1873-1894, IV, 33-34; on the date of the *ordo* itself, which precedes the epitaph of Abbot Aligern, see E. A. LOWE, *Scriptura beneventana*, 2 vols., Oxford 1929, Vol. I, commentary to plate XXXIX, who says that the epitaph of Paul the Deacon (which precedes the *ordo*, but not immediately), and that of Aligern, are «11th-century additions»; further on the epitaph of Aligern, see H. BLOCH, *Monte Cassino's Teachers and Library in the High Middle Ages*, in *La scuola nell'Occidente latino dell'alto Medioevo*, Spoleto 1972 (Settimane di studio del Centro Italiano di Studi sull'Alto Medioevo, 19), II, 601-605.

and two Beneventan antiphons for vespers; these directions match very closely the rubrics of the missal Lucca 606, which preserves much Beneventan music for Holy Week[14].

2. An «Ambrosian» Communion in Beneventan style for St. Benedict survives in a fragment in the Montecassino *Compactiones* XXII[15]. Probably this piece was composed at Montecassino itself; it is found in only one other source (see the next item), also connected with Montecassino.

3. The manuscript Vatican Ottob. lat. 145 may have been written for the use of Santa Sofia in Benevento, though it is modeled to some degree on sources from Montecassino[16]. It contains, among much else, six Beneventan antiphons for use in a *mandatum* ceremony; all six are used elsewhere as communions or offertories, and one is the communion just mentioned for St. Benedict, otherwise known only at Montecassino.

4. Casin. 361 preserves parts of a whole book of Beneventan

---

[14] The material from Lucca 606 is presented in facsimile in *PM* 14, plates XLI-XLIII. On the Greek-Latin antiphons, see *PM* 14, 309-311; HESBERT, *L'«Antiphonale missarum»* cit., «Ephemerides liturgicae» 60, 1946, 104-116.

[15] See J. BOE, *Old Beneventan Chant at Montecassino: Gloriosus Confessor Domini Benedictus*, «Acta musicologica» 55, 1983, 69-73.

[16] See E. M. BANNISTER, *Monumenti vaticani di paleografia musicale latina*, 2 vols., Leipzig 1913, text volume no. 348 (p. 122); J. BOE, *A New Source for Old Beneventan Chant: the Santa Sofia Maundy in MS Ottoboni lat. 145*, «Acta musicologica» 52, 1980, 122-133. A monastic vow (f. 121) contains the Cassinese phrase *in hoc sancto monasterio ubi sacratissimum corpus eius [i. e., of St. Benedict] humatum est*, but saints named in litanies suggest Santa Sofia; the Holy Twelve Brothers are named individually (f. 111v, as in the Santa Sofia litanies of London, British Library, Add. Ms. 23776, ff. 36, 39v, 45v and Naples, Bibl. Naz., Ms. VI E 43, f. 154v), as are Saints Graficus and Quineclus (f. 112; *3 non dec Nat. scorum grafici septimi et quinecli in sca sophia*, according to the Santa Sofia martyrology London 23776, f. 32, which also names the saints in the litanies just mentioned); Benevento, Bibl. Cap. Ms. 37 also names all these saints in a litany on f. 64 and in the martyrology as saints *in sancta sofia*. All twelve brothers, Saints Graficus, Septimus and Quineclus are named in a litany in the second (thirteenth-century) part of Naples, Bibl. Naz., Ms. VI G 31; the first part is a handsome book of monastic materials from the late eleventh century: not unlike the material in Ottob. lat. 145. The manuscript once belonged to the Biblioteca Vallicelliana, a rich source of Beneventan liturgical material.

chant, probably designed for use at Montecassino itself. The present manuscript is in the hand of Peter the Deacon, who was appointed librarian of Montecassino in 1131 or 1132[17]. In his untrained ordinary minuscule Peter the Deacon copied works of classical authors, to which he added a series of his own works[18]. But in making this book the Cassinese librarian preserved pages of a discarded volume of music for the Beneventan liturgy[19]. The presence of the Beneventan mass of the Holy Twelve Brothers in this Cassinese manuscript marks an early connection with Benevento.

5. The abbey of Santa Maria *de Mare* in the Tremiti Islands was claimed as a daughter house by Montecassino[20]. Its thirteenth-century cartulary is now Vatican Ms. Vat. lat. 10657. Four bifolia of the present manuscript are recycled leaves from an eleventh-century Beneventan gradual[21].

---

[17] See P. MEYVAERT, *The Autographs of Peter the Deacon*, «Bulletin of the John Rylands Library» 38, 1955-56, 129, 134 n. 1. On the subject of Peter the Deacon and his falsifications, see H. BLOCH, *Der Autor der 'Graphis aurea urbis Romae'*, «Deutsches Archiv für Erforschung des Mittelalters» 40, 1984, 61-66; MEYVAERT, *The Autographs* cit.; E. CASPAR, *Petrus diaconus und die Monte Cassinesischer Fälschungen*, Berlin 1909, esp. pp. 19-21; and the introduction to R. H. RODGERS, *Petri diaconi Ortus et vita iustorum cenobii casinensis*, Berkeley 1972.

[18] For a full list of the contents see M. INGUANEZ, *Codicum Casinensium manuscriptorum catalogus*, 3 vols., Montecassino 1915-1941, Vol. II, Pars 2, 208-212. The volume in its present form represents only about a third of Peter's original manuscript, whose structure has been largely reconstructed in BLOCH, *Der Autor* cit., 105-127.

[19] TH. F. KELLY, *Montecassino and the Old Beneventan Chant*, «Early Music History» 5, 1985, 64-69.

[20] On the disputed authority of Montecassino over Tremiti, see T. LECCISOTTI, *Le relazioni fra Montecassino e Tremiti e i possedimenti cassinesi a Foggia e Lucera*, «Benedictina» 9, 1949, 203-215; J. GAY, *Le monastère de Trémiti au XIe siècle d'après un cartulaire inédit*, «Mélanges d'archéologie et d'histoire» 17, 1897, 387-397; A. PETRUCCI, *Codice diplomatico del monastero benedettino di S. Maria di Tremiti (1005-1237)*, 3 vols., Rome 1960 (F.I.S.I., 98), Vol. I, XI-XLIX; G. PICASSO, *Montecassino e la Puglia*, in C. D. FONSECA, ed., *L'esperienza monastica benedettina e la Puglia. Atti del convegno di studio organizzato in occasione del XV centenario della nascita di San Benedetto (Bari - Noci - Lecce - Picciano, 6-10 ottobre 1980)*, 2 vols., Galatina 1983, Vol. I, 45-48; KELLY, *Montecassino* cit., 78-83.

[21] KELLY, *Montecassino* cit., 61-65.

6. I have shown elsewhere that a volume of Beneventan chant was commissioned by the monk Theobald, who became abbot of Montecassino in 1022 [22]. In his partly-autograph *Commemoratorium* [23], begun in 1019 and continued in subsequent years, Theobald details the objects that have been provided at his behest for San Liberatore [24]; the last item, added to the document after Theobald had been elected abbot, reads *et unum ingressarium*, doubtless a book of Beneventan masses, whose opening chant is always called *ingressa*. The music used at a dependent abbey was surely not unfamiliar at the mother house.

Montecassino, indeed, seems to have served as a source for the spread of Beneventan chant in monastic environments. Books were copied for daughter houses — Tremiti and San Liberatore — and Montecassino was used as a model for Santa Sofia in Ottob. lat. 145.

A sort of monastic conduit leads north through Subiaco and Lucca. Subiaco shows, in a thirteenth-century missal written at the abbey of Santa Scolastica (Ms. XVIII) [25], the full Beneventan vespers of Good Friday (though without notation), and the Beneventan melody of the *Exultet* [26]; the manuscript is written in northern script, but with Beneventan notation.

Beneventan notation is found often at Subiaco, both in fragments of manuscripts in Beneventan script and notation [27] and in sources in ordinary minuscule whose musical notation is Beneven-

---

[22] KELLY, *Montecassino* cit., 67, 70-71.

[23] The document is Montecassino, Archivio della Badia, Aula II, capsula CI, fasc. 1, no. 1. A complete facsimile and transcription are provided in E. CARUSI, *Intorno al Commemoratorium dell'abate Teobaldo (a. 1019-22)*, «Bullettino dell'Istituto Storico Italiano» 47, 1932, 173-190 plus plate.

[24] On these aspects of Theobald's life see *Chron.* II, 12, 42, 52, 56-58; BLOCH, *Monte Cassino's Teachers* cit., 577-578; J. GAY, *L'Italie méridionale et l'empire byzantin depuis l'avènement de Basile Ier jusqu'à la prise de Bari par les Normands (867-1071)*, Paris 1904 (Bibliothèque des Écoles françaises d'Athènes et de Rome, 90), 423-425, 438-441.

[25] See L. ALLODI, *Inventario dei manoscritti della Biblioteca dell'Abbazia di Subiaco*, Forlì 1891, 9 (no. 19).

[26] On the Beneventam Vespers see HESBERT, *L'«Antiphonale missarum»* cit., «Ephemerides liturgicae» 60, 1946, 136-141; *PM* 14, 335-337; on the *Exultet, PM* 14, 375-417.

[27] The fragment of a gradual — 11th-12th century — that now serves as the opening flyleaves of Ms. XX; two fragments of an antiphoner — 12th century? — in the folder labeled «Miscellanea» No. L.

tan [28]; at least one of these last was made for Subiaco (Ms. XXII), and thus it appears that there was at least one scribe writing Beneventan notation there. That elements of the Beneventan liturgy should survive into the thirteenth century is perhaps not so surprising, as Subiaco is the place of St. Benedict's earliest monastic life, and the place from which he journeyed to found Montecassino. Doubtless the Beneventan liturgical material, like its scribe, came north in a monastic connection with Montecassino.

The monastic missal Lucca 606 is a similar case from much farther north. The book is written in northern script and notation [29]; but attached to the main body of the missal is an appendix, written by the same text-scribe (ff. 150v-156v), which supplements the foregoing missal with certain special rites of Holy Week: rubrics, lessons, chants, etc. which are outside the normal scope of a missal [30]. Much of the material in this supplement is from the Beneventan liturgy, and the musical notation is Beneventan. This is by far our northernmost source of the Beneventan liturgy; but we can infer from the notation that the direction of travel was south to north. There is a further connection in Montecassino manuscript 175, whose Good Friday *ordo* matches Lucca's in many precise details [31]. Montecassino had a dependency (San Giorgio) in Lucca, though it can be dated only from the mid-eleventh century [32].

Thus music of the local Beneventan rite was being copied under Theobald only shortly before Desiderius' election as abbot; but by the time of Peter the Deacon the old books of Beneventan music were useful only as raw material.

But the music that supplanted the Beneventan chant, that repertory known as Gregorian, did not arrive at Montecassino only in the eleventh century. It had been in use in the region for a long time, evidently alongside the local chant dialect.

---

[28] These include fragments of three separate antiphoners in the Miscellanea; three bifolia from a late twelfth-century antiphoner bound into Ms. CCXLI; and the musical notation of the twelfth-century breviary Ms. XXII.

[29] One piece, however, is in Beneventan notation: the Alleluia *Adorabo*, f. 137.

[30] For facsimiles of parts of this appendix see *PM* 14, plates XXXIV-XLIII; see also the index, p. 470.

[31] See the Appendix to this paper.

[32] *Chron.* II, 90. See H. BLOCH, *Montecassino in the Middle Ages*, 3 vols., Rome 1986 [=*MMA*], I, 428-430.

The Gregorian chant must have been in place in south Italy in the eighth century. The version of the chant preserved in the region has so many features that had disappeared elsewhere by the end of the century and the early years of the ninth that a Gregorian liturgy including these features must have already been present before these changes took place elsewhere[33]. The arrival of the Gregorian chant in its surviving form, then, dates from the time of the Carolingian incursions into south Italy in the later eighth century. Exactly how this Gregorian influence came to the region, how it was received, and how it gradually overshadowed the Beneventan chant, will probably never be fully explained. But as a paradigm of Frankish influence on the church — perhaps, indeed, as a direct cause — we should not overlook the career of the eminent Paul the Deacon.

Paul, the famous historian of the Lombards and an important poet and teacher, is also a significant figure in eighth-century liturgical matters. He is credited with assembling a liturgical homiliary[34], and was connected with the mass-book that Charlemagne requested from Pope Hadrian I[35]; he is likely to have had further liturgical influence as well on the «Gelasian sacramentary of the eighth century[36]».

After his years at the Lombard court of Pavia, Paul was a significant presence at the court of Benevento from 763 to 774; his *Historia romana* was undertaken at the request of his pupil, Arichis' consort Adelperga (the daughter of King Desiderius), to whom he dedi-

---

[33] For a discussion of these features the reader is referred to the first chapter of TH. F. KELLY, *The Beneventan Chant* (forthcoming, Cambridge University Press); for another approach to the same subject, see K. LEVY, *Charlemagne's Archetype of Gregorian Chant*, «Journal of the American Musicological Society» 40, 1987, 1-30.

[34] See J. LECLERCQ, *Tables pour l'inventaire des homéliaires manuscrits*, «Scriptorium» 2, 1948, 205-214; R. GRÉGOIRE, *Les homéliaires du moyen âge. Inventaire et analyse des manuscrits*, Rome 1966 (*Rerum ecclesiasticarum documenta*, Series maior, Fontes, 6), 71-114.

[35] K. GAMBER, *Heimat und Ausbildung der Gelasiana saec. VIII (Junggelasiana)*, «Sacris erudiri» 14, 1963, 128-129; an Italian translation is K. GAMBER, *Il sacramentario di Paolo Diacono*, «Rivista di storia della chiesa in Italia» 16, 1962, 412-438.

[36] GAMBER, *Heimat und Ausbildung* cit., esp. pp. 109-112; see also C. MOHLBERG, *Note su alcuni sacramentarii*, «Atti della Pontificia Accademia Romana di Archeologia, Rendiconti», s. III, 16, 1940, 151-154.

cated an elaborate acrostic verse [37]. His verses in praise of Arichis and the prince's epitaph indicate Paul's devotion to the court of Benevento and its ruling couple [38].

After Pavia fell in 774 Paul became a monk of Montecassino, where he remained until his death in 799 except for three years at the court of Charlemagne (782-785/6). He was thus closely associated both with the Carolingian world and with the centers of primary importance to south Italy in this period [39].

We cannot be certain that Paul himself was the intermediary of the Roman rite in the South, but his career exemplifies the cultural currents that brought the Gregorian liturgy from the Carolingian North to the Lombard South. And when we consider the Lombard saints of Benevento we cannot fail to notice a coincidence: the Twelve Brothers in 760 have a Beneventan mass; St. Mercurius, translated to Benevento in 768, has none [40]: and the arrival of Paul the Deacon falls between the two, in 763.

When Paul moves to Montecassino that great abbey begins its active role as the recognized fountainhead of Western monasticism; its practices are studied as models; and perhaps under his influence it begins a rapprochement with the liturgy of Rome. Beginning in the later eighth century a series of *ordines* and letters relate the practices of Montecassino [41].

---

[37] Edited in *M.G.H., SS. Lang.*, 13-14; and in K. NEFF, *Die Gedichte des Paulus Diaconus*, Munich 1908 (Quellen und Untersuchungen zur lateinischen Philologie des Mittelalters, Band III, Heft 4), 9-10.

[38] Edited in NEFF, *Die Gedichte* cit., 15-18, 145-149.

[39] On Paul's activities at Benevento and Montecassino see *Chron.*, I, 15; *Chronicon Salernitanum. A Critical Edition with Studies on Literary and Historical Sources and on Language*, ed. U. WESTERBERGH, Lund 1956 (*Studia Latina Stockholmiensia*, 3), 10-13, 22, 24-25; BLOCH, *Montecassino's Teachers* cit., 567-572.

[40] On Mercurius at Benevento see H. BELTING, *Studien zum beneventanischen Hof im 8. Jahrhundert*, «Dumbarton Oaks Papers» 16, 1962, 157-160; surviving local liturgical materials for Mercurius include a mass assembled from the Gregorian common in London, British Library Ms. Egerton 2511 (formerly Benevento VI. 29), f. 281v; Naples XVI A 19 (f. 44; probably from Santa Sofia, at least in this part) provides a mass using largely metrical text adapted to Gregorian melodies.

[41] Many of these are gathered in K. HALLINGER ET AL., *Corpus consuetudinum monasticarum*, Vol. I: *Initia consuetudinis benedictinae*, Siegburg 1963, replacing in large part the edition of B. ALBERS, *Consuetudines monasticae*, Vol. III, Montecassino, 1907; this latter, however, includes some documents not in Hallinger.

400

That Montecasino had long-standing ties with Rome cannot be doubted, but liturgical connections can be verified only from Carolingian times. In the period between the Lombard destruction of Montecassino in 568/569 and its refounding by Petronax of Brescia in 717/718 the monks are reported to have resided in Rome under the protection of the Pope; but in fact very little is known about this period of Cassinese history[42].

Our knowledge of the history of Gregorian chant usage is not much clearer. No complete musical manuscript from Montecassino survives from before the age of abbot Desiderius in the later eleventh century[43]. Our earliest liturgical information is from the letters and *ordines* of the later eighth century — from the time, that is, of Paul the Deacon. A letter of Abbot Theodemar to the Emperor *Theodoric (778-797) repeatedly indicates Montecassino's fidelity to the Roman church[44]; and the same fidelity to Rome is expressed in

---

[42] See Paul the Deacon's *History of the Lombards*, in M.G.H., SS. Lang., 122 and 178-179; *Chron.* I, 2, 4; GREGORII MAGNI *Dialogi*, ed. U. MORICCA, Rome 1924 (F.I.S.I., 57), 106-108.

[43] For a chronological survey of the liturgical manuscripts preserved at Montecassino see F. AVAGLIANO, *I codici liturgici dell'Archivio di Montecassino*, «Benedictina» 17, 1970, 1-19. Of some 120 liturgical manuscripts now at Montecassino, no complete missal, antiphoner or gradual survives from before the Desiderian period. There are sparse musical notations in such earlier manuscripts as Casin. 230 and 446, and fragments of an eighth-century palimpsest uncial mass-book in Ms. 271 (cf. A. DOLD, *Vom Sakramentar Comes und Capitulare zum Missale*, Beuron 1943 [Texte und Arbeiten, 34]; A. CHAVASSE, *Les fragments palimpsestes du Casinensis 271 (Sigle Z 6)*, «Archiv für Liturgiewissenschaft» 25, 1983, 9-33). Surviving lectionaries, homiliaries, and sermons in Beneventan script are no older than the eleventh century. A mid-tenth century version of a Cassinese *ordo officii*, written in Capua, is preserved in Ms. 175 (edited in Hallinger: see below, note 47). This is perhaps the earliest precise information on liturgical practice at Montecassino (excluding, of course, the Rule of St. Benedict).
A convenient survey of liturgical manuscripts in the region is in K. GAMBER, *Codices liturgici latini antiquiores*, 2nd ed., 1 vol. in 2 parts, Freiburg/Schweiz 1968 (*Spicilegii Friburgensis subsidia*, 1), 238-58 (Nos. 430-99); 465-7 (Nos. 1170-9), 571 (No. 1593), 573-574 (No. 1599). From about the same early period (10th-11th c.) are several missals and fragments of missals, mostly without notation; see Nos. 431-434.

[44] *Nec ambigimus Romanum apud Gallias morem tam per singulas ecclesias quamque et monasteria in officiis et lectionibus, sicut et nos facimus, teneri* (HALLINGER, *Corpus consuetudinum* cit., 129); *Reliqua vero officia secundum morem Romanum explemus* (p. 130); ... *explentes omnia ordine Ro-*

---

* The reference here to "Theodoric" is erroneous. This sentence should read "A letter of Abbot Theodemar (778–797) to the Emperor Charlemagne repeatedly indicates ...."

a letter of Theodemar to Charlemagne (though this document is thought by some to date only from the ninth century); in some sources this letter is labeled as dictated (*dictata*) by Paul the Deacon[45]. The late eighth-century Montecassino *ordo officii* suggests that the abbey follows Roman practice[46], and a version of its text from the ninth century is full of liturgical details which make this clear[47].

These Montecassino documents are all written to provide outsiders with information about the practices of the abbey; they are for external use, and perhaps for that reason state the case for Roman fidelity as strongly as possible. That the Gregorian chant was used at Montecassino seems certain; but what is equally clear — but not mentioned — is that the Beneventan chant was used there as well.

This musical duality may have had additional political overtones. Conflicting Frankish and Lombard parties existed in ecclesiastical institutions: Ambrose Autpert, the Frankish abbot of San Vincenzo al Volturno, was harassed by a pro-Lombard faction in his monastery[48]; and northern influence is to be seen also at Montecassino, Santa Sofia, and other monasteries, which accepted the patronage of Charlemagne and a long series of northern emperors.

The history of the interaction between the two liturgical systems between the eighth century and the time of abbot Desiderius

---

mano (p. 130); *Unde et nos ... Romanam in legendis veteris ac novi testamenti per ordinem libris consuetudinem sequimur* (p. 132); etc.

[45] HALLINGER, *Corpus consuetudinum* cit., I, 157; on date, attribution, and authenticity see pp. 152-154; the text is edited on pp. 157-175.

[46] The *ordo* is edited in HALLINGER, *Corpus consuetudinum* cit., I, 105-123. An earlier *ordo* of the eighth century (ed. in HALLINGER, *ibid.*, 93-104) gives too little liturgical detail to be useful here.

[47] This second version is edited in Hallinger as text C, pp. 113-123. The second version does, however, name a Maundy Thursday antiphon (*Dum recubuisset Dominus Ihesus*) that survives only with a Beneventan melody and another (*Dominus Ihesus postquam cenabit*) that may have been sung to its Beneventan melody. See HALLINGER, 117.

[48] Autpert was elected abbot of San Vincenzo by its Frankish party in 777, while the Lombard monks elected Potone. A nationalistic controversy ensued, and Autpert abandoned his office in 778. Called to Rome, with others, by Hadrian I to clarify the matter of Potone's being accused of infidelity to Charlemagne, he died in 781. See *M.G.H., Epistolarum*, t. III, Berlin 1892, 594-597; M. DEL TREPPO, *Longobardi Franchi e papato in due secoli di storia vulturnese*, «Archivio storico per le province napoletane» 73 (n.s. 34), 1953-1954, 37-59; FALCO, *Lineamenti* cit., esp. pp. 463-469.

can only be traced roughly. The gradual independence of the church from the princes, increasing ecclesiastical contact with Rome, and the growing importance of Montecassino as an ecclesiastical, but also a temporal, power, all contributed to the eventual domination of the Roman chant. The earliest musical manuscripts of southern Italy date only from the end of the tenth century, and in these the Beneventan chant, if it is present at all, is in a secondary position, as an addition or an alternative to the Gregorian chant which soon supplanted it completely. The decline in importance of the city of Benevento during the ninth and tenth centuries contributed to the decline of the local chant, but it seems also to have fired a proud conservatism which contributed to the preservation of at least a portion of the Beneventan chant, as an element of Lombard history, until its ultimate disappearance, along with Lombard power itself, in the eleventh century.

Montecassino cannot have had a wide liturgical influence in the period after her destruction by the Arabs in 883 and during her subsequent struggle to regain lost possesions in the tenth century. But eventually she again became a fountainhead of the Roman liturgy as she had in the eighth century; her increasingly high position brought her in contact with distant winds from the wider world.

Imperial intervention in the election of abbots sought first to resist Byzantine influence through the counts of Capua, and subsequently to approve candidates associated with papal reform. Thus Theobald was appointed by Henry II in 1022; under Conrad II the monks elected their first foreign abbot, Richerius of Niederaltaich; and in 1057 the papal reform made itself felt at Montecassino. Leo IX, the first great papal representative of reform, was represented by his close adviser Cardinal Humbert, who oversaw the election as abbot of the papal chancellor Frederick of Lorraine, his fellow ambassador to Constantinople; Frederick had entered the monastery, along with his friend Desiderius, three years earlier; within a few weeks Frederick himself was elected pope, taking the name of Stephen IX [49].

At the election of Frederick, Montecassino was still using the Beneventan chant alongside the Gregorian. Theobald's *ingressarium*

---

[49] On this period in Cassinese history see BLOCH, *Monte Cassino, Byzantium* cit., 173-177, 187-193; *MMA* I, 15-19, 30-40.

had been copied only a few years earlier; the book which Peter the Deacon used to make Casin. 361 had perhaps not yet been erased; a Beneventan Communion for the founder was copied about now; and the rubric of Ottob. lat. 145 makes clear that the Beneventan chant is actually sung, not just recorded for archival purposes [50]:

Item quando non canimus ipse a[ntiphone] secundum romano.
Quo modo supra scripte sunt canimus secundum Ambro[siano]
hoc modo [51].

But there is already concern at Montecassino about the double employment of the two chants. The eleventh-century musical miscellany Casin. 318 includes a unique poem chronicling the triumph of Gregorian over «Ambrosian» chant by means of a musical ordeal [52]. It describes Charlemagne's efforts at musical uniformity and its effect in Italy [53]:

Insignis Karolus romanum pangere carmen
Omnibus ecclesiis iussit ubique sacris:
Unde per Italiam crevit contemptio multa,
Et status ecclesie luxit ubique sacre.
(Casin. 318, p. 244)

---

[50] The rubric may be designed for Santa Sofia in Benevento rather than for Montecassino; but its attachment to a monastic *mandatum*, and the presence in the Beneventan antiphons to follow of the Communion of St. Benedict, suggest a Cassinese origin.

[51] F. 124. See Boe, *A New Source* cit.

[52] The *Versi Gregorii, Ambrosii, Karoli, Pauli de canto romano vel ambrosiano* were published in A. Amelli, *L'epigramma di Paolo Diacono intorno al canto Gregoriano e Ambrosiano*, «Memorie Storiche Forogiuliesi» 9, 1913, 153-175 plus plate; and in E. Cattaneo, *Note storiche sul canto ambrosiano*, Milan 1950 (Archivio ambrosiano, 3), 23-26.

[53] On Carolingian liturgical reform, see C. Vogel, *La réforme culturelle sous Pépin le Bref et sous Charlemagne*, preceded by E. Patzelt, *Die karolingische Renaissance*, Graz 1965; C. Vogel, *Les échanges liturgiques entre Rome et les pays francs jusqu'à l'époque de Charlemagne*, in *Le Chiese nei Regni dell'Europa occidentale e i loro rapporti con Roma sino all'800*, Spoleto 1960 (Settimane di studio del Centro Italiano di Studi sull'Alto Medioevo, 7), I, 185-295; *La réforme liturgique sous Charlemagne*, in *Karl der Grosse. Lebenswerk und Nachleben*, ed. W. Braunfels, Vol. II, *Das geistige Leben*, ed. B. Bischoff, Düsseldorf 1965, 217-232.

The poem goes on to describe a contest in which two boys, one representing Gregorian and the other «Ambrosian» (for which we should read «Beneventan») chant, engaged in a singing duel in which the youthful Ambrosian representative was so outsung that he collapsed.

A *sententia* accompanying the poem expresses sympathy for the threatened «Ambrosian» chant:

Non est ita intelligendum ut cantus Ambrosianus abominandus sit; set annuente Deo, Romanus cantus est preferendus, pro brevitate et fastidio plebis (p. 245).

Although this poem itself may date from the eighth century[54], clearly some eleventh-century scribe of Montecassino chose to include these verses in a book of materials on liturgical music: the problem was a real one in his day[55].

But this was soon to change: Frederick was shortly to forbid the Beneventan chant, and Desiderius was to implement his wishes. The renewal of the liturgical books of Montecassino under Desiderius has left us some of the finest examples of Cassinese calligraphy[56]; but it succeeded, too — and probably not unintentionally — in eradicating almost all traces of the older Beneventan

---

[54] As least one scholar, Ambrogio Amelli, who first noticed it, was inclined to attribute the poem itself to Paul the Deacon. See note 52 above.

[55] Indeed, there survives a leaf of genuine Milanese music in a Cassinese hand, perhaps of the late eleventh century, as the front flyleaf of the Cassinese martyrology Vat. Ottob. lat. 3. See the facsimile in *PM* 14, plates XXXII-XXXIII; KELLY, *Beneventan and Milanese Chant* cit. (see note 3 above).

[56] Leo Marsicanus relates that before the time of abbot Theobald (1022-1035) Montecassino was but poorly supplied with books (*Codices ... quorum hic maxima paupertas usque ad id temporis erat*: Chron., II, 53). Though Theobald added much to the monastic library (*Chron.*, II, 53 names some 20 volumes), the contribution of abbot Desiderius (1058-1087) was by comparison enormous. The list in *Chron.*, III, 63 runs to some seventy books. And whereas Theobald is shown in miniature offering a book to St. Benedict (in Casin. 73, f. 4: facs. in BLOCH, *MMA*, fig 2; *Montecassino, Byzantium* cit., 218), the similar scene in the beautiful Cassinese lectionary Vat. lat. 1202 (f. 1: facs. in BLOCH, *MMA*, fig. 48; *Montecassino, Byzantium* cit., pl. 220) shows Desiderius offering not only churches but a whole heap of books.

chant[57]. All that remains now is an occasional fragment or palimpsest.

Indeed, from about the time of Desiderius, Montecassino's liturgical, not to say temporal, influence was substantial. The monastery that earlier had received the local chant from Benevento (as evidenced by the mass of the Twelve Brothers in Casin. 361) and had disseminated it as far as Subiaco, Tremiti, and Lucca, now becomes a source for the transmission of the official Gregorian chant. By the early twelfth century the books of Montecassino served as models for many liturgical volumes.

The presence of Cassinese influence in the ancient Lombard capital most clearly indicates the reversal of the liturgical flow. The *ordo officii* Benevento 66 is based on a Montecassino original adapted for the use of St. Peter's *intra muros* at Benevento; and Cassinese influence is to be seen in the two twelfth-century ordinals of Santa Sofia itself, Vat. lat. 4928 and Neap. VI E 43. Benevento also

---

[57] That so few liturgical manuscripts survive from the ducal church of Santa Sofia in Benevento and its monastery before the twelfth century may be a phenomenon similar to that at Montecassino. A new style of manuscript production at Montecassino, fitting the power and importance of the abbey, was a feature of the early twelfth century (see BLOCH, *MMA*, I, 71-82; *Montecassino, Byzantium* cit., 201-207; of primary importance will be the forthcoming study by Francis Newton on the scriptorium under abbots Desiderius and Oderisius), and it is not surprising that many liturgical books (and not just those containing Beneventan chant) should be replaced with more beautiful examples.

A similar replacement may have taken place at Santa Sofia in the twelfth century — a time of enrichment in which the beautiful cloister was added to the monastery by abbot John IV (on the date of the cloister and the identification of John, see A. PRANDI, (ed.), *L'art dans l'Italie méridionale. Aggiornamento dell'opera di Émile Bertaux*, 4 vols. (numbered IV-VI plus *Indici*) Rome 1978, V, 661). The books from this period are of an elegance and beauty parallel to those of Desiderius. The Veroli lectionary (see G. BATTELLI, *Il lezionario di S. Sofia di Benevento*, in *Miscellanea Giovanni Mercati*, VI, Vatican City 1946 [Studi e testi, 126], 282-291), like the Desiderian lectionary Vat. lat. 1202, is a splendid book containing only materials for the principal feasts of the church: in this case, St. Mercurius, the Holy Twelve Brothers, and the Dedication. Likewise the compendium of liturgical materials in Vat. lat. 4928, generously proportioned and decorated with gold, and the richly-illuminated cartulary Vat. lat. 4939, are books of a richness unknown at Benevento before this time. Further bibliography on all these books is found in the catalogue in *TBS2*, Vol. II.

adopted the trope repertory of Montecassino, to judge from the twelfth-century gradual-troper Benevento 34, whose repertory draws heavily on that in the palimpsest Cassinese troper Vatican Urb. lat. 602[58].

It is thus under Desiderius that Montecassino resolves a duality that had existed since at least the eighth century. The liturgical chant of Lombard Benevento, of the secular power in whose territory Montecassino lay, was preserved alongside the Gregorian chant, the music of the Carolingian reform and ultimately of the universal church. But by the time of Desiderius much had changed. Though Desiderius himself was of noble Beneventan origin, and indeed had been a monk of Santa Sofia, Lombard power had waned. Benevento itself had been handed over to the papacy, and secular power was now in the hands of the Normans. Montecassino had so increased in power that its abbots could expect to be made cardinals and even popes. In such an atmosphere, scented too with the winds of papal reform, it is little wonder that the ancient Lombard chant, once so proudly maintained, sank without a trace under the renewal of Desiderius. His characteristic diplomacy may have played a part, for renewing the liturgical books of the abbey did not necessarily require the obliteration of such complete books as the now-palimpsest Casin. 361; many older books of other kinds, after all, do survive; but the ancient Beneventan chant, once known throughout the region, is never heard again; the double chant tradition, now archaic and unsuitable, is resolved in keeping with Montecassino's high place in the wider world and the universal church.

---

[58] It is to the credit of Alejandro Planchart to have deciphered many of the now-palimpsest tropes of Urb. lat. 602, and to have shown that the tropes of Benevento 34 formerly thought to be *unica* are almost all present in Urb. lat. 602, in a paper presented at the *Fourth International Conference on Tropes* sponsored by the European Science Foundation, Perugia, September 1987.

APPENDIX

The Good Friday rites of Lucca 606 and Casin. 175 compared

The eleventh-century missal Lucca, Biblioteca Capitolare Feliniana Ms. 606 contains an appendix (folios 150v-156v) detailing the rites of the last three days of Holy Week, including extensive rubrics and many musical pieces from the Beneventan rite; the musical notation is Beneventan, though the writing is ordinary minuscule. The presence of much of the Beneventan rite in a northern manuscript is unusual; but its origin is southern, as witnessed both by the Beneventan notation of the musical pieces in this section and by the close relationship of its Good Friday rite with an *ordo* preserved in Montecassino, Archivio della Badia, Ms. 175.

Casin. 175, made under abbot John I (915-934) when the community was at Capua after the destruction of Montecassino by the Arabs, contains the commentary on the Rule of St. Benedict attributed to Paul the Deacon, as well as other liturgical *ordines*. The *ordo* edited here continues with a single sentence on Holy Saturday and a brief paragraph on Easter, with no reference to Beneventan chant and little relationship to the practices of Lucca 606; its chief purpose is evidently the details of Good Friday. This *ordo*, a later addition to the manuscript, may date only from the eleventh century (see note 13 above).

The close similarity of the two *ordines* is more apparent when they are compared with other south Italian rites for Good Friday; see the comparative tables in *Paléographie musicale*, XIV, Solesmes 1931 (repr. Berne 1971), 296-297, 300-301.

The two ordines are compared below. Angled brackets indicate the presence of musical notation in Lucca 606 (none is present in Casin. 175). Lections and musical pieces presented *in extenso* are abbreviated for the sake of comparison. Italics indicate the texts of items to be read or recited; abbreviations have been expanded, punctuation and capitalization have been normalized; an asterisk (*) indicates musical items from the old Beneventan liturgy.

408

The material from Lucca 606 is presented in facsimile in *Paléographie musicale*, XIV, plates XLI-XLIII; the *ordo* from Casin. 175 is edited in *Bibliotheca Casinensis*, IV, 33-34. More detailed information on the Beneventan rites of Good Friday may be found in René-Jean Hesbert, *L'«Antiphonale missarum» de l'ancien rit bénéventain*, «Ephemerides liturgicae» 60, 1946, 103-141; *Paléographie musicale*, XIV, 290-337. The abbreviation of Beneventan Good Friday vespers from four antiphons to two (as in the Montecassino *ordo* below) is to be seen in many manuscripts in the region; see the discussion forthcoming in my *The Beneventan Chant*.

Lucca 606, f. 155	Montecassino 175, p. 58

Incipit ordo officii in parasceven.
Expleto matutino cantent.
  *(Ant. Tristis est anima mea...)
Post hanc incip[iant] psalterium.
Facto vero aurora cantent prima.
  Ant. *Memento mei domine deus.*
  Ps. *Deus meus respice.*
  & *Beati immaculati* usque *legem pone.*
  Ν *Diviserunt sibi vestimenta.*
Item ad tertia.
  Ant. *Ait latro.*
  Ps. *Legem pone* usque *defecit.*
  Ν *Insurrexerunt in me.*
Ad sextam.
  Ant. *Tamquam ad latronem.*
  Ps. *Deficit in salutare* usque
    Mirabilia.
  Ν *Ab insurgentibus in me.*

Ordo qualiter agatur in parasceben.

Deinde legatur passio. secundum Marcum.
Ant. ad nonam.
  Latro de cruce.
  Ps. *Mirabilia testimonia* usque *Ad dominum dum tribularer.*
  Ν *Diviserunt sibi vestimenta.*

Expleta sexta
legatur passio secundum Marcum.

Finita nona pergant duo ante crucem et

sublato linteo cantent
  Ant. *Ecce lignum.*
Et respondentes eadem antiphona in choro,
Illi prosternantur ante ipsam crucem,
et ubi fuerit expleta,

Item nona completa, statim pergant duo
ante crucem et incurvati illam adorent;
et sublato linteo dicant antifonam:
  Ecce lignum crucis usque in finem.
Et respondente eandem antiphonam in cho[ro]
illi prosternantur ante ipsam crucem.
et ubi fuerit expleta,

erigant se et cantent illam totam,
et incipiant in choro
 Ps. *Deus misereatur.*

Iterum erigat se unus ex illis et dicat:
 Agios o theos.
Iterum erigat se alius et dicat:
 Sanctus deus.
 Iterum erigat se alius et dicit:
 Agios.
Iterum surgat alius et dicat:
 Sanctus fortis.
Iterum surgat alius et dicat:
 Agios athanatos.
Iterum surgat alius et dicat: [f. 155v]
 Sanctus et inmortalis.
Ubi fuerint explete tunc incipiant
in choro antiphonam:
 Popule meus.
Post hoc erigat se unus et dicat:
 Agios, ut supra.

Post hec incipiant in choro;
 Ant. *Quia eduxi te.*
Iterum erigat se unus ex illis et dicat:
 Agios, ut supra.
Post hec incipit in choro:
 Ant. *Quid ultra.*
Iterum erigat se unus ex illis et dicat:
 Agios, ut supra.
Hoc explete [sic] incipiant ipsi.
 Ant. *Popule meus.*
Respondeant in choro.
 Quid feci tibi.
Iterum incipiant ipsa improperia
et unus stet post altare et dicat semper
leni voce:
 Popule meus.
 ⟨*Ego propter te flagellavi... Popule
  meus.*
 Ego eduxi... Popule.
 Ego ante te aperui... Popule.
 Ego ante te preivi... Popule.
 Ego te pavi... Popule.
 Ego te potavi... Popule.
 Ego propter te chananeorum... Popule.
 Ego te pre ceteris... Popule.
 Ego tibi dedi... Popule.
 Ego te exaltavi... Popule.⟩

erigant se et cantent illam totam.
Et incipiant in choro
 psalmum *Deus misereatur nobis* totum.
Ubi autem fuerit expletus, erigant se
illi et dicant:
 Ecce lingum, [sic]
et respondeant in choro:
 Ecce lignum.
et iterum erigat unus ex illis et dicat:
 Agyos.
et iterum erigat se alius, et dicat:
 Sanctus deus.
Et erigat se alius, et dicat:
 Agios yschirros.
Iterum surgat alius et dicat:
 Sanctus fortis.
Et iterum surgat alius, et dicat:
 Agyos athanatos.
Iterum surgat alius, et dicat:
 Sanctus immortalis.
Ubi fuerit expletum, incipiant
in choro:
 Popule meus, usque *quia eduxi te.*
Iterum erigat se unus ex illis et dicat:
 Agios, ut supra.
Et iterum prosternantur ante crucem.
Iterum incipiant in choro:
 Quia eduxi te usque *salvatori tuo.*
Iterum erigat se unus ex illis, ac dicat:
 Agios o theos. Et ceteros omnes.
Iterum incipiant antiphonam in choro:
 Quid ultra debui facere tibi usque in finem.
Iterum erigat se unus ex illis et dicat:
 Agios, ut supra.
Hoc expleto, incipiant ipsi:
 Antiphonam *Popule meus.*
Respondeant in choro
 quid feci tibi usque *Responde.*
Iterum incipiant illi ipsa improperia.
Et unus post altare dicat semper:

 Popule meus.

Et dicente illo *popule meus,*

410

Respondeant in choro:
Quid feci tibi.

Post hec legat subdiaconus:
Lectio Ose prophete. *In tribulatione
sua*
Tractus. *Domine audivi*
sive
R. *Circumdederunt me.*
Item Lectio libri sapientie:
*In diebus illis,
Dixerunt impii de deo...*
[Tr.] *Eripe me domine ab homine.*

Item
passio secundum Iohannem.
Iterum orationes sicut in sacramentario
continentur.
Ubi fuerint explete
incipiant in choro:
*⟨Ant. *Adoramus crucem tuam...*⟩
Ps. *Deus deus meus.*
Et omnes adorent ipsam crucem.
[fol. 156]

* [Ant.] ⟨*Crucem tuam adoramus...*⟩
[Ps.] *Laudate deo* [sic].
* [Ant.] ⟨*Laudamus te christe..*⟩
[Ps.] *Cantate domino.*

Deinde canitur antiphona ante crucem:
⟨*O quando in cruce...*⟩
R. in choro antiphona
* ⟨*Omnes gentes*⟩

Postea pergat sacerdos ad altare
et dicat:
Oremus. Preceptis salutaribus moniti;
usque
pax domini sit semper vobiscum.
R. in choro: *Et cum spiritu tuo.*

Item vesperum.
*⟨Ant. *Heloy eloi lama sabathani...*
Ps. *Vocem meam* [sic].
N. A sexta autem hora...
*Ant. *Cum accepisset acetum...*
Ps. *Benedictus dominus deus meus.*

V. *Quod de passione dominica...*
*Ant. *Inclinato capite ihesus tradidit...*

respondeant ipsi
*quid feci tivi aut in quo contristavi
te responde mihi.*
Hoc expleto, legat subdiaconus
lectionem: *In tribulatione
sua mane consurgent ad me.*
tractu. *Domine audivi.*
sive responsum
Circumdederunt me.
Item lectio:

Dixerunt impii de deo.
Tractus. *Eripe me.*
sive
R. *Velum templi scissum est.*
Item
passio secundum iohannem.
Item orationes.

Ubi fuerint explete,
incipitur antiphona in choro:
**Adoramus crucem tuam.*

Et omnes adorent crucem.
Item psalmus:
Deus deus meus respice.
Alia antiphona
* *Crucem tuam adoramus.*
Psalmus. *Laudate dominum de celis.*
* Antiphona. *Laudamus te christe.*
Psalmus. *Cantate domino canticum nov
laudatio eius in ecclesia sanctorum.*
Deinde antiphona ante crucem:
O quando in cruce.
Item antiphona in choro
* *Omnes gentes quascumque.*
psalmus *Laudate dominum in sanctis e*
Postea pergat sacerdos ad altare
et dicat:
Oremus. Preceptis salutaribus moniti.
et dicatur usquequo dicatur
pax domini sit semper vobiscum.
R. *et cum spiritu tuo.*

Et sic incipiant antiphonam ad vesperum.
*[A.] *Eloy.*
Psalmus. *Voce mea ad dominum clamavi.*

et *Benedictus dominus deus meus
qui doces manus meas.*

XII

Ps. *Exaltabo te deus.*
V. *Ut nos a peccatorum vinculis...*⟩
℣. *Diviserunt.*
In evangelio:
 *⟨Ant. *Velum templi scissum est...*
 Ps. *Miserere mei deus.*
 V. *Postquam crucifixerunt iudei...*⟩

Ordo officii qualiter peragatur
in sabbato sancto...

Exaltabo te deus rex meus.

R. *diviserunt sibi vestimenta.*

 *Antiphona. *Velum templi.*
Psalmus. *Miserere mei deus secundum.*

In sabbato sancto...

Beneventan Liturgy and Music in Tuscany: Lucca, Biblioteca Capitolare Feliniana, ms. 606

In a manuscript from Lucca the evidence of south-to-north communication and in particular of southern italian cultural materials in Tuscany in the early eleventh century

The presence in Pisa, evidently for many centuries, of a famous south Italian Exultet roll[1], as well as the evidence that the Cathedral Library of Pisa once held a number of books written in the Beneventan script of southern Italy[2], raises questions about transmission from south to north. How did these documents come to Tuscany, and from where? Was the communication between monasteries, churches, political entities, individuals?

Portions of a Beneventan missal brought to Florence in the fourteenth century might seem to be further evidence of south-to-north transmission; but in fact this Neapolitan missal, or rather portions of it, were brought north by Giovanni Boccaccio purely as writing material, erased and dismembered pages being used by him for his own works; it never was sought or used in the north for its liturgical possibilities[3].

My object here is to call attention to further evidence of south-to-north communication, this time in Lucca. Here the evidence is not so obvious, because it does not involve the use of the characteristic south-Italian Beneventan script[4]; but it is significant in that it provides evidence of the importation of the old Lombard liturgy of southern Italy, and it is evidently written in Lucca and intended for use there. We do not know whether the south Italian Exultet in Pisa came there by accident or whether it was brought specifically for use there; nor do we know how the books in Beneventan script once

owned by the Cathedral library of Pisa were acquired: unlike the Pisa Exultet, they do not have liturgical functions. In the case of Lucca, however, it seems clear that a scribe of the eleventh century, well-versed in the Beneventan liturgy, and very likely trained in the South, has provided for use in Lucca a liturgical selection from a distant source.

The manuscript Lucca, Biblioteca Capitolare Feliniana 606, has recently been restored, and is now bound in brown leather with two paper flyleaves. It is a missal of 193 folios plus an opening parchment flyleaf from a later manuscript; the folios measure 620 by 450 mm, with a writing area 480 by 310 divided into two columns of forty or forty-one lines. The missal is written in ordinary minuscule of the early eleventh century; the rare musical notation is central Italian, with one exception to be mentioned below.

Preceded by a calendar and the *ordo missae*, the missal is complete for the entire year, temporal and sanctoral, concluding with votive masses and the order for the dead. A gathering is missing after folio 71, which contained the period from Maundy Thursday through Easter Tuesday; further *lacunae*, after folios 76 and 158 (1 folio), deprive us of a portion of the Easter season, and of a page of prayers.

Attached to the main body of the missal is an appendix (f. 150v-156v) which supplements the foregoing missal with certain special rites of Holy Week: directions and liturgical material for

Beneventan Liturgy and Music in Tuscany

the special ceremonies of Palm Sunday, Maundy Thursday, Good Friday, and the beginning of Holy Saturday; the rubrics indicate that the supplement, like the missal, is for monastic use. Much of the material in this supplement is from the Beneventan liturgy, and the musical notation is the same as that used by Beneventan scribes of the early eleventh century.

This supplement continues directly from the end of the missal: the text scribe who finishes the order for the dead begins the supplement (*Dominica in ramis palmarum . . .*) on the same folio. After the supplement the manuscript continues, always in the same hand, with votive masses and further monastic rites and benedictions. This supplement, then, was made at the same time and in the same place as the main manuscript: it is not a later physical addition.

The Holy Week supplement contains substantial portions of the ceremonies and the music used in the old Beneventan liturgy of south Italy. Many musical pieces are notated in this portion of the manuscript, and they are notated by a hand writing Beneventan musical notation: the same hand has added the notation to the Alleluia *Adorabo* in the main portion of the manuscript, folio 137.

The pieces supplied with musical notation in the supplement are listed in the Appendix; it should be noted that other pieces are indicated by incipits, but are not supplied with notation. Most of the notated musical pieces are not normally used in the standard Roman liturgy: they are from the Beneventan liturgy [5].

Evidently the supplement is an addition to a missal that already has the ceremonies for these days: Palm Sunday in the main missal is complete, and the supplement provides certain alternative ceremonies, with their liturgical forms. The lacuna after folio 71v makes it impossible to compare the Holy Week forms for Maundy Thursday, Good Friday, and Holy Saturday, but we may presume that they too were present in the main missal, and were provided with liturgical materials typical of an early eleventh-century central Italian missal.

The supplement, however, comes from another tradition: one that mixes Roman and Beneventan usage. Its scribe is not describing all the rites of Holy Week: he omits all the masses of Palm Sunday, of Maundy Thursday, of Holy Saturday, and the mass of the presanctified on Good Friday: he is consciously making a supplement, an alternative, not a substitute, for portions of the main missal.

In doing so, he has created one of the most important sources of the old Beneventan liturgy [6]. This supplement contains a very full

version of the Beneventan liturgy for these days; indeed, it is the only source which preserves the antiphon *Tristis est anima mea*. Some, but not all, of the sources from southern Italy preserve bilingual versions of certain antiphons, including the adoration antiphons *Adoramus, Crucem*, and *Laudamus*, as well as *Omnes gentes*, for Good Friday. In company with some Beneventan sources [7] and two missals of central Italy [8], the Lucca supplement presents these antiphons in their Latin version only [9].

Particularly disappointing for the study of the Beneventan liturgy is the fact that the supplement breaks off after the beginning of the rites of Holy Saturday. After presenting the Beneventan antiphon *Ad vesperum*, the scribe writes *quo expleto cum Gloria patri, dicat sacerdos oratio sicut in sacramentario continet*. And he does not go on to describe the lessons as they are read in the south, nor to include the four Beneventan tracts typical of Holy Satuday, nor to inform us about the use of the *Exultet*, which in the Beneventan rite is sung after the lessons and uses a text different from that normally employed elsewhere [10]. A complete *ordo* for Holy Saturday might have given us the opportunity to compare the *Exultet* of this supplement with the version found in the south Italian Exultet-roll at Pisa, which, although it uses the standard Roman text of the Exultet, retains the Beneventan melody and includes passages from the Beneventan text [11].

The importance of the Lucca supplement to the old liturgy of southern Italy, and the many liturgical peculiarities presented here that are typical of Beneventan practice, have long been recognized [12]; our purpose here is simply to point out the existence of this southern influence in a northern manuscript.

How did this Beneventan liturgy and music come to be written in a manuscript of Lucca? It appears that the scribe who wrote the music of the supplement, and who added the music of the Alleluia *Adorabo* on folio 137, was either a southerner himself or was trained in the south. His musical writing is in a style practiced nowhere in the north, and it does not resemble the music-hand of the rest of the manuscript. The scribe has as his source either a very good memory, or a written source from southern Italy. There is, however, no surviving source from which the Lucca supplement could have been copied directly. The musical contents of the supplement, rich as they are, are not precisely those of any other manuscript preserving Beneventan chant [13].

There is one aspect of the supplement that

seems to connect it with Montecassino. An *ordo qualiter agatur in parasceben* added to Montecassino, Archivio della Badia, ms. 175, pp. 587-8, in the late tenth or early eleventh century [14], describes a mixed Beneventan-Gregorian Good Friday rite, including the Latin versions of the three adoration antiphons used regularly in the Beneventan rite, and two Beneventan antiphons for Vespers; these directions match very closely the rubrics of the Lucca 606 supplement. I have presented these in parallel transcriptions elsewhere [15], and would only point out here that, despite their very close similarities, the liturgies they present are not identical: the Montecassino source, like some others from southern Italy, uses two antiphons for Good Friday Vespers, whereas the Lucca supplement uses four [16].

Montecassino is naturally a possible source for the information on the Beneventan chant contained in the Lucca supplement. The connection with Montecassino 175 is suggestive, as is the Cassinese aspect of the Pisa Exultet roll no. 2. We know that Montecassino used the Beneventan chant, although by the eleventh century it was already in decline there, and would soon be eradicated almost completely [17]. We know, too, that Montecassino had a dependency (San Giorgio) in Lucca, thought it can be dated only from the mid-eleventh century [18], hence earlier than the date of the Lucca supplement. What business might a monk of Montecassino have had at Lucca in the early eleventh century? Or is our scribe a Lucchese himself, recently returned from a period of training, or study; or some other mission, at Montecassino or some other significant abbey of the South?

There are other sources of Beneventan chant and liturgy, from Subiaco, and from other places as yet unidentified in central Italy [19]; but the Lucca supplement is by far the northernmost source, and it is a relatively early one. Whether its information traveled by some monastic conduit (this seems likely, given that Lucca 606 is a monastic book), or by some means related to the particular scribe involved, remains to be explained. But the supplement itself is evidence of the presence of southern Italian cultural materials at Lucca in the early eleventh century, and it adds to the growing evidence of the presence of southern Lombard culture in medieval Tuscany.

Appendix

Pieces with musical notation in Lucca 606, f. 150v-156v

Pieces from the Beneventan liturgy are printed in CAPITALS; pieces with an asterisk (*) appear with only an incipit with musical notation.

Palm Sunday
150v R. Ante sex dies

Maundy Thursday
151 Lectio ione prophete cum cantico (a few neumes, with included canticle Clamavi, f. 151v, fully notated)
152 a. Postquam surrexit (*)
    a. Domine tu mihi
    a. Mandatum novum (*)
    a. Si ego Dominus (*)
    a. In diebus illis mulier
152v a. CUM RECUBUISSET
    v. Ubi caritas
153 R. LAVI PEDES

Good Friday, adoration of the cross
155 a. TRISTIS EST ANIMA
155v v. Ego propter te flagellavi
    a. ADORAMUS CRUCEM TUAM
156 a. CRUCEM TUAM ADORAMUS
    a. LAUDAMUS TE CHRISTE
    a. O quando in cruce
    a. OMNES GENTES (*)

Good Friday, vespers
    a. HELOY HELOY
    a. CUM ACCEPISSET
    a. INCLINATO CAPITE
    a. VELUM TEMPLI

Holy Saturday
156v a. AD VESPERUM

NOTE

1. The Pisa Exultet is studied in detail and reproduced in Anna Rosa Calderoni Masetti, Cosimo Damiano Fonseca, and Guglielmo Cavallo, *L'Exultet «beneventano» del duomo di Pisa*, Pisa, 1989.

2. An inventory of Pisa cathedral of the last quarter of the thirteenth century lists a «totum biblie de littera beneventana»; a 1369 inventory adds two other Beneventan volumes to the bible: a «Librum Offitialis Amelai [=Amalarii?] in minori volumine» and a «Librum Canonum»; in 1394 two further volumes in Beneventan script are mentioned along with these three: an «Isidorum medicinalem» and a «Librum medicinalem»; in an inventory of 1433 only the Bible, the Isidore, and the Liber Canonum are mentioned. For citations of these inventories see Riccardo Barsotti, *Gli antichi inventari della Cattedrale di Pisa*, Pisa, 1959, p. 22 no. 4 (for the thirteenth-century reference); Pio Pecchiai, *Inventari della Biblioteca Capitolare del Duomo di Pisa*, «Miscellanea di erudizione», 1, Pisa, 1905, p. 138 no. 98, p. 139 no. 101 (1369 inventory); p. 138, n. XCVIII, p. 139 n. CI, p. 139 no. CII, p. 92 n. XCI, p. 138 no. XCVII (1394 inventory); p. 155 n. 58, p. 157 n. 86, p. 158 n. 104 (1433 inventory). All these are cited in Masetti, *L'Exultet*, cit., p. 73.

3. On this missal, whose remains are in Florence, Biblioteca Medicea-Laurenziana, ms. 29.8 and 33.31, see Virginia

Beneventan Liturgy and Music in Tuscany

Brown, *Boccaccio in Naples*, forthcoming in *Italia medioevale e umanistica.*

4. There is, however, a leaf in Beneventan script in Lucca: the final flyleaf (f. 270) of Lucca, Biblioteca Capitolare Feliniana, ms. 593, a lectionary-sacramentary of the 11th century, contains mass-prayers in Beneventan script of the second half of the eleventh century, partially erased and written over. See Elias Avery Loew, *The Beneventan Script; A History of the South Italian Minuscule. Second Edition prepared and enlarged by Virginia Brown*, 2 vols., («Sussidi eruditi 33-4»), Rome, 1980, Vol. 2 [= Brown, *TBS*], p. 54.

5. One of the musical pieces is the antiphon *O quando in cruce*, used for the Good Friday adoration of the cross. This piece is a translation into Latin of part of a Byzantine troparion; while not strictly a part of the Beneventan liturgy, is transmitted in a number of Beneventan manuscripts. See Egon Wellesz, *Eastern Elements in Western Chant. Studies in the Early History of Ecclesiastical Music*, «Monumenta musicae byzantinae. Subsidia», Vol. 2, No. 1, American Series, Oxford, 1947, pp. 68-77; *Paléographie musicale*, Vol. 14 [=PM 14], Solesmes, 1931, repr. Berne, 1971, pp. 305-308; Thomas Forrest Kelly, *The Beneventan Chant* [=TBC], Cambridge, 1989, pp. 207-209.

6. On the Beneventan chant and its sources see Kelly, *TBC*; comprehensive studies of a portion of the Beneventan music and its liturgy were made by René-Jean Hesbert, in PM 14, pp. 248-465, and in *L'«Anthiphonale missarum» de l'ancien rit bénéventain*, in «Ephemerides liturgicae», 52, 1938, pp. 28-66, 141-58; 53, 1939, pp. 168-90; 54, 1945, pp. 69-95; 60, 1946, pp. 103-41, 61, 1947, pp. 153-210.

7. Benevento, Biblioteca capitolare, ms. 33 (s. 10/11) and Benevento, Bibl. cap., ms. 35 (s. 12 in.).

8. Vatican., Bibl. Ap. Vaticana, mss. Vat. lat. 4770 (s. 10/11), Barb. lat. 560 (s. 10/11).

9. For the distribution of these antiphons in manuscript sources see the table in Kelly, *TBC*, pp. 56-57.

10. On the Holy Saturday rites of the Beneventan liturgy see Hesbert, *L'«Antiphonale missarum»*, in «Ephemerides liturgicae», 61, 1947, pp. 153-210; *PM*, 14, pp. 337-446.

11. The text of the Pisa Exultet from south Italy is transcribed in Masetti, *L'Exultet*, cit., pp. 22-25; the passages from the Beneventan text of the Exultet are (1) the passage *Flore utuntur coniuge [. . .] una augetur substantia* (Masetti, *op. cit.*, p. 24) and (2) the passage *Cuius odor suabis est et flamma ylaris, non tetro odore arvina desudat, sed iocundissima suabitate inficitur* (Masetti, *op. cit.*, p. 25). The full Beneventan text of the Exultet is found in *PM* 14, pp. 385-6; on the Beneventan text see also Henry Marriott Bannis-

ter, *The* Vetus Itala *Text of the Exultet*, in «The Journal of Theological Studies», 11, 1910, pp. 43-54.

12. The supplement is transcribed almost in its entirety in a series of tables in *PM*, 14, pp. 252, 284, 300, 308 n. 2; see also Kelly, *TBC, index* p. 337. Facsimiles can be found in Kelly, *TBC*, fig. 4 (2); *PM*, 14, plates XXXIV-XLIII (folios 150v-153, 154v-156); the forthcoming Volume 21 of *Paléographie musicale* contains facsimiles of all the musical pieces.

13. See Kelly, *TBC*, pp. 55-56, for a table of Beneventan music for Holy Week music in Lucca and other manuscripts.

14. The literature on this famous manuscript, written in tenth-century Capua and including Paul the Deacon's commentary on the Rule of St. Benedict, is large; see the bibliography in Brown, *TBS*, p. 74; the *ordo* is edited in *Bibliotheca Casinensis seu codicum manuscriptorum qui in tabulario casinensi asservantur series*, 5 vols., Montecassino, 1873-94, pp. 4, 33-4; on the date of the *ordo* itself, which precedes the epitaph of Abbot Aligern, see Elias Avery Lowe, *Scriptura beneventana*, 2 vols., Oxford, 1929, Vol. 1, commentary to plate XXXIX, who says that the epitaph of Paul the Deacon (which precedes the *ordo*, but not immediately, and that of Aligern, are «11th-century additions»; further on the epitatph of Aligern, see Herbert Bloch, *Monte Cassino's Teachers and Library in the High Middle Ages*, in «Settimane di studio del Centro Italiano di Studi sull'Alto Medioevo», 19, Vol. 2, Spoleto, 1972, pp. 601-5.

15. Thomas Forrest Kelly, *Desiderius and the Two Liturgical Chants of Montecassino*, forthcoming in the acts of the congress *L'età dell'Abate Desiderio.*

16. On the Good Friday Vespers antiphons see Kelly, *TBC*, p. 58.

17. See Thomas Forrest Kelly, *Montecassino and the Old Beneventan Chant*, in «Early Music History», 5, 1985, pp. 53-83.

18. Hartmut Hoffmann, ed. *Chronica monasterii Casinensis [Die Chronik von Montecassino]*, «Monumenta Germaniae Historica Scriptores», XXXIV, Hannover, 1980, II, p. 90. See Herbert Bloch, *Montecassino in the Middle Ages*, 3 vols., Rome, 1986, I, pp. 428-30.

19. For Subiaco see Kelly, *TBC*, p. 313 and *index* p. 339; the central Italian manuscripts are those mentioned above, note 8: Vat. lat. 4770 (see Kelly, *TBC*, p. 315 and *index*, p. 339) and Vat. Barb. lat. 560 (see Kelly, *TBC*, p. 313 and *index*, p. 339).

XIV

Non-Gregorian Music in an
Antiphoner of Benevento

In honor of Janet Knapp on her Sixty-fifth Birthday

Τhe *Corpus antiphonalium officii*, Dom Hesbert's
study of the early musical manuscripts of the Office, serves as the basis
for much modern research on the liturgy of the office hours. For it lists,
in two volumes, the liturgical contents of eight of the earliest antiphoners of the Office; and in two more, edits their texts.[1]

Because Hesbert's monumental study does not concern itself with
the music which accompanies the antiphons, the responsories, the invi-
tatories and the hymns, it lacks a dimension which must be filled out by
the musicologist: indeed, as many a medieval scribe discovered, knowing the music helps to avoid the traps that may escape the notice of the
non-musician.

One of the antiphoners studied by Hesbert is the subject of this article; this is Benevento, Biblioteca capitolare ms. 21 (Hesbert's manuscript L), a monastic antiphoner of the early thirteenth century written
in Beneventan text and musical notation.[2] Hesbert describes the manuscript as being written for the monastery of San Lupo in Benevento,
but in fact there is no evidence of this; the manuscript actually contains
no office for the monastery's patron. All we can say is that the manuscript is from South Italy, perhaps from the city of Benevento itself,
containing as it does offices for such local saints as Saint Barbatus,

---

[1] *Corpus antiphonalium officii* [hereafter *CAO*], ed. Renato-Joanne [Rene-Jean] Hesbert, 6 vols (Rerum ecclesiasticarum documenta, Series maior, Fontes, vii–xii, Rome,
1963–1979).

[2] Hesbert's inventory of the manuscript is in *CAO* II, *Manuscripti 'cursus monasticus'*; the
manuscript is described on pp. XX–XXIV; a facsimile is plate XII. In almost all literature
to date this manuscript has been designated with the shelf-number "V 21"; but we shall
refer here to the manuscripts of Benevento without their preceding Roman numerals, in
accord with the form of the new catalogue of the Biblioteca capitolare now in progress:
Jean Mallet and Andre Thibaut, *Les manuscrits en ecriture beneventaine de la Bibliothèque
capitulaire de Benevent*, Tome I: manuscrits 1–18 (Paris, 1984).

bishop of Benevento, and the Holy Twelve Brothers, martyrs buried in the Beneventan church of Santa Sofia.

Because of its inclusion in *CAO* this manuscript has become a model, one of the bases on which much research on the office is founded. But like many antiphoners of the Office—perhaps more than most—Benevento 21 has peculiarities that make it a less than perfect early example of the monastic antiphoner.

In the course of a systematic study of non-Gregorian music in South Italy, I have recently had occasion to study the many local antiphons in this manuscript—a task enormously facilitated by the *CAO*. Of the manuscripts in *CAO*, Benevento 21 has unique collections of antiphons for St. Scholastica, Gregory, Mark, Vitus, Januarius, Mercurius, John and Paul, Mary Magdalene, the Translation (to Benevento) of Saint Bartholomew, the Transfiguration, the Assumption, and others. Some of these (Bartholomew, Mercurius, Januarius) are saints of particular local importance, while others have particular Beneventan formularies for widely-celebrated feasts. In most of these cases the musical style is Gregorian—either imported music of limited circulation, or music composed locally in a Gregorian style.

But Benevento 21 also includes some music that is outside the Gregorian sphere—music of the Ambrosian rite, and music of the pre-Gregorian liturgy of Benevento. I propose here to show this non-Gregorian music in what is basically a Gregorian antiphoner. By looking at four offices of saints we can view the interaction of musical traditions in medieval southern Italy and consider some aspects of musical style.

1. To begin our survey of non-Gregorian music in Benevento 21 we turn to the feast of the Holy Twelve Brothers (1 September), the saints whose relics were collected by Duke Arichis II of Benevento and interred with great ceremony in the year 760 in his newly-founded church of Santa Sofia.[3]

Benevento 21 provides for this feast (108^2) the antiphons listed in Table 1. There are antiphons for use at Lauds and Vespers, with indications for their further use at the little hours; and an antiphon for the canticles at Matins: this is not the fullest version of an office, but it is a regular collection permitting a proper celebration of the day hours.

Most or all of this music is in the language of the Old-Beneventan chant—of the pre-Gregorian music of South Italy that must have been the local musical *lingua franca* in the middle of the eighth century when these saints' relics were dedicated.

---

[3] On Arichis and the foundation of Santa Sofia, see Hans Belting, "Studien zum beneventanischen Hof im 8. Jahrhundert," *Dumbarton Oaks Papers* XVI (1962), 156–57.

TABLE 1
Sanctorum XII Fratrum (*CAO* 108²)

Benevento 21	Melk 1012/1027	Benevento 66	Benevento 20	Vat. lat. 4928
a. Ecce quam bonum	a. Ecce quam bonum	a. Ecce quam bonum	a. Ecce quam bonum	a. Ecce quam bonum
a. Haec est vera	a. Haec est vera	a. Haec est vera	a. Haec est vera	a. Haec est vera
a. Beatus Donatus	a. Beatus Donatus	a. Beatus Donatus	a. Beatus Donatus	a. Beatus Donatus
a. Venit angelus		a. Venit angelus	a. Venit angelus	a. Venit angelus
			a. Sancti vero	
	a. Sancti vero		B. Septiminus	
a. Sanctissimus Arontius	a. Sanct. Aront.	a. Sanct. Aront.	M. Sanct. Aront.	a. Sanct. Aront.
B. Beatum Vitalem	/ / / / / / / / /	B/M. Beatum Vitalem		
M. Hos duodecim				B. Sancti vero
C. Sancti vero				M. Septiminus

EXAMPLE 1.

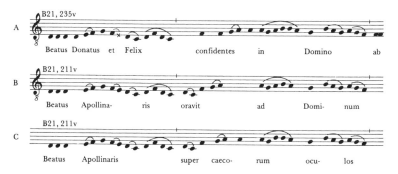

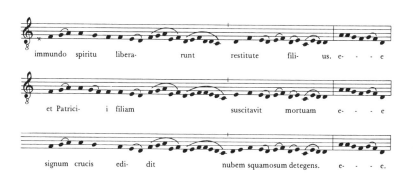

How do we recognize this Old-Beneventan music? First, one of the pieces here, the Magnificat antiphon *Hos duodecim,* is known elsewhere in the Old-Beneventan repertory: it is the Communion for the Old-Beneventan Mass of the Holy Twelve Brothers;[4] it survives in the eleventh-century gradual Benevento 40 (f. 122), one of two principal surviving sources for the Old-Beneventan liturgy, and also in the palimpsest Old-Beneventan gradual fragments in Montecassino 361.[5]

Second, two of the antiphons (*Beatus Donatus et Felix* and *Sanctissimus Arontius dixit*) have melodies which are shared by other Old-Beneventan antiphons (see Examples 1 and 2, respectively). Note the

---

[4] There are other examples of Old-Beneventan music serving both as Communion (or Offertory) and as Antiphon: see Thomas Forrest Kelly, "Une nouvelle source pour l'office vieux-beneventain," *Etudes Gregoriennes* (forthcoming), note 10; see also John Boe, "A New Source for Old Beneventan Chant. The Saint Sophia Maundy in MS Ottoboni lat. 145," *Acta musicologica* LII (1980), 122–33.

[5] On these palimpsest leaves from Montecassino see Thomas Forrest Kelly, "Montecassino and the Old-Beneventan Chant," *Early Music History* V (1985).

EXAMPLE 2.

Sanctissi- mus Aron- ti- us dixit

Beatis- si- mo interveniente Barbato ad nichilum redacta

Sanctissi- mus De- i cul-

Va- le- ri- a- no quemcumque nostrum presseris im- mo- la

sunt simulacra

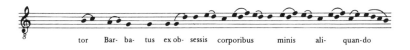

tor Bar- ba- tus ex ob- sessis corporibus minis ali- quan-do

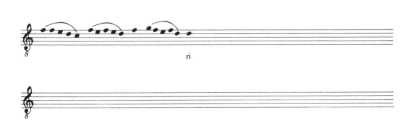

ri

vel fusis preci- bus immundo spiritu eici- e- bat

EXAMPLE 2. *(continued)*

similarity of the final cadences of all these antiphons, with their chains of falling podatus, even though they are directed towards different final notes.

And third, the antiphons display a variety of the Old-Beneventan turns of phrase which recur throughout this highly formulaic musical language.[6]

---

[6] The first two of these antiphons, both of extreme simplicity, defy conclusive assignment to the Old-Beneventan repertory. Unlike the other antiphons, their texts are not drawn from the legend of the saints; the first antiphon, a psalmic text widely used in the liturgy, is a logical choice for the compiler of an office in honor of twelve brothers; but the melody here is different from any setting of this text in the Gregorian Office. The second antiphon, *Hic est vera fraternitas*, begins like many liturgical texts (*CAO* 3003, 6804, 6805), but continues like a hymn-strophe; the same text is used as an Alleluia-verse in the twelfth-century gradual Benevento 34, f. 231v (facsimile in *Paléographie musicale* XV [So-

Most of the Old-Beneventan repertory is preserved in manuscripts without clefs, so that we must be cautious in estimating pitch. Benevento 21, though far removed in time from the creation of the Old-Beneventan chant, at least gives us a thirteenth-century view of how this music is assigned in a Gregorian context. The antiphons in Examples 1 and 2 fit the Gregorian modes 1 and 7. And in fact, to judge from the surviving sources, these are essentially the only modes of the Old-Beneventan chant, though the evidence of earlier manuscripts is that the two finals are not separated by a fourth as in the Gregorian *octoechos*, but only by a step. If the antiphons in Example 1 were written a fifth higher we would have a clearer representation of the unity of range and style in this music: though some pieces end on G, and others on the A one degree higher, there is no further distinction among the changes on the basis of the final note, and no formulas are shared by only one modal group.

We must be cautious about Beneventan psalmody, since our information is filtered almost entirely through manuscripts devoted to Gregorian music: but it seems likely that psalmody recites on one of three pitches: C, D, or E; and that a psalm-tone consists, like its Gregorian counterpart, of an intonation, a recitation (always the same pitch in each half-verse), and medial and final cadences.[7] Two psalmodic levels can be seen throughout the examples.[8] (But note that Examples 5C and 5D use Ambrosian psalm-tones).

These antiphons for the Holy Twelve Brothers are not unique to Benevento 21. From other musical manuscripts and ordinals we can gather a wider sense of their use. Table 1 shows these antiphons as they are provided in Benevento 21 and in four other sources.

At Melk Abbey are two flyleaves from an eleventh-century Beneventan antiphoner—our earliest source for this music;[9] Benevento 20, together with Benevento 19, is a two-part Gradual-Antiphoner of the twelfth century, evidently from a non-monastic environment; Benevento 66 is an *ordo officii* of the twelfth century; and Vatican lat. 4928 is the twelfth-century ordinal of the church of Santa

---

lesmes, 1937]). Both antiphons conclude with the falling-third cadence that is common to many Old-Beneventan antiphons: compare the antiphons for St. John the Baptist in Kelly, "Une nouvelle source."

[7] Further on Old-Beneventan psalmody see Kelly, "Une nouvelle source."

[8] Psalmody on C can also be seen, in Example 3C; on this psalmody see below, p. 488.

[9] For facsimiles of these Melk flyleaves, see Joachim F. Angerer, "Unbekannte Fragmente beneventanischer Provenienz aus der Stiftbibliothek Melk," *Ut mens concordet voci: Festschrift Eugene Cardine zum 75. Geburtstag*, ed. Johannes Berchmans Goschl (St. Ottilien, 1980), pp. 377–403. The relevant plates are on pp. 394 and 403; the author is not aware that these are successive leaves from the same antiphoner. Perhaps the rest of this Office will be revealed if someday this fragment is unglued from the binding of Melk 1027 and the verso can be read.

Sofia of Benevento (the antiphons listed here are for the vigil of the feast, the day itself being given over to a very full office in Gregorian style).

Though many of these antiphons are found in all the sources, the tradition is far from fixed. The first three antiphons occur regularly in order; and *Sanctissimus Arontius* appears usually (except in Benevento 20) as the last psalm-antiphon. The Old-Beneventan Communion *Hos duodecim* appears only in Benevento 21, and the antiphon *Septiminus beatus*, in fifth mode and clearly not part of the Old-Beneventan repertory, appears only in Benevento 20 and in the Santa Sofia ordinal.

Considering that the Holy Twelve Brothers are Beneventan saints, we should expect the manuscripts of Benevento to present a uniform tradition; yet what we find here is surprisingly fluid and unclear. Our oldest source, the Melk flyleaves, presents a pattern which is matched by none of the other sources. Nor does the ordinal of Santa Sofia—the church in which these saints are buried—serve as a model. These martyrs, probably since the dedication of their tomb in the eighth century, enjoyed a widely-extended cult in South Italy; and these manuscripts testify to a considerable variation in local practice.

2. The picture is entirely different for the office of Saint Barbatus (19 February), a seventh-century bishop of Benevento and a saint of purely local importance. Antiphons for Vespers and Lauds of Saint Barbatus are displayed in Table 2, which includes two ordinals and two musical sources (Benevento 22 is a twelfth-century noted monastic breviary). Letters in parentheses indicate the secondary assignment of an antiphon for the little hours.

This is a very firm tradition. Only the antiphon *O quam pretiosum* separates Benevento 21 from the other sources: and this antiphon—a doublet for the Benedictus at Lauds (though perhaps, as Hesbert thought, actually intended for the Magnificat at Vespers)—has the melody of the Gregorian O-antiphons of Advent.

The remaining music is largely Old-Beneventan. Four of the antiphons belong to two melody-types (Examples 2B and 2C, and 3A and 3B);[10] from each we can learn about the adaptation of texts to a melody.

Example 2, which also includes an antiphon of the Holy Twelve Brothers, shows a group of rather complex melodies. Opening and closing phrases are clear, but central phrases, where they exist, vary substantially. But antiphon 2B seems to be an unusual adaptation of

---

[10] One of the antiphons not represented here is *Accepta securi*: its musical style is not indisputably Old-Beneventan; and it ends on E: it would, if Old-Beneventan, be the only piece in the repertory in deuterus, with the possible exception of the Greek/Latin antiphon *Panta ta etni/Omnes gentes* (facsimiles in *Paléographie musicale* XIV [Solesmes, 1931], plates 59, XV, XXIII, XLIII; and in *Paléographie musicale* XX [Berne/Frankfort, 1983], f. 69v), which also may not be part of the Old-Beneventan repertory.

TABLE 2
Sancti Barbati (CAO 57²)

Benevento 21	Benevento 22	Benevento 66		Vat. lat. 4928	
a. Vir domini Barbatus	a. Vir domini	a. Vir domini	1	a. Vir domini	1
a. Clamabat beatus Barbatus	a. Clamabat beatus	a. Clamabat (P)	7	a. Clamabat (P)	7
a. Sanctissimus dei cultor	a. Sanctissimus (T)	a. Sanctissimus (T)	7	a. Sanctissimus (T)	7
a. Expletis missarum sollemnia	a. Expletis (S)	a. Expletis (S)	7	a. Expletis (S)	7
a. Accepta securi	a. Accepta (N)	a. Accepta (N)	3	a. Accepta (N)	3
B. Beatissimo interveniente	B/M. Beatissimo	a. Beatissimo	7	B. Beatissimo	7
B. O quam pretiosum					

EXAMPLE 3.

this melody. The opening phrase (probably called to mind by the similarity of opening words—note the same phenomenon in Example 1) is stretched significantly to span what is essentially two phrases of text. And although the text is long enough to accommodate a central phrase focused on D for *et catholica suscepta est fides Christi,* this clause is instead set to a perhaps overlong recitation in anticipation of the final phrase.

The antiphon *Clamabat beatus Barbatus* (Example 3B) represents a slight alteration of the normal four-phrase pattern characteristic of this melody: the second phrase (closing on B) is substantially lengthened, and the third and fourth are elided to make the single phrase *et Christo domino subicite colla.*

The tersest statement of this theme, Example 3C, does not represent its standard melody as clearly as does *Expletis missarum sollemniis* (3A) for St. Barbatus, for Example 3C opens in a very low range with the cry *"Heloy heloy."*[11] The psalmody for this antiphon (confirmed from the twelfth-century gradual Benevento 39, f. 25) is the only example presented here of psalmody reciting on C; no doubt the lower psalmody is chosen to match the low opening of the antiphon. One wonders, however, whether the scribe of Benevento 21, faced with this antiphon, would not have chosen the D-recitation of its melodic mates.

3. Two saints of particular importance in the rite of Milan are also found in our manuscript: Saint Apollinaris, bishop of Ravenna, and Saints Nazarius and Celsus, whose remains were discovered in Milan by Saint Ambrose himself.

The antiphons for Saint Apollinaris (23 July) in Benevento 21 are essentially in two series, one Old-Beneventan and the other Ambrosian, as seen in Table 3.[12] All the antiphons for Lauds and Vespers are Ambrosian. That is, they are found in Ambrosian antiphoners, and their melodies in many cases are widely used in the Milanese rite for other antiphons. In the Muggiasca manuscript (pp. 242–246), and in Oxford, Bodleian lat. lit. a. 4 (ff. 163–165v)—two related fourteenth-century Ambrosian sources with almost identical Offices for Saint Apollinaris—the six antiphons of Benevento 21 are all present, but not in the Beneventan order. Apparently the Ambrosian series is adjusted to the needs of the liturgy at Benevento, and the Ambrosian psalmody is not used. It should be noted perhaps that the Ambrosian tradition itself is not of exemplary purity, since the antiphon *O martyr domini* which appears in both manuscripts and at Benevento is in fact another relative of the Gregorian O-antiphons of Advent.

Particularly interesting is the double transmission of the antiphon *Apollinaris martyris festa recolimus/laudamus.* In Benevento 21 the antiphon appears twice with the same Ambrosian melody: first with the word "recolimus" among the Old-Beneventan antiphons, and later, with "laudamus," in the Ambrosian series. Benevento 66 and Vat. lat. 4928 also witness this reduplicated transmission: they indicate that the antiphons are in the seventh mode, true only for the Ambrosian melody. Benevento 20, however, has "laudamus" both times, and one anti-

---

[11] Not the same melody as that given for use in the reading of the Good Friday passion in Benevento 40, f. 14v (facsimile in *Paléographie musicale* XIV, plate XVII).

[12] The antiphons of Benevento 66, which are exactly those of Benevento 21, are omitted from Table 3.

TABLE 3
Sancti Apollonaris (CAO 57²)

Benevento 21			Benevento 20		Vat. lat. 4928	
ad noct.	Accipe spiritum sanctum	OB	ad noct.	Accipe spiritum	ad noct.	Accipe sp.
vig. i	Beatus Ap. super cecorum	OB		Beatus Apollinaris super		Beatus Ap. super
	Beatus Apollinaris oravit	OB		Beatus Apollinars oravit	vig. ii	Beatus Ap. oravit
	Ap. martyris festa recolimus	A		LEX DEI EIUS		Ap. m. festa recolimus
ad can.	Vere cognoscent	[OB]	ad can.	Vere cognoscent	ad can.	O QUAM METENDUM
				AP. MARTYRIS FESTA LAUDAMUS		
ad laudes			ad mat. laud.		ad mat. laud.	
et v.	Beatus Petrus apostolus	A	et v.	Beatus Petrus	et v.	Beatus Petrus
	Ap. egregius antistes	A		Ap. egregius		Ap. egregius
	Super cecorum oculos	A		Super *cecati*		Super *cecati*
	Ap. martyr per unigenitum	A		Ap. martyr per unig.		Ap. martyr per unig.
	Ap. martyris festa laudamus	A		Ap. mart. festa laudamus		Ap. m. festa laudamus
B/M.	O martyr domini Apollinaris	A	B.	O martyr domini Ap.	B/M.	O martyr domini

phon is Old-Beneventan, the other Ambrosian.[13] The two versions of this text, "recolimus" for Milan and "laudamus" for Benevento, have become confused in Benevento 21. The displacement of the order in Benevento 20 also suggests that there is something special about this antiphon. At the place where *Apollinaris festa* first appears in the other manuscripts, Benevento 20 provides the antiphon *Lex dei eius* (*CAO* 3611), a piece, evidently not from the Old-Beneventan repertory, used in our manuscript also for Saints Sixtus and Germanus of Capua (both local saints, but without Old-Beneventan music).

And so it appears that Benevento 21 really represents two pure series: Ambrosian antiphons for the day office, and Old-Beneventan for the night; but similarity of text allowed the Old-Beneventan version of *Apollinaris festa laudamus* to drop out.

4. The Ambrosian and the Old-Beneventan traditions meet also in the Office of Saints Nazarius and Celsus (28 July; see Table 4).[14] The final antiphon of Benevento 21, for the canticles of Lauds and Vespers, is a substantial piece in clear Old-Beneventan style; this antiphon also closes the series in Benevento 66 and Benevento 20. The other antiphons in Benevento 21, except for the two with question marks, are found in both our Ambrosian sources.[15] But though the antiphons are Ambrosian, they are not used in the Ambrosian order, nor with Ambrosian psalmody. And, unlike the two series, Ambrosian and Beneventan, for Saint Apollinaris in Benevento 21, the music here is almost entirely Ambrosian, except for the final antiphon.

Benevento 20 presents a curious contrast. For Saints Nazarius and Celsus it presents a series of six antiphons, all of them known from Benevento 21—or rather, their texts are known: but their melodies in several cases are Old-Beneventan where those of Benevento 21 are Ambrosian. In addition, the final Old-Beneventan antiphon from Benevento 21 and a new Old-Beneventan antiphon, *Accessit Nazarius,* gives this series a clearly non-Ambrosian flavor. One further antiphon (*Turbati sunt*) varies from Benevento 21—though the version here is not distinctly Old-Beneventan. And so only one antiphon, *Sancte vir dei,* retains the same melody as in Benevento 21.

Thus, while Benevento 21 presents an Ambrosian office and Benevento 20 a shorter Old-Beneventan series, the ordinal Benevento 66 is a sort of middle ground mixing the two styles: it includes several of

---

[13] Example 5B, the Old-Beneventan version of this antiphon, is unfortunately partly illegible in Benevento 20. The Ambrosian antiphon is a version of the melody in Example 5E.

[14] Benevento 21 alone of the manuscripts listed here does not include Celsus in the naming of the feast.

[15] Muggiasca, pp. 249–59; Oxford, Bodleian lat. lit. a. 4, ff. 166–71.

TABLE 4
Sancti Nazarii (CAO 1029)

Benevento 21			Benevento 66		Benevento 20		
ad M. et cant. et ad tert.	Apparuit thesauros	A	ad Mag.	Beatus Naz.			
ad noct.	DEMONSTRA MIHI	A	ad noct.	ACCESSIT NAZ.			
	Religio matris	A		Incompositi			
vig. ii	Annuit deus	A	vig. ii	Turbati sunt			
	Incompositi iudices	A		Sancte Naz. vir.			
			vig. ii [= ad cant.?]	Apparuit thesaurus			
ad laud. et vesp.	Turbati sunt nautae	A	ad laud. et vesp.	DEMONSTRA MIHI (?)	ad laud. et vesp.	DEMONSTRA MIHI	OB
	SANCTE VIR DEI	A		Religio matris		ACCESSIT NAZ.	OB
	Sancte Naz. vir dei	?		Annuit deus		TURBATI SUNT	OB?
	Benedicimus te	A		Benedicimus te		Sanct Naz. vir dei	? (= B21)
	Justi et sancti	?		Ecce vir dei		SANCTE VIR DEI	OB
M/B	BEATUS NAZ. UNA CUM	OB	B/M	BEATUS NAZ. UNA		BEATUS NAZ. UNA	OB

the Old-Beneventan antiphons of Benevento 20, though we cannot know which version of *Turbati sunt* is intended.

The antiphons which we know in both Ambrosian and Old-Beneventan guise are versions of the same basic melody, presented in one or another style. Example 4 shows the two versions of *Sancte vir dei*; and Example 5 shows various versions of *Demonstra michi* along with two related Old-Beneventan antiphons. In this latter case, though the Ambrosian and Old-Beneventan melodies are clearly parallel, we can see also that the Old-Beneventan version shares its melody with other antiphons in the Old-Beneventan repertory.[16]

Is the series of antiphons in Benevento 20 an abridgement and adaptation of the larger Ambrosian series of Benevento 21 or of the office as found in the Ambrosian sources? Then why not adapt *Sancte Nazari vir dei* as well?

In Example 5, the Old-Beneventan version of *Demonstra michi* is one of a group of Old-Beneventan antiphons that share the same melodic shape (Examples 5A, 5B, 5C). Likewise the Ambrosian melody (Examples 5D and 5E) is representative of an Ambrosian melody-type. The fact that both versions, Old-Beneventan and Ambrosian, belong strongly to their own repertories argues against their recent remodeling. Though melodies are related in the two traditions, they are not successive points along a developmental continuum: one is not derived from the other. More accurate is that they share a common ancestor: or, put another way, they are versions of a melody that is common to both rites—a melody transmitted, over time, in two traditions, variously adapted to local taste and style.

What we learn from these manuscripts adds to the picture of the relationship of Ambrosian and Old-Beneventan chant.[17] We know already that many parallels exist; that in earlier sources much of the surviving Old-Beneventan chant was actually called "Ambrosian" by its scribes[18]—who perhaps reveal more about the relationship than we have been willing to accept; and that at the time of Benevento 21 the two traditions were not the same: this is clear from the two distinct series of antiphons for Saint Apollinaris, and by the presence of both traditions in the Apollinaris antiphons.

---

[16] Example 5A, *Dum sanctificatus*, is a Lenten scrutiny antiphon found among the Gregorian music of Benevento 38. See *Paléographie musicale* XIV, pp. 243–48.

[17] On the relation between Old-Beneventan and Ambrosian chant, see *Paléographie musicale* XIV, 447–56; Terence Bailey, *The Ambrosian Alleluias* (The Plainsong and Mediaeval Music Society, Englefield Green, 1983), pp. 51–58; idem, "Ambrosian chant in southern Italy," *Journal of the Plainsong and Mediaeval Music Society* VI (1983), 1–7; Ambros Odermatt, *Ein Rituale in beneventanischer Schrift*, Spicilegium friburgense 26 (Freiburg/Schweiz, 1980), 66–69.

[18] For a list of these ascriptions, see Kelly, "Une nouvelle source," note 5.

EXAMPLE 4.

Our knowledge of the Old-Beneventan office is limited. Our earlier sources give us certain information because they are preserved probably with more integrity; but they are limited to one exceptional office for Vespers of Good Friday and a Vespers for St. John the Baptist.[19] From Benevento 21 and its relatives we learn of the wider distribution of this music; of its use throughout the yearly cycle; and something of its assimilation into Gregorian books.

[19] The Good Friday Vespers is found in Benevento 40 (facsimiles in *Paléographie musicale* XIV, plates XVII–XVIII), and in Benevento 39 and Lucca 606 (facsimile in *Paléographie musicale* XIV, plate XLIII); one of its antiphons, *Velum templi*, is also found in Benevento 21, f. 132. On this office see *Paléographie musicale* XIV, 335–37.

On the Vespers of St. John the Baptist, preserved in a series of eleventh-century flyleaves in a private Italian collection, see Kelly, "Une nouvelle source."

EXAMPLE 5.

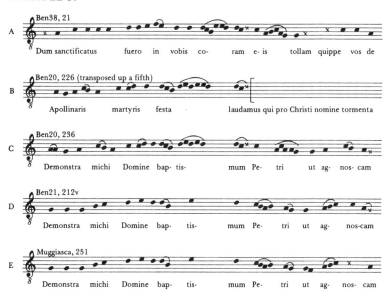

There was a time, surely, when a singer at Benevento would have been more familiar with the local music than with the imported Gregorian chant. And in the assembling of a book of music for the Office, lacunae in the received Gregorian series could naturally be filled with existing music: retaining the local rite for local saints, and allowing the Milanese saints to bring their own music.

Benevento 21 shows aspects of this amalgamation; but it represents a later, and possibly somewhat confused, stage. We cannot know how the music seemed to the compilers of Benevento 21; probably neither the scribe nor the singer is aware that one antiphon is Ambrosian, the next Old-Beneventan, and that both are foreign to the Gregorian tradition.

In addition to the retention and importation of non-Gregorian music we have seen, there are offices in Benevento 21 which include only one or two antiphons in Old-Beneventan style. (These include Saints Silvester, Sixtus, John and Paul, Vincent, and even Saint Benedict.) The present state of our knowledge does not permit us to say that in all cases these antiphons are the remnants of an ancient local practice: they may be newer compositions in local style, or remodelings of received music.[21]

[20] In several offices in this manuscript there are one or two antiphons that are clearly Old-Beneventan while the rest of the office is in Gregorian style, if not in universal use. Such offices include:

Saint Silvester:
    a. *Vir dei Silvester* (f. 36), the last antiphon, for the *Benedictus*, of the six presented for Lauds and the little hours. The antiphon is found also in Benevento 22, f. 76, and cued in Vat. lat. 4928, f. 33v.

Saint Sixtus:
    a. *Usque in senectam*, the last of the six antiphons for Vespers, found also in Benevento 20, f. 249.

Saints John and Paul:
    a. *Defuncto Constantino* (f. 192)
    a. *Mandaverunt Juliano Cesare* (f. 193?); the fifth and the last of nine Vespers and Nocturns antiphons. *Mandaverunt* is found also in a fragmentary noted breviary in Montecassino Compactiones V.

Saint Vincent:
    a. *Insigne preconium* (f. 66v), the antiphon for *Benedictus*, found also in Montecassino Compactiones V. With slightly different text and a different melody this antiphon is used in a number of other antiphoners (see *CAO* III, no. 3355).

Saint Benedict:
    a. *Nursia provincia* (f. 90)—see Example 3D; also in Ben19, f. 88; Ben22, f. 152v.
    a. *Ecce vir Dei Benedictus* (f. 90v); also in Ben19, f. 86v; Ben22, 153v.
    a. *Dum famis inopia* (f. 93v); also in Ben19, f. 93v; Ben22, f. 256; Vat. lat. 10646, f. 51.

Good Friday: a. *Velum templi* (f. 132) appears also in the Old-Beneventan Vespers of Good Friday in Ben38, Ben40, and elsewhere; see *Paléographie musicale* XIV, 335–37 and plates XVII and XLIII.

[21] An interesting case is the antiphon *Pater sanctus dum intenta* for Saint Benedict (f. 93v), which has a peculiarly Old-Beneventan version (shared with Ben19, f. 87, and Ben22, f. 156) of a melody that appears elsewhere in a version in Gregorian style (cf. *Liber responsorialis* [Solesmes, 1895], pp. 324–25).

Indeed, the musical traditions are not always kept separate even within a single piece. We can see Old-Beneventan musical elements insinuating themselves into other styles. Example 6 shows *Beatus Germanus*, the first antiphon for Saint Germanus of Capua from Benevento 21 (indicated also in Vat. lat. 4928, f. 81, as being in mode 7). We see a familiar Gregorian melody-type of the eighth mode: but the final cadence here, set to the words *mundo enituit*, is characteristically Old-Beneventan: the same ending can be seen in many of the foregoing examples. The creation of new music after the advent of Gregorian chant to Southern Italy undoubtedly creates conflations of style; in the ear of the creator of a local office, it is natural, perhaps inevitable, that echoes of familiar regional music should resound in an attempt, however earnest, to imitate the imported style.

In the context of Benevento 21, we are challenged to consider what is meant by a musical tradition, a musical dialect. We can distinguish the various rites of the Western church: Gregorian, Old-Roman, Mozarabic, Ambrosian, Old-Beneventan, and so on; this we do by facts of liturgical difference, by archaisms and idiosyncrasies; but when we come to characterize their musical styles we are sometimes on less secure ground. When an Ambrosian and an Old-Beneventan antiphon share the same melodic contour we postulate some underlying kinship: and from this it follows that the musical distinction is made by the surface detail, the filigree of local melodic motion.

And yet would we be willing to say that Ambrosian Chant, for example, is defined by the application of a certain repertory of surface details, and that what lies below that surface is immaterial?

It is true that the repertory of formulas, of turns of phrase, of "standard" means of melodic motion which are inflected in particular ways, is one of the chief ways by which we recognize such a musical style as the Old-Beneventan chant; but there is much more: characteristic ways of addressing range; limitations of final and of ambitus; a non-differentiated protomodality; repetitive melodic procedures for adjusting to longer texts; and many other features. Not all of these can be recognized in any given piece: and in fact some cannot be recognized at all without comparing two or many pieces. But together these qualities contribute to our modern, reconstructed understanding of what constitutes the Old-Beneventan musical style. It may be that to separate

EXAMPLE 6.

Beatus Germanus quasi sidus splendidus claritate plenus mun-   do e- ni- tu- it. e- - - e.

surface and structure is to divide an entity, and to create two falsehoods from a healthy and indivisible entity.

In that Benevento 21 adds substantially to our knowledge of Old-Beneventan music for the office, we can only lament its lack of purity in transmission. But in the larger sense of what it can teach us about the persistence of musical traditions, and indeed in terms of the manuscript's own objectives, we must acknowledge that it succeeds in weaving together the various musical threads of liturgical music in Southern Italy in the earlier Middle Ages.

XV

A BENEVENTAN NOTATED BREVIARY IN NAPLES
(ARCHIVIO STORICO DIOCESANO, FONDO EBDOMADARI,
COD. MISC. 1, FASC. VII)

It is to the great credit of Virginia Brown that we now have specific datable vidence of the scriptorium of the monastery of Santa Sofia in Benevento in the welfth century. It is she who, in one of her many spectacular moments, noted that he inner edge of a leaf in the Società Napoletana di Storia Patria matched a stub in volume of fragments across town in the cathedral archive. When she put those wo edges together there was a round of applause among the bystanders. 'aleographers are, I'll wager, not accustomed to spontaneous outbursts of pplause.

That happy conjunction conjoined also a book and a scriptorium, for the ingle leaf, the last one in its original monastic breviary, identifies the book as aving been commissioned by Albertus, *decanus*, and presented to the basilica of an Salvatore of Benevento, which he himself had constructed. San Salvatore, ituated next to the infirmary (the infirmary, evidently, of the monastery of Santa iofia), had been consecrated, the colophon tells us, in 1161 by Archbishop Henry f Benevento; on the tenth of September in the seventh year of the cardinalate of bbot John of Santa Sofia, its altar received the relics of several saints.

On the basis of this information, Professor Brown was able to date the olophon, and the manuscripts, to ca. 1161: the church was built then, and Albert, vhom we know from other documents as well, died in 1161[1].

Thanks to Virginia Brown, we now have the only securely datable and dentifiable Beneventan manuscript with neumes. She has also identified the hand f the scribe of the Naples breviary as that of a scribe of Benevento, Biblioteca Capitolare, 22, a notated winter breviary with neumes. This latter manuscript might e thought to be a companion volume to the Naples breviary, were it not for the act that there is duplicate material in the two manuscripts.

V. Brown, «Beneventan Fragments in the Biblioteca della Società Napoletana di Storia Patria», rchivio Storico per le Province Napoletane 113 (1995) 1-68 including 16 plates, esp. pp. 19-32 and lates 4-12; revised version in eadem, Terra Sancti Benedicti. *Studies in the Palaeography, History nd Liturgy of Medieval Southern Italy*, Edizioni di Storia e Letteratura, Roma 2005, no. 7, pp. 447-20, including the same 16 plates now renumbered, especially pp. 458-472 and plates 52-60. See also er «Origine et provenance des manuscrits bénéventains conservés à la Bibliothèque Capitulaire», in a Cathédrale de Bénévent, T.F. Kelly (ed.), Ludion, Ghent — Amsterdam 1999, pp. 149-165.

I propose here to consider the contents, liturgical and musical, of the Naple breviary, and to compare the contents with the liturgy of Santa Sofia, in order to find out what might have been the nature of the liturgy of San Salvatore.

Although we do not have any other musical books containing the office a practiced at Santa Sofia (except perhaps for Benvento 22), we do have two ordinals, one in Naples and one in the Vatican, which give us a clear idea of the Santa Sofia liturgy in the early years of the twelfth century. These are document that list the musical and other pieces to be performed in the office for the course of the year. Vaticano, Città del, BAV, Vat. lat. 4928 is a handsome book made for and surely at, Santa Sofia, at some point in the earlier twelfth century, thus fifty years or so before the Naples breviary; and Napoli, Biblioteca Nazionale Vittorio Emanuele III, VI E 43 is a similar volume made, a little earlier than the Vatican ordinal, for a dependency of Santa Sofia. From their contents we can have a good idea of what went on at Santa Sofia in the twelfth century, and a comparison with the Naples breviary can be quite instructive, even though the Naples manuscript is fragmentary.

Table 1 (see below, pp. 372-387) presents a side-by-side comparison of the two traditions. This is not easy reading, but is intended to show how closely the Naples breviary corresponds to the liturgy of Santa Sofia, and the ways in which it diverges.

There are ten separate surviving portions of the breviary, ranging from less than a bifolium to a complete fascicle. Each surviving portion runs continuously — there are no bifolia with discontinuous contents. Evidently the breviary was first disassembled into its continuous fascicles before pieces of the various fascicles were lost or removed, from the outside in. The losses are mostly the outer folios of fascicles.

The surviving portions are from the summer sanctoral, from Saints Philip and James (May 1) to St. Andrew (November 30), with substantial gaps. Andrew is normally the last saint in the sanctoral, so the few folios missing at the end of St. Andrew may well have been the last ones in the volume — unless there were such further materials as the common of saints and votive masses. The final leaf in the present ordering — whose cognate is the leaf with the colophon — is surely from a companion winter volume, since it contains material for Maundy Thursday. Were it not for the survival of this leaf, which duplicates material in Benevento 22, we would be tempted to posit that Benevento 22, almost identical in makeup with the Naples breviary, was the winter companion of this summer breviary.

Virginia Brown and Jean Mallet have both spent some time on these fragments, and what I have to contribute is essentially comparisons[2].

---

[2] See J. Mallet — A. Thibaut, *Les manuscrits en écriture bénéventaine de la Bibliothèque capitulaire de Bénévent*, 3 vols., CNRS, Paris 1984 (vol. 1); CNRS, Paris — Brepols, Turnhout 1997 (vols. 2-3);

A few remarks about the table may be helpful in making such comparisons. Breviaries and ordinals have different purposes, and different contents. The breviary intends to provide all materials for the office: hymns (usually without melodies), antiphons, responsories, lections, and prayers, in the order in which they occur in the liturgy. Such a book is not, of course, very practical, since the different functionaries (reader, celebrant, singers) would all require copies of the book, even though they would be better off with, respectively, a lectionary, or a collectar, or an antiphoner. A breviary is a book of reference, especially useful, perhaps, in transmitting the liturgy of one place for use in another, or for saying the office when away from home.

The ordinal, by contrast, is a book most useful in coordinating the liturgy of a place where the other books are all present. It consists of a series of cues, mostly but not exclusively to musical items, that are needed in the office in the course of the year. Nothing is complete, musical items do not have either complete texts or musical notation (although there is an indication of the musical mode for each antiphon). What is more, the ordinals of Santa Sofia (and other related ordinals from southern Italy) do not present materials in strictly liturgical order. In particular, the various elements of the night office are presented separately — antiphons together, responsories together, indication of the lections together.

This is difficult to present in a comparative table. At the offices of St. Juvenal, at letter C in the table, note that, in the case of the breviary, in the left column, I have given the incipit of the first lection «*Incipiunt miracula Sci Iuvenalis martyris. Quodam tempore*», and indicated that there are twelve lections. In fact the following eleven lections, with their complete texts, are found preceding the following eleven responsories. I have omitted them here so as to facilitate comparison of the liturgical parallels.

It can also be observed that there are feasts in the breviary that do not appear in the ordinal. Where there is nothing proper to a feast — no chants, no readings, no hymns — the feast is sometimes entirely ignored in the ordinal. This is the case for St. Juvenal, for example; it is a feast of some importance, which appears in the calendar, but its liturgical materials are drawn entirely from the common of saints. There is no indication of St. Juvenal whatever in the ordinal.

In the right-hand column, representing the ordinal, I give, not the office of St. Juvenal (which is not found in the ordinal), but the indications of what is to be done on *any* feast of a saint in Paschal time. Here, as in most feasts in the ordinal, the antiphons are listed first, and then all the responsories. Omitting the indented text in curly brackets produces the text of the ordinal as it stands. I have repeated

---

the contents of liturgical manuscripts in Beneventan script in the chapter library of Benevento (including Benevento 22 and the Benevento ordinal Benevento 66) are exhaustively indexed and compared in vols. 2-3.

XV

certain texts out of order so as to show that the same responsories and antiphons are used in both versions, even though the liturgical presentation is different. Similar adjustments have been made in other offices, where the ordinal gives some indication of lections.

It should be noted too that the ordinal is often quite vague as to the lections of the night office. It may say, for example, at the feast of the Holy Twelve Brothers of Benevento, «Lectiones vero legant octo de passione eorum», without saying what text is to be read, or how it is to be divided. Where a specific set of lections exists, it is provided *in extenso* in the breviary, even when there are no proper chants. Thus we have in the Naples breviary texts for Saints Boniface, Marcellinus and Petrus, Eleutherius, Matthew, Simon and Jude — feasts ignored or barely mentioned in the ordinals.

The ordinals compared here are, as I say, two ordinals closely related to Santa Sofia, both dating from shortly before Dean Albert's breviary for San Salvatore. But they form part of a larger group, and their context in that group is important for the understanding of the proximity of the breviary to the liturgy of Santa Sofia.

There are eight related ordinals from southern Italy, all of them deriving ultimately from the liturgy of Montecassino. (The long and not always amicable relationship of Santa Sofia to Montecassino should not obscure the fact that the liturgy of the Beneventan monastery is derived from that of Montecassino.) The manuscripts of the ordinal are listed in Table 2 (see below, pp. 388-389), with the *sigla* adopted from my forthcoming edition (in the series *Spicilegium Friburgense*) of all of the texts. Five of these ordinals reflect the liturgy of Montecassino, and three are versions of that text adapted for use at Benevento. Of the Beneventan ordinals, two are for Santa Sofia and for a daughter house, and the third is for the convent of San Pietro intra muros not dependent on Santa Sofia. The three ordinals help us to understand what is regional, what is Beneventan (that is, generally present in the city and region of Benevento, but not Montecassino), and what is specific to Santa Sofia.

In Table 1, the right column is the text of the Santa Sofia ordinals, C and D, with indications when their texts diverge. Differences from the tradition of Montecassino are not shown, but I will mention some of them below. What can generally be observed is similarity, not difference. This is a breviary of Benevento, certainly, and evidently of Santa Sofia. Small differences do exist. In box D, two responsories are in reverse order.

Two additional antiphons (Box F) are in the breviary for the Invention of St. Michael, a particularly southern Italian feast. But these antiphons, one of them universal and one purely local, are found in the Santa Sofia ordinals and in the Beneventan antiphoner, Benevento, Biblioteca Capitolare, 21, for the second nocturn. If they are provided here in Naples, it is presumably because they were ιot written earlier in the breviary, suggesting that there is some difference between he ordinals and the part of the breviary that does not survive. Perhaps, like the ιdditional materials later composed for the Holy Twelve Brothers and St. Mercurius, surviving in Napoli, Biblioteca Nazionale Vittorio Emanuele III, XVI A 9, there was newer, perhaps rhymed, material for St. Michael, which displaced hese two antiphons.

The translation of St. Bartholomew from India to Lipari (June 17), at letter ـ, is one of two translations celebrated at Benevento, where the Apostle's relics eposed in a basilica adjacent to the cathedral. The translation is not noticed at Montecassino. In our breviary — unlike the situation in the Santa Sofia ordinals — ιnly the third nocturn is given to Bartholomew, the first two being devoted to ïaints Nicander and Marcianus, whose feast falls on the preceding day according ιo the Santa Sofia calendars of Naples VI E 43 and Vat. lat. 4928. There is no nention of this feast of St. Nicander in any of the eight ordinals — nor of the feast ιf November 26, where the calendar of Santa Sofia has «S Nicandri mr in Sca ïoph»; this latter Nicander is evidently the one whose cult was centered on Capua. Γhis cult of St. Nicander might well be a clue to the destination of this manuscript, ïven though these saints are not among those whose relics are mentioned as being ιlaced in the altar of San Salvatore, were it not for the fact that these same lections, ïor this date, are found in other Benevento manuscripts (Benevento 2 and ïenevento 20).

August 29, at letter M, the feast of the Beheading of St. John the Baptist, is ιlso in Santa Sofia's calendar, «S Sabine, S Vitalis, S<atori> R<epositi>». These ιre acknowledged by a passion of Santa Sabina (though a different one, apparently, ι the breviary from what is specified in the ordinal) and, in one of the ordinals ιnly, by a twelfth lection «de sanctis». There is disagreement among three sources ιere.

At the Holy Twelve Brothers, letter N, the match between the breviary and he ordinals is extraordinary. Only the ordinal of Santa Sofia has a complete liturgy ïor the vigil of this feast, and substantial material for use during its octave. This is he Santa Sofia feast par excellence, the relics having been invented by Prince ïrichis II and interred in his palace church of Santa Sofia in 760[3]. The patrons of he Lombards had a wide cult in southern Italy, but only in the church where their ïelics repose is the feast ornamented with an elaborate vigil and octave. Not even at he dependent monastery for which ordinal C was made is this vigil observed. Our ιrdinal, however, has a proper sermon by archbishop Landolph of Benevento that ₋s not present in the Santa Sofia ordinal. And it allows us to recover the antiphon

---

On the relics and their importance for Benevento, see T.F. Kelly, *The Beneventan Chant,* Cambridge University Press, Cambridge 1989, pp. 11-12.

Beatus Honoratus, known otherwise only from its incipit in the ordinal and from fragment at Melk Abbey[4].

Other slight differences can be found in this feast; more significant is the indication, in the ordinal, of a set of antiphons for second vespers, beginning *Sancti viri supra Christum*; these are assigned in the breviary for use during the octave. They do not survive anywhere else, as far as I know, and they are evidently music sung only at Santa Sofia.

At letter V, the rubric about what happens when St. Matthew's day (September 20) falls on a Sunday is precisely the language of the ordinal. What is more, in both sources it is out of place, before St. Januarius (September 19) rather than after him. But it is doubly out of place in the breviary, since material for St. Matthew is presented also *after* that for Januarius. It appears that the ordinal is among the models for the breviary. Using the ordinal as model and inserting lections for feasts not in the ordinal would result in the split references to Matthew as we see them.

St. Januarius, at letter W, a Beneventan saint (or so the Beneventans imagined)[5], has the material common to both Beneventan ordinals, differing in this from the ordinals of Montecassino, which have a different sequence of materials.

St. Mercurius (Table 1 AA) is another saint particularly venerated at Santa Sofia, which held his relics. He is not mentioned at Montecassino, but he is venerated generally at Benevento, to judge from materials in Benevento 21. The Santa Sofia ordinals have extensive materials, and ordinal D had a complete vigil also, not present in ordinal C, or in any other manuscript. We cannot tell whether the Naples breviary had this vigil. I suspect it had, given that it includes the vigil for that other major feast of Santa Sofia, the Holy Twelve Brothers.

* * *

The above individual comparisons between the Naples breviary and the Santa Sofia ordinals serve to localize the Naples breviary within increasingly narrow circles. It is representative of the larger area of southern Italy which includes Montecassino and its orbit. There are the typically south Italian feasts of the Invention of St. Michael on Monte Gargano, and of Germanus of Capua. More

---

[4] On the Melk fragment (seven fragments of a Beneventan antiphoner preserved as flyleaves in various manuscripts of the Stiftsbibliothek in Melk; the antiphon is in Melk 1027, f. Z), see J.F. Angerer, «Unbekannte Fragmente beneventanischer Provenienz aus der Stiftsbibliothek Melk», in U mens concordet voci: *Festschrift Eugène Cardine zum 75. Geburtstag*, J.B. Göschl (ed.), Eos Verlag St. Ottilien 1980, pp. 377-403; *Paléographie musicale* 21: *Les témoins manuscrits du chant bénéventain*, T.F. Kelly (ed.), Abbaye Saint-Pierre, Solesmes 1992, plate 244 and commentary, pp. 378-379.

[5] See Kelly, *The Beneventan Chant*, pp. 28 and 72.

specifically it is representative of the city and region of Benevento, with its feast of the translation of St. Bartholomew, of St. Januarius, and of the Holy Twelve Brothers. Within the area of Benevento, it is representative of the liturgy of the family of monasteries dependent on Santa Sofia, given its major attention to the feasts of the Holy Twelve Brothers and Mercurius and its close similarity to the two ordinals of that group. But most specifically the Naples breviary represents the liturgy of the church of Santa Sofia itself: that specific church, with its vigil of the Holy Twelve Brothers, and not a dependent, or local, or regional church, which would not have the vigil.

Why would a manuscript made for the Basilica of San Salvatore reproduce the liturgy of Santa Sofia? Evidently the manuscript was made at Santa Sofia — we have Virginia Brown to thank for this discovery. But they made other manuscripts there also, which surely needed to be adjusted for their destinations. Virginia Brown has suggested, followed by Jean Mallet, that some manuscripts for the convent of San Pietro intra muros were made by the scriptorium of Santa Sofia. These include a missal (ex Benevento 29, now London, British Library, Egerton 3511), two chapter books (Benevento 26 and 37), and an ordinal (Benevento 66). These are all adjusted for use at St. Peter's, though they show — especially in the sanctoral of the martyrology of Benevento 37, that they are derived from the liturgy of Santa Sofia[6].

But there is no evidence of any adjustment in the Naples breviary. Surely nobody expected San Salvatore to imitate exactly what happened at Santa Sofia. As far as can be determined San Salvatore was not a monastic church, and even if it were staffed so as to perform the full liturgy, one would expect it to be adjusted either for a different monastery (as in the books for St. Peter's), or for a daughter house (as in the ordinal C).

It would be simplest to conclude that the breviary was made for Santa Sofia, were it not for Virginia Brown; and that it was the summer companion of the winter breviary Benevento 22, were it not for the survival here of a leaf of the Maundy Thursday liturgy — the very leaf whose cognate gives us the colophon that identifies Santa Sofia and San Salvatore. The first half of the leaf contains music for Maundy Thursday, and the rest of the fascicle — of which this must have been the outermost bifolium — would have contained the rest of the music for Holy Week, concluding the volume with Holy Saturday. It would have been a very large gathering. We could estimate the number of leaves in this fascicle from the companion volume Benevento 22, were it not for the fact that Benevento 22 finishes almost exactly where the Naples breviary does. It is perhaps only a coincidence, since the end of a volume is always more subject to damage than the

---

[6] Brown, in «Origine et provenance», pp. 164-165, provides a list of books created at the scriptorium of Santa Sofia.

middle, but it does make one wonder whether the Naples leaf might not have been a page originally intended for Benevento 22, but never finished. It certainly has the same division of lections as the (final) version of Benevento 22 — lections that are not matched in any of the eight ordinals. And perhaps it was used as a sort of flyleaf for the Naples breviary, given that it had a blank page which could protect the volume and on which the colophon mentioning Albertus could be written.

But if this breviary is meant to reproduce the liturgy of Santa Sofia in 1161 or so — as it evidently is — how do we account for differences between it and the ordinal of Santa Sofia, now Vat. lat. 4928?

Errors are one thing, and when a scribe miscopies Virgil we can often fix it. But divergences in the liturgy need to be accounted for in some other way.

Almost any liturgical book, by definition, is made to fulfill a new need, otherwise it would not be made. Such needs are created by a new person, a new place, a new way of writing, or a new liturgy. A person might need a book — a new bishop has a new pontifical made, or a novice entering a monastery provides himself with a psalter. A new place, a daughter house of a monastery, or a new church (perhaps like San Salvatore), would need to be provided with materials for performing the liturgy. Books might also be replaced in order to reflect new styles of production — in particular, changes in musical notation might account for the creation of many of the musical books of the eleventh and twelfth centuries. And changes in the liturgy will make current books increasingly obsolete. The creation of new hymns, of new rhymed offices, of new cults of saints, might render an office book susceptible of replacement; monastic reforms of various kinds — one thinks of Cluny, of William of Volpiano — would favor the replacement of one set of books with another. Nearer to home, the changes in the liturgy carried out by Desiderius of Montecassino, bringing his monastery closer to the practices of the Roman church, contributed to the wholesale replacement of liturgical books at Montecassino.

But this case is still puzzling. Surely San Salvatore was not so richly equipped with monks that it could perform the full liturgy of Santa Sofia (which was, after all, just across the street). It was made for the sick: «pro infirmis specialiter constructam». The presence there of a breviary (undoubtedly the intention, if not the fact, called for two volumes covering the whole year) describing exactly what was going on at Santa Sofia, evidently seemed a good idea to Dean Albert, even if that liturgy would not be performed at San Salvatore.

It must, then, reflect the liturgy of Santa Sofia; and the changes, greater and lesser, that we observe between the breviary and the ordinal of Santa Sofia must reflect changes that took place between the writing of Vat. lat. 4928 in the early twelfth century (the «annales beneventani» have their last addition for the year 1114), and the breviary, almost half a century later. The changes are in fact not many. The addition of some proper hymns, the rearrangement of one or two pieces, some changes in the hagiographical readings.

We would not have the slightest idea, however, that the breviary was intended for San Salvatore were it not for Virginia Brown's discovery of the colophon. Without it, one would have concluded, with certainty, that the Naples breviary was for use in Santa Sofia. And one would have been wrong.

Some liturgical books are made at one place for another; perhaps most of them are made in this way. In most such cases, it is the destination that we can determine, by facts of liturgical content. This book is rather the opposite of that, and in many ways a highly unusual book. The monks of Santa Sofia knew how to alter the liturgy for destination churches; they certainly did so for the books of St. Peter's, and for the ordinal now in Naples. If they made the secular missal-breviary preserved in Benevento 19 and 20, as Virginia Brown surmised they may well have done, they certainly did not simply mirror the liturgy of Santa Sofia.

So why did they do so for the Naples breviary? Perhaps it was because San Salvatore did not really have any liturgy of its own; as the infirmary church, mass might have been said there regularly, but surely not the full monastic office. That office was nevertheless present, and has now been recovered, in Albert's breviary.

Table 1: The Naples Breviary Compared with the Santa Sofia Ordinals

Napoli, Archivio storico diocesano, Fondo Ebdomadario, Cod Misc. 1, fasc. VII + Napoli, Biblioteca della Società di Storia patria, XXXIII A 1 (3)	Ordinals: C: Naples VI E 43 (dependent on Santa Sofia) D: Vat. lat. 4928 (Santa Sofia)
1. May 1- May 3 (ff. 33-36v)	
A	[<MAY 1> IN SANCTORUM APOSTOLORUM PHILIPPI ET IACOBI] ….
	Octo lectiones legantur de passione eorum. Quattuor autem de omelia sancti Augustini {episcopi *add. D*} *Erigenda nobis est.* Item responsoria . . .
R/ *Candidi facti sunt.*] V/ *In omnem terram.* Seq. Sci evg secdm Iohm: *In illo t. dixit I dis suis Non turbetur...* Or. *Sollempnitatis apostolice* Ant. ad laud. et ad vesperum. Ant. *Non turbetur.* Ant. *Vado parare.* Ant. T. *Ego sum via.* Ant. S. *Si cognovissetis me.* Ant. N. *Domine ostende.* Ant. Ad B. & M. *Tanto tempore* (VI). Or. *Deus qui nos annua apostolorum...* Ant. P. *Si dilexeritis me.*	R/ *Candidi facti sunt.* V/ *In omnem terram.*

Ant. ad Mat. l. et Vesp. Ant. *Non turbetur* (VI). Ant. *Vado parare* (III). Ant. T. *Ego sum via* (VIII). Ant. S. *Si cognovissetis me* (VII). Ant. N. *Domine ostende* (VII). Ant. Ben. Magn. *Tanto tempore* (VI).

Ant. P. *Si dilexeritis me* (VII). |
| **B** | Lect. Ad T. et ad T. et eadem ad Laud. *Stabunt iusti* Lect. Ad S. *Hi sunt quos aliquando* Lect ad N. *Scimus quoniam diligentibus* | |
| **C** | IN SANCTI IUVENALIS | <MAY 2> IN SANCTORUM FESTIVITATIBUS QUE SUNT A PASCHA USQUE IN OCTAVAS PENTECOSTES.

Ad vesperum antiphone *Alleluia* (VII) et psalmi de ipso die. |
	Lect. Ad V. *Stabunt iusti*	Lect. *Stabunt iusti.* Que ad matutinas laudes et tertiam et vesperam relegatur
	*Alleluia. V/ Pretiosa**	*Alleluia.* V/ *Pretiosa. Alleluia.* V/ *Confitebuntur celi. Alleluia.* V/ *Lux perpetua.* Iste tantum *Alleluia*
	Ym. Ad V. et ad Noct. *Paschalis dies colitur* (s. n.) v. *Lux perpetua lucebit sanctis tuis*	cantentur ad vesperum in vigilia sive in die et ad missam.

Ant. Magn. *Filie Ierusalem venite*	Ant. Magn. *Filie Ierusalem* (I).
Or. *Pretende nobis dne misericordiam.*	
Deinde ant. Per apostolis *Tanto tempore* v. et or. ut	
supra.	
In noct. Ant. Ad invit. *Alleluia.**	Ant. ad Invit. *Alleluia. Surrexit dominus* (VI).
	Ymnus pertinens ad ipsam festivitatem.
Ant. Ad noct. *Stabunt.**	Ant. ad Noct. *Stabunt iusti* (VIII).
*Ecce quomodo.**	Ant. T. *Ecce quomodo* (III).
v. *Sancti et iusti in domino.*	
Lec. 1 *Incipiunt miracula Sci Iuvenalis martyris.*	
Quodam tempore {*12 lections* }	{from below: Item responsoria
R/ *Beatus vir**	R/ *Beatus vir.*
R/ *Pretiosa**	*Pretiosa.*
R/ *Lux perpetua**	*Lux perpetua.*
R/ *Filie Ierusalem**	*Filie Ierusalem.*}
Vig. II.	Vigilia II.
Ant. *Lux perpetua**	Ant. P. *Lux perpetua* (IIII).
Ant. *Letitia sempiterna**	Ant. S. *Letitia sempiterna* (I).
v. *Lux perpetua**	
	{from below: Item responsoria . . .
R/ *Tristitia vestra**	*Tristitia vestra.*
R/ *In circuitu**	*In circuitu.*
R/ *Vidi civitatem**	*Vidi civitatem.*
R/ *Gaudete iusti**	*Gaudete iusti.*}
Ant. ad cantica *In civitate domini**	Ant. ad cantica *In civitate domini* (VII).
	Versus et responsoria *Sancti et iusti. Lux perpetua.*
	Letitia. Gaudete iusti.
	…
R/ *De ore prudenti**	Item responsoria R/ *Beatus vir. Pretiosa. Lux*
R/ *Ego sum vitis**	*perpetua. Filie Ierusalem. Tristitia vestra. In circuitu.*
R/ *Ego sicut vitis**	*Vidi civitatem. Gaudete iusti. De ore prudenti. Ego*
	sum vitis. Ego sicut vitis.

D	**R/ 12. *Martyrum purpureum* V/ *In civitate domini***	*Letabitur iustus.*
al. R/ *Letabitur iustus in domino* V/ *Protexit eum*	*Martyrum purpureum.* V/ *In civitate.*
[note reversed order of the 2 Rxx]	
Evg. *Ego sum vitis vera**	
Ant ad Mat. l. *Scimus quoniam.**	Ant. ad Mat. l. et ad Vesp. *Scimus quoniam* (VIII).
Ant. *Sancti tui domine.**	Ant. *Sancti tui domine* (VII).
Ant. *Sancti et iusti.**	Ant. N. *Sancti et iusti* (VIII).
Ym. *Gaudet sanctorum cetus supernorum* (s. n.)	Ad vesperum addatur antiphona hec: *Alleluia. Ego*
v. *Ecce quomodo computati sunt* R/ *Et inter sanctos*	*sum vitis vera* (I).
Ant. B. *Filie Ierusalem*	Ant. Ben. et Magn. *Filie Ierusalem* (I).
Or. *Pretende nobis domine* require retro.	

		Lect. ad S. *Hi sunt quos aliquando.*
		Ad N. *Scimus quoniam.*
E	INVENTIONE SANCE CRUCIS	<MAY 3> IN INVENTIONE SANCTE CRUCIS.
	Lec. Ad Vesp. *Fratres hoc <space> sentite*	Ad Vesp. Lect. *Fratres hoc {enim add. D} sentite.*
	Alleluia. V/ *Dulce lignum.*	*Alleluia.* V/ *Dulce lignum.*
	Ym. *Pange lingua** require in dnic de pass.	Ym. *Pange lingua.*
	v. *Hoc signum* R/ *Cum dominus.*	
	Ant ad M. *O crux splendidior.*	Ant. Magn. *O crux splendidior* (I).
	Or. *Deus qui in preclara salutifere*	
	Ant. De sanctis *Filie Ierusalem**	Deinde antiphona versus et oratio de sanctis.
	Or. *Presta qs om ds ut qui sanctorum tuorum*	
	Ant ad Invit. *Alleluia alleluia**	Ant. ad Invit. *Alleluia alleluia* (I).
	Ym. *Eterna Christi munera.**	Ym. *Eterna Christi munera.*
	Ant. ad Noct. *Stabunt iusti.**	Ant. ad Noct. *Stabunt iusti* (VIII).
	Ant. *Ecce quomodo.**	
	Lect 1. *Passio sanctorum martyrum Alexandri pape Eventi et Theodoli presbiterorum////*	In prima et secunda vigilia canantur responsoria de sanctis cum lectionibus eorum. ...

2. MAY 8- MAY 14 (FF. 37- 41V)		
F	[IN INVENTIONE SANCTI MICHAHELIS ...	<MAY 8> IN INVENTIONE SANCTI MICHAHELIS
		... Ant. ad Mat. l. et ad Vesp. *Dum sacra mysteria* (VIII). Ant. *Dum committeret* (I). Ant. *Dum preliaretur* (VII). Ant. *Angeli domini* (VIII). Ant. *Angeli et omnes* (VII). Lect. *Et proiectus est.* R/ br. *Stetit angelus.* Ym. *Christe sanctorum decus angelorum.* Ant. Ben. *Factum est silentium* (VIII).
	[Ant. *Angeli archangeli . . . do-*] *minum de celis alleluia.*	Ant. P. *Angeli archangeli* (VII).
	Lec. Ad Laud. *Et proiectus est draco*	Hora tertia induti albis lineis intrent ad missam
		Ant. T. *Celestis militie* (VIII).
	Ant. T. *Celestis militie.*	
	Lect. *Factus est prelium** (V)	Lect. *Factum est prelium* et ad Vesp.
	Or. *Deus qui miro ordine*	
	Ant. S. *Archangeli Michahelis.*	Ant. S. *Archangeli Michahelis* (I).
	Lect. *Factum est silentium in celo.*	Lect. *Factum est silentium in celo quasi medio*
	Or. *Perpetuum nobis dne tue*	
	Ant. N. *Angelus archangelus.*	Ant. N. *Angelus archangelus* (VII).
	Lect. *Et audivi vocem in celo.*	Lect. *Et audivi vocem in celo.*
	Alie antiphone	
	Ant. *Angelum pacis*	<CD, Ben21, vig. II, local>
	Ant. *Concussum est mare*	<CD, Ben21, vig. II, widely known>
	Ad Vesp. quartus psalmus *Confitebor tibi domine in toto corde.*	Ad Vesp. quartus psalmus *Confitebor tibi quoniam exaudisti.*

Alleluia. V. *Confitebor tibi domine*	
G SANCTI BONIFACII Ys. Ad Vesp. Et ad noct. *Adstat en turba* <s. n.; Ben 42> Ant. Magn. *Filie Ierusalem.* * Or. *Deus qui delinquentes* Ant. Ad invit. *Alleluia.* * Ant. Ad noct. *Stabunt.* * *Ecce quomodo.* * v. *Sancti et iusti in domino.* *Passio beati Bonifacii martyris. Temporibus Diocletiani {12 lections}* R/ *Beatus vir.* *<indicates the series as above at s. Iuvenalis> Vig. II. Ant. *Lux perpetua* * Ant. *Letitia sempiterna* * V. *Lux perpetua* * Ant. ad cantica *In civitate domini* * Ev. *Ego sum vitis vera* * Ad Mat. l. [et vesp.?] Ant. Stabunt iusti* Ant. [???] deo[?] Ant. *Sancti et iusti* * R/ br. *Gaudent iusti in domino* * Ym. *Sublime nobis imminet* (s. n.) R/ br. *Ecce quomodo* * Ant. ad Ben. *Filie Ierusalem* * Oratio ut supra.	<May 14: s. Bonifacii> Si venerit aliqua festivitas sanctorum cum duodecim lectionibus in his quattuor dominicis, aut in dominica post ascensionem in prima et secunda vigilia omnia fiant de sanctis. Vigilia tertia cum evangelio et matutine laudes et missa ad tertiam de dominica. Missa vero ad primam et reliqua omnia de sanctis. Preter festivitates sanctorum Marci, Philippi et Iacobi, inventionis sancti crucis, sancti angeli et sancti Bonifacii.
H <JUNE 2> PASSIO SANCTORUM MARCELLINI ET PETRI EXORCISTE B... salvatoris <incipit illeg., continues as Mallet Hag 71, BHL 5231, 12 lections >	<The dates of Marcellinus, Petrus and Herasmus are those of the calendar of Naples VI E 43; evidently the breviary celebrates them on the same day>
I <JUNE 1> PASSIO SANCTI HERASMI lecc. 9-12, BHL 2584	
J <JUNE 5> PASSIO SANCTI ELEUTHERII EPISCOPI ET MARTYRIS, ET ANTIE MARTYRIS. *Quinto et vicesimo anno imperii* <6 lections visible: BHL 2450>///	<The saint is barely known at Benevento, but appears in the caledar of Naples VI E 43; a collect in the 12c collectar of Ben 42, for a female monastery.>

	3. JUNE 15 – JUNE 17 (F. 42-43V)	
K	[IN SANCTI VITI///]	<JUNE 15> IN SANCTI VITI.
		Ant. Magn. *Confortavit dominus* (VI)
		Ant. ad cantica et T. *Florentia quedam* (VIII).
	Lec. 12. *Et facta est illi vox.*	
	Evg. *Ponite in cordibus vestris*	
	Ant. ad Mat. l. et ad Vesperum *Ingenuo ex genere.*	Ant. ad Mat. l. et ad Vesp. *Ingenuo ex genere* (VIII).
	Ant. *Cilicii indutus.*	Ant. *Cilicii indutus* (II).
	Ant. S. *Accersiri autem.*	Ant. S. *Accersiri autem* (I).
	Ant. P. *Carceris custodia.*	Ant. P. *Carceris custodia* (VII).
	Ant. N. *Succensus imperator.*	Ant. N. *Succensus imperator* (VIII).
	Ant. Magn. Ben. *Gloriosi etenim martyres.*	Ant. Ben. et Magn. *Gloriosis {-i D} etenim martyribus {-es D}* (VIII).
	Or. Da ecclesie tue qs dne intercedentibus	
L	TRANSLATIO SANCTI BARTHOLOMEI.	<JUNE 17> TRANSLATIO SANCTI BARTHOLOMEI
	Ad Vesp. R/ *Beatus namque apostolus.**	Ad Vesp. R/ *Beatus namque apostolus.*
	Ant. ad Magn. *Ut Christi discipulum.*	Ant. ad Magn. *Ut Christi discipulum* (II).
	Or. Ds qui apostoli tui Bartholomei corpus	
	Addita ant. Or. Et or de s Nicandro et Marciano.	
	Ant. *Gaudent in celis* <?>	
	Or. Sanctorum tuorum nos domine < Cfr. Ben 33, 106v, Mallet 3, 1428, no. 1539>	
	Passio Ss. Martyrum Nicandri et Marciani.	**In nocte omnia fiant de apostolis.**
	Gloriosa sanctorum… <8 lecc., BHL 6070?>	
	Ant. Ad cant. *Mirabilis et lucifer .*	
	Translatio s Bartholomei apli de Indi in Lypari <4 lections, BHL 1004>	
	Sermo venerabili Theodori abbati. *Beati Bartholomei* <Mallet 3,1329, no. 46>	
	/////	Ant. ad cantica *Mirabilis et lucifer* (vii T).
		Ant. ad Mat. l. et ad Vesp. *Dictum dei* (II). Ant. *Armenia predicat* (VIII). Ant. *Crudelitatem* (II). Ant. *Quemammodum* (VII). *Asperitatem* (I). Ant. ad Ben. et Magn. *Ut Christi discipulum* (II). Ant. P. *Ut lucrifaceres* (VIII). Ant. S. *Animas iubante* (VIII). Ant N. *Intercessione* (I). …

4. August 29 – September 8 (ff. 44-52v)	
IN DECOLLATIONE SANCTI IOHANNIS BAPTISTE.	<AUGUST 29> IN DECOLLATIONE SANCTI IOHANNIS BAPTISTE. Ad Vesp. lectio de uno martyre. R/ *Puelle saltanti* {-*s D}* Ym. *Almi prophete* et *Assertor equi.* Ant. Magn. *Die autem natalis* (II). In fine dicatur antiphona de sancto Augustino versus et oratio. In noct. Ant. ad Invit. *Regem martyrum* (III). Ym. *O nimis felix meritisque.* Ant. ad Noct. *Audivit Herodes* (VIII). Psalmi de uno martyre. Ant. *Hic est Iohannes* (IIII). Ant. *Herodes autem* (VII). Ant. *Dicebat Iohannes* (II). Ant. *Metuebat* (II). Ant. *Die autem natalis* (II). Vigilia II. Ant. *Die autem illa* (VII). Ant. P. *Quid petam mater* (IIII). Ant. S. *Da mihi in disco* (IIII). Ant. ad cantica et T. *Petiit puella* (VIII). Versus et responsoria de uno martyre. Septem lectiones legant de omelia Bede *Natalem beati Iohannis.* Octava vero passione SANCTE SABINE {*Cum tempus sevissime* add. C} Nona vero et decima et undecima ex commentario sancti Ieronimi *Quidam ecclesiasticorum.* Duodecima pro sanctis {C: Duodecima de sermone sancti Augustini de presenti capitulo.}
R/ *Iohannes Baptista…*] V. *Herodes enim.*	R/ *Iohannes baptista.* V/ *Herodes enim.*
Lec. 2 Hi siquidem <Bede>	
R/ *Metuebat* R/ *Et audito eo*	R/ *Metuebat.* V/ *Et audito eo.*
Lec. 3. Quatinus	
R/*Iustus germinabit**	R/ *Iustus germinabit.*
Lec. 4. Qui bene quidem	
R/ *Misit Herodes* R/ *Misso spiculatore*	R/ *Misit Herodes.* V/ *Misso spiculatore.*
Vig. II.	{From above: Vigilia II.
Ant. *Die autem illa.*	Ant. *Die autem illa* (VII).
Ant. *Quid petam mater.*	Ant. P. *Quid petam mater* (IIII).
Ant. *Da mihi in disco.*	Ant. S. *Da mihi in disco* (IIII).}
Lec. 5. Sed misere desipuit	
R/ *Puelle saltanti* V/ *Domine mi rex.*	R/ *Puelle saltanti.* V/ *Domine mi rex.*
Lec. 6. *Herodes enim tenuit*	
R/ *Contristatus est rex.* V/ *Herodes funestus.*	R/ *Contristatus est rex.* V/ *Herodes funestus.*
Lec. 7. *Ambo nanque continentes*	
R/ *Misso Herode spiculatore.* V/ *Cum autem audissent.*	R/ *Misso Herode spiculatore.* V/ *Cum autem audissent.*
Lec 8. Passio s. Savine mart. **Ilustrissima femina** <BHL 7407>	{From above: Octava vero passione SANCTE SABINE {*Cum tempus sevissime* add. C <BHL 7586b?>}

R/ *induit me dominus** Ant. Ad cant et T. *Petiit puella* Lec. 9. *Sci evg secdn Math. In il. t. Audivit Herodes.* Sermo beati Ieronimi pbri de eadem L. *Quidam* *eclesiasticorum.* R/ *In medio carceris* V/ *Misit rex.* Lec. 10. *Cunctique eo tempore* R/ *Accedentes discipuli.* V/ *Misso Herodes.* Lec. 11. *Vetus narrat historia* R/ *Magnificavit eum.** **Lec. 12. Quis sit autem hic Philippus** <continuation of sermon> R/ *Posuisti domine.** [Evg.] sec. Math. *In Illo t. Audivit Herodes* Or. *Sancti Ioh. Bapt. et martyris tui* Ad Mat. l. et ad Vesp. Ant. *Arguebat Herodem.* Ant. *Herodes enim.* Ant. *Puelle saltanti.* Ant. *Domine mi rex.* Ant. P. *Misit rex incredulus.* Lec. *Iustus cor suum.** R/ br. *Puelle saltanti.** Ymnus *Almi prophete* et *Assertor equi.** Ant. Ben. *Misso Herode spiculatore.** Or. *Deus qui precursorem filii tui* require retro	R/ *Induit me dominus.* {From above: Ant. ad cantica et T. *Petiit* *puella* (VIII).} {From above: Nona vero et decima et undecima ex commentario sancti Ieronimi *Quidam ecclesiasticorum.*} R/ *In medio carceris.* V/ *Misit rex.* R/ *Accedentes discipuli.* V/ *Misso Herodes.* R/ *Magnificavit eum.* {from above: **Duodecima pro sanctis** {C: Duodecima de sermone sancti Augustini de presenti capitulo.} R/ *Posuisti domine.* {(XI) D R/ *Hi pro dei amore* (XII, add. D} Ad Mat. l. et ad Vesp. Ant. *Arguebat Herodem* (II). Ant. *Herodes enim* (I). Ant. *Puelle saltanti* (I). Ant. *Domine mi rex* (III). Ant. N. *Misit rex incredulus* (VIII). R/ br. *Puelle saltanti.* Ymnus *Almi prophete* et *Assertor equi.* Ant. Ben. Magn. *Misso Herode spiculatore* (I). Deinde antiphona versus et oratio de sancta Savina et sancti Bartholomei. {Postmodum autem Ant. Beatum Vitalem versus et oratio *add. D*}

N	IN VIGILIA SANCTORUM DUODECIM FRATRUM	<AUGUST 31> D: IN VIGILIA SANCTORUM DUODECIM FRATRUM
	Ant. ad Invit. *Regem martyrum.** Ym. *Sacrum piorum.* Ant. ad Noct. *Predicantibus his.** Ant. *Victorem tribunum.** Ant. *Audax quidam.* **Lec. 1. Sermo ven. Landulfi [primi] Ben.** **Archiepiscopi** *In sollemnitatum vigiliis* <3 lections> R/ *Hi pro dei amore.*	ANT. ad Invit. *Regem martyrum* (VI). Ym. *Sacrum piorum.* Ant. ad Noct. *Predicantibus his* (II). Ant. *Victorem tribunum* (III). Ant. *Audax quidam* (IIII). psalmi de feria. Legantur tres lectiones de sermone sancti Augustini *Cum omnium sanctorum martyrum.* R/ *Hi pro dei amore.*

R/ *Hec est vera fraternitas.* R/ br. *Sanctorum velut aquile* \<over erasure> In secundo nocturno *Alleluia.* Lec. *Iustorum anime* V/ *Iusti confitebuntur* Or. *Beatorum martyrum tuorum duodecim* Incipantur ant. ad mat. l. et ad vesp. Ant. *Ecce quam bonum.* Ant. *Hec est vera.* Ant. T. *Beatus Donatus.* Ant. *Venit angelus.* Ant. *Sanctissimus Arontius.* Lec. *Fulgebunt iusti.* V/ *Letamini in domino* \<over erasure> Ym. *Rex gloriose martyrum.** Ant. Ben. *Sancti vero* (VIII). Or. *Concede qs omps ds ut sanctorum martyrum* deinde antiphona versus et oratio de sancto Bartholomeo. Alie Antiphone: Ant. **Beatus Honoratus** \<**found in D only, at** **Mercurius**> Ant. *Septiminus beatus* Ant. T. *Beatum Vitalem Satorum* Ant. ad. Vesp. *Ecce quam bonum.** quattuor antiphone. Lect. *Sancti per fidem.** R/ *Hec est vera fraternitas.** Ym. **Votis tuorum Christe fidelium (s.n.).** **Ant. Magn. Sancti vero*** Ant. de apostolo *Postquam Lycaoniam**	R/ *Hec est vera fraternitas.* R/ br. *Letamini in domino.* In secundo nocturno *Alleluia.* Finito nocturno incipantur matutine laudes. Ant. *Ecce quam bonum* (II). Ant. *Hec est vera* (II). Ant. *Beatus Donatus* (I). Ant. *Venit angelus* (II). Ant. *Sanctissimus Arontius* (VII). Ym. *Rex gloriose martyrum.* Ant. Ben. *Sancti vero* (VIII). deinde antiphona versus et oratio de sancto Bartholomeo. Ant. ad. Vesp. *Ecce quam* (II). quattuor antiphone. Lect. *Sancti per fidem.* R/ *Hec est vera fraternitas.* Ym. *Christi katerva pervigil.* Ant. Magn. *Septiminus beatus* (V) Ant. de apostolo *Postquam Lycaoniam* (VI) versus et oratio.
O \<IN SANCTORUM DUODECIM FRATRUM> In noct. Ant. ad Invit. *Eia fratres deo nostro.* Ym. *Christi caterva* (s.n.) Ad noct. Ant. *Africane.* Psalmi de pluribus martyribus. Ant. *Arbor bona.* Ant. *Christe generis.* Ant. *Hi paternis educati.* Ant. *Nam Christi sequentes.* Ant. *Sancto spiritu repleti* .	\< SEPT. 1. CD: IN SANCTORUM DUODECIM FRATRUM> In noct. Ant. ad Invit. *Eia fratres deo nostro* (II). Ym. *Christi caterva.* Ad noct. Ant. *Africane* (I). Psalmi de pluribus martyribus. Ant. *Arbor bona* (II). Ant. *Christe generis* (III). Ant. *Hi paternis educati* (IIII). Ant. *Nam Christi sequentes* (V).

	Passio scorum Donati et Felicis et fratrum eoru. *Dum fervor Maximiani* <BHL 2297, **TWELVE** lecc.>	Ant. *Sancto spiritu repleti* (VI). {from below: Lectiones vero legant **octo** de passione eorum.} Vigilia II. Ant. *Horum precibus opera* (VII). Ant. *Doctor magnus Cip.* (VIII). Ant. *Promovit rursum* (I). Ant. ad cantica. *Sancti vero uno ore* (VIII). Lectiones vero legant octo de passione eorum. Vigilia III. omelia sancti Gregorii pape *Cum constet omnibus nobis fratres.*
P	R/ 1. *Ingens christianis cunctis.* V/ *Claruerunt ergo.* R/ 2. *Civitas in monte sita.* V/ *Hi paternis.* R/ 3. *Hi paternis educati.* V/ *Sancto spiritu repleti.* <a folio missing>	R/ *Ingens christianis cunctis.* V/ *Claruerunt ergo.* R/ *Civitas in monte sita.* V/ *Hi paternis.* R/ *Hi paternis educati.* V/ *Sancto spiritu repleti.* R/ *Sancto spiritu repleti.* V/ *Predicantibus.* R/ *Predicantibus his duodenis.* V/ *Victorem tribunum.* R/ *Horum precibus operabatur.* V/ *Dextra mancis.*
	R/ 7. *Senatricis restitute.* V/ *Confidentibus in Christo.* R/ 8. *His ex aliis auditis.* V/ *Qui confestim.* At. ad cantica *Sancti vero* * R 9. *Sancti viri supra Christum.* V/ *Hos primum blandiri.* R/ 10. *Cum retrudi eos preses.* V/ *Ecce presens adsum.* R/ 11. *Sanctis presidi Valeriano.* V/ *Ad hec sanctis prompta mente.* **R/ 12 Hec est vera fraternitas.** * **Al. R/ Annuente Christo Ihesu. V/ Dominus per suos sanctos.** Ev. Sec. Lucam. *Convocatis Ihesus duodecim* Or. *Adesto nobis dne martium deprecatione*	R/ *Senatricis restitute.* V/ *Confidentibus in Christo.* R/ *His ex aliis auditis.* V/ *Qui confestim.* R/ *Sancti viri supra Christum.* V/ *Hos primum blandiri.* R/ *Cum retrudi eos preses.* V/ *Ecce presens adsum.* R/ *Sanctis presidi Valeriano.* V/ *Ad hec sanctis prompta mente.* **R/ Annuente Christo Ihesu. V/ Dominus per suos sanctos.** **R/ Hec est vera fraternitas.**
Q	Ant. Ad Mat. L. et ad Vesp. Ant. *Ecce quam bonum.* * Ant. *Hec est vera.* * Ant. T. *Beatus Donatus.* * Ant. *Venit angelus.* * Ant. *Sanctissimus Arontius.* * Lec. *Fulgebunt iusti.* * R/ br. *Venit angelus domini.* Ym. *Splendor diei* (s. n.) Ant. ad Ben. *Sampnium vetus insignis Benevente.* Or. *Deus qui nobis per singulos annos* Postea dic. antiph. V. et or. de sancto Bartholomeo.	Ant. ad Mat. l. *Ecce quam bonum* (II). Ut supra. {Ant ad V. *Sanctissimus Arontius* (VII) *add. in marg.* C} R/ br. *Venit angelus domini.* Ym. *Splendor diei.* Ant. ad Ben. *Sampnium vetus insig.* (VIII). Ant. P. *Beatus Honoratus* (I).

	Ant. P. *Beatus Honoratus.* *	Ad missam omnes pluvialibus induti intrent in choro et canent tertiam cum antiphona *Beatum Vitalem* (II). Finita tertia faciant sollemnem processionem. Ant. *Sancti vero* (VIII). R/ *Hec est vera fraternitas.* Ante ecclesiam Ant. *Septiminus beatus* (V).
	{above: Ant. T. *Beatum Vitalem.* *} Or. *Ds qui pro nobis singulos annos* *	
		Ant. S. *Venit angelus* (II).
	Ant. S. *Venit angelus.* * Or. *Germana nos qs dne scorum martyrum* Ant. N. *Extrahuntur duodeni .* Or. ut supra Ant. ad Vesp. *Ecce quam bonum.* * per ordinem Lec. *Fratres sancti per fidem.* *	Ant. N. *Extrahuntur duodeni* (VI). **Ant. ad Vesp. *Sancti viri supra Christum*** (II). **Ant. *Mox tirranus*** (II). **Ant. *Verum Christus*** (IIII). **Ant. *Ecce presens adsum*** (V).
	R/ br. *Venit angelus domini.* * Ym. *Votis tuorum* * Ant. ad Magn. *Sancti vero.* *	R/ br. *Venit angelus.* **Ym. *Christi caterva.*** Ant. ad Magn. *Sancti vero* (VIII). Postea dicant antiphonam et orationem de sancto Bartholomeo.
R	INTRA OCTAVAS Ant. ad Invit. *Regem martyrum.* * Ym. *Sacrum piorum.* * Ant. ad Noct. *Arbor bona* *	INTRA OCTAVAS {D ONLY} Ant. ad Invit. *Regem martyrum* (VI). Ym. *Sacrum piorum.* Ant. ad Noct. *Arbor bona* (II). Due sive tres dicantur per unamquamque noctem. Et legantur tres lectiones de sermonibus eiusdem festivitate. Lect. post noc. *Iustorum anime.*
	Lect. post noc. *Iustorum anime.* * Antiphone in laudibus *Ecce quam bonum* ut supra. Lectio, responsorium et hymnus ut supra. Ant. ad Ben. *Sancti vero.* * Ant. P. *His et aliis.* Ant. T. *Annuente Christo.* Ant. S. *Ad quem sancti.* Ant. N. *Ab humanis.* **Ant. *Discipulus* ad Vesp. Ant. *Sancti viri supra Christum.* Ant. *Mox tyrannus.* Ant. *Verum Christus suos servos.* Ant. *Ecce presents adsum.*** Ant. ad Magn. *Sanctorum duodenorum.* Alia ant. *Sampnium vetus.* *	Antiphone in laudibus *Ecce quam bonum* ut supra. Lectio, responsorium et hymnus ut supra. Ant. ad Ben. *Sancti vero* (VIII). Ant. *His et aliis* (VII P). Ant. *Annuente Christo* (VI T). Ant. *Ad quem sancti* (VII S). Ant. *Ab humanis* (V N). ad Vesp. Ant. *sancti viri* (II) ut supra. Ant. ad Magn. *Sanctorum duodenorum* (I). Ant. *Sampnium vetus* (VIII).
S		DOMINICA INTRA OCTAVAS . . . DOMINICA PRIMA KAL<ENDIS> SEPTEMBRIS . . .

T	IN NATIVITATE SANCTE MARIE.	<SEPT. 8> IN NATIVITATE SANCTE MARIE.
	Ant. ad Vesp. *Ante torum huius.* *	Ant. ad Vesp. *Ante torum huius* (IIII).
	Ant. *Hec est que nescivit.**	Ant. *Hec est que nescivit* (III).
	Ant. *Dum esset rex.**	Ant. *Dum esset rex* (III).
	Ant. *Nigra sum.**	Ant. *Nigra sum* (III).
	Lect. *Ab initio et ante.*	Lect. *Ab initio et ante.*
	R/ *Regali ex progenie.**	R/ *Gloriose virginis.*
	Ym. *Nunc tibi virgine.* /////	Ym. *Nunc tibi virgine.*
		Ant. Magn. *Nativitas tua* (I) { Deinde Ant. Sancti vero versus et oratio *add. D* }
		Ant. ad Invit. *Beatissime Marie* (IIII). Ym. *Quem terra pontus.* Ant. ad Noct. *Benedicta tu* (IIII). Require in purificatione. Sex antiphone. *Sancta dei genitrix* (I). Ant. ad cantica *Nativitas tua* (I). Canticum *Audite me.* Versus et responsoria *Nativitas est hodie. Corde et animo. Dignare me. Speciosa.*

5. September 14 – September 21 (ff. 53-55v)

U	IN EXALTATIONE SANCTE CRUCIS <ET SS. CORNELII ET CYPRIANI>.	<SEPT. 14> IN EXALTATIONE SANCTE CRUCIS <ET SS. CORNELII ET CYPRIANI>.
	//// Ev. …*omnia traham ad me …Filii lucis sitis.* {Jn 12: 32-36}	
	Or. *Adesto familie tue qs clemens et misericors deus ut in adversis*	
	Ant. ad Mat. l. et ad Vesp.	. . . Ant. ad Mat. l. et ad Vesp.
	Ant. *O magnum pietatis.*	Ant. *O magnum pietatis* (VII).
	Ant. *O crux admirabilis.*	Ant. *O crux admirabilis* (I).
	Ant. T. *Salva nos Christe.*	Ant. T. *Salva nos Christe* (III).
	Ant. S. *Nos autem gloriari oportet.*	Ant. S. *Nos autem gloriari oportet* (VII).
	Ant. N. *Sanctum nomen domini.*	Ant. N. *Sanctum nomen domini* (I).
	Lect. *Propter quod et deus.**	Lect. *Propter quod et deus.*
	R/ br. *Salva nos Christe salvator.*	
	Ym. *Eternus pater {illegible}**	Ym. *Crux fidelis.*
	V. *hoc signum crucis erit in celo.* R. *Cum dominus.*	
	Ant. Ben. *O crux sacratissima.**	Ant. Ben. *O crux sacratissima* (II).
	Or. Require retro *Ds qui nos hodierna die**	
	Deinde antiphona versuset oratio de sanctis.	Deinde antiphona versuset oratio de sanctis.
	Ant. *O quam pretiosus.**	
	V. *Exaltabunt sancti in gloria.*	
	Or. *Beatum martyrum.**	

	Ant. P. *In celestibus regnis.**{pl. mart.}	Ant. P. *Crux benedicta nitet* (VIII). Et canatur missa de sanctis. Ad missam maiorem omnes induti albis lineis intrent in choro . . .
	Ad vesp. Ys. {illeg.}* V. Hoc signum.*	Ad Vesp. Ym. *Vexilla.*
	Ant. ad Magn. *Sanctifica nos.** Deinde antiphona versus et oratio de sanctis	Ant. ad Magn. *Sanctifica nos* (IIII). Deinde antiphona versus et oratio de sanctis.
V	FESTIVITAS SANCTI MATHEI si venerit die dominco octava lectio fiat de libro Iudith; nona de omelia dominicali. Reliqua omnia de apostolo.	<SEPT 21> FESTIVITAS SANCTI MATHEI si venerit die dominco octava lectio fiat de libro Iudith; nona de omelia dominicali. Reliqua omnia de apostolo.
W	IN SANCTI IANUARII EPISCOPI ET SOCIORUM EIUS.	<SEPT 19> IN SANCTI IANUARII EPISCOPI ET SOCIORUM EIUS.
	Ant. ad Magn. *Domine rex cunctorum.* Or. *Intercessio qs dne beatorum martyrn tuorum Ianuarii* Ant. ad Noct. *Diocletianus cesar.* Ant. *Ante tyrannum.* Ant. *Precepto Timothei.* Ant. *Munitus crucem.* Ant. *In fornace ignis.* Ant. *Tunc de camino.*	Ant. ad Magn. *Domine rex cunctorum* (II). Ant. ad Noct. *Diocletianus cesar* (II). Ant. *Ante tyrannum* (VIII). Ant. *Precepto Timothei* (VII). Ant. *Munitus crucem* (II). Ant. *In fornace ignis* (VII). Ant. *Tunc de camino* (IIII).
	Passio sanctorum martyrum Ianuarii et sociorum eius. *Temporibus Diocletiani* <BHL 4115, 12 lec.> Vigilia II. Ant. *Ut iussus est.* Ant. S. *Dum sacrificare.* Ant. N. *Mira in sanctos.* Ant. ad cantica et T. *Domine rex cunctorum.** Evangelium de pluribus martyribus. Ant. ad Mat. l. et ad Vesp. Ant. *Ianuarius.* Ant. *Data preses.* Ant. *Timotheus.* Ant. *Post ignem.* Ant. *Ianuarius inopi.* Ant. ad Ben. *O quam pretiosis Beneventus.* Ant. P. *Ut sancti dei sunt.*	Vigilia II. Ant. *Ut iussus est* (I). Ant. S. *Dum sacrificare* (VII). Ant. N. *Mira in sanctos* (II). Ant. ad cantica et T. *Domine rex* (II). Psalmi et responsoria de pluribus martyribus. Ant. ad Mat. l. et ad Vesp. Ant. *Ianuarius* (VIII). Ant. *Data preses* (II). Ant. *Timotheus* (VI). Ant. *Post ignem* (VI). Ant. *Ianuarius inopi* (VII). Ant. ad Ben. et Magn. *O quam pretiosis Beneventus.* (II). Ant. *Ut sancti dei sunt* (VIII P).
X	PASSIO SANCTI MATHEI APOSTOLI ET EV. {4 lections}////	. . .
6. October 28 – October 30 (ff. 56-57v)		
Y	<OCT 28> {PASSIO SS SIMONIS ET IUDE...}///LEC 9-12. Ev. de pl. mart.*	

Or. Ds qui nots per beatos aplos tuos Symonem…	

Z	<Oct 30> In Sancti Germani R/ *Intempesta noctis** Ant. ad Magn. *Pater sanctus** Or. *Adiuvemus qs deus precibus b. confessoris tui Germani* *Vita vel obitus sci Germani epi et conf. Beatus Germanus patri Amantio…* <BHL 3465, 8 lections> Ant. ad cantica *Beatus vir** *Passio sancti Maximi martiris. Temporibus Diocletiani et Maximiani imperatorum sub Antonino* <BHL 5846, 4 lections, numbered 9-12>	In Sancti Germani. R/ ad Vesp. et octavum in nocte *Intempeste noctis*. Ant. Magn. *Pater sanctus* (IIII). In Noct. in prima et secunda vigilia omnia fiant de confessore. Vigilia III. Ant. ad cantica de uno martyre. Et legatur passio Sancti Maximi cum responsoriis suis. Ant. ad Mat. l. et ad Vesp. …

7. November 25 (ff. 58-61v)	

AA	[In natale sancti Mercurii Ym. *Ad martyris Mercurii…///* *sumpsit palmam..* Ant. ad Noct. *Mercuri noli ambigere.* Ant. *Accipe hanc lanceam.* Ant. *Dixit angelus Mercurio.* Ant. *Respondens martyr.* Ant. *Angelus domini apparuit.* Ant. *Beatus Mercurius dixit.* *Passio beati Mercurii martyris exposita ab Arechis principe. Decius ambitione…* <BHL 5933, 4 lections} R/ *Sollempnitatem annuis.* V/ *Glorioso certamine.* R/ *Clarus eros Mercurius.* V/ *Bellicosus in acie.* R/ *Romana militia.* V/ *Ad hoc enim.* R/ *Insignis athleta.* V/ *Cuius virtuti Decius.* Vigilia II. Ant. *Adiutus dei gratia.* Ant. *Apparens Ihesus.* Ant. *Veni iam miles.* Ant. *Martyr Mercurius.* Ant. *Glorioso certamine.* Ant. *Armenie populus.* {4 further lections} R/ *Angelus domini excitans.* V/ *Oportet enim te.*	<Nov 25> In natale {noct. C} Sancti Mercurii Ant. ad Invit. *Mercuri miles Christi* (II). Ym. *Ad martyris Mercurii.* Ant. ad Noct. *Mercuri noli ambigere* (VIII). Ant. *Accipe hanc lanceam* (VII). Ant. *Dixit angelus Mercurio* (II). Ant. *Respondens martyr* (II). Ant. *Angelus domini apparuit* (I). Ant. *Beatus Mercurius dixit* (VIII). {from below: Legantur undecim lectiones de passione eius edita ab Arechis principe. } {from below: R/ *Sollempnitatem annuis.* V/ *Glorioso.* R/ *Clarus eros Mercurius.* V/ *Bellicosus.* R/ *Romana militia.* V/ *Ad hoc enim.* R/ *Insignis athleta.* V/ *Cuius virtuti Decius.*} Vigilia II. Ant. *Adiutus dei gratia* (VIII). Ant. *Apparens Ihesus* (VI). Ant. *Veni iam miles* (II). Ant. *Martyr Mercurius* (VII). Ant. *Glorioso certamine* (II). Ant. *Armenie populus* (VIII). {from below: R/ *Angelus domini excitans.* V/ *Oportet enim.*

	R/ *Exibi{tur? –tus?} Decio.* V/ *Erat tunc viginti.* R/ *Adolescens egregius.* V/ *Deridens omnes Cesaris.* R/ *Fidelis Christi famulus.* V/ *Habeo galeam.*	R/ *Exibitus {-ur D} Decio.* V/ *Erat tunc {autem C} viginti.* R/ *Adolescens egregius.* V/ *Deridens omnes Cesaris.* R/ *Fidelis Christi famulus.* V/ *Habeo galeam.}*
	Ant. ad cantica. *Mercurii meritum.* Ant. *Armenia felix tellus.* Ant. *Ave beatissime.*	Ant. ad cantica. *Mercurii meritum* (II). Ant. *Armenia felix tellus* (II). Ant. *Ave beatissime* (VIII). Versus et capitula de uno martyre. Legantur undecim lectiones de passione eius edita ab Arechis principe.
	Lec. Nona. *Lec. S ev sec Lucam … Si quis venit ad me… Omel. B. Gregorii pape de eadem lec. Si consideramus fratres karissimi.*	Nona lectio legat omelie beati Gregorii pape *Si consideramus fratres karissimi.*
BB		R/ *Sollempnitatem annuis.* V/ *Glorioso certamine.* R/ *Clarus eros Mercurius.* V/ *Bellicosus in acie.* R/ *Romana militia.* V/ *Ad hoc enim.* R/ *Insignis athleta.* V/ *Cuius virtuti Decius.* R/ *Angelus domini excitans.* V/ *Oportet enim te.* R/ *Exibitus {-ur D} Decio.* V/ *Erat tunc {autem C} viginti.* R/ *Adolescens egregius.* V/ *Deridens omnes Cesaris.* R/ *Fidelis Christi famulus.* V/ *Habeo galeam.*
	R/ *Agonista invictissimus.* V/ *Cui angelus domini.* R/ *Videns impius Decius.* V/ *Ut vel sic.* R/ *Glorioso Mercurio.* V/ *Mox martyr predicat.* R/ *Sepultus extat beatus.* V/ *Omnes igitur humilitates.* *Secundum Marcum. In ill. t. Convocata turba Ihesus cum discipulis suis dixit eis si quis vult me sequi . . .////*	R/ *Agonista invictissimus.* V/ *Cui angelus domini.* R/ *Videns impius Decius.* V/ *Ut vel sic.* R/ *Glorioso Mercurio.* V/ *Mox martyr predicat.* R/ *Sepultus extat beatus.* V/ *Omnes igitur humilitates.*
		Ant. ad Mat. l. et ad V. Ant. *Omnis ad hoc* (I). ut supra. Ant. ad Vesp. *Mercurio Decius* (VII).{this Ant. *om. D}* Lect. *Iustus cor suum.* R/ br. *Veni iam miles.* Ym. *Laudes Mercurii.* Ant. ad Ben. et Magn.{Magn. *om. D} O quam speciosus* (VI). Ant. *Ortus in Armenia* (VI P). Ant. *Veni iam miles* (II T). …

		Ad Vesp. Ym. *Mercuri semper.* ...
	8. NOVEMBER 26 –NOVEMBER 29 (ff. 62-63v)	
CC	<S NICANDRI ET MARCIANI, NOV. 26> ...tunc Marcianus per salutem tibi... {refers to cenobium sancte Sophie, senior Gisolfus Beneventi princeps; BHL 6071? 6072? Cf B20, f 183v} Ev. et or. Require in pl. mart.	
DD	IN VIGILIA SANCTI ANDREE APOSTOLI. Ad Vesp. R/ *Venite post me.** Ym. *Post Petrum primum.* V/ *Andreas Christi famulus.** Ant. Magn. *Videns Andreas crucem.* Or. Qs omps ds ut beatus Andreas /// /// <a folio missing> [Ys. *Decus sacrati*] *Iam nos fovento ... Deo patri.* Ant. ad Noct. *Unus ex duobus.* Ant. *Dicit Andreas Symoni.* ///	<NOV 29> IN VIGILIA SANCTI ANDREE APOSTOLI. Ad missam addatur oratio SANCTORUM SATURNINI ET SISINNII. Ad Vesp. R/ *Venite post me.* Ym. *Post Petrum primum.* V/ *Andreas Christi famulus* Ant. Magn. *Videns Andreas crucem.* Ant. ad Invit. *Regem apostolorum* (III). Ym. *Decus sacrati nominis.* Ant. ad Noct. *Unus ex duobus* (I). Ant. *Dicit Andreas Symoni* (VIII). ...
	9. Maundy Thursday (ff. 64-64v)	
EE	[Vig. III ... Ant. *Terra tremuit* ...] *in iudicio deus.* Ps. *Notus in Iudea deus.* Ant. *In die tribulationis.* Ps. *Voce mea.* V/ *Homo pacis mee in quo sperabam.* R/ *Qui edebat* Lect. VII. *Convenientibus vobis in unum.* (I Cor 11: 20) R/ *Una hora non.* V/ *Quid dormitis.* **Lect. VIII. *Ego enim accepi a domino.*** (I Cor 11: 23) R/ *Iudas mercator.* V/ *Avaritie inebriatus.* **Lect. VIIII. *Quotiescumque manducabitis.* (I Cor 11:26)**	ITEM FERIA V. ... Vig. III ... Ant. *Terra tremuit* (VIII). Ps. *Notus in Iudea deus.* Ant. *In die tribulationis* (VII). Ps. *Voce mea.* V/ *Homo pacis mee in quo sperabam*{ R/ *Qui edebat* add. D} In tertia <legatur> de apostolo ubi ait ad Corinthios *Convenientibus vobis in unum.* {From below: R/ *Una hora non.* V/ *Quid dormitis*} **Alia *Similiter postquam cenavit.*** (I Cor 11: 25) {From below: R/ *Iudas mercator.* V/ *Avaritie inebriatus.*} **Alia *De spiritualibus autem nolumus vos ignorare*** usque *Et omnes in unum spiritum potati sumus.* (I Cor 12: 1 – 12:13) Item responsoria R/ *In monte oliveti.* V/ *Verumptamen.* R/ *Tristis est anima mea.* V/ *Ecce appropinquabit.* R/ *Ecce vidimus eum.* V/ *Vere languores.* R/ *Amicus meus osculi.* V/ *Bonum erat ei.*

		R/ *Unus ex discipulis.* V/ *Qui intingit mecum.* R/ *Eram quasi agnus.* V/ *Omnes inimici mei.* R/ *Una hora non.* V/ *Quid dormitis.* R/ *Iudas mercator.* V/ *Avaritie inebriatus.*
FF	Expleta autem nona lectione incipiant matutinas laudes	Expleta autem nona lectione statim incipiant antiphonam ad matutinas laudes qua incipiente … Item Ant. ad Mat. l.
	Ant. *Iustificeris domine.* Ps. *Miserere mei deus.* Ant. *Dominus tanquam ovis.* Ps. *Domine refugium.*	Ant. *Iustificeris domine* (VIII). Ps. *Miserere mei deus.* Ant. *Dominus tanquam ovis* (II). Ps. *Domine refugium.*
	Ant. *Contritum est cor.* Ps. *Deus deus meus* et *Deus misereatur nobis.* Ant. *Exortatus es.* Ps. *Cantemus domino.* Ant. *Oblatus est.* Ps. *Laudate dominum.* V/ *Homo pacis.** Ant. Ben. *Traditor autem.* V/ *Et accedens ad Ihesum.* Repetat *Traditor.*	Ant. *Contritum est cor* (VIII). Ps. *Deus deus meus* et *Deus misereatur nobis.* Ant. *Exortatus es* (IIII). Ps. *Cantemus domino.* Ant. *Oblatus est* (II). Ps. *Laudate dominum.* V/ *Homo pacis mee in quo sperabam.* Ant. Ben. *Traditor autem* (I). V/ *Et accedens ad Ihesum.* Repetat *Traditor.*
	Deinde tres clerici can. ante altare *Kyrieleyson.*	Qua finita mox incipiant canere *Kyrieleyson.* Et pergant tres clerici ante altare et cantent versum *Domine miserere. Kyrie.*
	Domine miserere. Kyrieleyson. *Qui prophetice…. Christe. Domine miserere.* *Christus dominus… Kyrie. Domine miserere.* *Qui expansis in cruce manibus… Christe. Domine miserere////*	Et chorus per unumquemque versum repetat *Kyrie* sive *Christe.* …

Table 2: Manuscripts

Ordinals of Montecassino:

N. Vaticano, Città del, BAV, Urb. lat. 585

A composite office book written at Montecassino 1099–1105; richly ornamented with miniatures and gold. The ordinal is in a hand of the middle of the twelfth century. The style of decoration is similar to that of manuscripts Mazarine 364 (O) and Getty 83.ML.97 (P).

O. Paris, Bibliothèque Mazarine, 364

A composite office book written at Montecassino 1099–1105 (based on the dates of Pope Paschal II and Abbot Oderisius; Hoffmann, «Studien», p. 127, suggests 1099–1105, based on the absence of the dedication of St. Stephen [1103] in the calendar); richly ornamented with miniatures and gold. The style of decoration is similar to that of manuscripts Urb. lat. 585 (N) and Getty 83.ML.97 (P).

P. Los Angeles, J. Paul Getty Museum, 83.ML.97 (formerly Ludwig IX.1, formerly Montecassino 199)

A composite office book written at Montecassino in 1153 by the scribe Sigenulfus; richly ornamented with miniatures and gold. The style of decoration is similar to that of manuscripts Mazarine (O) and Urb. lat. 585 (N)

Q. Montecassino, Archivio della Badia, 198

A copy of the *Breviarium sive ordo officiorum* from Montecassino (?), in a Beneventan hand of the twelfth or thirteenth century. The book once belonged to the Cassinese dependency of Sancta Maria de Albaneta.

R. Montecassino, Archivio della Badia, 562

A thirteenth-century copy, in Gothic script. Made for Montecassino, to judge from the reference to the dedication of the Church of St. Benedict and to the *dedicatio turris paradysi* contained in the second section.

Ordinals of Benevento:

C. Napoli, Biblioteca Nazionale Vittorio Emanuele III, VI E 43

A richly ornamented composite office book written 1099–1118 for a monastery of Santa Maria and based on the liturgy of Santa Sophia, Benevento.

D. Vaticano, Città del, BAV, Vat. lat. 4928

A composite office book written for, and probably at Santa Sophia, Benevento, in the twelfth century.

E. Benevento, Biblioteca Capitolare, 66

A late-twelfth-century copy of the ordinal made for the use of the convent of San Pietro intra muros, Benevento. The first part of the ordinal is a Montecassino text revised to suit the liturgy of Benevento, but the remaining portion is almost purely Cassinese.

)ther Manuscripts mentioned

Benevento, Biblioteca Capitolare, 21; antiphoner, saec. XII/XIII, from Benevento
Benevento, Biblioteca Capitolare, 22; breviary, *pars hiemalis* saec. XII;
  Benevento
Benevento, Biblioteca Capitolare, 26; chapter book with martyrology, saec. XII*in.*,
  for San Pietro intra muros, Benevento
Benevento, Biblioteca Capitolare, ex 29 (now London, British Library, Egerton
  3511); missal, saec. XII, for San Pietro intra muros, Benevento
Benevento, Biblioteca Capitolare, 33; notated missal, saec. XI*in.*, perhaps from the
  diocese of Salerno
Benevento, Biblioteca Capitolare, 37; processional, chapter book with
  martyrology, saec. XI*ex.*, for San Pietro intra muros, Benevento
Benevento, Biblioteca Capitolare, 42; composite office book, saec. XII 2/2
Napoli, Archivio storico diocesano, Fondo Ebdomadario, Cod Misc. 1, fasc. VII;
  fragments of a breviary, *pars estiva*, ca. 1161
Napoli, Biblioteca della Società Napoletana di Storia Patria, XXXIII A 1 (3);
  fragments of a breviary, ca. 1161, with colophon
Napoli, Biblioteca Nazionale Vittorio Emanuele III, XVI A 19; processional saec.
  XII; ff. 39-48, saec. XII/XIII, contains materials for Saint Mercurius and
  for the Holy Twelve Brothers.

XVI

MUSICAL RELATIONS BETWEEN
VENICE AND BENEVENTO

Perhaps I can make a small contribution to these proceedings by following the suggestion of my colleague Giulio Cattin, and speaking about connections between Venice and the liturgy of the Beneventan area. This is a proposition that at first appeared almost pointless: there would be very little to say on the subject. This should come as no surprise, but in fact a few observations may be useful in pointing out the nature of relationships between repertories, and giving suggestions about the transmission of medieval music.

Let me begin with a brief description of the musical situation of medieval Benevento, so as to provide further background to the comprehension of the very different situation at Venice.

The repertory we call Beneventan is the liturgical music of medieval southern Italy before the diffusion of the Gregorian chant, preserved in manuscripts from the Lombard duchy of Benevento. This music, like that of many other archaic repertories, was not written down earlier than the Gregorian chant; in fact, with rare exceptions the music comes to us from the hands of the same scribes who wrote the south Italian manuscripts of Gregorian chant in the tenth and eleventh centuries; it is these same sources that preserve the older repertory, disguised or added to the very music whose imposition provoked its ultimate suppression. There are, however, some ninety manuscripts or fragments which preserve at least some small element of Beneventan chant and which describe its considerable chronological and geographical diffusion throughout the south.[1]

---

[1]   On the Beneventan chant, see most recently Th. F. Kelly, *The Beneventan Chant* (Cambridge: Cambridge University Press, 1989); facsimiles of the sources of Beneventan chant are published in Th. F. Kelly, *Les Témoins manuscrits du Chant Bénéventain*, Paléographie musicale XXI (Solesmes: Abbaye Saint-Pierre, 1992). Earlier important studies of the repertory include R.-J. Hesbert, "L'Antiphonale missarum' de l'ancien rit bénéventain," *Ephemerides liturgicae* 52 (1938), pp. 28-66, 141-158; 53 (1939), pp. 168-190; 54 (1945), pp. 69-95; 60

The musical manuscripts of Benevento consist of a series of superimposed repertories, often contained within a single source. There is the Beneventan chant, whose origins go back to the sixth and seventh century; but superimposed on this is the so-called Gregorian chant, a repertory that arrived in a form essentially complete in the course of the eighth century. To this the local liturgists and musicians added a further layer in Gregorian style but for local usage. This "Romano-Beneventan" chant filled the voids in the received Gregorian repertory and furnished music for feasts of purely local importance: it is a repertory that deserves a study of its own. The creative spirit of the tenth, eleventh, and twelfth centuries turned from the creation of new liturgical chants toward the creation of a further musical layer of tropes and sequences.[2]

All these layers, then, are present in the manuscripts of Benevento and in many regional sources. But they are presented together in such a way that, for example, the mass of the Holy Twelve Brothers in manuscript 40 of the Biblioteca Capitolare of Benevento includes typical Gregorian chants, local Romano-Beneventan compositions, a rich selection of tropes, and an entire alternative mass in Beneventan style. Within this rich material the Beneventan chant itself is a single strand in a complex late-medieval fabric.

The situation at Venice is evidently different; the sources are later in date; we cannot now recognize traces of non-Gregorian liturgies or chants, despite the evident importance of the Patriarchate of Grado and Aquileia and that of Ravenna. Nevertheless, perhaps a brief review of what can be said may add one or two little details to this very interesting subject of liturgy at San Marco. Giulio Cattin has of course already considered this subject, in his magnificent work on music and liturgy at San Marco.[3] I intend here only to comment on some remarks that he has already made.

(1946), pp. 103-141; 61 (1947), pp. 153-210; Id., (writing anonymously), "La Tradition bénéventaine dans la Tradition manuscrite," in *Le codex 10 673 de la Bibliothèque Vaticane*, Paléographie musicale XIV (Tournai: Desclée, 1931, repr. Berne: Lang, 1971), pp. 60-465: 249-465.

[2] An edition of the tropes of Benevento is in progress under the editorship of Alejandro Planchart and John Boe, *Beneventum troparum corpus*, (Madison: A-R Editios, 1989-).

[3] G. Cattin, *Musica e liturgia a San Marco. Testi e melodie per la liturgia delle Ore dal XII al XVII secolo. Dal graduale tropato del Duecento ai graduali cinquecenteschi*, 3 vols. and index (Venezia: Fondazione Levi, 1990-92, Serie IV, Collezione speciale per la musica veneta. A. Monumenti, I).

Cattin says that there do not appear to be melodies from the old Beneventan liturgy present in the books from San Marco. In this, so far as my poor knowledge of Venetian sources goes, I agree with him. And this too should be no surprise, since the distance of geography and time between the Beneventan and the Venetian sources, and the deliberate eradication of the Beneventan liturgy, would make such a presence highly surprising.

However, I might just remark that Beneventan chant is present in Venice, though it may not have affected the Venetian liturgy.

A series of eleven folios in the Archivio di Stato of Venice all come from the same antiphoner in Beneventan script and notation from the end of the eleventh century. They include music for the Ascension, the Invention of the Holy Cross, the south Italian feast of the *Inventio sancti Michaelis* (8 May), and St. Eustachio.[4] But preceding St. Eustachio is the remains of some music in Beneventan style; this music is not otherwise known, and seems to be the end of a longer office. The remaining Beneventan music can be seen in the first six lines of Ex. 1.

Although there are a few other fragments in Beneventan script in the libraries of Venice (include a fragmentary page from a 13th-century missal in the Biblioteca Marciana),[5] this group of eleven folios is unique. We do not know, unfortunately, from what documents or volumes they were detached, but it seems likely that the parent volume, a significant antiphoner, was once more complete and was in Venice. One wonders why this should be so. Was there perhaps a particular interest in the music for sant'Eustachio, in whose honor the church of San Stae has been standing since at least the eleventh century? It is probably also important to remember the unusual manuscript Udine, Biblioteca Arcivescovile, 39 (Quarto 26),[6] a gradual with somewhat irregular contents, whose writing is ordinary minuscule, but whose notation is written in the Beneventan style. Evidently there was some penetration of books from the south, and of persons trained in the Beneventan style of notation, in the area of Venice.

Though there is little reason to expect a close connection between Venice and Benevento, there are nevertheless a few pieces

[4] Venezia, Archivio di Stato, Atti diversi, Ms. B. 159, n. 28. On these fragments see V. Brown, "A Second New List of Beneventan Manuscripts (II)," *Mediaeval Studies* 50 (1988), pp. 584-625: 619; Kelly, *Les Témoins manuscrits*, planche 329 and p. 404.

[5] Venezia, Biblioteca Nazionale Marciana, Marc. lat. XIV 232 (4257); see Brown, "A Second New List," pp. 619-620.

[6] C. Scalon, *La Biblioteca Arcivescovile di Udine*, Medioevo e Umanesimo vol. 37 (Padova: Antenore, 1979), pp. 109-110.

and groups of pieces where interesting comparisons can be made. These in turn may remind us of some basic questions about the uses and transmission of liturgical music in Italy.

1. *Alleluias*

The Alleluia *Qualis Pater talis Filius talis est Spiritus Sanctus*, which in Venice is the second of three Alleluias for the Trinity,[7] appears in a few French and Central Italian sources, as well as in Benevento. The melody used in Venice is the version also used at Benevento, which has a version of the jubilus longer than that used in the Aquitanian sources, but shorter than the version with repetitions used in central Italian sources of Pistoia and Volterra.[8]

The Alleluia *Veni sponsa Christi*, found in the Venetian gradual in Berlin[9] as the second Alleluia for St. Cecilia, has a melody known elsewhere only in Benevento 38, so far as I know. Curiously, in Benevento 38 this is the last Alleluia in the manuscript; like many older graduals, Benevento 38 closes with a series of Alleluias, first for Sundays, and then for the common of saints; *Veni sponsa Christi* is the last of several Alleluias for the common of Virgins. But the series once was much longer: the rest of this folio, and two further folios, have been erased to provide space for a later hand to write music for the ordinary of the mass. Is this mere coincidence, or is it possible that this last Alleluia was noticed, by somebody, precisely because it was last, and that some chance of transmission guaranteed its survival as far north as Venice? At any rate, Cattin's remarking of this Alleluia in the Berlin gradual allows us to verify the melody as it is found in the clefless notation of Benevento 38.[10]

The Alleluia *Herodes enim tenuit*, for the beheading of John the Baptist in the Berlin gradual, has the well-known *Dies*

---

[7] Berlin, Staatsbibliothek Preussischer Kulturbesitz Mus. Ms. 40608, fols. 213-213*v*; the manuscript is described and transcribed in Cattin, *Musica e liturgia a San Marco*, on this piece see II, p. 397.

[8] Sources for this melody are indicated in K.-H. Schlager, *Thematischer Katalog der ältesten Alleluia-Melodien*. Erlanger Arbeiten zur Musikwissenschaft, 2 (München: Walter Ricke), 1965, melody 278 (p. 199); the melody is transcribed from Benevento 39, fol. 138, in Schlager, *Alleluia-Melodien I bis 1100*, Monumenta Monodica Medii Ævi, 7 (Kassel-Basel: Bärenreiter, 1987), p. 402.

[9] Berlin 40608, fol. 195. On this piece at Venice see Cattin, *Musica e liturgia a San Marco*, II, p. 392.

[10] The melody of Benevento 38, fol. 165*v*, is edited in Schlager, *Alleluia-Melodien I*, p. 522.

sanctificatus melody, but with this text it is known to Schlager only in Benevento 39.[11] The other manuscripts of Benevento do not use this Alleluia for this feast; for the most part they have masses drawn from the common of saints; Benevento 39, however, includes a first mass from the common, but a second mass – *Alia Missa unde* – which has proper chants, and which includes not only this Alleluia but the Communion *Misit rex incredulus*, which is found also at Venice. How this melody came to Benevento remains to be discovered. There is little enough evidence that it came to Venice from the south.

The Alleluia *Deus nostrum refugium et virtus* appears in the Berlin gradual as one of the Alleluias in the series for Sundays after Pentecost;[12] with the text *Beatus Petrus* this melody is known only in Beneventan manuscripts and in Modena O. I. 7, and with this text *Deus nostrum refugium* only in Benevento 40, Benevento 35, and Modena.[13] The Beneventan version of the text is that used also at Venice, while the text in the Modena manuscript is longer (it adds the words "que invenerunt nos nimis"). The melody of Venice is essentially that of Benevento, except that the melisma which appears in the Alleluia and recurs in the verse is shorter at Venice: the Benevento melody has a repetition of a portion of the melisma, making an AAB form, where Venice presents the melisma in form AB. Whether the reduplication was removed by simplifying reformers before the copying of the Venice gradual, or added by earlier embellishes, remains to be seen, though Cattin has shown an evident tendency to the shortening in the Berlin gradual.

2. *Processional antiphon*

The processional antiphon *O pietatis Deus qui mundum universum* is used at Venice for the Greater litany, in a melody that according to Cattin is identical to that of Benevento 34.[14]

---

[11]   Berlin 40608, fol. 171*v*, is a version of Schlager, *Thematischer Katalog*, melody 27 (pp. 78-81); but with this text is known to Schlager only in Benevento 39, fol. 155*v*. See Cattin, *Musica e liturgia a San Marco*, III, p. 389.

[12]   Berlin 40608, fol. 203*v*, for the eighth Sunday after Pentecost. I am grateful to Giulio Cattin for providing me with a transcription.

[13]   Schlager, *Thematischer Katalog*, melody 309 (p. 212). The melody is transcribed in Schlager, *Alleluia-Melodien I*, p. 109; see Cattin, *Musica e liturgia a San Marco*, II, p. 394.

[14]   Berlin 40608, fol. 222*v*. On this piece at Venice see Cattin, *Musica e liturgia a San Marco*, II, p. 397.

This antiphon appears in fact in four Benevento manuscripts,[15] but it may not have been part of the core repertory. It does not appear in the central group of rogation antiphons in the two oldest graduals: in Benevento 38 it appears instead among the antiphons for the Lenten scrutinies, and in Benevento 40 one of a group of three added at the end the core repertory which appears in Benevento 38. It does not appear in three south Italian processionals which are based on the core series of antiphons used in Benevento 38 and Benevento 40 (these are Naples VI A 19, Naples VI E 43, and Vat. Reg. lat. 334); the antiphon does persist at Benevento, however, and appears in the later graduals Benevento 34 and 35 (but not in the brief group in Benevento 39).

These processional antiphons have always been curious pieces; and this is a place in liturgical books where a variety of interesting material may find a home. It appears that this piece was adopted at Benevento in the eleventh century, and it might have been composed there; but it is certainly not in the style of the old Beneventan chant, and its presence in the gradual of San Marco suggests that it may have had a wider circulation than we might otherwise suspect.

3. *The Office of St. Mark*

As Cattin has demonstrated, the office of St. Mark at Venice seems to be a compilation from several disparate elements. One of these elements, a group of antiphons for Lauds, is found elsewhere only at Benevento.

Music for the office of St. Mark in southern Italy is not limited to Benevento 21, as might appear from Hesbert's *Corpus Antiphonalium Officii*,[16] although it is limited. Of the small number of office books from early medieval southern Italy, many are lacking the portion that would have included St. Mark. These include the antiphoner Montecassino 542, the breviaries Benevento 22, 23, and 25, and the fragments in the *Compactiones* of Montecassino. The breviary-missal Benevento 20, however, does contain music for St. Mark. The south Italian elements for St. Mark are compared with the Venetian office in Table 1. Benevento

---

[15] Benevento 40, fol. 49*v*; Benevento 38, fol. 26*v*; Benevento 34, fol. 158*v*; Benevento 35, fol. 95*r*.

[16] Since the antiphons are found in Benevento 21, they are listed in R.-J. Hesbert, *Corpus Antiphonalium Officii*, 6 vols., Rerum ecclesiasticarum documenta, Series maior, Fontes 7-12 (Roma: Herder, 1963-79).

TAB. 1: *Music for the office of Saint Mark in Venice and Benevento*

Venezia, Archivio di stato, Procuratori di supra. Reg. 114. fols. 23v-30v: Cattin, III, p. 259 f.	Benevento 21, fol. 152	Benevento 20, fol. 256v

IN VIGILIA SANCTI MARCI APOSTOLI ET EVAN-GELISTE AD VESPERUM
 	
a. Egregius Christi Petrus apostolus
  V. Inde igitur
a. Doctrinam apostolicam
  V. Qui sacri statim
a. Ad hec disponente
  V. Hoc igitur
a. Beate sancte Marce
  V. Ad te devota
a. Sancte evangelista Marce
  V. Oves tuas
R. Pulchra facie V. Ut digni
ev. Post angelicam allocutionem
 	
[AD MATUTINUM]
Inv. Angelus domini astitit
a. Princeps apostolicus
  V. Quid hic moraris
a. Deus excelse metuende
  V. Qui filium tuum
a. Beatus Marcus plenus
  V. Cottidie autem
v. In omnem terram
		Passio sancti Marci evang.
		  Tempore quo dispersi erant
		  [*Passio* divided into 9 lections
		  with indication of R. *Beatus vir*
		  after the first lection]
		  ...cui est honor et gloria in secula
		  seculorum. Amen.

Venezia, Archivio di stato, Procuratori di supra. Reg. 114. fols. 23v-30v: Cattin, III, p. 259 f.	Benevento 21, fol. 152	Benevento 20, fol. 256v
R. Ecce evangelista Marcus V. Ecce vir	R. Beatissimus Marcus disc. V. Quod	
R. Beatissimus Marcus disc. V. Quod	R. Accepto evangelio V. Tante	
R. Accepto evangelio V. Tante		
R. initium evangelii V. Marcus ut alta	R. Cum autem venisset beatissimus	
	V. Multos denique infirmos	
	R. Multitudo populi crediderunt	
	V. Cum autem Alexandriam	
	R. Beatus autem Marcus in	
	V. Obsecro te homo dei	
	R. Credidit Annianus in Dominum Iesum	
	V. Et confestim baptizatus est	
	R. Cum autem tempus impleretur	
	V. Infirmos sanabat	
	R. Sanctus autem Marcus cum traheretur	
	V. Mittentes	
Non quiesco		
V. Ego ex iussione		
a. Cumque beatus Marcus		
V. Audientes vero		
a. Fili Marce		
V. Cernens ianitor		
v. Constitues eos		
R. Fili Marce V. Dominus Iesus		
R. Magnificavit eum V. Statuit illi		R. Famule Dei marce princeps
R. In medio carceris V. Cumque		V. Socius enim factus est

Venezia, Archivio di stato, Procuratori di supra. Reg. 114. fols. 23v-30v: Cattin, III, p. 259 f.	Benevento 21, fol. 152	Benevento 20, fol. 256v

a. Beatus Marcus cum traheretur
  V. Cum sacratissime
a. Famule Dei Marce
  V. Medie noctis
a. Socius enim
  V. Gratias tibi ago
v. Nimis honorati
R. Agmina sacra V. Potuit transgredi
R. Felix namque es, almifice V. Ora p
R. Posuisti domine V. Desiderium		

IN LAUDIBUS
a. Beatissimus Marcus evangelista
  V. Secuti sunt eum
a. Mox ut Dei famulus
  V. Quo audito
a. Expuens in terram
  V. Vir autem ille
a. Evangelizante sancto Marco
  V. Quo cognito
a. Positis genibus
ev. Ecclesiam namque
ev. Angelus autem Domini
alia a. O admirabile gaudium
alia a. O quam beata urbs
	AD L.
	a. Beatissimus Marcus evangelista
	a. Mox ut Dei famulus [ad T]
	a. Expuens in terram [ad S]
	a. Evangelizante sancto Marco
	a. Positis genibus [P]
	a. Angelus autem domini [ad B.]
	
	a. Famule Dei Marce [ad can.]
		AD MAT. L. ET V.
		a. Beatissimus Marcus evangelista
		a. Mox ut Dei famulus
		a. Expuens in terram
		a. Evangelizante sancto Marco
		a. Positis genibus beatus Marcus
		
		ad B. Beatus Marcus dum traheretur
		ad M. Famule Dei Marce pr. [ad can.]
		
		Introitus. Protexisti me deus. *per ordinem*....
		[texts of the mass follow, with incipits for the chants]

21 provides eight responsories for Mark: enough for two nocturns. This *Historia* shares two responsories with Venice: they both have texts from St. Jerome's *De viris illustribus*; the other responsories (except for one), have texts arranged from the *Passio sancti Marci* which is transmitted in Benevento 20. At Benevento and Venice these two responsories share essentially the same music, and both sequences of responsories seems to be assemblages.

The readings for matins are available at Benevento in Benevento 20, which provides the *Passio* divided into nine lessons. However, it is not possible to combine the music of Benevento 21 and the texts of Benevento 20 to produce a complete night office. For one thing, no proper antiphons survive. For another, the lections and responsories do not match when combined. The responsories of Benevento 21 (which is a monastic antiphoner, and normally provides four responsories per nocturn) provide a perfectly normal *historia*, telling the story of the life of St. Mark as drawn from suitable hagiographical sources. The lections of Benevento 20 do the same thing, providing a reading of the *passio* in nine lections. If these two series were combined, the result would not be that each responsory underscores with music some passage in the previous reading; more often it would anticipate, repeat, or be out of order. This is, by the way, a fairly normal situation in the office to find that responsories and lections do not correspond exactly.

Benevento 20 indicates that responsories from the common of saints will be sung, beginning with *Beatus vir*, and provides only a single final responsory proper to St. Mark.

Evidently Benevento celebrated St. Mark differently in its different churches. What was held in common at Benevento is a series of five antiphons for Lauds which appears in both manuscripts and which is shared with Venice. The antiphons *ad evangelium* vary at Benevento; Benevento 21 uses the *Angelus autem Domini* which is shared with Venice, but Benevento 20 provides other music. These antiphons shared with Venice are transcribed in Ex. 1. They are evidently the same melodies, but in slightly different versions. These five antiphons are drawn from the *Vita* which is found in Benevento 20. The antiphon *Angelus autem*, however, is not found in this version of St. Mark's life.

These five antiphons apparently travel as a group: even though they may have different canticle antiphons attached, the group of five is drawn in order from the *Vita* of St. Mark, and retains its integrity at Venice and in the two manuscripts of Benevento even though one of them is secular and one monastic. We cannot decide the origin of this series: there is no reason to think that it originated at Benevento. But the integrity of this little group serves to confirm Cattin's view of the composite character of the office of St. Mark at Venice. These antiphons have for the most part well-known Gregorian melodies. Antiphons 1 and 3 have a familiar eighth-mode melody, and each city is consistent in its version of it. In antiphon 3, *Expuens in terram*, Benevento lacks the phrase "esto sanus" (which is also lacking in the *Vita*); the Venice version, which allows for the decorated music of "Christi," is slightly confusing, since in the text that follows, "et confestim sanata est," the word "sanata," a reference to the hand rather than the person, is confusing. The text in the *Vita* reads: "Et expuens in terram, fecit lutum; unxit manum viri dicens: In nomine Ihesu Christi filii dei; et confestim sanata est manus eius."

What can we learn from these few comparisons? First, that the connection between Venice and the Mezzogiorno is not very strong, despite the presence in the region of Venice of scribes able to write Beneventan script. This lack of connection is not particularly surprising.

A number of rare Alleluias, in addition to one processional chant, seem to be unique to Venice and Benevento. This is a phenomenon which need not be explained by some transmission direct from Benevento to Venice (or perhaps from Venice to Benevento). More likely it underscores two important facts that we know but of which we need to be reminded: 1) our knowledge of the sources is incomplete, for two reasons: first, we have only a fraction of the manuscript sources which once existed; and secondly, our knowledge of existing sources, particularly in Italy, is far from complete. It seems likely that further information will show that these special chants are not unique at all, but that they are part of a more widespread phenomenon; 2) there seems to be a substantial repertory of chants which circulated in Italy, and which form, at least in part, an early layer of peninsular chant. The presence of the same music at Benevento and Venice suggests perhaps less a direct connection than the presence, never easy to detect, of a musical practice which was limited to Italy, and whose traces are only gradually being discovered.

Ex. 1. Anthipons for Saint Mark at Venice and Benevento.

V

1. Be-a-tis-si-mus Mar-cus e-van-ge-li-sta, ve-lut at-le-ta for-tis-si-mus ad cer-ta—men promptus, gra-di-e-ba-tur di-cens

B

1. Be-a-tis-si-mus Mar-cus e-van-ge-li-sta, ve-lut at-le-ta for-tis-si-mus ad cer-ta—men promptus, gra-di-e-ba-tur di-cens

V

fra—tri-bus: Do——mi-nus -us· lo-cu-tus est mi-chi ut A-le-xan-dri-am pro-fi-cis-car, al-le lu-ia. Se. u. e. u. q. e.,·

B

fra——tri-bus: Do——mi-nus e-us lo-cu-tus est mi-chi ut A-le-xan-dri-am pro-fi-cis-car, al-le lu-ia. c

V

2. Mox ut de-i fa-mu-lus A-le-xan-dri-am per-ve-nit, cal-ci-a-men-tum e-ius di-rup-tum est, quod su-to-ri tra-di-dit;

B

2. Mox ut de-i fa-mu-lus A-le-xan-dri-am per-ve-nit, cal-ci-a-men-tum e-ius di-rup-tum est, quod su to-ri tra-di-dit;

V

at il-le sus-ci-pi-ens in la-bo- ran- do si-ni-stram su-am for-ti-ter vul-ne-ra-vit et-ex-cla-ma-vit: u-nus de-us, al-le-lu-ia. Se. u. o. u. a. e

B

at il-le sus-ci-pi-ens in la-bo-ran- do si-ni-stram su-am for-ti-ter vul-ne-ra-vit et-ex-cla-ma-vit: u-nus de-us, al-le-lu-ia. c

V

3. Ex--pu-ens in ter-ram be-a-tus Mar-cus un-xit ma-num vi-ri di-cens: in no-mi-ne Ie-su Chri-sti fi-li-i De-i e-sto sa-nus;

B

3. Ex--pu-ens in ter-ram be-a-tus Mar-cus un-xit ma-num vi-ri di-cens: in no-mi-ne Ie-su Chri-sti fi-li-i De-i;

V

et con-fe- stim sa-na-ta est, al- le-lu- ia. Se. u. o. u. a. e.

B

et con-fe- stim sa-na-ta est, al-le-lu- ia. e————

V

4. E-van-ge-li-zan-te san-cto Mar-co Do-mi-num Ie-sum Chri- stum, cre-di-dit ho-mo il-le et bap-ti-za-tus est

B

4. E-van-ge-li-zan-te san-cto Mar-co Do-mi-num Ie-sum Chri- stum, cre-di-dit ho-mo il-le et bap-ti-za-tus est

V

cum to-ta do-mo sua, et magna multitu-di-ne lo- ci il-li-us, al-le-lu-ia. Se. u. o. u. a. e.

B

cum to-ta do-mo sua, de magna multitu-di-ne lo- ci il-li-us, al-le-lu-ia. e————

V

5. Po-si-tis ge-ni-bus be-a-tus Mar-cus laudem De- o di- ce-bat, qui-a rep-pe-rit

B

5. Po-si-tis ge-ni-bus be-a-tus Mar-cus laudem De- o di- ce-bat, qui-a rep-pe-rit

V

mul-ti- pli-ca- tos fra- tres in fi-de Chri-sti, al-le-lu-ia.   Se. u. o. u. a. e.

B

mul-ti- pli-ca- tos fra- tres in fi-de Chri-sti, al-le-lu-ia.   e————

V

Ev. An-ge-lus au- tem Do mi-ni de-scen-dit de ce- lo in cu-sto- di-am car-ce-ris et te-ti-git e-um di-cens:

B

Ev. An-ge-lus au- tem Do mi-ni de-scen-dit de ce- lo in cu-sto- di-a car-ce-ris et te-ti-git e-um di-cens:

V

fa-mu le De-i Mar- ce, ec-ce no- men tu- um in li-bro vi-te a-scrip-tum est, al-le-lu-ia.   Se. u. o. u. a. e.

B

fa-mu le De-i Mar- ce, ec-ce no- men tu- um in li-bro vi-te a-scrip-tum est, al-le-lu-ia.   e————

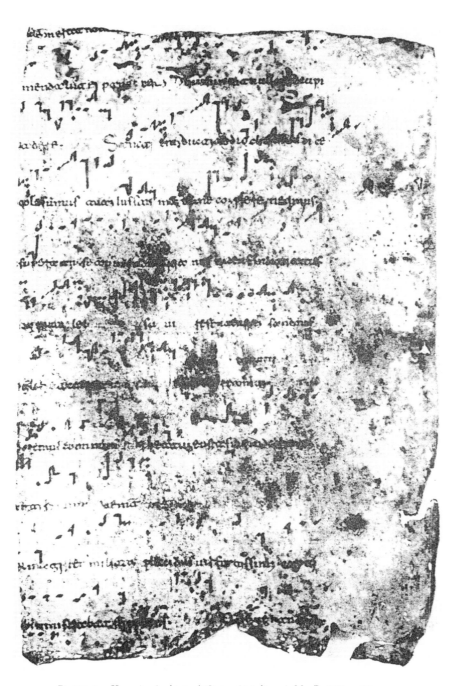

PLATE. 1.   Venezia, Archivio di Stato, Atti diversi, Ms. B. 159, n. 28.

XVII

Tradition and Innovation in the Antiphoner Benevento 848

Scholars of the chant will know that the Biblioteca Capitolare of the Cathedral of Benevento holds a series of medieval musical manuscripts of great significance. Written in the characteristic Beneventan script, these manuscripts were made between the 10th and the 13th centuries, and among them they contain several important repertories: almost all of the surviving music of the Old Beneventan Chant; a rich body of tropes and sequences; and a corpus of Frankish-Roman chant that appears from its style and its liturgy to represent a very early transmission. These manuscripts have been catalogued and studied in detail, and for very good reason.[1]

But there are other musical manuscripts in the Biblioteca Capitolare which have barely been noticed; mostly these are later volumes, many of which represent a generalized form of the liturgy that has little to teach us. But they are not without interest. In the eighteenth century, under the supervision of Cardinal Vincenzo Maria Orsini, archbishop of Benevento (1686–1724) and later Pope Benedict XIII (1724–1730), a uniform series of chant-books was assembled for the cathedral. These Orsinian books, combining manuscripts and printed volumes, essentially bring the Beneventan church into accord with that of Rome.[2]

One book, an antiphoner of the first quarter of the fourteenth century, is the subject of this report. It is a volume made for use at Benevento,

---

[1] On the books in Beneventan script see the exhaustive catalogue by Jean Mallet and André Thibaut, *Les manuscrits en écriture bénéventaine de la Bibliothèque capitulaire de Bénévent*, 3 vols. (Vol. 1 Paris: CNRS, 1984; vols. 2–3 Paris: CNRS and Turnhout: Brepols, 1997).

[2] There is no adequate catalogue of the books prepared under Orsini's direction. On the history of the library, see Mallet and Thibaut, vol. 1, pp. 7–34; Richard F. Gyug, "Les bibliothèques du chapitre et de l'archevêque," in *La Cathédrale de Bénévent*, ed. Thomas Forrest Kelly, Esthétiques et Rituels des Cathédrales d'Europe (Ghent and Amsterdam: Ludion, 1999), pp. 133–147.

and it is an important witness of local practice at a time when newly-made liturgical books tended to be reflections of a universal Roman liturgy.

This volume, labeled "848" in one series of numbers used in the library, is a parchment manuscript of 251 leaves, almost complete except for the serious mutilation it has suffered: 13 miniatures have been removed by cutting away a portion of a folio, and 12 entire folios which would have contained a decorated letter are now missing from the manuscript. The vandals missed three miniatures, of the Purification, of Saint Agatha, and of Saint Benedict (see figures 1–3); those that survive are handsome enough to suggest that the original miniatures had serious merit, and that the book had considerable value.

The volume is bound in leather over boards, and its inside cover bears the bookplate of Cardinal Orsini. An initial folio of added material for the invention of the Holy Cross[3] precedes the main body of the manuscript, which begins with a rubric "Incipit proprium et comune sanctorum secundum consuetudinem romane curie." After such a rubric, one expects a very standardized content, but in fact the manuscript is strongly local in character, retaining some music from the very earliest Beneventan sources of the office.

Table 1 compares the musical contents of Benevento 848 with that of the oldest complete south Italian antiphoner, Benevento 21.[4] Saints' feasts for which music is provided are listed in parallel columns; no mention is made of feasts with no proper music. Both manuscripts contain specifically local musical material which we might divide for convenience into five categories. I shall discuss each of these in summary below, and an appendix gives detailed lists and comparisons.

Feasts in **bold type** are those that have specifically southern Italian material.

---

[3] The leaf, numbred as folio 7, contains an invitatory, a single antiphon, and three responsories; it may be intended to supply material for a changing liturgy. In the main manuscript, f. 87, nothing is missing for the invention. A rubric indicates that the first two nocturns are "de sanctis," presumably of Saints Philip and Jacob two days earlier, the third nocturn of the cross. Perhaps the opening page is part of material to supply the first two nocturns.

[4] Ben21 is indexed, and its text edited, in René-Jean Hesbert, *Corpus antiphonalium officii* (=CAO), 6 vols., Rerum ecclesiasticarum documenta, Series maior, Fontes 7–12 (Rome, Herder: 1963–79). A facsimile edition is *Paléographie musicale* 22 (Solesmes, 2001).

Table 1: Musical contents of Benevento 21 and Benevento 848 compared

	Benevento 21 (sanctorale)	Benevento 848
July 6	Oct apostolorum	[lacuna?]
22	Marie Magdalene	M. Magdalene
?	Inv. S Stephani [Aug 3?]	
23	Apollinaris	Apollinaris
28	Nazarii	Nazarii et Celsi
August 1	[vincula Petri above]	S Petri ad vinc
3	[inv. Stephani above]	
5	Xisti ep: Transfiguratio	Syxti pp Felic & Agapiti; Transfiguratio
		Donati ep & m
7	Laurentii	Laurentii
10		[lacuna]
14	vig S Marie	
15	Assumptionis BMV	Assumptionis BMV
24		vig S Bartholomei
25	Passio S Bartholomei	Bartholomei
29	Decollatio S Ioh Bapt	Decollatio S Ioh Bapt
September 1	Duodecim fratrum	Duodecim fratrum
8	Nat S Marie	Nat S Marie
14	Exaltatio S Crucis	Exaltatio S Crucis
19	Ianuarii	Ianuarii
27	Cosme & Damiani	Cosme & Damiani
29		Dedic S Michaelis
October 25		Trans S Bartholomei de India ad Lipari [et ad Beneventum]
30	Germani ep ep Capue	Germani epi
31		vig Omn Scorum
November 1	Omnium sanctorum	Omnium sanctorum
11	Martini	Martini
22	Cecilie	Cecilie
23	Clementis	Clementis pp
25	[Mercurii in appendix]	Mercurii, Katherine
29	vig S Andree	
30	S Andree	Andree

	Benevento 21 (sanctorale)	Benevento 848
December 6	Nicolai	Nicolay
7	Ambrosii	
	lacuna	
13	Lucie	Lucie
20	Thome	
26	Nat dni	
27	Stephani	
28	Iohannis	
29	Innocentum	
31	Silvestri	Silvestri
January 14		
10		
15	Mauri abb	
20	Sebastiani mr; Marii et Marthe	Fabiani et Sebastiani
21	Agnetis	Agnetis
22	Vincentii	Vincentii
25		Conversione S Pauli
February 2	Purificatione S Marie	Purificatione S Marie
5	Agathe	Agathe
10	Scolastice	Scolastice
19	Barbati	Barbati
22	Cathedra S Petri	[Ih: Cathedra S Petri Pauli (error?)]
March 12	Gregorii	Gregorii
20	vig S Benedicti	vig S Benedicti
21	[in nat eiusdem]	Benedicti
25	Annunciatione	Annunciatione
April 26	Marci	Marci
May 1	Philippi & Iacobi	Philippi & Iacobi
3	Inventione s crucis	Inventione s crucis
6		S Iohannis ante p. latinam
8	Inv S Michahelis	Inv. S Michahelis
20	Eustasii	
June 15	Viti Modesti & Cresc	
17	Tr S Barth de India in Lipari	[cf. Oct. 25]
19	Gervasii et Protasii	
24	Iohannis Baptiste	Iohannis Bapt.
26	Iohannis et Pauli	Iohannis et Pauli
29	Petri & Pauli [+vinc s Petri]	Petri & Pauli
30	Pauli	Pauli

1. Musical offices for specifically local Beneventan saints include the Holy Twelve Brothers of Benevento, and saints Barbatus, Januarius, Mercurius, Michael, and Bartholomew. For Barbatus and the Holy Twelve Brothers, the music is, I think, a survival of the old Beneventan chant, and may have come into existence at a very early time, before the influence of the Frankish-Roman chant was felt at Benevento.[5] For Mercurius and Januarius, the music is of a newer, Frankish-inspired kind, and for Januarius, bishop of Benevento and patron of Naples, our manuscript provides a series of responsories not known elsewhere to my knowledge. Mercurius, the Byzantine warrior-saint dear to the fierce Lombards of Benevento, is provided with the traditional local music, and with a new rhymed gospel-antiphon.[6] The office of the Invention of Saint Michael, celebrating the apparition of the archangel on Monte Gargano, is likewise a Lombard-Beneventan feast of considerable antiquity; in this manuscript, however, as in Benevento 21, the musical material is essentially that used also for the more usual feast of St. Michael on September 29.[7]

Saint Bartholomew, whose relics came to Benevento in 838, is a special case. For his feast on August 25 Benevento 848 has the full office that is known in manuscripts elsewhere in Italy, but which may be a Beneventan creation.[8] To this our manuscript adds three apparently new

---

[5] On the music for The Twelve Brothers and Barbatus, see Thomas Forrest Kelly, *The Beneventan Chant* (Cambridge: Cambridge University Press, 1989), pp. 138–143; idem, "Non-Gregorian Music in an Antiphoner of Benevento," *The Journal of Musicology* 5 (1987), 478–497.

[6] The music for Mercurius is a subset of the pieces named in three Benevento ordinals (CDE: see the appendix) of the twelfth century, all of them based to some extent on Montecassino practice. Benevento 21 has material for Mercurius at the very end of the book in a supplement written in the original hand; its five responsories include three of those in Benevento 848, and it provides a different set of antiphons for lauds.

[7] Ben21 provides music for May 8 but not September 29, and includes some universal music, but also some local material, such as the responsory *Mons Gargane noli timere*. Benevento 20, a combined missal-breviary, pars estiva, of the twelfth century (a companion volume is Benevento 19; both are indexed in the CANTUS database: http://publish.uwo.ca/~cantus/), also provides music for May 8 but not September 29, but the music is the universal music for St. Michael.

[8] Essentially the same office is found in Ben20; a monastic version is in Ben21 and is specified in all the ordinals; the same repertory is found in British Library add. MS 30850 (CAO's MS S) and in Rome, Bibl. Vallicelliana MS C 5, and Florence, Arcivescovado, MS s.n., according to the CANTUS database.

Tradition and Innovation...

gospel-antiphons. For the feast of the Translation of Bartholomew from India to Lipari (June 17), Benevento 848 provides the series of local antiphons already known from Benevento 21 and from ordinals of Benevento.

    2. A second category consists of musical offices for saints associated with St. Benedict and his order, whose cults in southern Italy include music of specifically regional circulation, and which may have had their origin at Montecassino. These include Saints Benedict,[9] Scolastica,[10] and Germanus of Capua.[11] To this category might be added the office of Saint Vincent, whose unique south-Italian office may derive from the great abbey on the Volturno.[12] For some reason the south Italian office of St Maur is not present in Benevento 848.[13]

    3. Thirdly, there are musical offices of saints, mostly Roman saints, whose music in south Italian manuscripts includes unique musical items

---

[9] The office of Saint Benedict is too large a subject to cover here; the office in Ben848 includes the same materials, with the same south-Italian unica, as are found in other south Italian manuscripts. Ben848 does not, however, use the series of antiphons for first vespers, most of them local, beginning *Ecce vir dei Benedictus*, used in Ben19, Ben21, Ben22, Montecassino 542, and eight ordinals; but the antiphons involved are all found in the office except for *Euge beate pater*. South Italian offices of St Benedict are reproduced in *Paléographie musicale 21: Les témoins manuscrits du chant bénéventain*, ed. Thomas Forrest Kelly (Solesmes: Abbaye Saint-Pierre, 1992), hereafter PM 21, plates 11–17, 39–43, 69–76, 251–255.

[10] Ben848 includes mostly material unique to southern Italy and found in the local office of Scolastica: four responsories, and a series of antiphons for lauds and the little hours that includes all but one (*Hymnis et laudibus*). The antiphon-series is in an order slightly different from what is customary. A complete monastic office is prescribed in the ordinals; a similar version is provided in Ben22, and a secular office is found in Ben19; less extensive materials are provided in Ben21 and MC 542.

[11] The series of six antiphons found in Ben21 (see PM21 plates 58–59), and specified in the ordinals, is reproduced in Ben848. Ben21 adds a seventh antiphon, *Lex dei eius* (also used elsewhere), and Ben848 adds the Beneventan-style *Pater sanctus*, usually found at St. Benedict but included here because of its text.

[12] The south Italian propers for Vincent are found in Ben19, Ben21, MC542, MC CompV, and are specified in all eight of the ordinals. The same nine antiphons are prescribed for nocturns in all sources, and for lauds the first four antiphons are the same; variations thereafter are ones of ordering. Of a total of 17 antiphons, all are unique to southern Italy, except the text of the gospel-antiphon *Insigne preconium*, whose melody, however, is characteristically Beneventan. See PM21, plates 6–9, 34–37, 62–66, 246–247, 256–257.

[13] It is found in Ben19, Ben21, Ben22, MC542.

XVII

with Beneventan musical qualities. They include Saints Sylvester,[14] John and Paul,[15] and Xystus.[16] The music consists mostly of sets of antiphons, though the office of John and Paul is lengthier, including some responsories.

4. A special fourth category includes the offices of saints Apollinaris[17] and Nazarius and Celsus.[18] These are saints particularly revered in Milan, whose offices at Benevento contain unique items closely related to the Ambrosian and Beneventan chant.

---

[14] The manuscript transmits the series of six antiphons regularly found in southern Italy, of which four are found also in Ivrea 106 and Verona 98 (CAO manuscripts V and E); the final antiphon, *Vir dei Silvester*, has a particularly Beneventan aspect. The series is found, in precisely the order of Ben848, in Ben19, Ben21, Ben22, MC542, MC CompV; see PM 21, plates 5, 33, 61, 245, 255.

[15] The office of John and Paul retains many of the antiphons of purely local circulation; but it omits the Beneventan-sounding gospel-antiphon *Mandaverunt Iuliano*, found in Ben20, Ben21, and the MC CompV: see PM 21, plates 22, 41, 260.

[16] A series of six antiphons, precisely those of Ben20 (where the third antiphon, *Qui mihi ministrat*, was omitted in error and is entered in the margin) and Ben21, concludes with the characteristically Beneventan *Usque in senectam*. See PM21, plates 28, 54.

[17] The antiphons for vespers of St. Apollinaris in Ben848 are the series of six used in Ben20 and Ben21 for lauds and vespers, and they are drawn from the Milanese liturgy. Ben848 shares two variants with Ben20: "cecati" and "recolimus." On this latter, and the Milanese connection, see TBC 197–99; Kelly, "Non Gregorian Music," pp. 488–495.

The remaining proper antiphons, for nocturns and second vespers, include some antiphons from the common of one martyr, some repetition of previously sung antiphons, and five new antiphons, which are precisely the antiphons used for nocturns in Ben20 and almost the same as those in Ben21 except for the omission of the local antiphon *Lex dei eius* found in Ben20 and probably not part of the original series; *Lex dei* is perhaps a substitute for the Milanese *Apollinaris martyris festa recolimus* found in this position in Ben21 – see TBC, 198–99.

Particularly interesting is the presence in Ben848, in what is probably its original place, of the antiphon *Apollinaris martyris festa recolimus*, with its original text and Beneventan melody, which can now be completed from the incomplete version found in Ben20 (for a transcription of Benevento 20 see Kelly, *The Beneventan Chant*, p. 202, Ex. 5.14D).

This, then, is the only manuscript in which two series of antiphons, one Milanese and one Benventan, are presented separately and in order, even though the second series is interrupted by a variety of other material.

[18] The six antiphons for lauds and vespers in Ben848 are the antiphons, and the melodies, of Ben22; a longer series of antiphons in Ben21, using some of the same texts, has Milanese melodies (except for Ben21's final *Beatus Nazarius una cum Celso*, whose melody is Beneventan and matches that of Ben 20 and Ben 848). The series here, as in Ben20, has Beneventan

Tradition and Innovation...

5. Finally, the Transfiguration is provided with a very compete office; its antiphons are precisely those of Benevento 21, and of the two ordinals of Santa Sofia, Benevento;[19] the responsories are a subset of the twelve responsories given in Benevento 21.[20] It may be of significance that the office is not presented, as is usual in this manuscript, in breviary style, the antiphons and responsories of each nocturn being grouped together; instead, they are presented as they are in Benevento 21, all the antiphons of nocturns followed by all the responsories.

The office attributed to Peter the Venerable of Cluny in Paris, BNF lat. 17716, uses many of the texts found in the ordinals and in Benevento 21 – and also here –, but makes many revisions in the melodies.[21] Put another way, the Beneventan formularies are very similar in their order and their texts to that of Paris 17716, and date from a century earlier than the introduction of the feast into the Cluniac liturgy in 1132 by the venerable abbot. The relationship among these offices deserves a study of its own, but some comparisons suggest that the Cluny office, at least with respect to the selection and ordering of its texts, is not the work ot Peter the Venerable.

Unique materials for Saints Mark and for Saint Eustasius, present in Benevento 21 (and elsewhere) are not present in Benevento 848.

It is a striking confirmation of the persistence of local custom that this fourteenth-century antiphoner preserves in accurate form so much music from the earliest available sources at Benevento. An example is

---

melodies (with the possible exception of the antiphon *Sancte Nazari vir dei*, whose melodic aspect is not especially Beneventan). See Kelly, *The Beneventan Chant*, pp. 199–203.

[19] See the list of abbreviations in the Appendix.

[20] This is a particularly Beneventan office, since at Montecassino no antiphons are given for first vespers, and the first two nocturns are of saint Sixtus and companions. (For Montecassino practice, see my forthcoming edition of the Ordinal of Montecassino).

[21] On the diffusion of the office attributed to Peter the Venerable, cf. Mallet and Thibaut, *Les manuscrits en écriture bénéventaine*, vol. 2, p. 613 n1. See David Hiley, "The Office of the Transfiguration by Peter the Venerable, Abbot of Cluny (1122–1156) in the manuscript Paris, Bibliothèque nationale de France, fonds latin 17716," in *Chant and its Peripheries. Essays in Honour of Terence Bailey*, ed. Bryan Gillingham and Paul Merkley, Musicological studies; vol. 72 = Wissenschaftliche Abhandlungen Bd. 72 (Ottawa: Institute of Mediaeval Music, 1998), pp. 224–40. The text of the office of Paris, BNF lat. 17716 is published by Jean Leclercq as an appendix to his *Pierre le Vénérable* (Paris, Éditions de Fontenelle, 1946), pp. 382–388.

given in figure 4, which compares versions of the antiphon *Sanctissimus Arontius* for the Holy Twelve Brothers of Benevento, a melody of purely Beneventan aspect; the earliest source, a fragment now at Melk, as well as those of Montecassino and Benevento, preserve and transmit the same melody as is found in Benevento 848 – except that somehow the scribe of 848 has missed out a small but indispensable element of a Beneventan formula on the word *immolari*.

So much for tradition. There is also evidence of Beneventan creativity in this manuscript: music of local manufacture, evidently composed during the thirteenth century or the early fourteenth, to judge from its absence in earlier sources. These consist chiefly of music for Saint Barbatus, Saint Donatus, and Saint Bartholomew.

For Saint Barbatus the manuscript presents the series of ancient antiphons preserved elsewhere; six of the series of responsories preserved only in Benevento 21; and in a special insert (figure 5) it provides a new set of compositions, labeled "in tertio nocturno pro sancto Barbato," which gives not only three antiphons and two responsories for the third nocturn, but also a series of six antiphons for Lauds, in modal order, and a pair of gospel antiphons for second vespers.[22]

---

[22] An added portion of at least 8 leaves, now ff. 55-59 (leaves are now missing between f. 57/58 and 58/59), revises the original plan, completing the offices of St Barbatus (Feb 19) and of St Peter's Chair (Feb 22), and St. Paul. In the original manuscript,
1) St Barbartus is provided with two nocturns;
2) this is followed by a rubric about St. Valentinus (out of order, evidently), and
3) material for St Peter's Chair: musical items include a. M. *Tu es pastor* and inv. *Tu es pastor*, along with a lengthy rubric identifying the additional liturgical materials. Then follows
4) a rubric concerning feasts from St. Mathias to the beginning of St. Gregory (f 54v), which continues on f. 66.
Later alteration to this portions is achieved by inserting material after f. 54: (a) "In tertio nocturno pro S. Barbato", a complete third nocturn in verse; (b) The completion of the music for St. Peter's Chair, ff. 58-59. This consists of the full musical versions of the six responsories named in the rubric; they are numbers 1-3 and 6-8 of the office of St. Peter found at f. 105v ff, where they appear again, complete. The sixth responsory is incomplete, but the folio containing its completion would have had a great deal of blank space; (c) much of the office at St Paul, from the second antiphon of the first nocturn to the end of the office on f.65r, the verso being left blank. All of this music, in this order, is found later in the manuscript (ff. 111v-115). (d) The rubric, no. 4. above, is copied out again on f. 65r, and the original rubric, f. 54v, is marked "va- -cat" in a later hand.

Saint Donatus is provided with a full office. This is not the Saint Donatus of Benevento, not the Saint Donatus who is among the Twelve Brothers of Benevento, not any of the many other saints named Donatus: this is Donatus, bishop of Arezzo, whose relics, according to those is charge of the cathedral of Arezzo, repose in the famous *arca* on the high altar, as they have since the cathedral was built. There is an office of Saint Donatus from the eleventh century in Tuscan manuscripts,[23] and a metrical office found in the thirteenth-century choirbook A of the Archivio Capitolare of Arezzo.[24] But the Beneventan office is neither of those, and it celebrates the life of the martyred bishop of Arezzo, and tells of his translation to Benevento (see figure 6: note the mention of the city of Benevento). The office is unique, so far as I know;[25] its texts are based on the *Passio* of the saint,[26] and the music is composed in modal order. I expect to deal with this office in a separate study. The presence of relics of Saint Donatus at Benevento, a tradition not noted by scholars of the saint,[27] or acknowledged in Arezzo, was noted by Mario della Vipera in 1635, who was cited doubtfully by "J. B. S." in the *Acta sancto-*

It appears that the addition continued beyond what was intended. The supplying of the responsories of St Peter entailed an inattentive scribe who continued beyond St. Peter in his model, and copied also all of St. Paul.

[23] It is found, for example, in Lucca 603 and Florence, Arcivescovado, s. n., according to the CANTUS database.

[24] See Roberta Passalacqua, *I codici liturgici miniati dugenteschi nell'Archivio capitolare del duomo di Arezzo*, Inventari e cataloghi toscani, 3 (Firenze: Giunta regionale toscana & La Nuova Italia Editrice, 1980), pp. 49–55; see also Eun Ju Kim, "Historia Donati. L'ufficio ritmico di san Donato d'Arezzo," *Rivista internazionale di musica sacra*, n. s. 24/1 (2003), 29–43.

[25] I am grateful to Don Giovanni Alpigiano and Dr. Pierluigi Licciardello for their advice and expertise in the Tuscan offices of Saint Donatus, and in the various versions of the *vita*.

[26] *Bibliotheca hagiographica latina*, 2 vols. (Subsidia hagiographica, 6, Brussels: Socii Bollandiani, 1898–1901), vol. 1, p. 334, no. 2289; Doninus Mombritius, *Sanctuarium seu vitae sanctorum*, 2 vols. (Paris, 1910), 1:416–418; a copy of this life is in Benevento Biblioteca capitolare, MS 2, f. 33v–37v.

[27] There is no mention of Benevento in the article "Donato, vescovo di Arezzo" by Giovanni Lucchesi and Isabella Barsali, *Bibliotheca sanctorum* 4 (Roma: Istituto Giovanni XXIII della Pontificia Università Lateranense, [1964]), 774–785. On the various cults of Donatus at Benevento, and on later, and possibly deliberate, confusions between Donatus of Arezzo and Donatus, first of the Holy Twelve Brothers, see E. D. Petrella, "Per l'agiologia di S. Donato da Benevento," *Samnium* 12 (1939), 117–132.

rum;[28] another Beneventan ecclesiastical historian, Giovanni De Nicastro, in his manuscript "Benevento Sacro" of 1683, notes the tradition of the translation of Donatus, the location of his relics in the former church of Santa Maria dei Sanniti, now called San Donato, and indeed cites two texts from this office, from what he calls an "antico manoscritto Codice" in the Biblioteca Capitolare;[29] perhaps it is Benevento 848 that he has in mind.[30]

---

[28] "*Hactenus dictis in pacifica S. Donati sui possessione relinquerentur Aretini, nisi turbatio aliqua oriretur ex Samnitibus, dum lego apud Marium de Vipera, ubi Sancti elogium retulit ad hanc VII Augusti, hæc verba:* Deinde Beneventum translatum fuit [*corpus,*] quo vero tempore, a nemine expressum legitur, & in ecclesia S. Mariæ de Samnitibus collocatum; ex cujus corporis illatione ipsa ecclesia in cultum & nomen ipsius sancti Martyris nostri episcopi transivit, ubi magna populi frequentia veneratur, cujus festus dies uti ex præcepto Ecclesiæ servatur; & inter patronos Beneventanæ urbis eum cives sibi adscripserunt. Exstat officium translationis sancti Episcopi nostri in Ms. antiquo codice, quo ecclesia Beneventana ante Breviarii correctionem utebatur. *Non opinor, ægre laturos Aretinos, quod patronus suus etiam Beneventi & alibi celebretur; at sacro corpore sese privatos haud quaquam agnoscent. Magnus synonymorum Sanctorum numerus & hanc confusionem facile induxerit; sed earum hic sit finis.*" Acta sanctorum quotquot toto orbe coluntur : *vel à catholicis scriptoribus celebrantur, quae ex Latinis &Graecis aliarumque gentium antiquis monumentis collegit, digessit, notis illustrauit Ioannes Bollandus* (Antwerp: apud Joannem Mevrsium, 1643–), August II, col. 190, cited from the online text distribted by Chadwyck-Healey Ltd. The author is citing Mario Della Vipera, *Catalogus sanctorum, quos ecclesia Beneventana Duplici ac Semiduplici celebrat ritu, et aliorum sanctorum Beneventanae Civitatis Naturalium* (Naples, 1635).

[29] "DI S. DONATO. Fu questa chiesa dal bel principio della sua fondazione consagrata alla B. Vergine, sotto il titolo di S. Maria de Samnibus; ma / poi sendo stato in essa trasportato il Corpo di S. Donato Vescovo d' / Arezzo, e Martire, passò ella nel culto, e nome d'esso Santo. Ma / in che tempo seguisse tal Traslatione, no v'è alcuna memoria: Egli è ben vero che nella Biblioteca Beneventana in un / antico manoscritto Codice è asservato l'officio di questa traslazione, che s'usò ne tempi trasandati prima della Correttione del / Breviario, ove si leggono queste Antiphone. Ad Magnificat. O ineffabilis laetitia nobis divinitus edita / in B. Donati Episcopi, et Martiris Translatione incljta, quem / mente veneramur humillima, ut aeterna nobis impetret gaudia Alleluia. Ad Benedictus. O quam gloriosum est Donatus, de cuius Translatione gaudent Populi Samnitum, et collaudant Filium Dei Alleluia. Il di lui sagro Corpo è conservato con molto splendore, e veneratione sotto il Maggior Altare, e giova non poco a gl'oppressi da spiriti maligni. E egli protettore della Città, e fu ricevuto l'anno 1628 sotto il Ponteficato d'Urbano VIII; che perciò nel giorno della sua festività, che si solenizza come di / precetto e con Panegirico, e music a' 7 d'Agosto, la Città di / Benevento manda a tributar per il suo Sindico al Santo / Tutelare Due Torci." Giovanni De Nicastro, *Benevento sacro*, a cura di Gaetana Intorcia (Benevento, Stabilimento Lito-tipografico Editoriale De Martini, 1976), p. 197.

Tradition and Innovation...

Saint Bartholomew, the patron of Benevento since his relics arrived there in 838, is provided with a rich supply of music, for three separate feasts. The saint's *nativitas* of August 25, as mentioned earlier, has the proper office that regularly appears in Beneventan and some other Italian manuscripts,[31] to which this manuscript adds a new invitatory and three new Gospel antiphons.

Music for Bartholomew's translation from India to Lipari, celebrated at Benevento and Montecassino on June 17th, is present also, but out of place, being presented with material for the translation to Benevento on October 25. This first translation has a series of antiphons, two of which mention Benevento; they seem to have been created at Benevento towards the end of the twelfth century.[32]

Along with these antiphons is a new metrical office for the translation of Bartholomew to Benevento, celebrated in Benevento on October 25. Each antiphon's text is two rhyming hexameters; each responsory is two rhyming hexameters plus a third hexameter, not rhymed, for the verse. The nine antiphons for nocturns (prescribed also for vespers) are in modal order, returning to mode 1; the responsories, too, are in modal order, thought the order has been disturbed: the responsories are presented in modes 723456811. A series of antiphons for Lauds follows; they are not in modal order. The antiphon *O amirabile gaudium*, known from Benevento 21, closes the series.

Not all the new music here is great music. But there is plenty of evidence that new texts and music were being created for Benevento cathedral – and probably at Benevento cathedral – in the thirteenth and early fourteenth century. At the same time, the traditional music of the older

---

[30] But if it is, De Nicastro has mistranscribed one of the antiphons, and missed the affectation of the other.

[31] See above, note 8.

[32] The antiphons are not present in the twelfth-century Ben20, though they are called for in the Beneventan ordinals C and D and are present in Ben21. The restoration and enlargement of the shrine of St.Bartholomew by Archbishop Landolf I, dedicated in 1112, might be a likely time for the creation of this new music, but then we would expect it to be present in Ben20. (On the shrine's rededication in 1121 see Hans Belting, *Studien zur beneventanischen Malerei* [Wiesbaden: Steiner, 1968], p. 58.) The translation to Benevento is acknowledged in the rite of Montecassino by the use of music from the *nativitas*.

Beneventan antiphoners was being preserved: none of the new music in Benevento 848 replaces any older music.

Is it possible that this Benevento manuscript was made in Benevento? Art historians whom I have consulted have supposed the manuscript might have been made in Naples, given its date and obvious Beneventan contents – where else might such a well-illustrated book have been made?[33] And yet Andreas Bräm, whose substantial work on Neapolitan miniatures makes his opinion valuable, says in a private communication that he does not find the hand of this manuscript's artist among any of those in his forthcoming catalogue.[34] If the manuscript had been made in Naples, or in some other center, substantial liturgical and musical material would have to be sent from Benevento; if a whole Beneventan book had been used as the model for this one, that book has not survived, either at Benevento or elsewhere.

It seems simplest to suppose that the book was made where it was used: at Benevento, at the scriptorium of the cathedral, where all the relevant liturgical material was at hand. We do not actually have direct evidence of such a scriptorium, but Carmelo Lepore has posited the existence of a scriptorium in the thirteenth century, based on the large number of books available locally in the fourteenth century;[35] the volume under consideration here may well be a continuation of that tradition.

---

[33] I am grateful for their opinions to Andreas Bräm, Julian Gardner, Jeffrey Hamburger, and Valentino Pace.

[34] "Was die Lokalisierung betrifft, kann ich mich nicht zu einer eindeutigen Aussage entschliessen. Ich kenne die Malerhand aus meinen neapolitanischen Handschriften von 1320–1370 nicht. Das will aber nicht heissen, dass es sich nicht um einen Buchmaler Neapels handelt. Vielleicht war er auf Illumination von Gesangshandschriften spezialisiert. Ich kenne allerdings kaum illuminierte Gradualien und Antiphonarien aus der Mitte des Trecento, die nach Neapel zu lokalisieren sind. Deshalb ist es gut möglich, dass ein Neapolitaner in Benevent oder in einem anderen städtischen Zentrum gemalt hat." Electronic message from Dr. Bräm of January 6, 2004.

[35] Carmelo Lepore, "Scriptoria beneventani. Produzione libraria d'età medievale in Benevento e sua persistenza nell'area sannito-irpina della diocesi," in Pax in virtute. Miscellanea di studi in onore del cardinale Giuseppe Caprio, ed. Francesco Lepore and Donato D'Agostino (Vatican City: Libreria Editrice Vaticana, 2004), pp. 809–838.

Tradition and Innovation...

In any event, this volume confirms for Benevento what has often been observed elsewhere, namely the persistence of tradition in local practice, and the real possibility that a book of relatively late date may transmit elements of a much older tradition. When that tradition is of considerable antiquity and has been suppressed locally and elsewhere, the survival of such a book is particularly noteworthy.

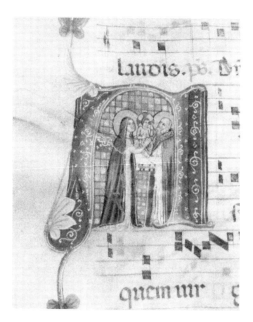

Fig. 1.   Benevento 848, f. 36v. Purification of the Virgin

Fig. 2.   Benevento 848, f. 42. Saint Agatha

Fig. 3.   Benevento 848, f. 70. Saint Benedict

Fig. 4. The antiphon *Sanctissimus Arontius*

Fig. 5.   Benevento 848, f. 55. Additional material for St. Barbatus

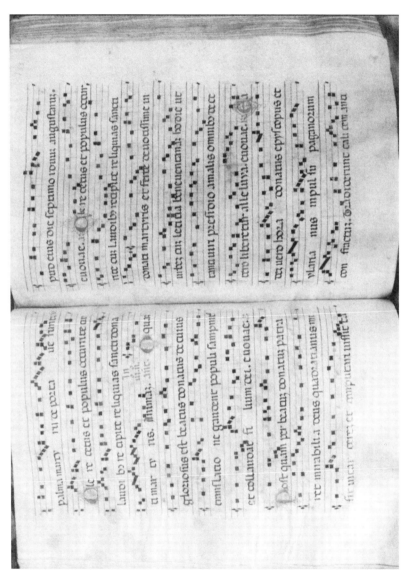

Fig. 6. Benevento 848, f. 132v–133. Office of St. Donatus of Arezzo

Appendix: Offices of Benevento 848

Offices of particular local interest appearing in Benevento 848 are compared here with other south Italian sources with brief abbreviated commentary. The offices are presented in alphabetical order. The following abbreviations are use:

Manuscripts cited in abbreviated form

Ben19	Benevento, Biblioteca capitolare MS 19, missal-breviary, winter portion, 12th c., Benevento; indexed in CANTUS database: http://publish.uwo.ca/~cantus/
Ben20	Benevento, Biblioteca capitolare MS 20, missal-breviary, summer portion, 12th c., Benevento; indexed in CANTUS database: http://publish.uwo.ca/~cantus/
Ben21	Benevento, Biblioteca capitolare MS 21, antiphoner, 12/13th c., Benevento; facsimile in *Paléographie musicale* 22.
Ben22	Benevento, Biblioteca capitolare MS 22, notated missal, 12th c., Benevento
Ben42	Benevento, Biblioteca capitolare MS 42, psalter-hymnar with other materials, second half of 12th c.
MC542	Montecassino, Archivio della Badia MS 542, antiphoner, winter portion, incomplete. 12th c., Montecassino; indexed in CANTUS database: http://publish.uwo.ca/~cantus/
MC CompV	Montecassino, Archivio della Badia, Compactiones V, many loose folios, recovered from bindings, from a single notated breviary, 12th c.

Ordinals of Montecassino

N	Vatican City, Biblioteca Apostolica Vaticana MS Urb. lat. 585, Montecassino 1099–1105
O	Paris, Bibliothèque Mazarine MS 364, Montecassino 1099–1105
P	Los Angeles, Getty Museum MS 83.ML.97 (Ludwig IX.1; ex Montecassino MS 199), Montecassino 1153
Q	Montecassino, Archivio della Badia MS 198, Montecassino (?), 12/13 c.
R	Montecassino, Archivio della Badia MS 562, Montecassino, 13th c.

Ordinals of Benevento

C   Naples, Biblioteca nazionale MS VI E 43, 12th c., for a dependency of Santa Sofia, Benevento

D   Vatican City, Biblioteca Apostolica Vaticana MS Vat. lat. 4928; 12th c., Santa Sofia, Benevento

E   Benevento, Biblioteca capitolare MS 66, 12th c., St. Peter's *intra muros*, Benevento

Bibliographical abbreviations

CAO   René-Jean Hesbert, *Corpus antiphonalium officii* (=CAO), 6 vols., Rerum ecclesiasticarum documenta, Series maior, Fontes 7–12 (Rome, Herder: 1963–79)

Mallet   Jean Mallet and André Thibaut, *Les manuscrits en écriture bénéventaine de la Bibliothèque capitulaire de Bénévent*, 3 vols. (Vol. 1 Paris: CNRS, 1984; vols. 2–3 Paris: CNRS and Turnhout: Brepols, 1997).

PM21   *Paléographie musicale* 21: *Les témoins manuscrits du chant bénéventain*, ed. Thomas Forrest Kelly (Solesmes: Abbaye Saint-Pierre, 1992)

TBC   Thomas Forrest Kelly, *The Beneventan Chant* (Cambridge: Cambridge University Press, 1989)

XVII

Apollinaris (July 28), f. 119v

ad v. a.

a1. Beatus Petrus apostolus
a2. Apolinaris egregius antistites
a3. Super cecati oculos
a4. Apolinaris martyr per unigenitum
a5. Apolinaris martiris festa recolimus
    ad M.
a6. O martir domini Apolinaris
    ad noct.
a. In lege *per ordinem* [of one martyr]
a7. Accipe spiritum sanctum
a8. Beatus Apolinaris super cecorum
a9. Beatus Apolinaris oravit ad dominum
R. Iste sanctus*
    ad laud.
[a1.] Beatus Petrus*
    Ipso die ad ves. ant. per ordinem.
[a8.] Beatus Apolinaris super*
[a9.] Beatus Apolinaris oravit*
a10. Vere congnoscent omnes qui sanctus A.
a11. Apolinaris martiris festa laudamus
[a2.] Apolinaris egregius*
    ad M.
[a4.] Apolinaris martir*

Antiphons for vespers, a1–a6, are the series of 6 used in Ben21 and Ben20 for lauds and vespers, and they are drawn from the Milanese liturgy. Ben 848 shares two variants with Ben 22: "cecati" and "recolimus." On this latter, and the Milanese connection, see Kelly, *The Beneventan Chant* (=TBC), pp. 197–99; Kelly, "Non Gregorian Music." The remaining proper antiphons, for nocturns and second vespers, include some antiphons from the common of one martyr, some repetition of previously sung antiphons, and five new antiphons, a7–a11. These are precisely the antiphons for nocturns in Ben20 (almost the same as Ben21), except for the omission of the local antiphon *Lex dei eius* found there and probably not part of the original series, perhaps a substitute for the Milanese *Apollinaris martyris festa recolimus* found in this position in Ben21 – see TBC, 198–99.

Particularly interesting is the presence, in what is probably its original place, of the antiphon *Apollinaris martyris festa recolimus*, with its original text and Beneventan melody, which can now be completed from the incomplete version found in Benevento 20 (for a transcription of Benevento 20 see TBC 202, Ex. 5.14D).

Tradition and Innovation...

This, then, is the only manuscript in which two series of antiphons, one Milanese and one Beneventan, are presented separately and in order, even though the second series is interrupted by a variety of other material.

Benevento 21		Benevento 20	
ad noct.		*ad noct.*	
vig. i			
Accipe spiritum sanctum	BEN	Accipe spiritum sanctum	
Beatus Ap. super cecorum	BEN	Beatus Ap. super cecorum	
vig. ii			
Beatus Apollinaris oravit	BEN	Beatus Apollinaris oravit	
Ap. martyris festa recolimus	MIL	LEX DEI EIUS	
ad can.			
Vere cognoscent	[BEN]	Vere cognoscent	
		AP. M. FESTA LAUDAMUS	
ad laudes et v.		*ad mat. laud. et v.*	
Beatus Petrus apostolus	MIL	Beatus Petrus apostolus	
Ap. egregius antistes	MIL	Ap. egregius antistes	
Super cecorum oculos	MIL	Super cecati	
Ap. martyr per unigenitum	MIL	Ap. martyr per unigenitum	
Ap. martyris festa laudamus	MIL	Ap. martyris festa recolimus	
B/M		*B.*	
O martyr domini Apollinaris	MIL	O martyr domini Apollinaris	

Barbati (Feb. 19), f. 50–54

The new music here includes the music for the third nocturn, a7–a9, R7–R8; a series of 6 antiphons in modal order for lauds; and two antiphons for second vespers

[*i. n.*]

a1. Vir domini Barbatus
a.2 Clamabat beatus Barbatus
a.3 Sanctissimus Dei cultor

R1. Vir domini Barbatus v. Cumque eodem tempore {mode 7}
R2. Sanctissimus dei cultor v. Quanquam sacri baptismatis {7}
R3. Piissimus autem deus v. Nam ex obsessis {4}

ii. n.

a4. Expletis missarum sollempniis
a5. Accepta securi
a6. Beatissimo interveniente

323

R4. Cumque viri dei predicationibus v. Ut qui salutaria {7}
R5. Ablata salutis v. Abite filii cecitatis {3}
R6. Astante beato Barbato v. Eorumque principi {7}

f. 55: *In tertio nocturno pro sancto Barbato*

a7. Iste sanctus habitat in tabernaculo {1}
a8. Magna est gloria eius {6}
a9. Benedictionem accepit a te domine {7}

R7. Fideli Theodore suasit presul v. Accepto itaque simulacro {7: special}
R8. Dum explevisset missarum sollempnia v. Vir dei ostendi principi {2}

ad laudes et per horas

a10. Sacerdos dei Barbatus satagebat {1}
a11. Confitemini domino et servite illi {2}
a12. Fugite filii et abicite simulacra {3}
a13. Beatus Barbatus oratione facta {4}
a14. Romualdo princeps vis dei genitrice {5}
a15. ad B. O venerande pontifex ad cuius preces {6}

in secundis v. ad M.
a16. O beatum pontificem cuius anima {2}
alia a17. Barbatus vir sanctissimus suis precibus {unknown}

Ben21 gives 9 responsories (including the first 6 here), and gives a1–a6 at lauds, repeating them over the day hours, and an additional ant. *O quam pretiosis Beneventus*. Antiphons for vespers and nocturns are of confessors.

Ben 22 has 12 readings but no responsories, followed by a1–6, some marked for day hours, and a6 marked "ad B et M."

The ordinals have a1–a6 only, "reliqua omnia de confessore"
Vatican City, BAV Vat. lat. 14446 has a1–a6 only: see PM21, p. 327–328.

Tradition and Innovation...

Bartholomei (25 August), f. 146v

in vigilia s Bartholomei ad vesp.	*in iii. n.*
a. Rex in xpm credens *sn	a. Clamabat plebi apostolus
ad M.	a. Ut iussu apostoli
a. Gloriose Bartholomee splendor et lux	a. Orante sancto Bartholomeo
[one piece missing?]	R. Precepto apostoli destructis v. Propterea
[*in i. n.*]	prophanas ymagines
[inv.?] a. Sancte Bartholomee a///-cede pro	R. Beatus namque apostolus v. Cum autem
nobis.	nunciatum
	R. Postquam Licaoniam v. Ibi lux sine fine
a. Intravit Bartholomeus apostolus	
a. Seustius per annos plurimos	*ad laud.*
a. Polimii regis filiam	a. Rex in xrm credens
R. Ingressus Bartholomeus apostolus ulteri-	a. Precepto apostoli
orem	a. Dixit regi Astrigi
v. Cumque ut peregrinus	a. Iussu regis Astrigis
R. Per os Seustii v. Per multos enim	a. Revelante apostolo Polimiu[m] {cf.
R. Vocatus a Polimio v. Regis filiam lunaticam	Ben21/233, which has Polimius, last letter
in ii. n.	erased}}
a. Beatus Bartholomeus ait Polimio	*ad B.*
a. Aurum et argentum	a. Benedictus oriens dator
a. Cogente apostolo	*in secundis ves. ad M.*
R. Dum precibus apostoli v. Terrena quidem	a. Suum suscepit israhel puerum///
R. Obsecrante sancto apostolo v.	
Circumvolans igitur	
R. Videns rex Pollimius V. Statim ut	
a demonio	

Benevento 21 has all nine antiphons (more than needed) and all 9 Rxx for matins, plus three more

R.Angelus dni sicut sol
R. Felix namque ap.
R. O quam precipuis laudibus

Ben21, Ben20, and the ordinals lack the last 2 antiphons of lauds a. *Benedictus oriens,* a. *Suum suscepit;* but all have:

a. B. Postquam Licaoniam
a. O quam multiplicibus

Ben20 has the antiphons and responsories of matins as Ben848

Ordinals have essentially the same office as in CAOs MS S, but not elsewhere in CAO. At least one responsory is in CAO's MS E.

The office is in Vall C5, I-Far, according to CANTUS

The new pieces in Ben848 are the invitatory and the three Gospel antiphons
a. M. Gloriose Bartholomee splendor et lux
a. B. Benedictus oriens dator
a. M. Suum suscepit israhel

In translatione sancti Bartholomei de India in Lipari (17 June), f. 178v (out of order)

ad ves.
a1. Dictum dei fide servasti
a2. Armenia predicat
a3. Crudelitatem mortificabas
a4. Quemammodum pisces
a5. Asperitatem peremisti
a6. Ut lucrifaceres
ad M.
a7. Ut xri discipulum
ad B. et ad M.
a8. Mirabilis et lucifer
a9. Animo iuvante

Ben21 has all these, in this order, plus
a. O ammirabile gaudium
a. Intercessione fac
Ben20 has no proper music: "Omnia require in apost."

Only **CD** of the ordinals have all of the 848 antiphons:
Translatio sancti Bartholomei. Ad Vesp. R/ *Beatus namque apostolus*. a. ad Magn. *Ut Christi discipulum* (ii). In nocte omnia fiant de apostolis. a. ad cantica *Mirabilis et lucifer* (vii T). a. ad Mat. l. et ad Vesp. *Dictum dei* (ii). a. *Armenia predicat* (viii). a. *Crudelitatem* (ii). a. *Quemammodum* (vii). *Asperitatem* (i). a. ad Ben. et Magn. *Ut Christi discipulum* (ii). a. P. *Ut lucrifaceres* (viii). a. S. *Animas iubante* (viii). a. N. *Intercessione* (i).

Tradition and Innovation...

In translatione sancti Bartholomei de Lipari in Beneventum (Oct 25), f. 180v

ad processionem	R. Ecce dies remeat v. Hec est illa dies {7}
a. Adest christi discipulus {this has had	R. Insula vastatur v. Hec iacet afflicta {2}
much of its text rewritten, and has some	R. Dum monachus quidam v. Promens hec dicta {3}
notational peculiarities...}	R. Cautus ad hec monachus v. Ignis splendorem {4}
ad matutinum	R. Complet mandatum V. Quem mox pagani {5}
inv. Plebs devota deo canat ymnum	R. Vela tument ventis sequitur v. Perdere nituntur
ad noct. et and vesperum.	{6}
a. Corporis adventu {mode 1}	R. Dextera dei patris v. Et sic aiuti veniunt {8}
a. Lux nova descendens {2}	R. [O veneranda...]structa beatis. v. Suscipe {1}
a. India dat sanctum {3}	R. [T?]u celeber vita. v. Imperio dignus {1}
a. Exultat mundus sumendo gaudia {4}	*prosa* Rosa recens et iocunda
a. Iudicii sedem {5}	forma decens rubicunda...
a. Martyrii titulum {6}	*ad laudes*
a. Ossa beata nitent {7}	a. Bartholomeus adest fulgens {1}
a. Apulie metas {8}	a. Transeat iste dies {2}
a. Huius in adventu {1}	a. Esto pius turbis {7}
	a. Plebs veneranda deo {8}
	a. Laus sit in excelsis domino {2}
	ym ad laudes et ad vesper.
	y. Exulta satis sampnia*sn
	ad B.
	a. O bone protector iudex rectorque benigne
	{2 O-ant}
	ad M.
	a. O amirabile gaudium de tanto munere {6; not in
	verse; also in B21}

Ben21 has nothing; Ben42 has indications of three ants, M. *Ut Christi discipulus* (= *Adest Christi discipulus* here?), *O admirabile gaudium* (= *O mirabile* here?)

Ordinals: Montcassino ordinals ENOPQR have 3d nocturn of Bartholomew; Santa Sofia ordinals CD repeat antiphons of June 17, two nocturns of Bartholomew.

ENOPQR:	CD: Translatio sancti Bartholomei.
Deinde a. ad cantica *O quam multiplicibus*	Ad Vesp. R/ *Beatus namque apostolus.*
Item responsoria.	a. ad Magn. *Ut Christi discipulus* (II).
R/ *Ingressus.* R/ *Obsecrante.*	In nocte vero due vigilia fiant de apostolo.
R/ *Precepto apostoli.*	Secunda autem de sanctis Chrisanti et Darie.
R/ *Postquam Licaoniam.*	a. ad cantica *Ut Christi discipulus* (II).
a. ad Mat. l. *Rex in Christum.* per ordinem.	a. ad Mat. l. et ad Vesp.
	a. *Dictum dei* (II).

ENOPQR:	CD: Translatio sancti Bartholomei.
	a. *Armenia predicat* (viii).
	a. *Crudelitatem mortificabat* (ii).
	a. *Quem ad modum* (vii).
	a. *Asperitatem peremisti* (i).
	a. ad Ben. et Magn.
	a. *O admirabile gaudium* (ii).
	a. *Ut lucrifaceres* (viii P).
	a. *Mirabilis et Lucifer* (vii T).
	a. *Animas iubante* (viii S).
	a. *Intercessione* (i N).

Benedicti (March 21), f. 69v

Ordinals of Montecassino

+ = unique to L (=Ben21) in CAO

In vigilia sancti Benedicti. a. *ad*	R1. Fuit vir vite. *V/* Recessit igitur.
Invit. Regem confessorum *(vi).*	+R2. Nursia provincia. *V/* Ne si de scientia.
ad Mat. l.	+R3. Hic itaque cum iam. *V/* Relicta domo.
+a1. Ecce vir dei *(i).*	+R4. Puer domini Benedictus. *V/* Recessit igitur.
a2. Cumque in specu *(i)*	+R5. Benedictus dei famulus. *V/* Nutricem suam.
+a3. Aquam de montis *(i).*	+R6. Vir dei mundum. *V/* Tribusque.
+a4. Mulier quedam *(vii).*	+R7. Ceperunt postmodum. *V/* Nomen itaque.
+a5. Euge beate pater *(i).*	+R8. Misereatur vestri. *V/* Tunc ad locum.
ad Ben.	+R9. Cum beatus Benedictus. *V/* Quem mox.
a6. Sanctissime confessor *(iiii).*	+R10. Non aspicias. *V/* Vix in oratione.
	+R11. Intempesta. *V/* Mira autem.
<*In sancti Benedicti*>	+R12. Vir enim domini. *V/* Cuius si quis velit.
ad Vesp.	*ad Mat. l. et ad Vesp.*
+a1. Ecce vir dei *(i). Quattuor ut supra.*	a19. Hic itaque *(ii).*
ad Magn.	a20. Predicta nutrix *(viii).*
a7. Pater sanctus dum *(iiii).*	a21. Inito consilio *(ii).*
ad Invit.	+a22. Dum panis inopia *(i).*
+i1. Laudemus dominum *(ii).*	a7. Pater sanctus *(iiii).*
ad Noct.	*ad Ben.*
a8. Fuit vir vite *(ii).*	a23. Hodie sanctus Benedictus *(ii).*
a9. Ab ipso pueritie *(vii).*	
a10. Nursia provincia *(vii)*	+a24. P. Hec via immensis *(i)*. [not even in L]
a11. Relicta domo *(vii).*	a6. T. Sanctissime confessor *(iiii).*
a12. Recessit igitur *(vii).*	*Hac hora omnes fratres induti pluvialibus*
a13. Benedictus dei famulus *(vii).*	*faciant sollempnem processionem*
Vigilia ii.	*et cantent has antiphonas*
+a1. Ecce vir dei Benedictus *(i).*	a7. Pater sanctus *(iiii).*
+a2. Cumque in specu *(i).*	a17. Non aspicias *(vi).*
a14. Frater Maure *(vii).*	R7. Ceperunt postmodum *V/* Nomen itaque.

Tradition and Innovation...

+a3. Aquam de montis *(i)*.
a15. Intempeste noctis *(i)*.
+a4. Mulier quedam *(vii)*.
    ad cantica
a16. Vix optinui *(iii)*.
a17. Non aspicias *(vi)*.
+a18. Immensi regis *(vi)*.
	Ante ecclesiam
	a25. Hodie sanctus Benedictus.
	
	a5. *S.* Euge beate pater *(i)*.
	a13. *N.* Benedictus dei famulus *(vii)*.
	    a. *Magn.*
	a25. Hodie sanctus Benedictus *(ii)*.
	
	FROM B848
	i2. Regem confessorum

MC542, PM 21, pl. 251–255
vesp: 1 2 3 4 5 7(M)
noct: i1, 8 9 10 11 12 13 1 2 14 3 15 4 16 17 18
    R1 2 3 4 5 6 7 8 8 9 10 11 12
laudes: 19 20 21 22 7 23(B) 24(P)

Ben21, f. 90, PM 21, pl. 39–43
vesp: 1 2 3 4 5 6(M)
noct: i1, 8 9 10 11 12 13 1 2 14 3 15 4 16 17 18
    R1 2 3 4 5 6 8 7 9 10 11 12
laudes: 19 20 21 22 7 23(B) 6(BT) 5(S)

Ben22, f.152v, PM 21, pl. 69–76
vesp: 7(M)
noct: 8 9 10 11 12 13, 1 2 14 3 15 4, 16 17 18
    R1 2 3 4, 5 6 7 8, 9 10 [11?] 12
l & v: 19 20 21 22 7 24(infra8) 23(B) 6(T) 5(S)

Ben19, f. 86v, PM 21, pl. 11–17
vesp: 1 2 3 4 5 7(M)
noct: i1, 8 9 10, 11 12 13, 1 2 14
    R1 2 3, 4 5 6, 8 7 12
lauds: 19 20 21 22 7 23(B) 24(P) 6(T) 5(S)

Ben848, f. 69v
vesp: 8 9 10 11 12 1(M)
noct: i2, 8 9 10, 11 12 13, 1 2 14
    R1 2 3, 4 5 6, 8 7 9 10
laud: 19 20 21 22 7 25(B)
vesp: 3 14 15 16 4 7(M)

Donati episcopi et martyris (August 7), f. 129v

This office is apparently unique; it is not either of the offices known elsewhere. There is an office of San Donato found from the eleventh century in Tuscan manuscripts (for example, in Lucca 603 and Florence, Arcivescovado, s. n.), and a metrical office found in the thirteenth-century choirbook A of the Archivio Capitolare of Arezzo (See Roberta Passalacqua, *I codici liturgici miniati dugenteschi nell'Archivio capitolare del duomo di Arezzo*. Inventari e cataloghi toscani, 3 (Firenze: Giunta regionale toscana & La Nuova Italia Editrice, 1980), pp. 49–55.)

ad ves.
a. Donatus vir catholicus {mode 1}
a. Ab ipsa pueritia {2}
a. Sub Iuliano cesare {3}
a. Sanctus Donatus pontifex {4}
a. Expellitque demonia {5}
  ad M.
a. O ineffabilis letitia nobis {6}

  inv.
a. Donate martyr Christi
  ad noctem ant. In lege dni *per ordinem de uno martyre.*
R. Erat quidam puer v. Tempore quo Iuliano {1}
R. Suscepit eum quidam Ylarinus v. Diebus ac noctibus {2}
R. Multi egrotates venientes V. Syranna ceto annis ceca visu {6}
R. Beatus Donatus pro libertate Eustasii v. Et ceperunt omnes unanimiter {3}
R. Post ut dormitonem acciperet v. At vero Donatus proclamabat {5}
R. Perfidus Quadratianus v. Clere cetus et populus {7}
  in iii. n.
a. O quam pretiosus est beatus Donatus {6}
a. Postquam per beatum Donatum {6}
a. Clere cetus et populus …Beneventanam {1}
R. Eadem vero hora v. Quod videntes Cristiani {4}
R. Quadratianus ira repletus v. Qui cum diu pateretur{8}
R. Hic est vere martyr qui pro Xristi nomine*
  an B.
a. Postquam per beatum Donatum

Tradition and Innovation…

Duodecim Fratrum (Sept 1), f. 156v

Ben848 preserves a series of antiphons, descending probably from the Beneventan liturgy, and based perhaps on an original set of four, which survives in various combinations. The combination seen here is found only in the fragments now at Melk. According to the ordinals C and D there was a full Santa Sophia office of the Holy Twelve Brothers, but it apparently does not survive.

The arrangement in Ben848 is curious; it presents psalmody as though for vespers, but the Magnificat antiphon continues with psalmodic cues, and is followed by (at least) four further antiphons. These are likely to be psalms for matins, where the full series of nine could be used.

a1. Ecce quam bonum
a2. Hec est vera fraternitas
a3. Beatus Donatus et Felix
a4. Venit angelus domini
a5. Sancti vero uno ore
    ad M.
a6. Sanctissimus Arontius
a7. Beatus Honoratus et Fortunatianus
a8. Septiminus beatus
a9. Beatum Vitalem sa[nc]torum/ / / [ends incomplete, next leaf missing]/ / /

Melk (PM 21, pl. 243–244): 1 2 3 4 5 6 7/ / /
Ben20: laud & vesp: 1 2 3 4 6 8(B) 6(M)
Ben21: 4(M); 5(ad cc.); laud & vesp: 1 2 3 4 5 9(B) + *Hos duodecim*
MCCompV: 1 2 3 4 6 9(B)
Ordinals:
    C: vesp: 1 2 3 4 8(M)
    D: lauds: 1 2 3 4 6 5(B) *Sampnium insig.* (B) 7
    CD have complete set of antiphons and responsories for nocturns, not known elsewhere
    ENOPQR (Montecassino): vesp: 4(M); laud & vesp 1 2 3 4 6 9(BM)

Germani episcopi (Oct 30), f. 185v

Antiphons only, all known from Ben21

Ben848:
a1. Beatus Germanus quasi sydus
a2. Suadenti filio
a3. Cunctis annitentibus
a4. Sublimatus gloria mundo
a5. Hodie sanctus Germanus
a6. En qui flamis caritatis
    ad B.
a7. Pater sanctus dum intentam (usually for Benedict)

    From Ben21:
a8. Lex dei eius

The office is not in Ben19/20, Ben22

_Ben21, f 251 (PM 21, pl. 58–59)
    L+V: 1 2 3 4 5(erased) 6 8

    Ordinals
    L+V: 1 2 3 4 5 6(BM)

Ianuarii (Sept 19), f. 165

All these antiphons were known in the 12c, although we did not have a version of *Ianuarius inopi orarium* until now. The order of antiphons at lauds is not attested in the 12th century. These responsories are not known at Benevento or Montecassino. Are they by chance known at Naples?

Ben848

a1. Diocletianus cesar
a2. Ante tyrampum ductus
a3. Precepto Timothei fornax///
    [Lacuna]
    R. ...crucem divini in fronte fixit, et ingemiscens in celum sursum aspexit..
    V. In caminum ignis
R. Beatus Ianuarius ingressus V. Domine deus
R. Omnes promissionem v. Qui deus salvasti
R. Beatus Ianuarius oravit v. Adesto nunc michi

Tradition and Innovation...

R. Sanctus Ianuarius sicut bonus pastor v. Ita vero affuit
R. Per beatum Ianuarium martirum v. Erat autem ipse
R. Beatum Ianuarium martiris tui v. Beato Ianuario suffragante
R Claruit beati Ianuarii maxima v. Bonum certamen
R. Ante pedes martiris. Eya fratres arripite
    ad laudes
a4. Data preses
a5. Timotheus tunc
a6. Domine rex cunctorum
a7. Post ignem demptosque
a8. Ianuarius inopi orarium
    ad M. [the M is erased, as is the *Magn* originally written with the differentia]
a9. O quam pretiosis Beneventum
a10. Ut sancti dei sunt decollati
    ipso die ad vesperas
a3. Precepto Timothei*

Ben 20 has the a1–a3 plus others, responsories from common; lauds series compared below
Ben21 has a1–a3 of nocturns, plus others, no responsories; lauds series compared below
Ordinals have a1–a3 of nocturns, plus others; two different lauds series, compared below

Lauds (+ vesp) series compared:

aA. Ianuarius cum sociis
aB. Decollatus

Ben 20: A 4 5 6 7 9
Ben21: A 5 6 10 8 7
CD: A 4 5 7 8 9 10
ENOPR: A 4 5 B 10 7
Ben848: 4 5 6 7 8 9 10

Inventionis s Michahelis (May 8), f. 89v

Ben20, Ben21, use most of these pieces, generally widely known.

ad M.	*ad lauds et per horas*
a. Dum sacrum mysterium	a. Stetit angelus
ad mat.	a. Dum preliaretur
inv. Regem archangelorum	a. Archangele Michael constitui te
in i. noc.	a. Angeli domini dominum
a. Concussum est mare	a. Angeli archangeli throni
/////	*ad B.*
...dixit michi. Hic.	a. Factum est silentium
in ii. n.	
a. Michel archangele	Rbr. Stetit angelus
R. Factum est silentium v. Milia milium	Rbr. Ascendit fumus
R. Stetit angelus iuxta aram v. In conspectu	Rbr. In conspectu
R. In conspectu angelorum v. Super miser.	*ad M.*
in iii. n.	a. Princeps gloriosissime Michael
a. Angelus archangelus	
R. In conspectu gentium v. Stetit angelus	
R. Hic est Michael v. Angelus Michael prepositus	

Ben 21, f. 159

ad M.	R. Factus est sil v. Et proiectus
a. Princeps gloriosissime	R. Stetit v. Factum est
	R. Nunc facta est salus v. Et proiectus est diabolus
[inv.] Alleluia alleluia	R. Fidelis sermo v. Michael et angeli eius
ad noc.	R. Michahel et angeli eius v. Qui dicebat in corde
a. Stetit	R. In conspectu gentium v. Angelus qui fuit
a. Data sunt	R. In conspectu ang. v.Deus meus es tu
a. Ascendit fumus	R. Hic est Michahel v. Angeli archangeli throni
a. Michahel archangele	R. Venit Michahel arch. v. Emitte dominum
a. Gloriosus apparuisti	R. Docebo te que ventura v.Ex die qua posuisti
a. Archangele Michahel	R. Numquid scis quare v. Nunc ergo egressus
vig. ii.	R, Mons Gargane noli timete v. Non livet vobis
a.Michahel prepositus	R. Summi regis archangele v. Audi nos Michael
a. Michahel gabriel	*ad laudes*
a. Laudemus dominum quem	a. Dum sacra mysteria
a. Angelum pacis	a. Dum committeret bellum
a. Concussum est mare	a. Dum preliaretur
a. Celestis militie	a. Angeli domini dominum
[*ad can.*]	a. Angeli et omnes virtutes
a. Princeps glo.*	*ad B.*
	a. Factum est silentium
	ad P. a. Angeli archangeli throni
	ad S. a. Archangeli michahelis intercessione
	ad T. a. Celestis milities

Tradition and Innovation...

Iohannis et Pauli (June 26), f 101.

Many of the antiphons are local, known also from Ben21 and Ben 20

Ben848

+ = unique to L in CAO	*ad laudes et per horas*
ad v.	a12. Paulus et Iohannes dixerunt Iuliano
+a1. Iohannes et Paulus martyres	{CAO}
+a2. Constantia Constantini filia	a13. Paulus et iohannes dixerunt ad Terentia-
+a3. Gallicano in angustia	num [CAO]
a4. Ioh et Pulus dixerunt Gallicano {universal}	a14. Iohannes et paulus cognoscentes {CAO}
+a5. Sanctorum concilio Ioh et P	a15. Sancti spiritus et anime iustorum
ad M.	{comune: no mention of Ioh et P}
a6. Astiterunt iusti ante dominum {comune}	a16. Iohannes et Paulus dixerunt ad Gallica-
	num {CAO}
ad noct. [ants.1 2 4 cued from previous]	*ad B.*
R1. Isti sunt duo viri v. Isti sunt due olive	a17. Isti sunt sancti qui pro Christi
R2. Beati martyres christi v. Una fides	amore{comune: no mentionof Ioh et P}
R3. Isti sunt duo olive v. Isti sunt viri miseri-	*ad M.*
cordie	a18. Isti sunt due olive et duo{various saints
in sec. noc.	in CAO; no mentionof Ioh et Paulus}
a5. Scorum concilio*	
+a7. Dominum tibi preponimus	
+a8. Defuncto Constantino	
R4. Vidi coniunctos v. Vidi angelum dei	
[2 more Resp. cued]	
in iii noc.	
+a9. Christus vester dicit	
+a10. Reversus est Terentius	
+a11. Omnes fideles Christi	
[3 Resp. cued]	

From Ben21:
+a.19. Non tibi facimus hanc
+a20. Mandaverunt Iuliano cesare
+a21. Numquam ad salutationem
+a22. Missus Terentius
+a23. O ammirabile indicium sanctorum meritis Ioh et P [O-ant]

Ben 848

vesp et noct: a 1 2 3 4 5 6
noct: a 1 2 4 [R 1 2 3] 5 7 8 [R 4 R* R*] 9 10 11 [R* R* R*]
laudes et vesp: a 12 13 14 15 16 17(B) 18 (M)

Ben 21, f. 192

vesp et noct: a 1 2 3 5 8 9 12 19 20
R 1 2 3
laud: 7 21 22 10 11 23(B)

Ben 20, f. 200

noct: a 1 2 3 [R1 R* R*] 4 5 8 [R* R* R*] 9 12{or 13? mode 1} 19 [R2 R* R3]
laud: 7 21 22 20 10 11
vesp: 23

Ordinals

vesp: a 20 (M)
noct: a 1 2 3 4 5 8, 9 12 (or 13?) 19, 20
R 1 2 3
laudes et vesp: a 7 21 22 10 11 23 (B M)

Mercurii (Nov 25), f. 205v

This is all traditional music at Benevento except for the rhymed antiphon *O Mercuri piissime martir*

Ben 848

a. ad Magnificat////
[a folio missing at beginning]
a1. Beatus Mercurius dixit si sic
R1. Insignis athleta Mercurius v. Cuius virtute Decius
R2. Angelus domini excitat dompno v. Oportet enim te
R3. Exhibitus Decio v. Erant tunc viginti
   in iii. n.
a2. Adiutus dei gracia
a3. Apparens Ihesus xpristus dominus
a4. Veni iam miles fortissime
R4. Adolescens egregius v. Deridens omnis cesaris
R5. Fidelis xpisti famulus v. Habeo galeam
R6. Sepultus extat beatus Mercurius v. Omnes igitur v. Gloria {with prosa in B21}
   ad laudes et per horas
a5. Omnis adhoc populus {these 4 not rhymed}
a6. Miles agone
a7. Angelus inquid ei presens
a8. Ortus in Armenia
a9. Mercurio Decius nunc verbera

ad B.
a10. [O] Mercuri piissime martyr {rhymed}

Ben21 has Mercurius material at the very end of the book in a supplement, original hand
There are 5 responsories, including nos. 2 5 6 above
a different set of Lauds antiphons

Ben20 does not have this office

Benevento ordinals have
a5–a8 for vespers, same set for lauds, with the fifth ant *Mercurio decius* (CE) or
a. *Mercurio decus* {mode 7, MS D} for vigil (same ant? SAME AS 848?)
The responsories of Ben848 are a subset, nos. 4 5 6 7 8 12, of the monastic series in CDE
The matins antiphons of Ben848 are a subset of the monastic series in CDE

Nazarii et Celsi (July 28), f. 121v

ad vesperas et ad laudes
a. Demonstra michi domine
a. Accessit Nazarius
a. Turbati sunt naute
a. Sancte Nazari vir dei
a. Sancte vir dei libera nos {Melody = Ben20, not Ben21}
  ad M. et B.
a. Beatus Nazarius una cum Celso

These are the antiphons, and the melodies, of Ben20; a longer series of antiphons in Ben21, using some of the same texts, has Milanese melodies (except for Ben 21's final *Beatus Nazarius una cum Celso*, whose melody is Beneventan and matches that of Ben 20 and Ben 848). The series here, as in Ben 20, has Beneventan melodies. {With the possible exception of the antiphons *Sancte Nazari vir dei*, whose melodic aspect is not especially Beneventan. See TBC 199–203.}

Scolasticae (February 10), f. 47v

The office here is similar to that of MC 542, using the same 4 responsories and a similar series of antiphons. None of the material in B848 is new, but most of it is of south Italian origin.

List from the Montecassino ordinals:

Ad Vesp.	*ad Mat. l. et ad Vesp.*
+A1. Dilecte mi (III).	+a1. Dilecte mi (III).
a2. Sanctimonialis (VI).	+a8. Quid est quod loqueris (VII).
+A3. Tunc inclinato. (VII).	a2. Sanctimonialis (VI).
ad Mag	+a3. Tunc inclinato (VII).
+A4. Celsa secreta (IIII).	+a9. In ymnis et laudibus (I).
ad noct	*ad Ben. Magn.*
Invit. Regem virginum (III). .	+a4. Celsa secreta (IIII).
+a5. Rogavi te (VII).	a2. T. Sanctimonialis (VI).
+a6. S. Egredere (VII).	+a9. N. Ymnis et laudibus (I).
+a7. P. In columbe (I).	
+R1 Sanctimonialis. V/ Tanta fuit.	From Ben 21:
+R2 Rogavi te ut. V/ Egredere.	
+R3 Egredere. V/ Rogavi te.	R13 Audivi vocem*
R4 Simile est regnum celorum homini.	
R5 Pulcra facie.	
R6 Specie tua.	
R7 Simile est regnum celorum decem.	
R8 Quinque prudentes.	
R9 Hec est virgo sapiens.	
R10 Cumque sanctus Benedictus.	
V/ Qui tante eius.	
R11 Non eris inter virgines.	
+(alsoV) R12 Beata es que. V/ Audi Scolastica Christi	

Ben848, f. 87v	**Ben19, f, 57**
vesp: a1* 4*(M)	vesp: a4
noct:	noct: I,a 1 5 6 7 9
R1 2 10 3	R 1 2 3, 7 5 10, 4 11 12
laud et per h: a1 8 2 3 5 6 4(B) 7(M)///	laud & vesp: 1 8 2 3 9 4(M) 5 6 7(P)
MC542, f. 100	**Ben22**
vesp: a4(M)	vesp: R2 a4(M)
noct: a5 6 9	noct: a1(ad cc)
R 1 2 3 10	R 1 2 3 4, 5 6 7 8, 9 10 11 12
laud: a1 8 2 3 7	laud: a1 8 2 3 9 4(B) 7(P) 2(T) 6 (S) 9(N) 4(M)
Ordinals (NPQR)	**B21, f. 73v**
vesp: a1 2 3 4(M)	vesp: R2, a4(M)
noct: I, a5 6 7	noct: 5(ad cantica)
R1 2 3 4, 5 6 7 8, 9 10 11 12	R1 2 3 10 11* 13* 12
laud & v: a1 8 2 3 9 4(BM) 2(T) 9(N)	laud: a1 8 2 3 9 7(P) 4(BM) 6(S)

Silvestri (December 31), f. 20v

Ben848, f. 20v

ad laudes
a1. Infantulus dum esset
a2. Sylvester beatissimus
a3. Timothei Christi martyris
a4. Ad hec sanctus Sylvester ait
a5. Sylvestro autem in carcere
 ad B
a6. Vir dei Sylvester

Antiphons 1 3 4 5 also in CAO E and V

The same series of antiphons is also found in

Ben19, f. 12 (PM 21, pl. 33)
Ben21, f. 35v–36 (PM 21, pl. 5)
B22, f. 78 (PM 21, pl. 61)
MC542, f. 30 (PM 21, pl. 245)
MC Compactiones 5 (PM 21, pl. 255)

Sixti papae (August 5), f. 123

Ben 848, f. 123

 + = unique to L in CAO
 ad vesp. et ad laudes
+a. Iunior fui
a. Volo pater ut ubi
a. Qui mihi ministrat
+a. Lex dei eius
+a. Syxtus epyscopus dixit
+a. Usque in senectam

B20, f. 249 (PM 21, pl. 28): Same, except that a3 is entered in the margin
B21, f. 216 (PM 21, pl. 54): Same as Ben848

XVII

Transfigurationis (August 5), f. 124

The transfiguration is provided with a very complete office in Ben848; its antiphons are precisely those of Ben21, and of the ordinals C and D; the responsories are a sub-set of the twelve responsories given in Ben21. This is a particularly Beneventan office, since at Montecassino no antiphons are given for first vespers, and the first two nocturns are of saint Sixtus and companions.

{The text that follows is excerpted from my forthcoming edition of the Ordinal of Montecassino}

The transfiguration is provided with a very complete office in the manuscripts of Benevento (CD) and in manuscript O. At Montecassino no antiphons are given for first vespers, and the first two nocturns are of Saints Sixtus and companions (though only manuscript N names the saint). At Benevento, Sixtus is commemorated with three lections on the vigil of the Transfiguration.

Manuscript O, which follows the Beneventan practice rather than the Cassinese for most of this feast, nevertheless adapts the third nocturn for several martyrs, evidently commemorating in the third nocturn what in other Cassinese ordinals is celebrated in the first two.

The Transfiguration is apparently of higher rank at Benevento than at Montecassino, since in manuscripts C and D it is listed among feasts on which all wear copes; at Montecassino the feast is in albs. The ordo given for Christmas mass in CEO is applicable, according to the ordo, to other major feasts which are enumerated: only manuscript E (but not C) gives the Transfiguration as such a feast. This is curious both because C gives such a complete liturgy, and also since by the time manuscript E arrives at the Transfiguration it has altered its allegiance to provide the Cassinese version of the office. In the rubric given at the octave of Pentecost in CEO about feasts falling on Sunday, the Transfiguration is among those of which nothing of the Sunday is to be said.

The office of the Transfiguration was a relatively recent addition to the liturgy at the time of the ordinal. The office attributed to Peter the Venerable of Cluny in Paris, BNF lat. 17716, uses many of the texts found in the ordinal and in Benevento 21, but makes many revisions in the melodies. But the formularies in the ordinals, and in Benevento 21, are very similar in their order and their texts to that of Paris 17716, and date from a century earlier than the introduction of the feast into the Cluniac liturgy in 1132 by the venerable abbot. The relationship among these offices deserves a study of its own, but some comparisons suggest that the Cluny office, at least with respect to the selection and ordering of its texts, is not the work ot Peter the Venerable.

The antiphons of matins at Cluny and in the ordinal are shown below. This series is in modal order at Cluny, at least for the first eight antiphons. Some of these are texts already known in the liturgy, but set to new melodies at Cluny. Some of these

Tradition and Innovation...

melodies have the effect of achieving the modal series for the first eight antiphons. In the second nocturn several antiphons are imported, text and melody, from elsewhere in the liturgy.

The antiphons of the ordinal and of Benevento 21 are uniform in the first nocturn, but manuscript O (of Montecassino) varies in the second and third. There does seem to be a common pattern, and least at the beginning of this series, that antedates the Cluny series, and perhaps influenced it. There is no evidence of modal ordering in the ordinals.

O	CD	Ben 21	Paris lat. 17716
Ant. Assumpsit Ihesus (II).	Ant. Assumpsit Ihesus (II).	Ant. Assumpsit Ihesus (II).	+Ant. Assumpsit Ihesus. 1
Ant. Hodie dominus (II)	Ant. Hodie dominus (VIII).	Ant. Hodie dominus (VIII).	Ant. Hodie dominus. 2
Ant. Ante duos vates (VIII).	Ant. Ante duos vates (VIII).	Ant. Ante duos vates (VII).	Ant. Ecce nubes lucida. 3
Ant. Respondens Petrus (II).	Ant. Respondens Petrus (II).	Ant. Respondens Petrus (II).	+Ant. Petrus et qui cum illo. 4
Ant. Domine bonum est (IIII).	Ant. Domine bonum est (IIII).	Ant. Domine bonum est (III).	+Ant. Respondens Petrus. 5
Ant. Ecce nubes lucida (VIII).	Ant. Ecce nubes lucida (VIII).	Ant. Ecce nubes lucida (VIII).	Ant. Accedente discipuli. 6
Vigilia II.	Vigilia II.	Vigilia II.	in II noct.
Ant. Vox de celo (III).	Ant. Celi aperti sunt (V).	Ant. Celi aperti sunt (V).	+Ant. Ante duos vates. 7
Ant. Audientes (I) .	Ant. Vox de celo (III).	Ant. Vox de celo (III).	+Ant. Celi aperti sunt. 8
Ant. Nemini (I) .	Ant. Audientes discipuli (I).	Ant. Audientes discipuli (I).	Ant. Quam discipuli vocem. 5
			*Ant. Vox de celo sonuit. 4
			*Ant. Domine bonum est. 1
			*Ant. Visionem quam vidistis. 1
ad cantica	ad cantica	ad cantica	ad cantica
Ant. Fulgebunt (II).	Ant. Visionem quam.	Ant. Visionem quam. (cued)	Ant. Ihesus ad discipulos. 6

+ = reused antiphon-text with new (?) music in 17716
* = reused antiphon-text with older melody in 17716

The antiphons of lauds consists of a series of four new texts, with a fifth antiphon which varies with the sources. This series has melodies in modal order in Paris lat. 17716, though these melodies are not those of Benvento 21. It appears that the texts were assembled specifically for a Tranfiguration office – its earliest witness may be the ordinal edited here – whose music was substituted at Cluny a century later.

Tradition and Innovation...

CDEOPQR	Ben 21	Paris lat. 17716
Ant. ad Mat. l. et ad Vesp.	Ant. ad Mat. l.	in laudibus
Ant. *Accessit Ihesus* (VIII).	Ant. *Accessit Ihesus* (VIII).	Ant. *Accesit Ihesus* 2
Ant. *Ut testimonium* (VIII).	Ant. *Ut testimonium* (VIII).	Ant. *Ut testimonium* 3
Ant. *Lex per Moysen* (II).	Ant. *Lex per Moysen* (II).	Ant. *Lex per Moysen* 4
Ant. *Descendentibus* (VIII).	Ant. *Descendentibus* (VIII).	Ant. *Descendentibus* 5
(or VI, or I)		
N: no fifth antiphon	Ant. *Visionem quam* (VI)	Ant. *Celi aperti sunt* 6
CD: Ant. *Nemini dixeritis* (I).		
EOPQ: Ant. *Visionem quam* (VI)		
		Ant. Ben. *Tribus discipulis* 7
Ant. ad Ben. Magn. *Hodie transfi-*	Ant. ad Ben. *Hodie transfigurato*	Ant. Magn. *Hodie ad patris*
gurato (I).	(I).	*vocem.* 1

Vincentii (January 22), f. 32–34v

Antiphons only, all found in 11/12c sources

[+ = L only in CAO]	*ad laudes*
ad noc.	+a10. Dum pateretur beatus Vincentius
+a1. Satis est laudabile	+a11. O{MS: A} felicem me inquit
+a2. Valerius epyscopus	+a12. Vincentius sanctus stramentis
+a3. Ad civitatem Valentinam	+a13. Quid agis sevissime
+a4. Mecum decertet	+a14. Exclamans Vincentius custodibus
+a5. Beatus Vincentius ait ad Datianum	*ad B*
+a6. Tu solus maxime	a15. Insigne preconium
in iii. n.	*ipso die ad vesperas*
a7. Ecce iam in sublimibus	[4 antiphons cued from earlier]
+a8. Nolo cesses	+a16. O beate passionis venerabilis
+a9. Ecce iam de apparitoribus	*ad M.*
responsoria de plurimorum martirum	+a17. Odor sancti Vincentii
	***
	a18 (Ben 21) Hodie beatus Vincentius ex hoc mundo

Ben19

Noct: 1 2 3 4 5 6 7 8 9
Laudes: 10 11 12 13 16 15 14(P) 17(S)

Ben21

Noct: 1 2 3 4 5 6 7 8 9
Laudes: 10 11 12 13 16 15(B) 18(M) 17(S)

Ben 22

Noct: 1 2 3 4 5 6 7 8 9
L et V: 10 11 12 13 16 15(BM) 14(P) 17(S)

MC546

Vesp: 15(M)
Noct: 1 2 3 4 5 6 7 8 9
Laudes: 10 11 12 13 16 14(P) 17(S)

MCCompV

Vesp: 15(M)
Noct: 1 2 3 4 5 6 7 8 9
(L et V?) 10 11 12 13 16 15?(BM) 14 17

Ordinals

Noct; 1 2 3 4 5 6 7 8 9
Lauds et V: 10 11 12 13 16 15(B) 14(P) 17(s)

INDEX OF INCIPITS

Compiled by John Z. McKay

INDEX OF MANUSCRIPTS

Compiled by John Z. McKay

INDEX OF NAMES AND PLACES

Compiled by John Z. McKay